A Language Suppressed: The Pronunciation of the Scots Language in the 18th Century

Dedicated to the Memory of
Kathleen Frew
Irrepressible Advocate for the Scots Language

A LANGUAGE SUPPRESSED

THE PRONUNCIATION OF THE SCOTS LANGUAGE IN THE 18TH CENTURY

Charles Jones

Forbes Professor of English Language
University of Edinburgh

JOHN DONALD PUBLISHERS LTD
EDINBURGH

The publisher acknowledges subsidy from the Scottish Arts Council
towards the publication of this volume.

John Donald Publishers Ltd,
138 St Stephen Street, Edinburgh, EH3 5AA.

ISBN 0 85976 427 3

A catalogue record of this book is available from the British Library.

Printed in Great Britain by Bell & Bain Ltd, Glasgow.

Contents

INTRODUCTION

The resurgence of interest in historical phonological explanation and description over the past thirty years has led to a considerable increase in our understanding of the processes of innovation and decay in pronunciation habits across a wide range of English language materials. Yet there is no doubt that almost all the important scholarship has been biased in favour of the period which spans the earliest records to around 1700. The study of phonological change in the temporal span covering the past two hundred and fifty years or so has been much neglected, partly because earlier materials are somehow perceived to manifest more significant innovations in the phonological system than do those which are closer in time to the modern observer. The lack of interest in this later period may result too from a perception that 18th and 19th century materials are sufficiently well treated in contemporary grammars and dictionaries to warrant any more detailed description superfluous. The prescriptive nature of many of the 18th and nineteenth century data sources has also had a negative effect on the investigative priorities of many modern scholars. This is not to say that there has been no interesting work carried out on historical English phonology from 1700-1900, but it has not been seen as part of the mainstream of scholarly endeavour.

This negative response to 18th and 19th century materials is even more strong when we turn to consider Scots language sources. The historical study of the phonology (as well as most other aspects of the grammar) of Scots has always been on the periphery of the linguistic scholarly tradition, and what we have claimed for early period bias in the English materials is, if anything, even more pronounced in Scots language studies. Despite the fact that the 18th century in Scotland saw a major cultural and social revival, the enormous interest in matters linguistic in Scotland throughout the Enlightenment and beyond has been often seen as an embarrassment by many observers, since it has been viewed as yet one more mechanism through which the indigenous culture and language of Scotland was coming to be actively and deliberately suppressed by an overbearing English social and linguistic model. Some writers on grammar in Scotland have come to be viewed as part of a de-culturing conspiracy, as effective an Anglicising agent as the Treaty of Union itself. Even were this to have been the case, the mechanisms of its operation and dissemination would still provide a great deal of interest for the sociolinguist concerned with linguistic conformity and accommodation (Kerswill:1994). However, a recurrent theme in this book will be to show that in some ways, the Scottish grammatical tradition was as much an influence for linguistic preservation and enhancement as it was a medium for standardisation of an English stereotype.

This book should be seen as only a very preliminary effort to capture the flavour of the grammatical tradition in Scotland in the 18th century. It makes no claims to inclusiveness and by no means does it attempt to cover the full range of source materials available. Indeed, such a coverage is at the present time an impossibility, given the depressing fact that no adequate bibliography of Scottish school and grammar book materials exists for the period and that most primary source materials are extremely difficult to come by. At the same time, so popular were many of the grammatical treatises and schoolbooks in their lifetime that daily wear and tear has meant that a great many have not survived despite the quantities in which they were produced and the very large number of editions many of them went through. We suffer too from the library acquisition policies of past generations which considered many of the school grammar books as unworthy of collection. A massive amount of work awaits to be done in the bringing together and collation of every type of source material relating to Scots in the 18th century alone. The same can be said too concerning the vast amount of contemporary comment upon the status of and attitudes to Scots pronunciation which is available in a wide range of diverse source materials.

We know next to nothing of the majority of the individuals who composed the schoolbooks, grammars and pronouncing dictionaries which are the object of our study in this book. Not all of their authors were Scottish and even those who were frequently give us little information about contemporary Scots pronunciation; in many instances this has to be gleaned indirectly. It has to be borne in mind too that several of the most prestigious Scottish writers on matters grammatical were writing in England for an English audience, while a large number of such works printed and published in Scotland for Scottish schoolchildren were the work of imported English schoolmasters and grammarians. But we shall endeavour to show that sufficient evidence can be assembled from even such diverse source materials to enable us to have a good feel for the principle characteristics of the Scots pronunciation of the period. But what kind of Scots? We might be tempted to think that systematic attempts at the correction of a non-standard dialect might concentrate upon the eradication of the least prestigious of its manifestations; while it is true that many authors exemplify only the 'grossest barbarities' of Scots pronunciation some others, it seems, were eager to illustrate what was a socially acceptable model for socially mobile Scotsmen and (importantly) women; one which reflected the characteristics of an acceptable Scottish phonological output rather than that one which originated in the speech habits of the London Court. Indeed, it is possible to see in many of the prestige pronunciations of the 18th century upper class Scot, the ancestors of present day, prestigious local norms such as the Morningside and Kelvinside varieties.

This book makes no attempt to describe the enormous output of grammars and dictionaries emanating from England in the 18th century, nor does it try to establish in any systematic fashion, genealogical or typological links between the Scottish and English source materials.

However, wherever it is relevant or enlightening, reference will be made to the comments and descriptive techniques of the most eminent English grammarians, notably Walker, as well as those - like Kenrick, Sheridan and Nares - who, for a variety of different reasons have import for Scottish materials.

It is rare indeed to find another scholar smitten by the bug of the eighteenth century Scottish grammatical tradition. To discover one in Volker Mohr who is so generous in sharing his erudition and enthusiasm is even more unusual. His comments and observations have been of enormous help to me on many occasions in writing this book. Needless to say, any misrepresentations of these are entirely my responsibility.

1

SCOTS IN THE EIGHTEENTH CENTURY

Dhe hoal pollished pepel ov Grait-Brittain will forguet, dhat evver Barbarrity waz dhare
James Elphinston: *Propriety Ascertained in Her Picture* (1786:160).

1.1 The Scots Orthoepists' Dilemma

> A provincial phrase sullies the lustre of the brightest eloquence, and the most forceful reasoning loses half its effect when disguised in the awkwardness of a provincial dress. (Sylvester Douglas:1779)

> There is a limited conformity in the present union of heart and interest of the two great kingdoms, beyond which total similarity of sounds would not be desirable, and dissonance itself has characteristic merit. (James Adams:1796)

These two quite different points of view were held by linguistic observers who, in their different ways, profess to be both patriotic Scotsmen as well as strong supporters of political Union with England. They highlight the dilemma Scots writers and observers of the language faced throughout the 18th century. On the one hand there was a highly organised and influential group of grammarians and linguistic commentators who were seeking after what can only be described as a 'language death' situation, where what they called the Scotch method of pronouncing English was seen as not merely a social inconvenience, but as a barbaric relic of a backward society and, as such, to be suppressed in much the same way as was Erse. On the other hand, and it has to be admitted that their voice has been largely ignored by most modern writers, there was also a substantial group who found this 'linguistic cleansing' profoundly distasteful and even un-patriotic. While this latter group of commentators often acknowledged the fact that linguistic preservation and fixing were impossible, and that there were indeed social advantages arising from the adoption of a London metropolitan standard pronunciation, they nevertheless saw that the situation on the ground in Scotland was much more complex than many of their contemporaries (notably those imported from London) claimed. They realised that there was a strong practical case to be made for the preservation of Scots as a linguistic entity and for the resistance of any supplanting of Scots habits of speech production with those originating from the giddy heights of London Society. The linguistic concerns so typical of the Enlightenment had important political, as well as social ramifications. Political events in Scotland throughout the 18th century had contributed to movements embracing both linguistic and cultural uniformity and diversity. The two Scottish rebellions - even though they were perpetrated by political groups whose primary linguistic allegiance was neither Scots nor English - as well as the Bute Controversy of 1762, had led in England to a suspicion of and dislike for the Scots and their language and even to demands for its suppression. There is, for instance, the apocryphal evidence from Boswell's *London Journal* entry of December 8th, 1762: 'At night I went to Covent Garden and saw *Love in a Village*, a new comic opera...Just before the overture began to be played, two Highland officers came in. The mob in the upper gallery roared out, 'No Scots! No Scots! Out with them!" (Basker :1993:85)

We find a pronounced Scotophobia too in the dialectal Bowdlerising of all traces of perceived 'Scotticisms' in the writings of Hume, Boswell and Smollet (Basker:1993:85-87; Rogers:1991:56-71; Lettley:1988; Walker:1968 and 1981). Yet, on the other hand, there were many influential individuals and groups who believed passionately that political union had brought with it (at least - but not entirely - on the Scottish side) a sense that a national British language would be a major cultural, social and - perhaps above all - economic gain. This janus-like attitude had the ironic effect of producing a situation where some of the most eminent and important grammatical observers and teachers of English in England itself were Scotsmen - notably James Elphinston and James Buchanan - while, in the cause of promoting 'good English' in Scotland, there was an extensive importation of schoolmasters and grammar teachers into a multitude of language schools in Edinburgh and other major Scottish conurbations throughout the 18th century. Indeed, some of the most ardent proposers and supporters of an *English Academy* where the linguistic rectitude of 'correct' English would be maintained, were Scotsmen - Smollet, Kames, Hugh Blair, Adam Smith and Hugh Robertson.

1.2 The Search for a Linguistic Norm

> It has been remarked as a phœnomenon in the literary world, that, while our learned fellow subjects of Scotland and Ireland are making frequent attempts to ascertain, and fix a standard, to the pronunciation of the English tongue, the natives of England themselves seem to be little anxious either for the honour of improvement of their own language: for such the investigation and establishment of a rational criterion of English orthoepy, must certainly be considered.
>
> It is indeed more natural for foreigners and provincials to see the use and necessity of such criterion. The natives of a country, and particularly of the metropolis, meet with none of those difficulties, which occur to others. Custom renders everything easy and familiar, nor do they perceive any of those irregularities and apparent improprieties, that strike the ear of such as are accustomed to different dialects. At the same time, however, that these are most sensible of the difficulties and defects, they are the least qualified to obviate them. There seems indeed a most ridiculous absurdity in the pretensions of a native of Aberdeen or Tipperary, to teach the natives of London to speak and to read.

Kenrick's typically condescending introductory remarks to his *A Rhetorical Grammar of the English Language* (1784) in many ways encapsulate the recurrent themes of the 18th century grammarian, orthoepist and linguistic commentator. We see the desire for a 'normative criterion' for orthographic representation and the imperative of both ascertaining and of fixing a 'standard' of pronunciation (recall Samuel Johnson's statement of intent in the introduction to his *The Plan of a Dictionary for the English Language* (1747) that 'one great end of this undertaking is to fix the English Language') a standard which is to be based on the 'best practice' of a certain group of speakers in the English capital and whose most 'vicious' expression is to be found among provincials of all types, but notably those speakers from Ireland and (particularly in Kenrick's case) Scotland (1784:56:footnote):

> By being *properly* pronounced, I would be always understood to mean, pronounced agreeable to the general practice of men of letters and polite speakers in the Metropolis; which is all the standard of propriety I concern myself about, respecting the arbitrary pronunciation of quality of sound given to monosyllables.

Yet nevertheless Kenrick observes that 'Setting this caution aside, I know of no rule to determine, whether the provincial method of pronouncing such words be not as proper as that of the Metropolis'. This is an interesting aside. On the one hand, while he admits to the lead taken by 'our learned fellow subjects in Scotland' in this normative and regularising crusade, Kenrick still lets it be known in no uncertain terms that such individuals should refrain from pontificating (from what he sees as their position of inherent ignorance) upon the normative use of English. His admission that he knows of 'no rule to determine, whether the provincial method of pronouncing...be not as proper as that of the Metropolis' may infer that the recommendations of the Scottish (as well as Irish and American) writers should ideally relate to the means whereby their own, national standards should be 'ascertained' and 'fixed', perhaps even a recognition of a set of valid and non-valid norms (Bartsch:1878:76ff). Even the Scot James Beattie (1788:92) rather uncompromisingly asserts that 'The language, therefore, of the most learned and polite persons in London, and the neighbouring Universities of Oxford and Cambridge, ought to be accounted the standard of the English tongue, especially in accent and pronunciation'. Yet we should not be surprised to read from the pen of that great supporter of national language that, despite everything, provincial linguistic manifestations are still liable to persist even in the heart of 'standard' speaking country: 'Scotch men have lived forty years in London without entirely losing their native tone. And it may be doubted, whether it is possible for one, who has lived the first twenty years of his life in North Britain, ever to acquire all the niceties of English pronunciation' (1788:94). Written in a context where there had been a century of prescriptive grammar, spelling and pronouncing manual writing by the most eminent linguists of both countries, this amounts almost to an admission of failure. The notion that usage, even 'vicious' regional and provincial usage, will persist despite the best efforts of the reforming grammarian, is a recurrent theme in writing of the Scottish divine George Campbell. In his *The Philosophy of Rhetoric* (1776) Campbell strikes an anti-grammarian (but not anti-standard) pose by asserting the primacy of usage over prescription: 'use, or the custom of speaking, is the sole original standard of conversation as far as regards the expression'. It is only in 'the last resort' he claims that we are 'entitled to appeal from the laws of and the decisions of grammarians; and that this order of subordination ought never, on any account, to be reversed' (1776:130). Yet 'Reputable Use' is taken from the 'conversation of men of rank and eminence' and, is to be seen in a national context since 'National language' is 'found current, especially in the upper and the middle ranks, over the whole British empire' (1776:133):

> Thus, though in every province they ridicule the idiom of every other province, they all vail to the English idiom, and scruple not to acknowledge its superiority over their own. For example, in some parts of Wales, (if we may credit Shakespeare) the common people say *goot* for *good*: in the South of Scotland they say *gude*, and in the North *gueed*. Whenever one of these pronunciations prevails, you will never hear from a native either of the other two; but the word *good* is to be heard every where from natives as well as strangers. The provincials may not understand one another, but they all understand one who speaks properly.

Alongside 'Reputable Use' there was a recognition by many 18th century scholars not only of the existence of other widely spoken social and regional varieties, but of the fact that the standard language itself was open to alternation and change. Recall Buchanan's (1762:58-59: footnote) comment: 'In the English Tongue, as in all living Languages, there is a double Pronunciation; one cursory and colloquial, the other regular and solemn. The cursory Pronunciation, as the learned Mr. Samuel Johnson observes, is always vague and uncertain, being made different in different Mouths by Negligence, Unskilfulness, or Affectation. The solemn Pronunciation, though by no Means immutable and permanent, is yet less remote from the Orthography, and less liable to capricious Innovation. We shall observe, however, that although the best Speakers deviate least from the written Words, yet the more precise and severe Part of the solemn Pronunciation is seldom used in ordinary Conversation: For what may be suitable and becoming in a Pulpit, Desk, or on the Stage, or in other public Declamations, would often be exploded as formal and pedantic in common Discourse'. While we recognise in this statement all the assumptions which gave rise to the notion that fixing the orthography would restrain language change, nevertheless we see too a recognition that linguistic innovation is unstoppable and that a single prescriptive variety can compromise speakers in certain social contexts. Sheridan, while admitting of the existence of a situation where there are sets of individuals 'speaking one common language, without agreeing in the manner of pronouncing it' (even in a metropolitan situation where there is a 'cockney' versus 'court-end' contrast) still, as we might expect, concludes that there is always one version which will become fashionable: 'it will of course fall to the lot of that which prevails at court, the source of fashion of all kinds' (1762:30); he even sets out 'the difficulties of those who endeavour to cure themselves of a provincial or vicious pronunciation', difficulties which for him arise mainly through educational neglect. But his attitude to non-metropolitan varieties is surprisingly tolerant: 'With respect to the rustic pronunciation, prevailing in the several counties, I mean amongst the gentry, and such as have a liberal education, there does not seem to be any general errour of this sort' (1762:34). We shall see below in several places how this magnanimous attitude to the speech of educated speakers away from London prevailed among several of the Scottish writers, who at least acknowledge the existence of (and one even describes in detail) what must be a 'provincial' urban educated type of usage.

Even among the Scottish observers themselves there were some who saw it as a *desideratum* to be worked towards and which in any case would transpire through the general climate of 'improvement', that there should be a single, shared language between Scotland and England. As Sinclair (1782:9-10) claims: 'During the reign of James the First, the Scotch and English dialects, so far as we can judge by comparing the language of the writers who flourished at that time, were not so dissimilar as they are at present. Time, however, and commerce, joined to the efforts of many ingenious men, have since introduced various alterations and improvements into the English language, which, from ignorance, inattention, or national prejudices, have not always penetrated into the north. But the time, it is hoped, will soon arrive, when a difference, so obvious to the meanest capacity, shall no longer exist between two countries by nature so intimately connected. In garb, in manners, in government, we are the same; and if the same language were spoken on both sides of the Tweed, some small diversity in our laws and ecclesiastical establishments excepted, no striking mark of distinction would remain between the sons of England and Caledonia'. The power of language to amalgamate the inhabitants of Scotland and England into a homogenous society is strongly stressed by Buchanan (1766:xi-xii) who recommends that 'both clergy and laity enjoin the school-masters over that part of the united kingdom, to acquire and teach a proper Pronunciation...it will be joining them into one social family, and connecting them by much more benevolent and generous ties than that of political union'.

For Elphinston it is the lack of an accurate representational orthography which has led to the language's 'immediate corrupcion in her verry vitals' and has, indeed, led to the differences between 'dhe *Inglish* and dhe *Scottish* Dialects'. Given the lack of an appropriate orthography, he argues, *Inglish Truith*, the standard language, is unavailable to the provincial, 'Hwile all endowed widh speech, ar dhus interested in propriety; such members ov dhe Metropolis, az hav had dhe good-fortune, (hweddher from dellicate edducacion, or from incorruptibel taste) ov keeping equally free from grocenes, and from affectacion; hav doutles a chance, if stil but a chance, for purity. But dhe distant hav no possibel chance, unless from repprezantacion' (1786:xiii). There is little doubt that Elphinston saw as one of the gains of his orthography its potential to 'standardise' the provincial method of pronunciation upon the model of *Inglish Truith*. Ever confident in the benefits of education, it is Buchanan (1770:46) who is perhaps the most sanguine of all the 18th century grammarians on the power of the schoolmaster to significantly over-ride social and geographical linguistic variation: 'There are Scotch gentlemen indeed in London, whose pronunciation, and consequently tone of voice, cannot be distinguished from natives of the place: But then they applied themselves vigorously to the study of it under the best masters, and with the advantage of not imbibing the least tincture of the provincial dialects, to which the generality of South-Britons are subjected. For the manner of pronouncing, which is usual among the polite and learned, who are natives of the metropolis, is, in every country the standard'.

As is well known, the 18th century fondness for 'scientific' attempts at linguistic normalisation resulted in various endeavours to set up an English Academy modelled (however loosely) upon those in France and Italy (Monroe:1910; Freeman:1924; Emerson:1921; Read:1938). Jonathan Swift's *A Proposal for Correcting, Improving, and Ascertaining the English Tongue* in his famous letter to Lord Oxford of 1712 was one of several in the century; recall Addison's suggestions in his *Spectator* (no. 135) article of the same year. While the proposal for the establishment of an English Academy was not universally popular, Sheridan refers to it as 'so noble a work' (1762:xvi), and Elphinston embraces the idea wholeheartedly for the opportunities he thinks it would bring for the establishment of orthographic homogeneity: 'Dhe Italian Acaddemiscians had set dhe exampel; and rendered dhe eldest daughter ov dhe Lattin tung, consistent and communicative az her parent. Dhey fixed her Orthoggraphy, beyond dhe power ov chainge; and went immediately fardher, dhen even dhe French hav yet been abel to' follow. Inglish Orthoggraphy must pas like firy trial' (1786:vi-vii). Sylvester Douglas too sees the advantage of an Academy model for orthographic regularisation: 'Indeed the numerous and judicious alterations which have been made from time to time in Italian and French orthography, by the Academia della Crusca, and the French Academy, are sufficient to demonstrate that such improvements are both practical and advisable' (Jones:1992:109).

It is Sheridan in his *Heads of a Plan for the Improvement of Elocution and for the Promoting of the Study of the English Language* (the sequel to his *Two Dissertations on the State of the Language in Different Nations*) who pleads most eloquently for the setting up of public and private institutions for the promotion of English Language study. While the establishment of University lectureships may be arrived at through the generosity of private endowment, such funding sources, he argues, are not always reliable. In his opinion, much more preferable is the 'new mode' of promoting the same end, namely 'the institution of societies for encouraging such arts, sciences, manufactures, and studies as are most wanting' (1762:200): 'This practice, which was first begun in Ireland, and soon adopted by the sharp-sighted people of Scotland, in both which kingdoms most excellent effects have been produced from it'. These endeavours were the result of a twofold impetus: to improve the general level of reading and writing skills among the young and to provide a model of pronunciation for social groups which included in particular the legal profession, the clergy and the politician. The 'excellent consequences' and 'good effects' which would result from his endeavours he claimed (1762:205-206) would be:

> I The establishment of an uniformity of pronunciation throughout all his Majesty's British dominions.
> II The facilitating the acquirement of a just, proper delivery, to such as shall apply to it; and the enabling all such as are to speak in public, to deliver their sentiments with due grace and force, in proportion to their talents for elocution.
> LASTLY, the refining, ascertaining, and establishing the English language on a durable basis.

There can be little doubt that Sheridan's visits to Scotland were the catalyst for much of the interest in both English and Scots language there in the later part of the 18th century. Of his visit in 1761, the *Scots Magazine* comments:

> Mr Sheridan proposes to read two courses of LECTURES; the first, on ELOCUTION, the second, on the ENGLISH TONGUE; consisting of eight lectures each.

In the first, he will treat of every thing necessary to a GOOD DELIVERY, under the following heads: ARTICULATION, PRONUNCIATION, ACCENT, EMPHASIS, PAUSES or STOPS, PITCH and MANAGEMENT of the VOICE, TONES and GESTURE. In the second, he will examine the whole state and constitution of the English Tongue, so far as relates to sound; in which he will point out its peculiar genius and properties, and specific differences from others, both antient and modern.

In order to do this in the clearest and most effectual manner, he will begin with the very first elements of speech, and thence proceeding through syllables and words, to sentences and verses, lay open the principles of composition and numbers in a manner hitherto unattempted. In this course he will point out the true source of the difficulty (at present thought to be insuperable) which all foreigners as well as natives of different kingdoms and counties, that speak a corrupt dialect of English, find in the attainment of the right pronunciation of that tongue.

In the close he will point out an easy and practicable way of reducing the living tongue to a standard, and establishing such a method of teaching it, that the adult may become masters of it with more ease and certainty, than of any other modern tongue; and that the rising generation in this country may be taught to speak it in its utmost purity.

The price of a ticket, which will admit one person to both courses, will be a guinea.

Sheridan's lectures and various publications excited much interest in Edinburgh and beyond and attracted a great deal of review comment, notably in the *Scots Magazine,* where we find remarks relating to his *Dissertation on the Causes of the Difficulties which occur in the Teaching of the English Tongue,* like the following: 'We applaud Mr Sheridan's Scheme for teaching all the British subjects to speak with such propriety, as may remove those broad, uncouth accents, which disgrace, and very often destroy, the effect of a very sensible discourse; nay, indeed, throw such an air of ridicule on the speech, and the speaker, as bring both into contempt with the audience. Disgrace of this type daily happens in the metropolis, to the natives of Ireland, Wales, Scotland, and even to the English pronunciation of Yorkshire, Somersetshire, and other remote counties'. We see here what very much looks like an 'in your back yard too' attitude to linguistic impropriety, an attitude which brings with it considerable doubt concerning the practicality of achieving Sheridan's stated aims: 'Whether such an uniformity of pronunciation can possible be established, we must question' (*Scots Magazine*; July, 1762: 372). The fact that Sheridan's visits to Edinburgh were not altogether without incident perhaps added to their popularity; the reviewer of the *Scots Magazine* (1762:vol 24:481) points to a controversy over Sheridan's financial dealings with his Scottish audiences in the publication of his *Course of Lectures on Elocution*: 'A correspondent observes that those who attend Mr Sheridan's lectures at

Edinburgh have not been handsomely used by him; in as much as they were drawn in, by his making them believe that they were to get his book at half price, to pay the full price *per* advance upwards of a year before they got it; and that, in this instance he but ill exemplifies the extraordinary reformation in morals which he says might be expected from due cultivation of oratory - We shall be glad of an opportunity of vindicating him in this particular; the rather that, so far as we heard, his behaviour, while at Edinburgh, was altogether gentlemanly'. There were, in fact, some five hundred subscribers to the *Course of Lectures;* however, that there was something of a general air of confusion attached to the organisation of the lectures themselves, is highlighted by Sheridan's admission in the preamble to the subscriber's list that 'As many of the Names in this List were hastily taken down at the door of the several places where the Lectures were delivered, and but very few were written down by the subscribers themselves at any of the other places, it is to be feared that many mistakes have been committed in point of spelling, as also in assigning the proper title, stile, or distinction to each name. There being likewise a deficiency of more than one third of the names of those who attended the Lectures, occasioned by the casual loss of some of the lists, the editor, in order to fulfil the conditions mentioned in his proposals, to the best of his power, is obliged to publish this list, under all these disadvantages'.

Almost certainly as a result of Sheridan's high profile stance and the interest it engendered in many of Edinburgh's middle and upper classes, the *Scots Magazine* (July, 1761:vol 23:390) records that 'Notice was given in the Edinburgh papers of July 27, that on the Tuesday following, the plan of a new establishment for carrying on, in that country, the study of the English tongue, in a regular and proper manner, was to be laid before the Select Society. Mention was made of this by Mr Sheridan, on the Friday before, in the last lecture of his first concourses' (McElroy and McElroy:1959). The *Select Society* of Edinburgh is described by Henry Mackenzie (Thomson:1927:40) as 'A literary, or properly speaking a philosophic society, for they discussed all manner of subjects; initiated and supported by the principal literary men of Edinburgh. The regulations were like those of other debating societies: a subject was given out; if a question of doubt arose, a supporter and impunger were appointed who opened the discussion, and then the members and the few strangers admitted spoke at their discretion'.

Consequently, in 1761 we find the publication in Edinburgh by the *Select Society* of a special set of Regulations 'for promoting the reading and speaking of the English Language in Scotland':

> As the intercourse between this part of GREAT-BRITAIN and the Capital daily increases, both on account of business and amusement, and must still go on increasing, gentlemen educated in SCOTLAND have long been

sensible of the disadvantages under which they labour, from their imperfect knowledge of the ENGLISH TONGUE, and the impropriety with which they speak it.

Experience hath convinced SCOTSMEN, that it is not impossible for persons born and educated in this country, to acquire such knowledge of the ENGLISH TONGUE, as to write it with some tolerable purity.

But, with regard to the other point, that of speaking with propriety, as little has been hitherto attempted, it has generally been taken for granted, that there was no prospect of attempting any thing with a probability of success; though, at the same time, it is allowed to be an accomplishment, more important, and more universally useful, than the former.

The *Select Society* included among its members such notables as Hugh Blair, William Robertson, John Adams, Adam Ferguson and Lord Alemoor, of whom Sheridan (*A Rhetorical Grammar of the English Language,* 1781:142) rather condescendingly observes: 'And yet there was still a more extraordinary instance which I met with at Edinburgh, in a Lord of Session (Lord Aylmoor), who, though he had never been out of Scotland, yet merely by his own pains, without rule or method, only conversing much with such English men as happened to be there, and reading regularly with some of the principal actors, arrived even at an accuracy of pronunciation, and had not the least tincture of the Scottish intonation'. This Edinburgh group may have been the closest Sheridan came to the realisation of his scheme to establish a society (an enhanced version of that proposed by Swift in his letter to Lord Oxford) for the 'refinement and establishment of the English Language' (Sheridan 1781:229). The Select Society's aim was to ensure that 'a proper number of persons from ENGLAND, duly qualified to instruct gentlemen in the knowledge of the ENGLISH TONGUE, the manner of pronouncing it with purity, and the art of public speaking, were settled in EDINBURGH: And if, at the same time, a proper number of masters, from the same country, duly qualified for teaching children the reading of ENGLISH, should open schools in EDINBURGH for that purpose.' In these aims the Society was largely successful and numerous pedagogical establishments were set up not only in the capital, but also in Glasgow, Dundee and Aberdeen (Law 1965:144-192). Their existence was widely advertised in the press of the day, as the following from the *Edinburgh Evening Courant* for November 10th, 1781, on behalf of William Scott, testifies:

ENGLISH LANGUAGE

Mr Scott proposes next week, to open the following CLASSES: - A Class for Gentlemen attending the UNIVERSITY - Another for young Gentlemen attending the HIGH SCHOOL - and a third for Young Ladies - The terms of admission will be moderate, and may be known by enquiring at Mr Scott's house, in the Trunk Close, any day between 11 and 12, Saturdays excepted - PRIVATE TEACHING as usual.

> ☞ Mr Scott intends to begin a COURSE OF LECTURES on ELOCUTION, in St Mary's Chapel, Niddry's Wynd, on *Monday the 26th current,* at 7 in the evening. - The number of lectures will be SIX; one lecture to be delivered each Monday till the course be concluded. - Tickets of admittance to the *whole* course, 5s. each Lady and Gentleman; to a *single* lecture, 2s.

In the same newspaper for May 12th, 1781, the entrepreneurial Scott assures his readers that 'The very great encouragement which Mr Scott has met with in the teaching of English, has determined him to attend more particularly to that branch of education in future; on which account he will give up his *public writing school* the beginning of next August. - Young Ladies and Gentlemen are instructed in a just and graceful pronunciation, at his own house, in separate classes; and, in boarding-schools and private families, he continues to teach English, writing, and accounts'. It was an educational climate like this - increasingly stressing not only language enhancement and improvement but also uniformity and conformity - which undoubtedly led to the production of so many of the spelling books, grammars, treatises on language and dictionaries which we shall describe in detail in the next chapter. It should be recalled too that several proselytisers of the Scots language saw in the recent foundation of the Society of Antiquaries of Scotland (a 'Temple of Caledonian Virtue') in 1780, another institution whereby that language's cause could be furthered; Callander of Craigforth (1781:16) concludes his Preface with the following remarks: 'We cannot conclude these cursory remarks without congratulating our readers on the establishment of a Society, which promises to revive a taste for the study of national antiquity. The worthy nobleman [the eleventh Earl of Buchan:CJ] to whose truly patriotic spirit it owes its institution, and the gentlemen associated for so laudable a purpose, it is hoped, will look with indulgence upon this poor attempt to second their endeavours, in restoring and explaining the ancient language of Scotland'.

1.3 Attitudes to the Scots Language in the 18th Century

All the observations we have made in the preceding section point to an officially held perception that the 'variety' of English spoken in Scotland in the 18th century was, at best, stigmatised and if possible best eradicated and replaced by some southern, metropolitan linguistic model of propriety. Sinclair (1782:4) indeed sees 'the Scotch dialect' as 'a dialect of the Saxon or Old English, with some trifling variations' and, taking a kind of utilitarian stance not unlike that expressed by the *Select Society*, recognises the 'quaintness' of the Scotch variety, but recommends its abandonment in the cause of personal advancement and the political advantages of a 'national language' (1782:1-2):

> To many it seems of no importance, whether this or that word expresses, with

> the greater purity, a particular idea; and, perhaps, it is of little consequence to any individual, who lives in a retired or distant corner of the country, in what stile his sentiments are given. His highest ambition generally is to be understood, not to please his hearers. But such as wish to mix with the world, and particularly those whose object it is to have some share in the administration of national affairs, are under the necessity of conforming to the taste, the manners, and the language of the Public. Old things must then be done away - new manners must be assumed, and a new language adopted. Nor does this observation apply to Scotchmen only: the same remark may be extended to the Irish, to the Welsh, and to the inhabitants of several districts in England; all of whom have many words and phrases peculiar to themselves, which are unintelligible, in the senate-house, and in the capital.

Throughout the 18th century, attitudes to the Scots language, both from English and Scottish writers range from the downright condemnatory, through the apologetic, to the patronising. In a 'they can't help themselves' frame of mind, Buchanan (1757:xv:footnote), describing 'that rough and uncouth brogue which is so harsh and unpleasant to an English ear', is moved to express the view that 'The people of North Britain seem, in general, to be almost at as great a loss for proper accent and just pronunciation as foreigners. And it would be surprising to find them writing English in the same manner, and some of them to as great perfection as any native of England, and yet pronouncing after a different, and for the most part unintelligible manner, did we not know, that they never had any proper guide or direction for that purpose'. Scots speech is usually characterised as containing 'errors' requiring correction or the repository of 'barbarisms' and vulgarities' and only occasionally do we find appeals like those of Beattie (1788:91) for tolerance in the area of linguistic plurality: 'we may learn, that, as every nation and province has a particular accent, and as no man can speak intelligibly without one, we ought not to take offence at the tones of a stranger, nor give him any grounds to suspect, that we are displeased with, or even sensible of them. However disagreeable his accent may be to us, ours, it is likely, is equally so to him. The common rule of equity, therefore, will recommend mutual forbearance in this matter. To speak with the English, or with the Scotch, accent, is no more praiseworthy, or blameable, than to be born in England, or Scotland: a circumstance, which, though the ringleaders of sedition, or narrow-minded bigots, may applaud or censure, no person of sense, or common honesty, will ever consider as imputable to any man'. Yet he sees no contradiction to this 'forbearance' in immediately rejecting the idea that 'all provincial accents' are 'equally good', recommending as the 'standard of the English tongue' what he characterises as 'The language..of the most learned and polite persons in London, and the neighbouring Universities of Oxford and Cambridge'.

But often what is stressed is the socio-economic disadvantage the Scots speaker will find himself under when unable to produce a pronunciation acceptable to an English audience: 'There are. I believe, few natives of North-Britain, who have had occasion either to visit or reside in this country, that have not learned by experience the disadvantages which accompany their idiom and pronounciation [sic:CJ]. I appeal especially to those whose professions or situations oblige them to speak in public. In the pulpit, at the bar, or in parliament, a provincial phrase sullies the lustre of the brightest eloquence, and the most forceful reasoning loses half its effect when disguised in the awkwardness of a provincial dress' (Jones:1992:99). These remarks of Sylvester Douglas almost exactly mirror those of Buchanan: 'Their [the people of North Britain:CJ] acquiring a proper accent and graceful pronunciation, would embellish and set off to far greater advantage the many excellent and rhetorical speeches delivered by the learned both from the pulpit and at the bar' (1757:xv:footnote).

Yet there remains a perceptible sense that something has been lost under the pressure of the tide to abandon the vulgar Scotch vernacular for some regularised English model. Henry Mackenzie's remarks (1780:174) are fairly typical when he complains that 'the old SCOTTISH dialect is now banished from our books, and the ENGLISH is substituted in its place. But though our books be written in ENGLISH, our conversation is in SCOTCH....When a SCOTSMAN therefore writes, he does it generally in trammals. His own native original language, which he hears spoken around him, he does not make use of; but he expresses himself in a language in some respects foreign to him, and which he has acquired by study and observation'. Indeed, Sheridan's hypothesis that the decline of standards in spoken English are the result of inadequate school and university teaching is echoed by Alexander Scot in a Scottish context, 'thaut poalisht *lengo*, whoch ez noat spoc en Scoatlaund' being unattainable there owing to the fact that (Jones:1993:125-26):

> Oy haiv massalf tnoan dip-lairned profassours oaf fowr destengueshed oonavarsetays, caupable oaf coamoonicatten airts aund sheences auss w-al auz laungages auncient oar moadarn, yet endefferent auboot, aund froam thance oonauquant woth thaut sengle laungage whoch ez auboov ainay laungage alz; aund en whoch auloanne thase maisters ware tow empairt tnoalege. Foar moy share, oy moast aunoalege oy caunnoat winder ev Cauladoneaun paurents sand cheldren tow Yoarksheir foar leeberaul adecatione, aund paurteekelarlay foar thaut poalisht *lengo*, whoch ez noat spoc en Scoatlaund.

1.4 The 'Leave Our Language Alone' School

Several writers in the period protest that had Scots been left to its own linguistic devices and been unaffected by English, then it would have developed (indeed, had been developing) along the lines of a classical dialect with its own linguistic and literary integrity. Sylvester Douglas is an enthusiastic espouser of this position. Noting that Edinburgh, the 'Capital of the Kingdom. After the Union..sunk from that distinction, and became, at most, the first provincial town of Great Britain', a fact, he claims, to be seen as the chief cause 'which completely established the English dialect of our language as the standard of what is considered as classical' (Jones:1993:98). However, 'If the two kingdoms had continued as distinct, as they had been until the death of Queen Elizabeth, it has been thought probable, that two dialects might gradually have been formed, bearing that sort of relation to each other which subsisted between those of ancient Greece: that we might have possessed classical authors in both'. Such a view is still to be heard at the end of the century: 'Had we retained a Court and Parliament of our own, the tongue of the two sister kingdoms would, indeed, have differed like the Castilian and the Portuguese; but each would have had its own classics, not in a single branch, but in the whole circle of literature' (James Ramsey of Ochtertyre:1800:74). A similar position is taken by Alexander Geddes (1782:404): 'if the Scots, remaining a separate nation, with a King and court residing among them, had continued to improve and embellish their own dialect, instead of servilely aping the English, they would at present be possessed of a language in many points superior to the English': and again (1782:448):

Had Jammie never seen the Thames,
Nor chang't the Abbey for St James',
Edina's Court had nou been fund in
As geud a plight, as that of Lundin:
And nowther PIT or FOX had been
Politer speakers than MACQUEEN

Clearly such a position is in direct contrast to Elphinston's 'Inglish Truith' and Sinclair's 'national language'.

There can be no doubt that there was another side to the somewhat stereotypical view that all Scots usage was seen as impropitious and vulgar, requiring refinement by some kind of accommodation to a self-proclaimed English metropolitan norm. On the one hand, there is some evidence to suggest that what was being advocated by several of the most important 'Pronouncing Dictionary' type publications produced by Scots in the period was not a wholesale abandonment of Scots language characteristics by the socially aspirant, but rather the adoption of some kind of contemporary 'Standard Scots' based perhaps upon the language of the legal, clerical and academic professions in Edinburgh, or even other large Scottish conurbations (Jones:1993). It is interesting to record that Sylvester Douglas appears to admit that variation can exist between different kinds of Scots speakers dependent upon the degree of exposure they have had to 'polite' varieties (Jones:1992:101):

> Let it be understood however that it is by no means my intention to observe upon all the grosser barbarisms of the vulgar Scotch jargon. This would be an useless and an endless labour. I only mean to treat expressly of the impurities which generally stick with those whose language has already been in a great degree refined from the provincial dross, by frequenting English company, and studying the great masters of the English tongue in their writings: Of those *vestigia ruris* which are apt to remain so long; which scarce any of our most admired authors are entirely free from in their compositions; which, after the age of manhood, only one person in my experience has so got rid of in speech that the most critical ear cannot discover his country from his expression or pronounciation [sic:CJ].

At the same time, there were groups of individuals who, far from being apologetic for any perceived 'impropriety' or 'impurity' in Scots, actively advocated its use, promoted its survival and pointed to its long and legitimate historical pedigree; Elphinston. for instance, apparently seeing his contemporary Scots as a survival of an earlier form of the language spoken in England: 'In *Langhams* Inglish, az in dhe prezzent Scotch (hwich iz indeed littel else dhan dhe Inglish ov his days....' (1786:303). John Callander of Craigforth in the *Preface* to his *Two Ancient Scots Poems* (1781) recommends the 'usefulness and importance of investigating..our ancient language', which he sees mainly in terms of the ways in which it justifies the study of comparative/historical etymology. Commenting on the necessity of producing a comparative Germanic language dictionary, he comments (1781:12): 'It is high time that something of this kind were attempted to be done, before the present English, which has now for many years been the written language of this country, shall banish our Scottish tongue entirely out of the world', and Callander, as we shall see like several other contemporary Scotch language apologists, appeals to what he sees as the language's pristine state of preservation and originality (1781:8-9): 'Our language, as it is at present spoken by the common people in the Lowlands, has maintained its ground much longer than in England, and in much greater purity. This must be owing to the later cultivation of this part of the island, and its less frequent communication with strangers....we, in Scotland, have preserved the original tongue, while it has been mangled, and almost defaced, by our southern neighbours'. Two scholars stand out in this second group, both Roman Catholic clergymen, one an Englishman turned Scotophile, the other a native born of Buchan stock - James Adams and Alexander Geddes - both of whose lives spanned the period 1737-1802. In 1792 the members of the Society of Antiquaries of Scotland saw published in their *Transactions* a long essay by the Reverend Alexander Geddes,

LL.D... entitled *Three Scottish Poems, with a Previous Dissertation on the Scoto-Saxon Dialect.* The *Dissertation* is a long justification and history of what Geddes describes as the 'Scoto-Saxon Dialect' (a term which may have been the invention of Geddes, although the somewhat similar *Scoto-English* was coined by Zacharaias Collin (1862)) and is followed by an energetically chauvinistic *Epistle* extolling the virtues of the same. Of great interest to the student of historical Scots and historical dialectology and an important source for contemporary Scots pronunciation, there also appear in the piece two translations into 'Skottis vers' of classical Greek poetry, one in a form representing the dialect of Edinburgh, the other in the Buchan dialect ('which may be called the Scottish Doric' (Geddes 1792:462:footnote)). The special orthographic method used in these 'translations' and the information they provide for the nature of late 18th century Scottish regional language will be explored in Chapters Two and Three. Geddes' outspoken support for Scots is everywhere evident in *Three Scottish Poems* and he takes the customary anti-provincial argument turning it against English itself (1792:447):

Let bragart England in disdain
Ha'd ilka lingo, but her a'in:
Her a'in, we war, say what she can,
Is like her true-born Englishman,
A vile promiscuous mungrel seed
Of Danish, Dutch, an' Norman breed,
An' prostituted, since, to a'
The jargons on this earthly ba'!

What he describes as the Scoto-Saxon dialect was until recent times, Geddes claims 'the general language of the low-lands of North Britain, and is still prevalent among the people of the north east provinces' (1792:402). Despite his criticisms of the heterogeneity of English, he sees contemporary Scots itself as an amalgam of several different languages and dialects (1792:415-416):

> On analysing the Scoto-Saxon dialect, I find it composed; First, and chiefly, of pure Saxon; Secondly, of Saxonized Celtic, whether Welsh, Pictish, or Erse; Thirdly, of Saxonized Norman or old French; Fourthly, of more modern French Scoticized; Fifthly, of Danish, Dutch, and Flemish, occasionally incorporated; Sixthly, of words borrowed from the learned dead languages. It must not however be supposed, that all these are blended together in the same proportion in every Scottish provincial dialect. The Welsh words are principally to be found in the more southern provinces, the Pictish and Erse in the more northern; the Danish, Dutch, and Flemish all along the eastern coast, especially in the trading towns and fishing villages: terms relative to the arts, politeness, and luxury, are mostly French; and Greek and Latin words are rarely to be found but in authors.

In a transparent effort to prove the respectability, antiquity and authenticity of the Scots language, Geddes produces a lengthy (if occasionally somewhat speculative) history of the Scots language and an appeal for the construction of a Scots lexicon. He attempts to justify the linguistic integrity of Scots by referring to its possession in equal measure with English of what he sees as the linguistically advantageous 'properties' of *richness*, *energy* and *harmony*. With respect to the first two of these, he demonstrates that his contemporary Scots shows as complex and various a lexical inventory and morphological structure as its English cousin, although it has to be admitted that some of his observations are somewhat fanciful (1792:420): 'The superior ENERGY of a language (independent of peculiarity of stile) seems to consist in this, that it can express the same sentiments in fewer words, and with fewer symbols, than any other, and this, I apprehend, is the just boast of the English. Our numerous monosyllables, rough, rigid, and inflexible as our oaks, are capable of supporting any burthen; whilst the polysyllables of our southern neighbours, tall, smooth, and slender, like the Lombardy poplar, bend under the smallest weight. From this, no doubt, arises the confessed superiority of our poetry; especially of the higher kinds, the *epic* and *tragic*. This, also, gives a peculiar strength to our apophthegms, and to every sort of composition, where strength is a chief ingredient. '

Criteria relating to *harmony* on the other hand are principally of a phonetic and phonological nature, and together with his *Tables* and *Observations* form the core of his comment upon contemporary Scots pronunciation. Like Elphinston, Geddes is unashamedly a spelling reformer (1792:430):

> On the whole, then, I am of the opinion, that if a philosophical grammarian had existed in Scotland, prior to the reign of Mary, or about that period, and turned his attention to this object; it would have been no hard matter for him to reduce the Scottish orthography into a system of equal perfection with that of the Italian. But I will go a step farther; and, supposing myself to be such a grammarian, will attempt to do, what I fancy he might have done: or rather what I would do at this day, if I had to reform the Scottish orthography. If this be accounted a folly, it is at least an innocent one. I do not expect that my system will ever be followed; but it pleases myself, and cannot well displease any one besides. It is on occasions like this, that theory may take its free swing; because its swings can do no injury.

His interest in Scots is not antiquarian or sentimental; it centres on the spoken language itself and he disdains attempts at artificial creation and maintenance (1792:403): 'Thus, to write Scottish poetry...nothing more was deemed necessary than to interlard the composition with a number of words and trite proverbial phrases, in common use among the illiterate; and the more anomalous and farther removed from the polite usage those words and phrases were, so much the more apposite and eligible they were accounted. It was enough that they were not found in an English lexicon to give them a preference in the Scottish glossary'.

It is the English Jesuit James Adams (1737-1802) who provides the most powerful antidote to the 'pure' English language apologists in the period. Written in 1799 while enjoying 'the summer's recess at Musselburgh' his *Pronunciation of the English Language* - especially its Appendix on *The Dialects of all Languages and Vindication of that of Scotland* - provides a rationale for the preservation of 'non-standard', regional varieties (especially that of Scotland 'which is so remarkable and original') in the face of the normative, standardising culture of the period. A native of Saffron Walden, it is difficult to find in the period an Englishman more admiring of the 'noble race' of Scotland. A Jesuit priest and 'ancien professeur d'human a S. Omer' in France, Adams was compelled to abandon France during the French Revolution, settling in Scotland at Edinburgh and Musselburgh where he wrote in addition to *The Pronunciation of the English Language Vindicated* (1799) his *Euphonologia Linguae Anglicanae* (1794). Adams follows the example of Geddes - a 'learned and reverend Friend' (1792:162) - in referring to Scots as the 'Scoto-Saxon', which 'triumphs, to the present day, in its contrast with our Anglo-Saxon', and he is one of the very few commentators in the 18th century who actively argues against the abandonment of provincial speech habits in favour of some metropolitan standard (1799:159):

> For, if the fair daughters of Scotia laid aside all distinction of accent, and wholly adopted our refined sounds, they would frequently, both at home and abroad, be challenged for natives of our South. How ready are Englishmen to claim every affinitive perfection for their own; and how ready is a Scotchman to give up what genuinely appears not to be his own.

All this in a context where 'the Scotch accent yields in the Capital, and in Universities, to refined English' (1792:148). His appeal for the retention in Scotland of a recognisably distinct regional usage is not the result of some xenophobic nationalistic outlook, since his appeal is addressed to 'British readers....for he that names himself English or Scotch, names but one half of what he is by the bond of Union,' yet it is none the less forceful, persistent and uncompromising (1799:157):

> The sight of the Highland kelt, the flowing plaid, the buskin'd leg, provokes my antagonist to laugh! Is this dress ridiculous in the eyes of reason and common sense? No: nor is the dialect of speech: both are characteristic and national distinctions. National character and distinction are respectable. Then is the adopted mode of oral language sanctioned by peculiar reasons, and is not the result of chance, contemptible vulgarity, mere ignorance and rustic habit.

His insistence on the importance of and need to recognise the status of regional language (especially where it brings with it some kind of claim to nationhood) represents the antithesis of Elphinston's 'Inglish Truith' and would doubtless have caused Kenrick to shudder with apprehension; not only is regional variation of value in its own right, its destruction and modification under the dictates of a 'national language' is physically impossible (1799:161):

> The learned, even in remoter days, yielded to the impulse of literary conformity, and now honour the classical English, and perfect it by their writings; but mere local dialectal sound *never should, never will, never can be*, totally removed; the effort would be as vain, and the prejudice is as unjust, as to attempt to change the green colour of the eye in the natives of the Orknies.

However, it would be wrong and over simplistic to assume that Adams (and, as we shall see, some other Scottish contemporaries) was merely intent upon promoting the vernacular in some kind of reaction to Sheridan's defence of a London standard. On the contrary, Adams' writings reveal a consciousness of the existence of a prestigious form of Scots in the 18th century (possibly one which was Edinburgh based), a *regional Scottish standard* and not the 'refined' London form of speech which many Scottish grammarians (and, we might assume, schoolteachers) were promoting as the form of language appropriate to the educated and professional classes. Adams himself is quite explicit on this matter. While asserting that the 'broad dialect rises above reproach, scorn and laughter', he claims that there is another form of the Scots language, its 'tempered medium' which is 'entitled to all the vindication, personal and local congruity can inforce, by the principles of reason, national honour, and native dignity' (1799:157). He argues that 'refined English is neither the received standard of that country, and its most eminent scholars designedly retain the variation; retain it with dignity, subject to no real diminution of personal or national merit' (1796:158). Yet the 'refined' metropolitan standard of London, advocated by so many contemporary commentators as the linguistic paragon, is not - Adams argues - the only 'standard' available to the Scots speaker, since the Scots 'dialect manifests itself by two extremes. The one is found in the 'native broad and manly sounds of the Scoto-Saxon-English; the terms of coarse and harsh are more commonly employed. The other is that of a tempered medium, generally used by the polished class of society' (1796:156-157). The implication being that there is no need to import a London standard to Scotland, since its own prestigious native norm is already flourishing, flourishing in particular among the members of the Scottish Bar (1796:160):

> The manly eloquence of the Scotch bar affords a singular pleasure to the candid English hearer, and gives merit and dignity to the noble speakers who retain so much of their own dialect, and tempered propriety of English sounds, that they may be emphatically named *British Orators*. In fine, there is a limited conformity in the present union of heart and interest of the two great kingdoms, beyond which total similarity of sounds would not be desirable, and dissonance itself has characteristic merit.

Adams is almost unique in his time in recognising that a 'polite and mitigated dialect' and the 'common and broad mode of speaking' Scots 'both have their merit, and give room for fair vindication'. Yet his justification and support are primarily based on patriotic feeling and some sentimentality, since 'every liberal and well educated observer will admit that there is something pleasing in the tempered dialect of the Scotch; that it is graceful and sweet in a well tuned female voice: that it would be a pity, nay an injury, to local merit, wholly to forgo it' (1796:159). Indeed, not at all unlike Sylvester Douglas, he is willing to recognise that some 'provincial sins' are worse than others: 'every word has some particular twang, or twist discordant with received classical English sounds, and that there is a dialect of dialect in different quarters, and it is this kind of local dialect alone that locally sinks into vulgarity among the illiterate Scotch, and may rank with our provincial corruptions' (1796:154); a view reflected too by Henry Mackenzie (Thomson:1927:15): 'There was a pure classical *Scots* spoken by genteel people, which I thought very agreeable; it had nothing of the coarseness of the vulgar *patois* of the lower orders of the people'. Interesting too in this context are the remarks by Walter Scott in his letter of February 25th, 1822 to Archibald Constable of Castlebeare Park, Ealing in Middlesex: 'By the way did you ever see such vulgar trash as certain imitators wish to pass on the world for Scotch. It makes me think myself in company with Lothian Coal carters - And yet Scotch was a language which we have heard spoken by the learned and the wise and witty and the accomplishd and which had not a trace of vulgarity in it, but on the contrary sounded rather graceful and genteel. You remember how well Mrs Murray Keith - the late Lady Dumfries - my poor mother and other ladies of that day spoke their native language - it was different from English as the Venetian is from the Tuscan dialect of Italy but it never occurd to anyone that the Scotish [sic:CJ] any more than the Venetian was more vulgar than those who spoke the purer and more classical - But that is all gone and the remembrance will be drownd with us the elders of this existing generation and our Edinburgh - I can no longer say our Scottish gentry - will with some study speak rather a worse dialect than the Newcastle and Sheffield riders. So glides the world away'.

But above all, it is Adams who raises the loudest voice proclaiming *la difference* and with it the need, the desirability of a separate and identifiable Scotch system of orthographic representation; hence his sympathy for orthographic reformers like Elphinston and, especially, Geddes, since (1799:162): 'How, in the name of wonder, can Scotch Schoolmasters teach poor children to read their Bible printed the English way? They use no other. Hence every word is a stumbling block; and, from early youth, the Scotch are taught *that our pronunciation is anomalous and capricious*, the prejudice is deeply rooted, and has cost me all my past labour to endeavour to eradicate the notion'.

2

THE SOURCE MATERIALS AND THE NATURE OF THE EVIDENCE

2.1 Types of Evidence Available for 18th Century Scots Pronunciation

Great Pedagogue, whose literanian lore,
With syllable and syllable conjoin'd
To transmutate and varyfy, has learn'd
The whole revolving scientific names
That in the alphabetic columns lie,
Far from the knowledge of mortalic shapes,
As we, who never can peroculate
The Miracles by thee miraculiz'd,
The Muse silential long, with mouth apert
Would give vibration to stagnatic tongue,
And loud encomiate thy puissant name,
Eulogiated from the green decline
Of Thames's banks to Scoticanian shores,
Where Loch-lomondian liquids undulize

If we detect in the rhetoric of these lines Fergusson's (1773) parody of Anglicisation and linguistic description, it only reflects the almost obsessional characteristic of 18th century linguistic scholarship for linguistic normalisation, dialect suppression and the pedagogic methodology required to eliminate linguistic non-conformity. One positive result of this obsession for the historical phonologist is that there is little shortage of tools available for the reconstruction of the pronunciation of Scots especially in the latter half of the 18th century, and an extensive range of different types of evidence is ready to hand. The sources we can turn to are as plentiful and varied as those for English language materials and, while many of them may be said to be an imitation of English models, others are unique to a Scottish linguistic descriptive context. Outstanding in this latter group is *A Treatise on the Provincial Dialect of Scotland,* written by Sylvester Douglas (Lord Glenbervie) around 1779 (Jones:1992); James Elphinston's essay on the characteristics of the Scotch dialect in the second part of his *Propriety Ascertained in Her Picture,* 1787; Alexander Geddes' *Three Scottish Poems, with a Previous Dissertation on the Scot-Saxon Dialect* (1792) (Jones:1994) and James Adams' *Appendix* on *The Dialects of All Languages and Vindication of that of Scotland* in his *The Pronunciation of the English Language* (1799). All of these are direct accounts of the salient characteristics of a range of Scots pronunciation in the period, often showing considerable phonetic insight and detail. Although we are extremely fortunate in having data sources of this type, it has to be admitted that they are not typical of the majority of source collections at our disposal in the period. The bulk of these, even when written by Scots orthoepists and grammarians and published in Scotland, very often are mainly concerned to treat with what their authors perceived to be 'polite' metropolitan London usage, although misconceptions and misinterpretations arising from some of those perceptions can sometimes provide valuable insights into pronunciation habits in Scotland itself.

We can divide the evidence-providing materials into at least four main types, although within these there are overlaps as well as clear subdivisions: 1 short lists and catalogues of Scots pronunciation characteristics, constructed mainly, it has to be admitted, to point to their supposed shortcomings in comparison with some standard, usually London metropolitan, norm; 2 specialised orthographies; 3 spelling books, usually aimed at an audience of schoolchildren; 4 pronouncing dictionaries; 5 grammar books and grammatical treatises; 6 general essays on the nature of language.

2.2 Short Lists and Catalogues

Under this head we might include those sets of brief, generalised (and on occasion very informative) lists of Scots pronunciation characteristics, mainly of the kind indicating where Scottish speakers are 'prone to err'. Although some of these accounts are fairly detailed, others are tantalisingly brief, notably the one provided by the northern Englishman Nares (1784:212): 'Mistakes in quantity are not uncommon, and indeed a very principal error in the pronunciation of our northern neighbours is that of lengthening the vowels which we pronounce short, and of shortening those which we make long: thus for *heăd*, they say in Scotland, *hēde* or *heēd*, for *tāke tak*, etc'. Perhaps the best known of the more extensive summaries is Walker's 'Rules to be Observed by the Natives of Scotland for attaining a just Pronunciation of English' in his *A Critical Pronouncing Dictionary* (1791:xi-xii): 'That pronunciation which distinguishes the inhabitants of Scotland is of a very different kind from that of Ireland, and may be divided into the quantity, quality, and accentuation of the vowels. With respect to quantity, it may be observe that the Scotch pronounce almost all their accented vowels long. Thus, if I am not mistaken, they would pronounce *habit, hay-bit; tepid, tee-pid; sinner, see-ner; conscious, cone-shus;* and *subject, soob-ject.*' Despite the limitations of Walker's re-spelling system and descriptive terminology (notably his syllable boundary placement conventions and conflation of vowel quantity and quality) we shall see that his observations are not without merit and provide much more helpful information than the parallel, but less immediately clear, section in Sheridan's *Appendix* to his *A General Dictionary of the English Language* (1780:61): 'With regard to the natives of SCOTLAND - as their dialect differs more, and in a greater number of points, from the English, than that of any others who speak that language, it will require a greater number of rules, and more pains to correct it. The most material difference in point of pronunciation, and which pervades their whole speech, is that of always laying the accent on the vowel, in words where it ought to be on the consonant....for it is in this that the chief difference between the Scotch and English pronunciation consists'.

What we shall come to recognise as an extremely helpful list of 'words in which the Natives of North Britain are most apt to err' is to be found in the anonymous *A Spelling-Book upon a New Plan* (1796:*Preface*:vii), whose author proclaims that 'It may not be improper here to set down a few of those words in which the Natives of North Britain are most apt to err, in order that the teacher may be particularly on his guard to prevent the ....children from falling into these common errors'. Some examples of 'Common' versus 'True' versions are given in Table 2.1:

TABLE 2.1

A Spelling Book Scotticisms

Spelling	Commonly Pronounced	True Pronunciation
Act	Ack	Act
and	ând	ănd
arm	ārm	àrm
art	ārt	àrt
base	bāze	bāce
beau	bew	bō
beaux	beux	boz*e*
card	cārd	càrd
charge	*ch*ār*ge*	*ch*àr*ge*
corps	corpse	cōr*e*
cough	coch	còff
dost	dōst	dŭst
doth	dōth	dŏth
fact	fack	făct
guard	g*u*ārd	g*u*àrd
has	hās	hăz
him	hum	hīm
his	huz	hīz
in	un	īn
it	ut	īt
juice	joic*e*	jûc*e*
large	lār*ge*	làr*ge*
laugh	lach	lăff
mourn	mŭrn	mōrn

What is arguably the most full and detailed summary of contemporary Scots phonetic characteristics is to be found Volume Two of Elphinston's *Propriety Ascertained in Her Picture* in a section entitled *Anallysis ov dhe Scottish Dialect* (1786:1-35). Summarising this section under DHE

CONSEQUENT CONFUZION, Elphinston (1786:11-12) concludes:

> Infinite must be dhe confuzion from dhe Scottish interchainge (or coincidence) ov different or even oppozite vowels; dhe interchainge ov *pike* and *pic*, *titel* and *tittel*, az ov *duke* and *duc*; dhe coincidence ov *wake* and *walk*; *walks*, *wakes* and *wax*; *take*, and *tac*, almoast widh *talk*; *bade* and *bad*, almoast with *bawd*; *scarc* [sic:CJ] with *scar*, boath uttered *scaur*; *hope* and *hop*, *sope* and *sop*, *note*, *knot*, and *not*; *coat* and *cot*, *rode*, *road*, and *rod*, *toad* and *tod*, *cloke* and *cloc*, or dhe like; dhe vocal gradacion ov *peat*, *pit*, *pet*, *pat*; into' *pit*, *pet*, *pat*, *pot*: like dhe Inglish jargonnic *sat out* for *set out*; or interchainge ov *set* and *sit*, *lay* and *ly*. If *came* and *cam* be equally distinct from *calm*; dhe last, prolonging *a* slender shut, cannot also prolong *a* broad, more dhan can *a* slender open be interchainged widh *a* slender shut prolonged. *Calm* cannot dhen be *caum*, *psalm* cannot chime widh *shawm*, nor *alms* and *aums* coincide. *Salvacion* similarly can no more be strained into' *salvahcion*, dhan into' *salvaucion*. .

Elphinston even attempts to provide 'A faithfool specimen ov Scottish colloquial iddiom' (1786:119-120): 'Ye'r aw wrang: he's up e' dhe buckel (or weel at hemsal). But I dread he'l gae af at dhe nail wih hemsal: I wos he mayna faw awstaps, or gang a gray gate. He leves on nae deaf nets: he fists at hac an mainger, ev no on wein an wastels. Aw dhes'l coast hem monny a saut tear, though he let na on, an kens I hev sin hez hairt gret afore noo. Its el yoor comon to' spic sae: ev he be en sec a tacking, he spoails (or speils) good (*u* French) leikly. Bat deed, he woz ey a spelt bairn: nabody cud tal hwat he wod baut, or thought he sud be last at hiz ain haund.' This passage, Elphinston asserts, 'may run into' Inglish dhus: 'Yoo ar all in dhe wrong: he iz wel to' pas, or in good condiscion. But I dred hiz running riot: I wish he may not fall to' pieces, or go to' pot. He livs on no hollow nuts: he feats at rac and mainger, if not on wine and walnuts. All dhis wil cost him manny a briny tear, dho he poots a good face on it, hwile he knows I hav seen hiz hart redy to' burst before now. It il becoms yoo to' talk so. If he be in such a case (or such a taking), he belies hiz appearance. But indeed, he waz always a spoil'd child: noboddy cood tel hwat he wood be at; or thaught he shood be left at hiz own dispozal'.

It is, of course, difficult to tell how contrived such a representation is, especially since it occurs in a section where Elphinston (1786:4) is decrying the use of non-native lexical intrusion into Scots and highlighting peculiarities of Scottish phraseology. Indeed, it may be an instance of what he calls 'dhe old dialect' (1786:80) or 'true (dhat iz, braud) Scotch', and thus represent a version of the language at the more vernacular end of the formality scale. It is under his discussion of plural morphology in [s]/[z] that Elphinston comments upon the contemporary use of *'Scots'*, *Scotch'*: 'Dhat *Scots* iz onely a plural or an appropriative, every *Scotchman* may now know; hweddher from *Mary Queen ov Scots* or dhe *Scots Maggazene*, dhe rival ov dhe *Gentelmans*. Dhe *Scots* and *English tongues*, dhus lost in dhe *Scotch* and *Inglish*, must emerge like dhe respective nacions, widh blended purity, in dhe *British tung*' (1786:134).

Given his well attested anti-Scottish bias, Kenrick's rendering of a passage from Johnson's *Idler*, translated by 'an essayist [who:CJ] must be a North-Briton, and not a native of England' perhaps smarts of parody:

> Eezy poeetry iz that in wheetsh nateuril thots air expressed without violins too the langwidsh. Thee diskriminaiting karitir ov eez konsists principilly in the dikshun, for awl trew poeetry reequirs that thee sentimints be nateuril. Langwidsh suffirs violinss by harsh or by dairing figurs, by unshootibl transpozeeshun, by uneuzyl aksptaishuns ov wurdz, and any lisins wheetsh wood bee avoided by a ritir ov proz.

There is too the summation of 'The common and striking differences between the Scotch and English accent' (again containing some of the descriptive confusions of Walker and Sheridan) provided in the anonymous *A General View of English Pronunciation: to which are added EASY LESSONS for the use of the English Class* (1784:11-12) - probably wrongly ascribed by Alston to William Scott:

> The difference between the Scotch and English, in the sound of these vowels, lies chiefly in this, - that the former confound the *a*^{1} with *e*^{1}, as b*a*^{1}d for b*e*^{1}d, and back again, as h*e*^{1}b-it, for h*a*^{1}b-it; *e*^{1} with *i*^{1}, as f*e*^{1}t for f*i*^{1}t ; bliss (made a verb) for bl*e*^{1}ss, r*i*^{1}d for r*e*^{1}d: - o^1 short with o^2 long, as l*o*^{2}-ng for l*o*^{1}ng, and m*o*^{1}st for m*o*^{2}-st. The common and striking differences between the Scotch and English accent, is in the former generally making short syllables long, as bo^2-nd for bo^{1}nd, pri^2-vy for pri^{1}v-y; ta^{2}lent for ta^{1}l-ent; te^3-pid for te^{1}p-id: and long syllables short, as po^{1}st for po^{2}st; no^{1}t-ice for no^2-tice; cra^{1}dle for rca^2-dle; ca^{1}d-ence for ca^2-dence.

Not unlike this are the comments of Fulton and Knight in their section dealing with the *Principles of English Pronunciation* in their *A General Pronouncing and Explanatory Dictionary of the English Language* (1813:xi), a work extremely well received by the educational, legal and religious Establishment of Edinburgh, if its Advertisement is to be believed: 'These Recommendations are founded, not merely on a critical examination of the Books themselves, but on the knowledge of their Practical Effect in the Instruction of Youth':

> The Scots confound the sounds of the vowels in almost every instance. Instead of Rāce rēed rōad rûde, they say Ràce, rèed, ròad rŭde; and instead of Hat hem hill hog, they say HA̋t ham hell hòg. This remark, however, applies only to the retainers of their native dialect, for many of the Scots (as

> well as of the Irish and Provincial English) can pronounce the language as correctly as the most cultivated inhabitants of London.

In his *A Plan for an English Grammar-School Education* (1770:44), James Buchanan shares the recurring concern of some of the above commentators for the significance of differences of 'length' or 'quantity' of vowel segments in distinguishing the idiosyncratic nature of contemporary Scots: 'Quantity is the measure of sounds, and determines them to be long or short. A long syllable takes double the time in pronouncing, that a short one does, as mat, mate; her, here; fir; fire; rob, robe; tune, tune'. We shall, of course, at a later point discuss the significance of assigning a durational distinction to what might be vowel quality differences of an [a]/[e], etc. type, but it is interesting to notice how Buchanan criticises Scots pronunciation (much after the fashion of Elphinston) on the grounds that it 'confuses' short for long, and vice versa, although other important alternants are clearly signalled as well (1770:45):

> I shall adduce but a few examples, out of a multitude, to shew how North-Britons destroy just quantity, by expressing the long sound for the short, and the short for the long; as abhōr for abhŏr, abhōrrence for abhŏrrence, abōlish for abŏlish, thrōn for thrōne [sic], m:unt for mount, muntain for mountain, funtain for fountain, amunt for amount, tўp for tȳpe, cairy for căṙry, mairy for mărry, apostateeze for apostatīze, sympatheeze for sympathīze, ceevil for cĭvil, civileeze for cīvilize, cōmfōrt for cŭmfŭrt, eetem for īitem, eer for īre, leer for lȳre, breer for brīar, deemond for dīamond, maijesty for măjesty, &c, &c.

Recall too his comment in the *Linguae Britannicae Vera Pronunciatio* (1757:x:footnote) to the effect that 'The difference betwixt accent and pronunciation is not only evident from the above definitions, but also by numberless examples that might be produced; such as *clī'ent, socīe'ty, varīe'ty, vīo'lent, canonī'ze, sympathī'ze,* &c, &c. which the Scots accent the same way as the English; but the former pronounce thus, *clee-ent, socee-ety, varee-ety, veeolent, canoneeze, sympatheeze'*. Utilising a very different method of arrangement and presentation, an extensive, vowel by vowel set of those 'words in which the Natives of Scotland are very apt to err' appears in William Scott's new edition of *A New Spelling, Pronouncing, and Explanatory Dictionary of the English Language* (1807:xxv-xxvi), although there are, as we shall see, severe difficulties in interpreting Scott's observations. John Callandar of Craigforth was one of the first to recognise the necessity of producing a comprehensive Scots lexicon with a full set of contrastive references to related Germanic languages; in his discussion of his proposed 'Scoto-Gothic glossary' he laments the extent to which English has 'deviated' from its Germanic origins, largely owing to its contact with Latin based languages. As part of this discussion he provides a set of examples showing the close relatedness of what he perhaps sees as especially salient Scots characteristics to German cognates (1781:11):

GERMAN	SCOTS	ENGLISH
Beide	Baith	Both
Eide	Aith	Oath
Kiste	Kist	Chest
Meiste	Maist	Most
Brennan	Bren	Burn
Gehe	Gae	Go

Brief and usually anecdotal descriptions of Scots usage and the prevalent attitudes towards it are often to be found in letters addressed to the editors of periodicals such as *The Gentleman's Magazine, The Scots Magazine* and *The Weekly Magazine,* reminiscent of a practice still common in the letters pages of the modern *Scotsman* and *Glasgow Herald.* Such 18th century materials have never been fully investigated and even a cursory glance at them suggests that they contain a rich collection of interesting materials. Some fairly typical examples of the periodical letter genre are to be found in Appendix Three below. While we shall obviously discuss them individually and in detail in the chapters which follow, the most salient characteristics of 18th century Scots pronunciation which seem to emerge most frequently from the summaries we have been outlining seem to be

SCOTS	STANDARD ENGLISH
[e]	[ɛ]
[o]	[ɔ]
[e]/[ɛ]	[ɑ]/[a]
[ɑ]	[a]
[i]	[ɩ]
[i]	[ɑɩ]
[ü]/[ʏ]	[ʊ]

By no means representative of the total number of Scots/English alternations to be found in the period, these nevertheless appear to point to a tendency for Scots speakers to raise short vowels, to fail to apply the *English Vowel Shift* to pure palatal vowels and to centralise and front labial vowel sounds.

2.3 Specialised Orthographies

While 18th century writers on Scots pronunciation did not develop the innovative phonetic alphabet type of representation manifested by Thomas Spence of Newcastle's *New Alphabet* in his *The Grand Repository of the English Language* (1775), there are at least two sustained attempts at modifications to and manipulations of the existing orthographic set in an attempt to represent the spoken word in a more phonetic form. These are to be found in the well known innovations of James Elphinston in his two part *Propriety Ascertained in Her Picture; (or, English Speech and Spelling Rendered Mutual Guides, Secure Alike from Distant, and from Domestic, Error*) (1786, 1787) as well as in the lesser known (and in some ways more phonetically revealing) orthographic method invented by Alexander Scot and illustrated in his *The Contrast* of 1779 (Jones:1993). While both these writers are particularly interesting in that they use innovative orthographies to illustrate Scots language characteristics, we should bear in mind too the occasional 'respellings' and 'naive' spellings which surface in several treatises where an author fails to use specialised phonetic representations. A good example is the way James Dun manipulates conventional orthography throughout his *The Best Method of Teaching*, wherein is included a list headed: 'The *English* Commonly Sound the following Words thus':

Ah	*sounded*	A
Awry		Ary
Circle		Surcle
Circuit		Surket
Done		Dun
Eight		Ait
Bishop		Bushop
First		Furst
Fire		Fiur
Four		Fore
Gorgeous		Gorjus
Handkerchief		Henkecher
Hierarchy		Hirarky
Housewife		Huzzit
Key		Ke
Folly		Fally
Mastiff		Mastee
Myrrh		Mur
Ought		Awt
Serjeant		Sarjant
Sevennight		Sennet
Sheriff		Shreeve
Sword		Soord

However, Kenrick (1784:iii-iv) is extremely wary of representations of the 'respelling' type, commenting that 'this method of disfiguring the orthography is very prejudicial to the learner; who, in thus being taught to speak and read, will forget, or never learn, how to write: an accurate method of spelling words being attained chiefly by reading books correctly printed; in which the word is literally presented in its due proportion of number and character to the eye....The celebrated Mr Sheridan has avoided falling into this erroneous practice, and very judiciously proposes to distinguish the sound of words by certain typographical marks to be placed over particular syllables'. Indeed, the vast body of evidence to be gleaned from the many writers of grammars in Scotland throughout the century exists in a form where the more customary devices of super/subscripted identifying numerals or acute/grave and other marks are used to represent pronunciation shapes and we shall explore their significance fully below. We shall have an opportunity to examine in some detail one important and unique representative of this group; the work of a scholar using the Sheridan/Kenrick type system in a specific and sustained effort to characterise Scots pronunciation both in the Capital and in his native Buchan - Alexander Geddes in his *Three Scottish Poems* (1792).

2.4 Spelling Books

There are, of course, several other kinds of evidence for 18th century Scots pronunciation although, in general, they tend to be of a rather less reliable nature and are certainly much more indirect. While the evidence from rhyming poetry, lists of 'Scotticisms' and the often apocryphal comments of lay observers can all serve to both verify and constrain the information gleaned from the more direct kinds of evidential materials described above, there can be little doubt that our major sources of evidence - in terms of the quantity of surviving materials - for contemporary speech habits (and the attitudes towards them) are to be found in spelling and writing textbooks, in general and as well as specialised pronouncing dictionaries, in compendia of linguistic and social behaviour, as well as in general works on grammar and dissertations by linguistic specialists expressing and detailing their views on language, universal grammar, their personal as well as 'standard' pronunciation and the orthographic conventions used to represent the same.

There are, of course, a great many instances of the Spelling Book genre produced in England, a typical example being Thomas Tuite's *The Oxford Spelling-Book (Being a Complete Introduction to English Orthography)* (1726), with sections on the letters of the alphabet, vowel, diphthongal and consonantal sounds; division of syllables; lists of words *Alike in Sound but Different in Spelling and Signification*; rules for points and abbreviations, the whole illustrated by moral and religious exercises. At the same time, there were many Spelling Books and Spelling Catechisms produced in Scotland (and particularly in Edinburgh) for the instruction of school children in both private and public educational establishments set up in the period (Law:1965:148-61). Not all of their authors were Scottish, nor were they always specifically describing Scots usage, but very often it is possible to deduce features of the phonology/phonetics of contemporary Scots from the comments they contain. Unquestionably the response to a perceived educational necessity (and an associated set of commercial opportunities linked with this), not least promulgated by the educational and social aims of groups like the *Select Society* as well as the proselytising of the religious Establishment - notably the *Scottish Society for the Propagation of Christian Knowledge* - these Spelling and Writing guides were produced in considerable quantities and from a range of publishing houses throughout Scotland; their popularity (Lennie's *Principles of English Grammar*, first published at the beginning of the 19th century, saw an eighty fifth edition in 1886: Volker Mohr, *personal communication*) and day to day use in the classroom is testified by their scarcity today. Some reasons for their great popularity in Scotland itself are proposed by Buchanan (1757:6-7) who, after criticising teachers of English south of the border - where 'Great numbers set up for Teachers of English (when they fail in the business they were brought up to) without a preparative education, or being the least qualified for the execution of such an important trust' - proceeds to rhapsodise on the advantages of Scottish education: 'Let us but travel North of the Tweed, and we will find these grand errors in a very great measure repudiated as scandalous: for, 1. The generality of Teachers of English have had a liberal education, especially those in cities and big towns, a qualified teacher of English being as much esteemed as those who teach Latin or Greek. 2. The harmony that subsists amongst not only them, but teachers of all the several branches of literature, and their frequent and friendly conversation one with another, must of necessity improve their knowledge, so as to arrive to the greatest perfection in their respective professions. Hence it is, that that rational and expeditious method of teaching to read by the powers of the sounds, has been so long practised in that part of the united kingdom'. Buchanan, of course, was a strong advocate of an English rather than a Latin and Greek based education, eloquently argued in his *A Plan for an English Grammar-School Education* (1770). His enthusiasm for the vernacular surfaces everywhere, notably in his sycophantic Dedication to Queen Charlotte in his *The British Grammar* (1762): 'Permit me to lay at Your Majesty's Feet an Essay towards Speaking and Writing Grammatically, and Inditing Elegantly the Language of the bravest, wisest, most powerful, and respectable Body of People upon the Face of the Globe! Highly distinguished with the additional Glory, of being the Vernacular Tongue of the most Virtuous, most Potent, and best Beloved MONARCH upon Earth! A Language, MADAM, which has received fresh Lustre from its being now spoken by a QUEEN the Darling of a People, whose Tongues joyfully proclaim their Gratitude, and whose Hearts (united in the firmest and most dutiful Attachment) will always exult to hear Your MAJESTY express Your ineffable Goodness and all-attracting Affability in the refined and comprehensive English Energy! in the manly Diction of Britons!'

For the historical Scots linguist the interest of these Spelling Books varies enormously, since the kinds of information they provide on matters phonetic and phonological can range from the level of the almost insignificant - for instance, James Gray's *A Concise Spelling Book for the Use of Children* (1809) - to one where there is detailed description of phonetic segments (sometimes even in a specifically Scots context) notably in *A Spelling-Book Upon a New Plan* (1796) and *A New Spelling-Book: In which the Rules of Spelling and Pronouncing the English Language are exemplified and explained* by William Adie, Schoolmaster in Paisley, published there in 1769. It is clear from several of these works that certain educators viewed skills in pronunciation, writing and spelling as more important than those involving comprehension; 'Children are first to be thoroughly grounded in pronunciation: when that is once gained, then it is time to allow them to read such books as are suitable to their understanding' (Warden:1756:*Preface*:x); 'children would learn to read much sooner and easier, were they taught (while the organs of speech are flexible) to pronounce properly from the beginning; and to acquire a graceful delivery, they should, all the while, be taught just quantity, proper accent, emphasis, cadence, and pause. These being the first principal requisites towards a just and eloquent pronunciation, I shall treat of each as briefly as is consistent with perspicuity' (Buchanan:1770:43-44).

Works in this genre, perhaps the most typical of which is William Adie's *A New Spelling-Book* of 1769, conform to a rather general pattern, some stressing matters linguistic more than others, while what detail provided for phonetic description there is varies widely both in quantity and (as we shall see below) typology. As we have already noted, some of these books make little pretence at providing any significant level of linguistic information; notably the Aberdeen published *The Child's Guide* (1795) - 'by a Lover of Children' - is replete with religious materials, with prayers and proverbs, a short catechism, graces, psalms, a history of the Bible, Solomon's *Precepts*, a young man's library, examples of the punishments for breaking the ten commandments (many, it might seem to a modern reader, quite unsuitable for the minds of very young children), lessons in arithmetic and a Latin glossary. In his *A Spelling Book*, Warden (1753:xv) is unrepentant of this heavy emphasis on Christian materials: 'The *Mohametans* carefully preserve every piece, every loose bit of paper of their *Alcoran*, and why should we be behind hand with these infidels, in shewing a veneration for that book which God himself has penned?' Much in the same vein is the anonymous *The Instructor: or An Introduction to Reading and Spelling the English Language*, published in Glasgow in 1798. This work has many Moral

Lessons outlining the duties of Children, Fables, lists of the Books of the Old and New Testament, lists of the principle countries of Europe, measures of time and numerals, although there are also occasionally instructions to the child on the best pedagogical methodology (1798:23):

> You must not think that you will can [sic:CJ] say your talk if you read it once or twice. You must read it till you can say it well, though you should have to read it six times. If there are some words that you can not read, spell them with care and then try to read them. At all times be sure not to pass by a word till you can say it; for if you do so you will not learn to read well.

This book may have been modelled on a work like *The English Instructor* (1728) by Henry Dixon, a school book popular in Scotland and which saw many editions as far as the early 19th century. It consists mainly of lists of words of varying syllable length, religious and moral fables, a catechism and exercises on the Duties of Religion and the like. Quite typical of the contents of the Spelling Book genre is the following from William Scott's *A Short System of English Grammar* (1793:Lesson xvi):

> The Little Prat-A-Pace
>
> Leonora was a little girl of quick parts and vivacity. At only six years old, she could both work and handle her scissars [sic:CJ] with much dexterity, and her mamma's pincushions and huswifes were all of her making. She could read, with ease and readiness, any book that was put into her hand; She could also write very prettily, and she never put large letters in the middle of a word, nor scrawled all awry, from corner to corner of her paper. Neither were her strokes so sprawling, that five or six words would fill a whole sheet from the top to the bottom; as I have known to be the case with some other little girls of the same age.

However, Scott still manages to find a large set of other faults even in such a paragon of youthful behaviour.

Many of these books have a practical, social, utilitarian set of goals considered best achieved through the possession of good linguistic skills of all types. Such an attitude is clearly to be seen in George Fisher's *The Instructor or Young Man's Best Companion* (1751) [the twenty fifth edition] which contains, alongside much information concerning the pronunciation of vowels and consonants, *The Family's Best Companion* 'with Instructions for making linen; how to *pickle* and *preserve*; to make divers sorts of wine; and many excellent *Plasters*, and *Medicines*, necessary in all families' together with a *Compendium of the Sciences of Geography and Astronomy*. Fisher (1789:1-2) claims: 'The Design of this Book being to instruct Mankind, especially those who are Young, in the Method of conversing and transacting Business in the World; therefore the most necessary Accomplishment of spelling and writing, good and proper *English*, claims the first Notice; for let a Person write ever so good a Hand, yet if he be defective in Spelling, he will be ridiculed, and contemptibly smiled at, because his writing fair will render his Orthographical Faults more conspicuous'. Even Alexander Barrie's otherwise useful *A Spelling and Pronouncing Catechism* published in Edinburgh in 1796 is prefaced by almost thirty pages of religious catechism exercises, containing no less than one hundred and ninety five questions and answers of the type: Q. 'What is the chief end of man?' 'A Man's chief end is to glorify God, and to enjoy him for ever'. Perhaps not unexpectedly - since it was commissioned by the *Scottish Society for the Propagation of Christian Knowledge* - James Gray's *A Concise Spelling Book* (1809) is replete with religious materials. Many of the Lessons selected for pronunciation and spelling practice have a strong religious flavour and many pages are devoted to hymns and prayers in this most extensive of all the Scottish Spelling Books.

Instructions to the teacher on the use of the Spelling Book are not, in general, particularly common, a notable exception being Barrie who in his *The Tyro's Guide* (1815:4) gives detailed instructions to the school teacher as how best to use the work in a practical situation:

> After the scholar is well acquainted with the above key, together with the directions prefixed, the teacher may select a few words out of every lesson, as he goes along, and order the scholar to spell them, to point out the number of syllables, and where the accent is placed; to mention the number of vowels, and their respective sounds, according to the key; to point out the diphthongs, where they occur, whether proper or improper, and to give the reason why they are said to be so. Take, for example, the word *Reason*. *Teacher*. Spell reason. *Scholar. r, e, a, rea, s, o, n. son*. How many syllables are in it? *Two, rea, son*. Which is the accented syllable? *rea*. How do you know the accent is upon *rea*? Because it is most forcibly uttered in pronouncing the word. How many vowels are in it? *Three*. Point them out; *e, a*, in *rea*, and *o* in *son*. How do you know there are only *two syllables* when there are *three* vowels in it? Because *ea* is a diphthong, or double vowel. What kind of diphthong is *ea*? An improper diphthong. How do you know that it is improper? Because only one of the vowels is sounded. Which of them is it? *e*. What does *e* in *rea* sound like? *e* in *these*. What does *o* in *son* sound like? It is indistinctly sounded, like *e* in *able*,

Recall too the rather similar exercise in James Gray's *A Concise Spelling Book* (1809:102-103):

> *A Short Exercise on the Principles*
>
> *How many Syllables, or distinct sounds, are there in* considered? Four; Con-sid-er-ed.
> *How do you know that there are four Syllables in* considered? Because there are four Vowels in it.

Point them out. *O* in *con*, *i* in *sid*, *e* in *er*, and *e* in *ed*.
Which is the accented Syllable? Sid.
How do you know that the Accent is upon sid? Because there is most Stress laid upon it, in pronouncing the Word.
What does o *in* con *sound like?* *O* in not.
What does i *in* sid *sound like ?* *I* in King.
What does e *in* er *sound like?* *E* in her.
What does e *in* ed *sound like?* *E* in men.
What does c *in* con *sound like?* *C* in cost.
What does s *in* sid *sound like?* *S* in thus.

In much the same vein, James Dun's *The Best Method of Teaching to Read and Spell English* published in Edinburgh in 1766, provides what, for the genre, is a wealth of information to the prospective teacher on how to instruct the child according to the method proposed by the writer: 'The Method I would observe in teaching this little Book is this, I would begin with the Vowels, and teach them by themselves, then the consonants by themselves, that the Child may the sooner know what Letters are Vowels, and what Consonants, and understand, when he is told, there can be no Syllable or perfect Sound without a Vowel' (1766:*Preface*:x). The author of *A Spelling-Book Upon a New Plan* is typically realistic concerning the role of the teacher: 'In teaching the lessons at the end of the spelling columns, much useful and important information may be communicated to the children, by catechising them upon the facts contained in the individual lessons, as they go along; but this must be left to the discretion and good sense of the teacher' (1796:6) and he knows, perhaps from practice, how the skill of a good teacher can often transcend the best written material; describing the phonetics of the <d> in items like <soldier>, he comments: 'But a good teacher would do more to describe its power by one word of his mouth, than five pages in writing' (1796:28:footnote). The importance of the skill and professionalism of the teacher is very clear from Buchanan's (1757:7:footnote) observation of how 'It is common with the vulgar and illiterate to imagine, that any one who can read tolerably well, is surely a person proper enough to teach little children. But the learned and more judicious part of mankind know better; and that it requires the utmost skill and ability in a teacher, to lay the foundation of a child's education, as it is then, the dawning genius can be either strengthened, and properly cultivated, or enervated and utterly marred'. His pedagogic methodology appears to been rather enlightened as well (1770:30): 'Children should be taught the alphabet, and the combination of letters into syllables, as it were by way of diversion; and, in all their progress in syllabification, in order to preserve the genuine sweetness and benignity of their dispositions, the teacher will put on the bowels of a parent, and instruct them with the utmost mildness, benevolence, and affability'.

In general, the intentions of the authors of these Spelling and Writing manuals were centred in the area of the enhancement of the linguistic skills and abilities of schoolchildren which they often perceived as a route to a way of life which was virtuous and god fearing. Typical are the sentiments of William Scott in the *Advertisement* to his *A New Spelling and Pronouncing Dictionary* (1807), describing his work as 'particularly calculated for the Improvement of Natives and Foreigners in the Proper Speaking and Writing of the English Language'. Again in the *Advertisement* to his *An Introduction to Reading and Spelling* (1796), Scott declares 'the compiler hopes it will be found particularly well-adapted to initiate young people in the Knowledge of the English Language, and at the same time to form their minds to the love of learning and virtue'. It is in the *Preface* to what is surely the technically best developed of all the Scots Spelling Books - the anonymous *A Spelling-Book Upon a New Plan,* published in Edinburgh in 1796 - where we find the educational ideal of the genre expressed:

> The Design of this Book is, to render the teaching and acquiring of the English Language easy and agreeable, both to teachers and taught; and to introduce an uniformity of pronunciation into the different parts of the country where it may be used, in a manner never before attempted. The importance of such an object will be allowed by all. - How far the following Treatise is calculated to accomplish it, time alone can tell; - sure it is, however, that the right pronunciation of a word is easily learned by a child, as a wrong one: and upon that principle this book proceeds.

Yet we must bear in mind that although it is tempting to see the intentions of the authors of these Spelling Books as religion and 'standard' pronunciation conformist and prescriptive (recall Perry's stated intention in the dedication to *The Only Sure Guide to the English Tongue* (1776) that 'the following Spelling Book [is:CJ] intended to fix a standard for the pronunciation of the English language, conformable to the practice of polite speakers in the city of London') there was at the same time a strong sense of the practical social and economic benefits of refined linguistic skills. Even Perry composed *The Man of Business and Gentleman's Assistant* (1774) with advice on bookkeeping, accounts and general business management techniques, a work heavily subscribed to by the land holding and business community around Kelso and beyond. Fisher strongly identifies with this utilitarian effect of language improvement: 'the most necessary accomplishment of spelling and writing good and proper English, claims the first Notice; for if a Person write ever so good a hand, yet if he be defective in Spelling, he will be ridiculed, and contemptibly smiled at, because his writing fair will render his Orthographical Faults more conspicuous' (1789:1-2). It is perhaps Buchanan in his *Linguae Britannicae Vera Pronuntiatio*

(1757:xii:footnote) who sees the advantage in rectifying non-standard pronunciation at the earliest possible age:

> It ought to be, indispensably, the care of every Teacher of English, not to suffer children to pronounce according to the dialect of that place of the country where they were born or reside, if it happens to be vicious. For, if they are suffered to proceed in it, and be habituated to an uncouth pronunciation in their youth, it will most likely remain with them all their days. And those gentlemen who are so captivated with the prejudice of inveterate custom, as not to teach to read by the powers of the sounds, ought in duty, at least, to make their scholars masters of the various formations of the vowels and diphthongs, and of the natural sounds, or simple contacts of the consonants both single and double, whereby they may form the various configurations of the parts of the mouth, and properly apply the several organs of speech in order to speak with ease and propriety. And as children do not commence scholars so soon as their capacities admit, or often on account of their speaking but badly, if they were taught the mute sounds or simple contacts of the consonants, it would immediately enable them to pronounce with a peculiar distinctness. I had a child lately under my care, of about nine years of age, whose speech from the beginning was unintelligible to all, but those who were acquainted with her manner of expression. After I had taught her the sounds of the consonants, and the proper motions that were formed by these contacts both in her own, and by looking at my mouth, I brought her by a few lessons to pronounce any word whatsoever. And by a short practice, she spoke with perfect elocution. This method effectually cuts stammering or hesitation in speech, either in young or old; especially if a grown person be taught to speak for some time with great deliberation.

The general shape of the 18th century Spelling Book genre is fairly standard. There is normally a *Preface* or *Introduction* setting out the author's intentions and any claims for innovation in presentation and methodology. Here too we normally find exemplification of the letters of the alphabet and how they should be pronounced, arguments in favour of and opposing VC and CV alphabet pronunciations often set out at some length and justified on historical, educational and mnemonic criteria. In his discussion of the teaching of the consonantal components of the alphabet, Telfair, in recommending *eb*, *ec*, *ed*, etc rather than *bee*, *cee*, *dee*, comments: 'Others there are who make the Scholars mouth (as they call it) all the consonants, and pronounce them as much as possible without either a vowel before or after them. This is a very trifling bad innovation: it is a method no ways easier for the Scholars than that of putting the vowel before the consonant; and by making children force out the sounds too hard, it becomes sometimes a cause of stammering' (1775:2). Again in the same section he notes: 'What connection has the name *aitsh* with the breathing represented by that letter? or how does it convey the sound? It is surely the most absurd name for it imaginable: and it happens frequently that a child has been three or four months at school, before he can be made to comprehend, how *aitsh* (i.e. *ch*) *a*, *t*, comes to sound *hat*. To avoid so great a difficulty, I would prefer to call it *hee*, which is a name similar to that of the other letters *bee*, *cee*, &c.'

It is in the introductory sections too that we also occasionally find examples of handwriting styles, font types and sizes. The bulk of many Spelling Books is taken up in the post Preface section dedicated to lists of lexical items (some invented especially as illustrative material) which purport to demonstrate the syllabic, morphophonemic and accentual characteristics of the language. Nearly all authors, but notably William Scott (*An Introduction to Reading and Spelling* (1796)), the anonymous authors of *A Spelling-Book Upon a New Plan* and *The Instructor*, and Gray (*A Concise Spelling Book for the Use of Children* (1809)), begin their handbooks with an illustration of the various syllable combinations the language allows in monosyllabic words: VC, CV, VCV, followed by lists of items (and often ingeniously devised prose *Lessons*) illustrating the same, with the recommendation that these be read aloud by the pupil.

Many Spelling Books (notably those by Barrie and Gray) also provide extensive lists of words of varying syllable lengths, on some occasions marking what they see to be syllable boundaries (as in *tes-ti-mo-ny*) on others showing them what they describe as 'undivided'. It is perhaps these 'long and useless tables of words' which Telfair criticises so strongly (1775:2) and which also arouse the concern of Warden (1753:vii) who condemns 'the present spelling books, I mean, the tabular part of them' as 'nothing but a confused heap of words'. Perhaps the classic shape of the 18th century Spelling Book can best be seen from a perusal of the Contents lists of James Robertson's *The Ladies Help to Spelling*, published in Glasgow in 1722. Robertson, 'School-Master at Glasgow', informs us that the 'Contents are taught to Ladies and Gentlewomen by the Author, in *Gibson's Close* in the *Salt-Mercat*, betwixt the Hours of 4. and 6. at Night':

> Of the Various Sounds of the Letters with their Exceptions; Of Right Dividing of Words by Syllables; The Use of Capital Letters; Abbreviations; Numeral Letters; Of Stops and Points; Notes of Direction; A Catalogue of Words, almost equal in Sound, but very much different in sense and Spelling; Of Missive Letters; How to Write to Persons of all Ranks; How to begin Letters upon any Subject; How to end Letters upon any Subject; Of Folding Letters upon any Subject; Of Directing Letters; Of Sealing Letters; A Catalogue of the Proper Names in the Bible.

The Ladies Help takes the form of 'A Dialogue betwixt a Young Lady and her School-Master Concerning Orthography; or the Art of Spelling, &c' and is largely in the form of a set of questions and responses, such as the opening: '*Master*: I suppose you can Read well enough'; *Lady*: 'It's but a supposition, for I Read by Chance, or like a Parrot - pronouncing words, not knowing, whether the Letters be right or wrong plac'd'. *Master*: 'You ought to know the different sounds of the Letters, Especially the Vowels'. *Lady*: 'That's my great trouble, for sometimes I find the Letters sounding one way, and sometimes another, as *tion* frequently sounds *shon*: *tial* as *shall*, *can* as *kan*: These, and many others, are so uncertain in their pronounciation [sic:CJ], that in Writing, I know not what to Write' (1722:2-3). We should not be surprised at the production at this date of a spelling and writing manual aimed specifically at females, since there appears to have been considerable anxiety in some sections of the educational establishment that a concentration of literacy skills amongst males led to a gross injustice and, indeed, social and economic loss. Buchanan, in particular, loudly and vehemently argued the case of female education (1762: *Preface*:xxix): 'It is greatly to be lamented that the Fair Sex have been in general so shamefully neglected with regard to a proper English Education. Many of them, by the unthinking Part of the Males, are considered and treated rather as Dolls, than as intelligent social beings.' And again in his *A Plan of an English Grammar School Education* (1770:118) he thunders:

> With such an English education, we dismiss our female pupils, committing them to the care of proper governesses of boarding-schools; where they may now learn French to great advantage, and other accomplishments peculiar to their sex, and suitable to their rank in life
>
> It is a woe-ful draw-back on the interest and future happiness of society, and consequently to be lamented, that the fair sex have been, in general, so shamefully neglected with regard to proper English education. For though in point of genius, they are not inferior to the other sex, yet due care is not always taken to cultivate their understanding, to impress their minds with solid principles, and replenish them with useful knowledge.
>
> Pray, is a young lady of birth or fortune to be cruelly deprived of the lasting pleasure resulting from a capacity of expressing herself with fluency and accuracy in speaking and writing her mother-tongue? A qualification which would so eminently distinguish, add a lustre to, and place in every point of view all her other accomplishments?

However, Scottish women were not quite so subservient as these observations suggest, since as early as 1720 we find the ladies of Edinburgh founding (on the model of and as a rival to the all male Athenian Club) *The Fair Intellectual Club*: 'In the month of May 1717, three young Ladies happened to divert ourselves by walking in *Heriot's Gardens*, where one of us took Occasion to propose that we should enter into a Society, for Improvement of one another in the Study and Practice of such Things, as might contribute most effectively to our Accomplishment...We thought it a Great Pity, that Women who excel a great many others in Birth and Fortune, should not also be more eminent in Virtue and good Sense, which we might attain unto, if we were as industrious to cultivate our Minds, as we are to adorn our Bodies'. The Club's founders were certainly conscious of the fact that their venture might attract the hostility of men: 'Ignorance of Human Nature, (whereof Women partake of as well as Men) Malice, Weakness or Want of Thought, may occasion a great many Objections against us, such as, that we go out of our Sphere, that we neglect more proper Business, &c...'. In consequence, their club was originally intended to be a secret society whose members were neither to be under fifteen years of age, or over twenty; there was to be no politics or religion discussed (although they took a strong Christian position against non-religious painting, music and poetry) while censure and ridicule were not to be tolerated among members; death or marriage terminated membership of the Club. The aim of Club members 'sensible of the Disadvantages that our Sex in General, and we in particular labour under' was 'to imitate the laudable Example of some of our Brethren, that make the greatest Figure in the learn'd and polite World'. However, the secrecy of the *Fair Intellectual Club* was compromised when its Secretary revealed its existence to a member of the all male *Athenian Club* with whom she was in love. The interests of the Club were not confined to a narrow Edinburgh social circle, since it published at least two volumes of *The Edinburgh Miscellany* which included writing from contributors from several parts of Scotland. It is important to stress too, that one of the major concerns of the Club's Constitution was the linguistic competence of its members:

> Nor do you confine your Studies so much, as to neglect the *French* and *Italian* languages, which are accounted so polite and fashionable in this Age. But when I consider the Improvements all of you have made in the *English* Language, I can never cease to admire your Judgement and Application. As nothing less than a right Taste of the Excellency and Beauty of Writing and Speaking well, could determine you to be at due Pains to attain them; so, without great Industry and Application, it had been impossible for you to have become Mistresses of the *English* Language in such Perfection; especially considering how difficult it is for our Country People to acquire it. And here I cannot cease to reflect with Indignation on the Negligence of our Sex, in this Particular: What a Shame is it, that *Ladies* who value themselves for Wit and Politeness, shou'd yet be ignorant of their Mother Tongue? How many set up for Wits, that can't write good Sense, in proper Language? And how few can pronounce what they read, or deliver themselves, with a proper Grace? The more trivial these Faults appear, the greater Reproach to those who cannot correct them. Few, very few of the *Ladies* I have had Occasion to know, can so much as spell. Good God! What have they to boast of?: How can they censure others with the least Assurance, who can scarce do any Thing to Purpose themselves? Pardon me then, *Ladies*, tho' I gratefully acknowledge my Duty to Heaven and you, on this Occasion, for the Privilege of being admitted to share the Blessings of your Conversation, who have distinguished your selves from the common Herd of Women, by your Diligence to acquire such admirable Qualities as you now possess'.

In many respects it is James Dun's *The Best Method of Teaching to Read and Spell English (Demonstrated in Eight Parts)* (1766) which is the spelling book stereotype of the period. In its one hundred and eighty three page bulk, it embraces a great many exercises in pronunciation and spelling of words of varying syllable length, has page after page of word lists illustrative of the pronunciation of the letters <c> and <g>, <ch>, <th> and so on, sections on the pronunciation of vowels and diphthongs with a question and answer format used to illustrate much of this, closed with a section of illustrative *Lessons* encompassing more than half of the bulk of the entire work. Many of these, as we have noted, have a strong religious bias, while others are aimed at instilling good behaviour and manners in the young population, one headed *Upon Occasion of the Complaints of some Parents, of their Children's unmannerly Behaviour, and of some old Scholars, advanced in Years, being sent to the School again, to learn Civility and good Manners* (1766:117-118):

> If you are in a standing Posture, let your Body be upright, not lolling upon another's Shoulders, as if you wanted a Supporter; nor sink your Head into your Shoulders. Do not play with your Fingers, nor shuffle with your Feet, nor stand so near the Person you speak to, as to breathe in his Face, or bedew him with your Breath. Do not speak through your Nose, nor with any affected unhandsome Gesture.

2.5 Pronouncing Dictionaries

While there is no doubt that the Pronouncing Dictionary exists as an identifiable and separate genre in the 18th century, it has to be borne in mind that several other of the primary source types contain within them sections with long lists of words variously marked for pronunciation and which could be labelled 'pronouncing dictionaries' in their own right. Notable among these is the extensive list of items in *A Spelling-Book Upon a New Plan* (1796) where especially the lists of Disyllables (pp 25-43), Trisyllables (pp. 49-59), Four Syllables (pp. 73-79) and Five Syllables (pp. 87-89) show a substantial level of phonetic (as well as stress placement) information which, given their alphabetical presentation, could readily be used to discover the recommended pronunciation of a substantial part of the contemporary lexicon: āgĕnt; căpăble; Năvĭgā*ti*òn; prōlōcûtor; obsēqŭĭ*o*ŭsnĕss. So too John Warden's *A Spelling Book* contains extensive 'collections of words' wherein, for example 'where *c* before *e*, *i* or *y* is sounded like *s*; wherein the diphthongs *ou*, *ow*, sound as in *loud* or *now*; where *u* sounds *u*[1] as in *endu*[1]*re*', and so on. Again, Barrie's *A Spelling and Pronouncing Catechism* (1796) contains lists of lexical items clearly marked for pronunciation values: dâu*gh*\tèr, ŏût\wărd, hêi\noŭs. Perhaps to a lesser extent we could include under this head the lists of words which appear in many Spelling Books, notably in Dun's *The Best Method* illustrative of recommended pronunciations for specific phonetic types: '*H* has the sound of *each*, or *ch* has the Sound of *etch*, in such words as the following: Chap, chaff, chat.....', so that *chap* sounds *tshap*, &c. and so *ch* sounds in: *Chìn-a, Cho-sen, Rich-es*' (1766:20).

Pronouncing Dictionaries proper range from those in which there is a minimal degree of phonetic information provided, with almost none of it showing any direct inference for 18th century Scots pronunciation, to those where not only is the information provided specifically in a Scots context, but it is couched in considerable phonetic detail and descriptive sophistication. In the first category falls the *Linguae Britannicae Vera Pronunciatio* or *An English Pocket Dictionary* written by James Buchanan in 1757 and published in London, which he regarded as 'a *vade mecum* for grown persons' in which (1757:*Advertisement*):

> Every Word has not only the common Accent to denote the Emphasis of the Voice, but, in order to a just Pronunciation, every Syllable is marked with a long or short Accent to determine its quantity; and the quiescent Letters, various sounds of Vowels, &c. are so distinguished, that any Person, Native or Foreigner, who can but read, may speedily acquire an accurate Pronunciation of the English Language.

Buchanan makes the claim for his Dictionary that 'with respect to orthography, I have been very solicitous in correcting the antiquated manner of spelling in former dictionaries: and that I have reduced the English orthography to the standard of the best writers of the present age, the rules for spelling prefixed, will, as a specimen, sufficiently evince' (1757:iv-v). However, the 'long or short Accent' marks he employs in the Dictionary entries themselves have little to do with quantity and represent in no principled way differences in vowel quality and monophthong/diphthong contrasts, as is clear from such entries as *Cāne* ('to beat with a stick or walking stick'), *Cănīne* ('Dog-like') and *Că´nĭster* ('A vessel of tin or silver to hold tea'). In these instances the <ā>/<a> alternation appears to represent some kind of [e]/[a] contrast while the <i>/<ĭ> seems to signify a diphthongal [aɩ] versus [ɩ] alternation with little significance for stressed vowel durational differences. Buchanan is, of course, aware that the long/short nomenclature reflects phonetic facts other than those relating purely to duration: 'Can any one, for example, when he knows the long sound of (*i*) is like the pronoun (*I*) marked with the long accent over it thus (ī); and that the long sound of (*u*) is like (*eu*) with the long accent thus (ū), and sees them so marked in such words as *piety, diameter, irony, purity, universe, unity*, &c. I say, can he miss of pronouncing them thus, *pIety, dIameter, Irony, peurity, euniverse, eunity*?' However, he continues: 'And also when he sees the short sound of (*i*), which is almost (*ee*) with the short accent over it thus (ĭ)....in such words as *dĭvĭsĭbĭlĭty*....*w*ill he not with certainty pronounce them as if wrote *deĕveĕseĕbeĕleĕty....'* (1757:ix), a recommendation which may have struck his English contemporaries as a blatant Scotticism.

Writing at the very end of the 18th century, William Angus produced several works of a Pronouncing Dictionary nature, notably his *A Pronouncing Vocabulary of the English Language* (1800:second edition) which provide us with more reliable and systematically presented phonetic description. Despite its title, this work has an overall shape not all that unlike a Spelling Book, with its lists of Greek and Latin Proper Names, Scriptural Names, rules for the use of commas, full stops and other points, as well as lists of 'Words similar in Orthography, but different in Signification and Orthoepy' (1800:108-112):

Orthography	Signification	Orthoepy
Does v.	Doth	duz
Does n.	Plural of *doe*, a she-deer	dōz
Form n.	External appearance	fÂrm
Form n.	A long seat or a class of students	fōrm

At the same time, he includes lists of 'words similar in Orthoepy, but different in Orthography and Signification', such as *adds, adze; burrow, borough; soared, sword,* etc. (1800:112-114). But the bulk of the work consists of an alphabetically arranged list of words ('which frequently occur') in two columns, one representing 'Orthography', the other 'Orthoepy', with the phonetic significance of the symbols in the latter explained in the *Key to the Sounds* (1800:7), so that we find entries such as:

Orthography	Orthoepy
abstemiousness	ab-stē'mė-us-ness
shrewdly	shrûd'lė

Both Angus' *An English Spelling and Pronouncing Vocabulary* (1814) and *An Introduction to Angus' Vocabulary and Fulton's Dictionary* (1814) (both published in Glasgow) were 'Intended to facilitate the Acquirement of Uniform English Pronunciation and a Correct Delivery'. Central to these works are long, specially selected (and occasionally alphabetically arranged) sets of lexical items grouped under headings of particular vowel types. Thus, <a>, <o> and <au> are to be pronounced as his Â (possibly [ɒɒ]): *all, fall, call, salt, dwarf, warm, quart, daub, laud, vault, taught, saw, draw, thaw, yawning,* etc. (1814:6), while the following are to be rendered with his <â> (possibly [ɑɑ]): *bar, jar, star, march, path, partner, farmer*, etc. Barrie's *A Spelling and Pronouncing Dictionary of the English Language for the Use of Schools* (1794) follows a very similar pattern, with long lists of words arranged under o^1, o^2, a^3, etc. headings, a representational system he abandoned in favour of superscripted accents, acutes, graves and macrons in the later *A Tyro's Guide* and *A Spelling and Pronouncing Catechism*.

John Burn's *A Pronouncing Dictionary of the English Language* published in Glasgow in 1796 (the second edition) is set out in a much more conventional dictionary format, heavily influenced by the approach taken by William Johnston, Kenrick and Buchanan. The dictionary entries take the form of conventionally spelt lexical items, 'undivided' as to syllable composition, and marked for accent by acute and grave superscripts: 'Accent is the raising of the voice in some particular syllable of a word. It is marked thus (ʹ) or thus (ˋ). The first is called the acute, the last the grave accent. The acute denotes a short, and the grave a long syllable. These two accents, with the characteristical figures, sufficiently distinguish the long and short syllables in every word in the Dictionary' (1796:vi-vii). His 'characteristical figures' refer to no less than seventeen numerical superscripts denoting vowel quality (set out in his table entitled *Of the Vocal or Vowel Sounds in the English Language* (*Introduction*:v)) in this instance placed at the end of the word (in the case of monosyllables and disyllabic words), or at the end of syllables in polysyllabic items, thus: 'Bèat^{14} *n* to strike, knock, conquer, rouse, throb' and 'Be^{15}lèa^{14}guer^{1}ʹ, v, to besiege, block up'.

James Douglas' *Treatise on English Pronunciation* (c 1740) (Holmberg:1956) might also be treated as a type of Pronouncing Dictionary to the extent that it is set out in a fashion which enables the reader to find examples of the pronunciation of vowels, diphthongs and consonants arranged in their alphabetical sequence. The entire *Treatise* is structured on a Question/Answer routine basis. For instance, 'How is the Vowel *E* Sounded in the first Syllable of a Word? I The Vowel *E* is Sounded Long in the first Syllable of a Word. 1. When *E* final follows a Single Consonant in Words of one Syllable, as GLĒBE, GLĒDE, HĒRE, MĒTE, THĒSE, SCĒNE, RĒRE, THĒME, BĒDE, VĒRE. *Except* WĚRE which is sounded short. 2. When the Vowel *E* terminates the first Syllable, as, BĒSOM, MĒDIATE, PĒTER, FĒVER, FRĒQUENT, RĒCENT, VĒNAL' (Holmberg:1956:141). Obviously, it would be difficult to 'look up' any lexical item in a work like this without knowing the place in word or syllable of the particular vowel or consonant whose pronunciation the reader was anxious to ascertain: *How is the Vowel O sounded in the End of a Word*? I. The Vowel *O* is Sounded like *OO* Long in the following Words. DŌ, THRŌ, TŌ, WHŌ, INTŌ, UNDŌ, UNTŌ. II. In the End of all other Words this Vowel is sounded like *o* Long, 1. In English Words, Ō, FRŌ', GŌ, HŌ, LŌ.' (Holmberg:1956:179).

While there may be some doubt as to the suitability of classifying James Douglas' *On English Pronunciation* as a Pronouncing Dictionary, there can be little doubt as to the appropriateness of that label for the substantive part of his namesake's *A Treatise on the Provincial Dialect of Scotland* (1779). Sylvester Douglas' insightful work has three chapters dealing in turn with the nature of sounds and their orthographic representation; the pronunciation of the sounds represented by the letters of the alphabet and a long discussion on the nature of rhyme. However, the section which has the greatest interest for the student of late 18th century Scots pronunciation is that which lies at the heart of the *Treatise*: *A Table of Words Improperly Pronounced by the Scotch, Showing their True English Pronounciation* [sic:CJ] (Jones: 1992:158-233). This alphabetical list of items is unique in the 18th century for the way in which it reveals specifically Scots pronunciations, albeit to point out how 'improper' they are, and for the detail of phonetic description which it incorporates. Consider the following entries which are fairly typical as instances of Douglas' pronunciation recommendations:

ABOVE

The *o* has the second or short sound of *u*, exactly as in *rub, sunk*. The Scotch are very often apt to sound it like the long vocal *u* or *oo*; so as to make *above*, rhyme to *groove*. There are a considerable number of words of this termination, and they are pronounced in three different ways. Some of them in the manner we have just described. In some, as *strove, rove, grove*, the *o* has its long close sound as in *abode*. And in some, as *move, prove*, it is sounded in the manner in which the Scotch pronounce it in *above*. As these three sounds are generally confounded in Scotland, so that the words pronounced in England in one way, are, in that country, pronounced in an other, it will be useful to attend to the following lists, where they are arranged according to their true pronounciation. *Love* which they sound properly, and which rhymes to the true pronounciation of *above* will serve as the leading word in the first list. *Move* which rhymes to *groove* in the second. and *Jove* (which is also properly pronounced by the Scotch) in the third.

1. *Love, above* (pronounced by the Scotch like *move*) *dove* (by the Scotch like *Jove*) *shove*, noun and verb (by the Scotch like *Jove*) *glove, True-love*.

2. *Move, amove, approve, behoove, disapprove, improve, prove,* (*remove, reprove*) All often pronounced by the Scotch like *love*.

3. *Jove, alcove, cove, clove* (verb and noun,) *drove* (verb and noun,) *grove, hove, rove, strove* verb and noun, *throve, wove*. The following is a perfect rhyme

O! witness earth beneath, and heav'n above;
For can I hide it? I am sick of love.

BOUGHT

In this and similar words, as *sought, thought, fought, drought*. The *ough* has the long open sound of the *o* in *corn*, or of *oa* in *broad*. This sound, if at all, is but just distinguishable from the long broad *a* in *all, malt* or *au* in *Paul*. Some writers on pronounciation consider them as entirely the same. They are generally made to rhyme with such words as *taught*, and *fraught*, but that is no proof that their sound is exactly the same.

> If e'er one vision touch'd thy infant thought
> Of all the nurse, and all the priest e'er taught.

The Scotch, after they get rid of the more barbarous pronounciation in which the *gh* is pronounced as a strong guttural, generally fall into the mistake of using the long close sound of *o*, and making (for instance) *bought*, and *boat*, the same word to the ear. And this they do so generally that in endeavouring to mimic the Scotch pronounciation I have observed that the English are apt to hit upon this particular way of sounding this class of words. Yet this, in truth, is not part of the vernacular pronunciation of Scotland.

2.6 Grammar Books and General Essays on Language

There are extant at least three major Grammar Books composed by Scottish writers in the 18th century, works whose primary aim it was to provide an analysis and categorisation of the main characteristics of English syntax (and occasionally morphology) primarily based upon Latin stereotypes (Michael:1970:9-23). Probably the most important of these was James Buchanan's *The British Grammar* published anonymously (Kennedy:1926) in 1762 written, its advertisement boasts, 'towards Speaking and Writing the English Language Grammatically, and Inditing Elegantly'. The bulk of this work is a treatise on the syntax of English, with lengthy sections on Noun and Verb structure, including discussions upon case, gender, tense and modality. Rules for concord are set out and the whole is concluded with extensive exercises upon False Syntax. However, the work has some interest for the historical phonologist in that its *Introduction* contains a discussion of the language's sound system, in a format we are by now familiar with from our discussion of Spelling and Writing Books. Buchanan begins with a description of the alphabet symbols, proceeds to examine the various 'powers' of these symbols as vowels, diphthongs, triphthongs and consonants. There is a discussion of syllabicity and the principles of syllable division, concluded by a section on Prosodic structure. This overall model is followed by John Burn's *A Practical Grammar of the English Language*, published in Glasgow in 1766, 'In which the several parts of Speech are clearly and methodically explained; their concord and government reduced to grammatical rules, and illustrated by a variety of examples'; an almost identical format appears too in William McIllquam's *A Comprehensive Grammar*, likewise published in Glasgow, in 1781 and republished as *A Compendious Grammar* (1789, 1797, 1802), although this work is distinctive for its (often rather odd) *Concise*

Historical Account of the English Language (1781:1-8). Since these latter grammar books, like Burn's, are clearly intended 'for the Use of Schools', they too attempt to cover much of the ground normally associated with Spelling Books. McIllquam's works is exceptional, however, for its attention to vowel quantity, emphasis and cadence and for its attempts at a derivational morphology and its detailed examples of the parsing technique.

General treatises on the nature of language are, of course, the hallmark of the 18th century Enlightenment (Dwyer:1987; Michael:1970), and there were several notable Scottish contributors to the genre. Not all of these have direct interest for the student of contemporary Scots phonology (Monboddo (1774)); - but *The Theory of Language* (1788) by James Beattie - Professor of Moral Philosophy and Logick in the Marischal College and University, Aberdeen - contains much sophisticated information on matters relating to pronunciation, syllabification, prosody and linguistic standards. While they do not perhaps fit too neatly into the *Essay on Language* category, the two essays on pronunciation by James Adams: *Euphonologia Linguae Anglicanae* (1794) and *The Pronunciation of the English Language* (1799) are not only replete with valuable information concerning general phonetic and phonological description, but contain many observations, as we have already noted, specific to contemporary Scots phonetic values.

2.7 Miscellaneous Sources

Infrequent information concerning matters phonological and phonetic can be found in the pages of 'near alike' lists and catalogues of Scotticisms, as well as in other, often anecdotal and indirect contexts. Perhaps the best instance of the last is the anecdote by James Adams (1799) concerning contemporary habits of Latin pronunciation. Commenting upon the pronunciation *ankshus* for <anxious>, he recounts (1799:115-116):

> This hissing English contraction extended to Latin words, shews another absurdity in our pronunciation of Latin. In the year 1755, I attended a public Disputation in a foreign University, when at least 400 Frenchmen literally hissed a grave and learned Doctor (Mr Banister) not by way of insult, but irresistibly provoked by the quaintness of the repetition of *sh*. The Thesis was the concurrence of God in *actionibus viciosis*: the whole hall resounded with the hissing cry of *sh* (*shi, shi, shi*) on its continual occurrence in *actio, actione, viciosa - ac-shi-o, vi-shi-osa*. Strange, that our great Schools will not adopt the laudable precedent of the Scotch; for we render all the vowels, syllables and words absolutely unintelligible, exemplified in this phrase: *Amabo, Domine refer mihi quae curatio dari possit huic aegro uti cito sanetur, - emebo, Dâm - ine reefur meihei quee curaisho heic eegro dairei pawssit yutei ceito sai- neetur*. This pronunciation would make a French Doctor think the address was abusive, Hebrew, or High Dutch; the first hearing would go far to puzzle the ablest Latin scholar in Scotland, the eminent Doctor Gregory. The

> French may laugh at us, not so much indeed on account of the singularity of native pronunciation, as our want of good sense in not imitating their example of tempering the sounds of their own tongue in speaking Latin; for any Latin phrase, articulated by the strict laws of French nasal sounds, monotonous, and final accent, would be equally unintelligible to Italians, Spaniards, Germans. English and Scotch Literati.

A 'Scotch' pronunciation of *sanetur* as what Adams' 'respelling' suggests is [senitur] highlights, as we shall see in detail below, two of the most typical features of Scots 18th century vowel phonology, the raising of [a] and [e] to [e] and [i] respectively.

The extremely popular lists of 'Scotticisms' in the period (Basker:1993; Rogers:1991), seem most often to have been the product of abashment at provinciality, many writers - notably Smollet - systematically expurgating their writings of any trace of what were perceived as Scots characteristics of syntax, morphology or vocabulary. However the lists themselves - notably those of Hume (1760), Sinclair (1782), Beattie (1787), William Scott (1793), William Angus (1813) and Elphinston (1787) - do provide us with some phonological information, notably in the areas of the suprasegmental (metathesis phenomena) and at the phonology/morphology interface. Many authors of spelling books include lists of lexical items which are homophonous or near homophonous under general titles such as *A Collection of Words similar in Sound, but different in Spelling and Signification* (*The Instructor*: 1798); *Words of the same Sound, though widely different in the Sense and Signification* (Fisher:1762);*Words nearly the same in sound; but different in signification and spelling* (*A Spelling Book on a New Plan*:1796); *Words the same in Sound, or nearly so, but different in Spelling and Signification* (Barrie:1794); *Words the same in Sound, but different in Spelling and Signification* (William Scott: 1793), *Of Words having very near the same Sound, tho' they are of a different Signification* (Dun:1766), *Words the same in Pronunciation, but different in Spelling and Significance* (Gray:1809:104-106), while Barrie also includes a list of items in which 'the Pronunciation varies from the Spelling' and even the otherwise rather unhelpful *The Child's Guide* (1799:32) tells us that 'there are many words like one another in letters and sounds; for example, 'let us drink our *wine*, for the *wind* blows'. With the possible exception of the extensive 'Catalogue of Words, almost equal in Sound, but very much different in sense and Spelling' in Robertson's *The Ladies Help to Spelling* (1722:41-62), with 'near alikes' such as <Bruise>/<Bruce>; <Bread>/<Breed>/<Bred>; <Brow>/<Brew>, these (near) homophone lists are not always insightful in terms of contemporary Scots pronunciation, often reflecting characteristics of non-Scots phonology, in pairings such as <Rome>, <room>; <air>, <e'er>, <ere>, <Heir>; <bile>, <boil>, although some sets (notably those of

Fisher, Warden and *A Spelling Book on a New Plan* [which also includes phonetic detail in its extensive list]) appear irregularly to highlight items which might be most likely homophonous in a Scots context: <ship>/<sheep>; <babel>/<babble>; <char>/<chair>; <near>/<ne'er>; <tall>/<toll>. Only in John Drummond's *A Grammatical Introduction to the Modern Pronunciation and Spelling of the English Tongue* (1767) do we find lists of near alikes based upon pronunciation divergence rather than convergence: 'The following words are different, if rightly pronounced' (1767:79ff): <ax>/<acts>; <doer>/<door>; <home>/<whom> etc.; 'Words that Differ in the First Syllable, if rightly pronounced' (1767:78ff): <better>/<bitter>; <rabble>/<rebel> etc.

3

Orthographic Innovations and Their Interpretation

'Can the shades and gradations of sound be painted?' Sylvester Douglas (1796)

3.1 Methodologies

The level of sophistication to be found in 18th century handbooks on pronunciation as regards the description and classification of speech sounds is, as we have suggested, somewhat variable. On the whole, we look in vain for detailed articulatory or acoustic description of the speech mechanism, although there are some notable exceptions, especially Beattie (1788:20-21):

> Human Voice is air sent out from the lungs, and so agitated, or modified, in its passage through the windpipe and larynx, as to become distinctly audible. The windpipe, wezand, or rough artery, is that tube, which, on touching the forepart of our throat externally, we feel hard and uneven. It conveys air into the lungs for the purpose of respiration and speech. It consists of cartilages, circular before, that they may the better resist external injury; but soft and flattish on the opposite side, that they may not hurt the gullet, or esophagus; which lies close behind, and is the tube whereby what we eat and drink is conveyed into the stomach. These cartilages are separated by fleshy membranes; by means of which the windpipe may be shortened or lengthened a little, and, when necessary, incurvated, without inconvenience.

While we should not expect to find in 18th century spelling books and the like the types of elaborate description characteristic of the modern treatise on phonetics, what we do find is the type of information suggestive of the introductory materials to modern dictionaries and the kind of description often to be seen in elementary books for non-native speakers of English. In general, descriptive techniques for sound systems in the 18th century centre around three main areas: 1. manipulations of the standard alphabet, through the introduction of diacritic marks or through some re-organisation of recognised alphabetic symbols. Only occasionally do we find the introduction of new, non-standard orthographic symbols. 2. the utilisation of metaphorical descriptive terminology such as *broad, acute, fat, grave, slender*, and so on. 3. the use of homophonous exemplification, notably through the medium of rhyme. The complexities of the endeavour are fully appreciated by Sylvester Douglas (Jones:1992:100): 'Minute discussions concerning pronounciation, [sic:CJ] or phraseology, are of a dry and forbidding nature....The task of ascertaining and correcting the peculiarities of provincial pronounciation is as difficult as it is uninviting. If we suppose a person perfectly acquainted with all the vices of the Scotch, and perfectly master of the proper English pronounciation how is he to convey his knowledge to the others by the eyes? Can the shades and gradations of sound be painted? Or what adequate means can he employ to communicate a just idea of two different sounds which two different sets of men represent by the very same combination of letters?'

Before we can proceed to interpret in detail the kinds of evidence supplied by the source materials outlined in the previous chapter for their significance for the pronunciation of contemporary Scots, we must first examine in some depth the descriptive techniques employed by 18th century observers of pronunciation involved in what Samuel Johnson, in his *A Plan of a Dictionary for the English Language* (1747) calls 'the great orthographical contest'. In this way we can arrive at some feeling for the accuracy and detail of the observational adequacy of those who introduce innovations in the system of symbol/sound representation and arrive at some kind of assessment of the ways those representations can be best interpreted as data for actual contemporary usage in all its complexity.

3.2 The Phonological Inventory: General Characteristics
Vowel Sounds: Monophthongs
Diacritic Numerals and Accent Marks

The use of superscripted numerals and other diacritic marks to denote the (close to) surface phonetic value of vowel and even consonantal segments was not, of course, an invention of the 18th century orthoepist. Writers like Hart and Gil in the previous two centuries had utilised such devices to enhance the descriptive power of phonetic alphabets, alongside their use of non-standard orthographic shapes, which they so successfully introduced. The spelling reformer *par excellence* in the seventeenth century who relied almost entirely on diacritic devices was, as is well known, Richard Hodges, whose *The English Primrose* sets out to 'shew tẖe inconvenienčiė and unčertaintiė, in our expressiňĝ— tẖe Eňglish Tọňḡụẹ; and tẖen tô shew how the säme may be remedięd, without infriňğiňḡ of custọm.......and yet ûṣẹ our äñçient and ûṣûâl cḥaracters, and adḍẹ ônely tô tẖem sọmẹ marks oḟ distiňcṭion.' (Hodges 1644:2-3) It was perhaps the difficulty of setting up and especially of proofing an elaborate system like this which acted against its wholesale adoption as a reformed alphabet, and there is little to match it in the 18th century for extravagant use of super and sub scripted emblems. Orthoepists and dictionary compilers in the later period were content to use a considerably simpler system of bars, accents, macrons and cedillas or a set of numerical markers to register vowel quality (and occasionally consonantal) contrasts. Although, as we shall see, there was considerable variation in usage by individual spelling reformers, the greatest influence in the promotion of diacritic numerical marking in the 18th century was undoubtedly Thomas Sheridan, whose *Scheme*, set out in various places but notably in the *Dissertation on the Causes of the Difficulties, which occur, in Learning the English Tongue*, published as part of his *Course of Lectures on Elocution* in 1762 was intended 'to facilitate the Attainment of the English Tongue, and establish a *Perpetual Standard of Pronunciation*'. Sheridan's *Scheme* (1762:239-40) was to be based on four major principles the aim of which was to produce a system of phonetic representation where the standard of 'one symbol, one sound' predominated, and where digraphs were to be employed only where they represented genuine bi-vocalic (diphthongal) transitions:

> the four following rules should be strictly observed:
> 1. No character should be set down in any word, which is not pronounced.
> 2. Every distinct simple sound, should have a distinct character to mark it; for which, it should uniformly stand.
> 3. The same character should never be set down, as the representative of two different sounds.
> 4. All compound sounds, should be marked only by such characters, as will naturally, and necessarily produce those sounds, upon being properly pronounced, in the order in which they are placed.

Yet the *Scheme* is essentially characterised by its overall reliance upon the symbolic content of the standard orthography, for while Sheridan had clearly become more than despondent over its ability to reflect spoken usage, in the *Rhetorical Grammar* we still find more than a hint of disapproval of the efforts of earlier scholars to remedy this defect by parting too radically from any in-use system of orthography: 'Such indeed is the state of our written language, that the darkest hierogliphics, or most difficult ciphers which the art of man has hithertoo invented, were not better calculated to conceal the sentiments of those who used them from all who had not the key, than the state of our spelling is to conceal the true pronunciation of our words, from all except a few well educated natives' (1780:13). Even as late as 1818 we find Fulton and Knight in their *Principles of English Pronunciation* (1818:vii) expressing a similar view:

> Letters, to answer perfectly the end of their invention, should be proportioned to the number of simple sounds; that every sound may have its own character, and every character a single sound. Such would be the orthography of a new language, to be formed by a synod of grammarians on principles of science. But who can hope to prevail on nations to change their practice, and make all their old books useless? - Every attempt, therefore, to render the orthography of the English Language conformable to its orthoepy, must prove preposterous and impracticable; as this could not be done without new moulding our alphabet, and making a considerable addition to its characters.

However, despite his 'four rules', the *Scheme* set out by Sheridan in the *Dissertation* still contained several ambiguities:

	1st	2nd	3rd
A	hat	hate	hall
E	bet	there	here
I	fit	bite	field
O	not	note	prove
U	cub	bush	cube

	4th	5th
E	her	
I	stir	birth
O	love	
U	busy	

The attempt to preserve the traditional orthography and to extend its descriptive power by means of numerical classification clearly has the consequence of violating Sheridan's second principle; the third sound of <I> and the third of <E> both represent some kind of [i], while the second sound of <E> and the second of <A> both appear to represent a low mid [ɛ] type segment. This ambiguity is removed, or at least disguised, in the *Scheme of the Alphabet* as presented in Sheridan's *A Rhetorical Grammar* (1780) where there is a division of the vocalic inventory into nine as follows: a^1, *hall*; a^2 *hat*; a^3 *hate*; e^3 *beer*; o^2 *note*; o^3 *noose*; e^1 *bet*; i^1 *fit*; u^1 *but*, with a closer match between symbol and phonetic shape, although there are still outputs from the phonology which the inventory does not appear to account for, notably any kind of [ɑ]/[a]/[æ] contrast. Sheridan's influence on the grammarians and spelling reformers in Scotland was especially strong, due in part to the popular lecture series he delivered there from 1761 and which, in turn, led in the same year to the publication by the *Select Society* of *Regulations for Promoting the Reading and Speaking of the English Language in Scotland;* the Society was to have a profound influence upon the progress of spelling reform and the status of study into pronunciation in Scotland (Law: 1965:158; Jones: 1992:97-98).

While Kenrick's *A Rhetorical Grammar of the English Language* of 1784 uses a numerical system of vowel (and consonantal) classification not unlike Sheridan's grammar of the same name, his is a much extended inventory, listing no less than sixteen vowel sounds, each distinct phonetic output exemplified by appropriate lexical items, thus avoiding any ambiguity of the type so clear in Sheridan's *Dissertation*. Yet Kenrick appears to have been influenced more by Sheridan's *Scheme of the Alphabet* in the *Rhetorical Grammar*; discussing the inherent lack of symbol/sound matching in the standard orthography, he observes (Kenrick: 1784: *Introduction*: iv):

> The celebrated Mr Sheridan has avoided falling into this erroneous practice, and very judiciously proposes to distinguish the sound of words by certain typographical marks to be placed over particular syllables.

Unlike Sheridan's system, Kenrick's does not attempt to provide a set of different kind of *e*'s or *a*'s, but simply lists what he considers to be the contrastive vocalic inventory of vowel sounds, sixteen in all plus 'the indistinct sound, marked with a cypher thus [0] [a *zero* symbol:CJ], as practised in the colloquial utterance of the particles *a* and *the*, the last syllables of words ending in *en*, *le*, and *re*; as *a garden*, *the castle*, &c. also in syllables frequently sunk in the middle of words of three syllables, as *every*, *memory*, *favourite*, &c.' (*Introduction*:viii). So, for an item like <Fascination>, Kenrick proposes a dictionary entry for 'correct' pronunciation purposes such as [fa^{11}s-*c*i^{15}-na^{12}-*ti*o^{1} n].

One of the Scottish grammarians most influenced by Kenrick's methodology seems to have been William Scott, 'Teacher of English Language' and 'Teacher of Elocution and Geography in Edinburgh' whose *A New Spelling, Pronouncing, and Explanatory Dictionary of the English Language* (the revised edition of 1802 appears to be the only extant version) was intended as 'an agreeable and valuable Companion for the Youth of both Sexes, and particularly calculated for the Improvement of Natives and Foreigners in the proper Speaking and Writing of the English Language'. Scott lists no less than fifteen different primary vowel segments, like Kenrick using the standard orthography in combination with a numeral to differentiate the various types:

> 1, blab, had; 2, babe, place; 3, web, beg; 4, glebe, cede; 5, rib, bid; 6, bribe, ride, mice, smile; 7, God, job, log; 8, robe. mode, joke; 9, cub, cud, mug; 10, cube, duke, muse; 11, star, garb, half, calf, can't, shan't, ah ha, father, command, rather; 12, hall, wall, bald, scald; 13, hopeful, mindful, full, bull, bush, food, room; 14, voice, void, spoil; 15, loud, foul, noun, out.

Since such a complex system would make the interpretation of dictionary entries a difficult mnemonic exercise even for the most motivated of scholars, Scott prefaces the top of each verso and recto page of the dictionary section with headings containing examples of vowel and consonantal types, thus

> lad^{1}, lade^{2}, met^{3}, mete^{4}, fin^{5}, fine^{6}, hop^{7}, hope^{8}, cub^{9}, cube^{10}, far^{11}, call^{12}, full^{13}, join^{14}, rout^{15}, e-ven^{0}, lin*e*l, q*u*art, ra*g*e, ro*s*e, na*t*ion, e*x*alt, pun*ch*, *th*em.

where the superscripted zero denotes vowel reduction, and the italicised consonantal and vowel graphs (again following Kenrick) represent various characteristics ranging from non-realisation in the case of vowel segments, to voicing, and various stages of continuancy adjustment in the consonants. As we shall see below, one of the most interesting features of Scott's *A New Spelling, Pronouncing, and Explanatory Dictionary of the English Language* lies in its inclusion of a substantial list of 'Words in which the Natives of Scotland are very apt to err' (1802:xxv-xxvi), a list in some way perhaps compensating for Scott's embarrassment as a Scotsman in prescribing polite English usage, a feeling surfacing self consciously and perhaps overstatedly in the *Preface* (1802:xii):

> Should an attempt of this nature be thought too presuming in one who is a native of Scotland, it need only be observed, that, in early life, he went to London, and resided many years in its neighbourhood with his worthy uncle, the late Mr Burgh, as his assistant; during which time, one part of his business was to instruct the young gentlemen of the academy in the proper reading and reciting of the English language. To this he might further add, that, ever since, he has been constantly engaged in the same branch of teaching, and that his pronunciation has been approved by the most undoubted judges, particularly by the first of English speakers, Mr Garrick, to whom he had the honour of reading several times.

It would be difficult to ascribe to John Warden any desire to emulate some numerically based representational system of the type advocated by Sheridan and Kenrick, since his *A Spelling Book* 'wherein the pronunciation and spelling of the English Tongue are reduced to a very few principles and general heads' was published in Edinburgh in 1753. Described as a 'Teacher of English in Edinburgh' Warden sets out to produce the customary 'systematic' guide to the teaching of English pronunciation for native speakers, claiming that 'the present spelling books, I mean the tabular part of them.....are nothing but a confused heap of words' (1753:*Preface*:xvii). Perhaps it will be to the dismay of many present day educators of primary school children, that Warden vigorously advocates the primacy of spelling and pronunciation over skills in meaning recognition and interpretation; to that end, he devises a standard orthography plus numerical marking system which has the aim of making a child 'of quick capacity...master of the pronunciation of the English tongue in the space of three or four months, and in six or eight be an accurate reader, so far as regards pronunciation and quantity'. It is perhaps worth citing his explanation of his methodology in full (1753:*Preface*:xii):

> I have denoted the names of the letters by figures. They will be a guide to those who are not thoroughly conversant in the *English* pronunciation; because when they observe any particular letter marked, they are certain, where-ever the same figure is annexed to the same *letter*, that it is to have the same name. The same method is observed in the sounds of the diphthongs where both the vowels are pronounced, the sound of each vowel is expressed by the figure denoting that sound. Thus in so^2u^2nd *o* is marked o^2, being the same name it is expressed by in so^2t; and *u* is marked u^2, being the name it is expressed by in tru^2e.

Warden's *Spelling Book* provides what he describes as a 'few principles' and 'general heads' relating to the pronunciation of vowels, diphthongs, 'letters not named', terminations at the ends of words, the phonetic realisation of <e> after <c>, <g>, <s>, etc.; divided diphthongs (<aim>, <create>); collections of words where <z>, <h> are pronounced, where <c> is sounded [s]; diphthongs <ou>, <ow> sound as *loud*; <au>/<aw> sound as [ɔ] or [o]. The whole is closed by Tables of words of near alikes in pronunciation as well as an unusual Table of 'those words, which, if properly pronounced, are different, but, by a wrong pronunciation, are the same in sound.' Every section relating to vocalic and consonantal segments is followed by 'exercises' comprising apparently random lists of lexical items with the numerical values of vowels, diphthongs and consonants variously superscripted or subscripted: 'each letter having as many figures placed either above or below as it has different names'. Thus, for monophthongal vowels and the consonants we have:

a^{123} e^{123} i^{123} o^{123} u^{1234} y^{1234} c^{123} g^{12} $s^{123}$$t^{12}$ ch^{12} sh^{12} th^{12}

with examples such as :

Ha^2s^3 tha^2t^1 o^2f ho^1ly^4 a_2ft_2er $na_1t_2i_2o_1na_2l$ we_3ll

It would appear that a child had to be able to recite the various 'names' associated with each letter and, presumably, provide some kind of phonetic equivalent for each segment. But Warden provides no 'key' for his numerical system, no set of model lexical items illustrating the sound in question and the teacher is left to work out the values for the numerical equivalent of the three different kinds of <a> or four different kinds of <y> which the standard orthography signals. Of course, such a system - while it may have its uses as a means of teaching spelling - has the kinds of drawback we saw so typical of Sheridan's model: the same sound could be represented by a set of different symbols, while there were phonetic segments which (given the complete reliance upon standard orthography) could not be realised at all: notably, in Warden's case, the [ɑ]/[a] contrast. Warden's system may have been the model for that of Drummond (1767:19) who likewise uses up to four superscripted numerals to denote vowel quality (a^{123}, e^{123}, i^{123}, o^{123,} u^{1234}, y^{123}), plus superscripted ', denoting a letter 'not sounded': '*u* has his first sound in *music*, his second sound in *murder*, his third sound in *figure*, his fourth sound in *bull*'; a system, as we shall see below, he - again like Warden - applies to consonantal segments as well.

Alexander Barrie ('Teacher of English, Writers Court, Edinburgh') was one of the most prolific and successful writers of pronouncing dictionaries and pronunciation guides in Scotland in the second half of the 18th century. In his popular *A Spelling and Pronouncing Dictionary of the English Language for the Use of Schools*, published in Edinburgh in 1744, he utilises a descriptive system very much after the fashion of Sheridan, although enlarging it to include more vowel values, especially those indicating what might be length and lowering in pre-[r] contexts (1754:v):

SOUNDS OF THE VOWELS

a	ha^{1}te	ha^{2}t
e	the^{1}se	the^{2}m
i	pi^{1}ne	pi^{2}n
o	no^{1}te	no^{2}t
u	cu^{1}be	cu^{2}b
w	w^{1}e	few^{2}
y	try^{1}	hy^{2}m*n*

a	ha^{3}ll	la^{4}rge
e	the^{3}re	he^{4}r
i	si^{3}r	gi^{4}rd
o	do^{3}	do^{4}ne
u	bu^{3}sh	

However, reflecting a trend in many of the Scottish Spelling Book and Dictionary writers in the later part of the century, Barrie's subsequent works, notably *A Spelling and Pronouncing Catechism* (1796) and *The*

Tyro's Guide to Wisdom and Wealth (1815:9th edition) utilise a diacritic method which employs superscripted accents, graves, acutes, cedillas, etc. in place of numerals. Compare the system he favours in both the *Tyro's Guide* and the *Spelling and Pronouncing Catechism*:

	First	Second	Third
a	hāte	hăt	hâll
e	thēse	thĕn	thêre
i	pīne	pĭn	sîr
o	nōte	nŏt	störm
u	cūbe	cŭb	bûsh
w	we	few̄	
y	trȳ	hy̆m*n*	

	Fourth	Fifth
a	làrge	
e	hèr	
i	gìrd	
o	dô	dòne

where again it is worth noting the addition of the <störm> shape to denote the contrast between what are probably, as we shall see below, low back segments such as [ɔ] and [ɒ]. In such a system, items such as <daughter>, <heinous>, <down> and <outward> are realised symbolically as <dâu*gh*`tèr>, <hèi′noŭs>, <döw̆n>, <öût′w̆ârd>, although we should note the addition of grave accent marks to denote stress placement, underlined consonantal components denoting non-realisation and perhaps the inadvertent retention of the standard orthography in the <u> symbol in <daughter> and the <i> in items like <fruit>: <frûit>. From time to time too, Barrie will use 'respellings' to re-inforce his symbolic representations as in <êi*gh*th> with the addition of 'pr. êi*gh*tth'. To enable the user of *The Spelling Catechism* effectively and easily to utilise this rather complex system of diacritic symbols, each recto and verso page is headed by the hāte, hăt, hâll, làrge, etc. set. Barrie even provides an exercise in *False Spelling* (1815:250-51) based upon the *Story of a Fox, witch whoever amazin, is sed to be a fact*:

> Sum ears ago a yung fox was kept at the Golden Bear inn at Reading, and imploied in a weel to turn the Jak; after a konsiderible wile imploied their, Reynard gave his kiper the sleek, and reganed his native feelds, this very fox was afterwards purswed by the hounds, and fyndin himself in grate danjer, he began to rekolect his former hapy situashun, and imeditely direkted his coarse toard the kitshin, gimped into his weel, resumed his former okupashun and safed his lyfe.

Possibly the most developed version of Barrie's system is to be found in the various writings by William Angus, notably in his *An English Spelling and Pronouncing Vocabulary on a New Plan* (1814:5th edition) and *A Pronouncing Vocabulary of the English Language* (1800) both published in Glasgow. Angus' method of representing the vowel system is in some ways more elaborate than Barrie's, more regularly marking as it does stressed and unstressed variants and attempting to show differences in vowel duration

VOWELS
NAME SOUNDS
SHORT OR LONG QUANTITY
ȧ *or* ā, *as in* vacate vāk´ȧt
ė *or* ē, *as in* revere - rė-vē r,
ï *or* ī, *as in* finite - fī´nït
ȯ *or* ō *as in* promote - prȯ-mōt´
u̇ *or* ū *as in* future fū´tu̇r
GENERAL SHORT SOUNDS
UNMARKED
a e i o u *as in* fan fen fin fon fun
OCCASIONAL SOUNDS
SHORT QUANTITY LONG QUANTITY
ă *as in* pass Â *as in* all
ĕ *as in* her â *as in* arms
ŭ *as in* bush û *as in* rule
DIPHTHONGAL SOUNDS
oy - toil, toy ow, noun, town.
w *as in* wet y *as in* yet

This elaborate system - 'intended to facilitate the Acquirement of A Uniform English Pronunciation, and a Correct Delivery' - results in representations for items such as <articulate> as <âr-tik´-ŭ-la´t> - representations where (despite the traditional long/short nomenclature wrongly used for monophthongal/diphthongal contrast), stressed and unstressed syllable values are accorded a different diacritic; to the extent where the 'unaccented' value of whatever entity is represented by the 'long Â *as in* all' is realised without the circumflex mark, thus <im-pAr-tūn> '*importune*'. Angus' system is very similar to that found in *A General Pronouncing and Explanatory Dictionary of the English Language* by G Fulton and G Knight, published in Edinburgh in 1818 and running to at least thirteen editions by 1825. Fulton and Knight employ the Name Vowel and Occasional Sounds nomenclature, also utilising different symbols for stressed and unstressed values. However, they use the term *shut* for Angus' 'general short' and label the Occasional Sounds thus:

Italian â	Lârd, lăst
Broad Â	WÂrd, wăst
or ô	Lôrd, lost
Italian û	Rûle, fŭll
Obscure ĕ	Hĕr

Commissioned for and published (in Edinburgh in 1796) by that most linguistically chauvinistic body in the 18th century - *The Society in Scotland for the Propagation of Christian Knowledge* - the anonymous *A Spelling-Book Upon a New Plan,* has been much neglected by the scholarly tradition. This *Spelling Book* attempts 'to render the teaching and acquiring of the English language easy and agreeable, both to teachers and taught; and to introduce an uniformity of pronunciation into the different parts of the country where it may be used, in a manner never before attempted' (*Preface*:i). For the student of 18th century phonology this work has two great interests: the first, a lengthy dictionary of words of varying syllabic length whose pronunciations are indicated by a straightforward system of superscripted accent marks of the familiar kind: secondly, it provides (as we have seen: p 24) an extensive list of 'words in which the Natives of North Britain are most apt to err' (*Preface*:vii). The claim to novelty made by the *Spelling Book* rests mainly in the way its *Scheme* presents information about the pronunciation of individual vowel sounds. The *Scheme* is a two dimensional display, the left hand vertical column containing the various standard orthographic marks familiar to the reader, against which there is an invitation to read off two types of information. The first is a set of lexical items with vowels marked by various superscripted accents; these are arranged in columns under 'model' heads which indicate the 'true pronunciation'. All the lexical items arranged in the columns under each of these heads have the same pronunciation, despite being marked by a diverse set of orthographic and superscripted symbols. The author provides a user friendly guide to his system (*Preface*:vi):

> Suppose then, you wish to know the true pronunciation of the word *conceive*, written thus [in the lists containing disyllables and polysyllables: pp 25-43: CJ] cŏncēive: look in the *Scheme* for the vowel *o* - follow the line upon which it stands, till you find a word which it has the same mark as in the syllable cŏn; and on the top of the column immediately above that word, you see the word *top*. Now all the words in the same column downwards, have exactly the same sound; so ŏ in *blot* must be sounded like *o* in *top*, the sound of which, everyone knows; and ŏ in cŏn having the same mark with ŏ in *blŏt*, must be sounded like it: Again, for the other syllable cēive - look for the diphthong *ei*, and follow the line on which it stands, till you find a word in which it is marked in the above syllable - at the top of that column you see the word *me*, which

shews that *ei* in *conceive* must be pronounced like *e* in *me*, the sound of which also everyone knows: - *c* being written in the *Italic* character, shows it to be soft; and *e* final written in the same way, shows it to be silent.

Such a system would require constant cross reference between the word list and the *Scheme*, and perhaps in an effort to avoid this, the *Spelling-Book* contains conventional sections describing the various sounds of individual vowels, thus: 'The vowel *e* has three sounds: 1. an open sound, similar to that of *ai*, in *Beck, bell, belt*...2. a long sound like *ei*, in *be, he, me*...3. short, similar to short *u*, in *erst, fern, her*...(1796:6). However, the (somewhat unreasonable) claim is made that the 'marks in the Scheme...any man of an ordinary capacity may [learn:CJ] in less than half an hour' (*Preface*:i).

There were writers such as McIllquam who endeavoured to use an extremely simple and restricted form of accentual diacritic marking. In his *A Comprehensive Grammar: in which the Principles of the English Language are Methodically Digested into Plain and Easy Rules*, published in Glasgow in 1781, we find a traditional characterisation of vocalic segments based largely on their orthographic shapes which are seen as having different values. Thus, there are three sounds of <a>, two of <y> and so on. McIllquam's *Scheme* is a follows:

SCHEME of the VOWELS

a	lā- lāte	gắt	mâlt
e	hē hēre	hĕr	thêre
i	fī- fīne	fin	fíeld
o	nō nōte	nŏt	prôve
u	dū- duke	dŭck	bûll
y	mȳ tȳre	fy̆n- -ty̆	

Crude directions as to length 'by position' are provided (with vowel length and vowel quality typically conflated) and, as with all such standard orthography based systems, ambiguities have to be treated separately: 'ê sounds ā: as *there, were, where, ere, ne'er*; î sounds ē; as, *capuchine, machine, magazine*; ô sounds û; as, *do, to, who, move, prove*; û sounds ô; as, *bush, full, pull, true, truth*' (1781:11). In the same way there are lists of orthographic digraphs (false) and 'true' diphthongs mapped against the diacritically marked single vowels (1781:12-15); the values for <ou>, for instance, given as:

sounds â — as, bou*gh*t, fou*gh*t, nou*gh*t,
sounds ŏû — as, bou*gh*, sound, gout, thou, our
sounds ō — as, dou*gh*, thou*gh*, four, course
sounds ŏ — as, clough, cough, trough
sounds ô — as, group, gourd, gou*t*, throu*gh*
sounds ū — as, you, your, youth, youthful
sounds ŭ — as, enough, rough, scourge,
and in the terminations, *ous*;
as, hideous, bounteous, duteous.

In his *Three Scottish Poems, with a Previous Dissertation on the Scoto-Saxon Dialect* (1792) - published in the first volume of the *Transactions* of the Society of Antiquaries of Scotland - Alexander Geddes also chooses to use a system of diacritic grave and acute and other superscripts to denote variations in both vowel quality and quantity. The system (like McIllquam's) is relatively undeveloped and relies heavily upon a descriptive backup where individual vocalic segments are simultaneously characterised by the metaphorical descriptive epithet, such as *broad slender a, open or broad a* and so on. However, as we shall see below, it provides us with one of the most detailed descriptions of Scots geographic variants in the 18th century: 'I am perfectly sensible that this novel orthography will, at first, have an uncouth appearance, even to Scottish readers; but I flatter myself, that such of them as are capable of reflection, and can read with both ears and eyes, will soon recover from their astonishment; and confess that my symbols represent their sounds more properly and distinctly than their present orthography' (1792:438). Partly in this vein too is the descriptive method of James Adams who, in his tirade in support of 'The Dialect of Scotland', an *Appendix* to his *The Pronunciation of the English Language Vindicated* (1799), uses a simplified diacritic accentual system in combination, as we shall see, with a crude form of 'respelling'. Indeed, under his discussion of the vagaries of pronunciation associated with the digraph <ou>, Adams pontificates (1799:79-80):

> Now, these, and some similar difficulties, might be facilitated to strangers, shorten our grammars, and render our pronunciation *visibly* plain and easy, by introducing four accents, the grave, the acute, the circumflex, and the jugum. This alone would express the common variations of our vowels and diphthongs. If we absurdly reject them as a French precedent, the Hebrew and the Greek will free us from the self reproach of introducing French modes of literature. But why, after all, do we not introduce them in our new publications? It is an object worthy the attention of our universities; the Scotch Literati would have great merit, and be followed, if they would boldly bring forward this great desideratum in our language, now solely confined to our dictionaries.

On the other hand, Adams (1799:162) (with what looks like a side swipe at Elphinston) is very enthusiastic for Geddes' diacritic system: 'His plan is a desideratum, and would at once proscribe the apparent inconsistency of the Scotch pronunciation, solely manifested by retaining our mode of spelling, and deviating from it in a manner not to be conceived by any powers of English combination of the letters. How, in the name of wonder, can Scotch Schoolmasters teach poor children to read their Bible printed the English way? They use no other. Hence every word is a stumbling block; and, from early youth, the Scotch are taught *that our pronunciation is anomalous and capricious*, the prejudice is deeply rooted, and has cost me all my past labour to endeavour to eradicate the notion; for it was chiefly with reference to the Scotch I made the past arduous attempt'.

It is probably fair to say that the most elaborate system of diacritic marking was that produced by William Perry. Originally 'Master of the Academy at Kelso', Perry produced there a fairly typical late 18th century guide to accountancy and business method, *The Man of Business and Gentleman's Assistant* (1774), a work heavily subscribed to by local businessmen, farmers and landowners. However, on moving to Edinburgh, Perry produced two major works on the pronunciation of contemporary English: *The Only Sure Guide to the English Tongue* (or *New Pronouncing Spelling Book*) of 1776 and the *Royal Standard English Dictionary* ('Designed for the use of schools, and private families') of the same year. The latter, dedicated to the Duke of Buccleuch, is 'intended to fix a standard of the pronunciation of the English Language, conformable to the present practice of polite speakers in the city of London'. It is in the *Only Sure Guide* that we see Perry's representational system at its most developed, where he provides, after the style of Kenrick and Barrie, a *Key* to 'the different sounds of the vowels', but where numerical and alphabetic superscripts are simultaneously employed: see Table 3.1. However, a system like this has all the disadvantages of Kenrick's and Sheridan's in being unable to produce a 'one symbol/one sound' mapping, explicitly admitted by Perry in his footnotes to the *Key*, where he observes 'the *o* in *lost* has the sound of *a* in *hall'*, and that *'a* in *wash* sounds like *o* in *not'*. Indeed, so concerned is he with this shortcoming, that he is forced to turn to an even more elaborate system of representation:

> Having found it difficult to convince several teachers in this country of the propriety of giving the various sounds to the Vowels, as mentioned in the *Key*, and particularly that the vowels *a, e, i, o, u* and *y* in the following words: li*a*r, h*e*r, sh*i*rt, d*o*ne, b*u*ck, h*y*rst, have all one and the same sound, viz. like ŭ in *buck*, I thought it proper to add the following scheme of the vowels, in which those that have the same sound have the same figure over them.

TABLE 3.1

Perry's *Key*

A1	2	3
ā	ă	â
hate	hat	hall/wash
E 1	2	3
ē	ĕ	ê
mete	met	there
I 1	2	3
ī	ī	î
pint	pin	field
O 1	2	3
ō	ŏ	ô
note	not/lost	prove
U 1	2	3
ū	ŭ	û
duke	buck	bush
Y1	2	3
ȳ	y̆ or y	ý
by	beauty	hyrst

A4	5
à	á
part	war
E 4	
é	
her	
I4	
í	
shirt	
O 4	5
ò	ó
book	done
U1	2
w̄	ŵ
new	now

The *Scheme of the Vowels* which Perry produces has all the combined complexity of the Kenrick/Sheridan and Warden models, as set out in Table 3.2 below. Nor does the complex detail of phonetic representation in Perry's system end here. In addition to the common custom of representing 'vowels not sounded' by italicisation, thus <Laˆboŭr>, <preāch>, etc., he attempts to mark 'indistinct vowels' by the same method: <āble>, <pàr`son>, <făt'ten>, while he takes special care to try to show durational differences: '*a, e,* and *o without any of the above characters* either alone, or before or after a consonant, are the same in quality as *a, e* and *o* in the words *hate, mete, note* but different in quantity; that is, they are the long sounds contracted' (1776:x).

TABLE 3.2
Perry's *Scheme of the Vowels*

ā[1]	ă[2]	â[3]
hate	hat	hall
ē[5]	ĕ[6]	ê[1]
mete	met	there
ī[7]	ĭ[8]	î[5]
pint	pin	field
ō[9]	ŏ[10/3]	ô[11]
note	not/loft	prove
ū[12]	ŭ[13]	ô[14w]
duke	duck	bush
ȳ	y̆	ỳ
try	beauty	hyrst, martyr

à[4]	â[10]	á[13]
part	wash	liar
	é[13]	
	her	
	ì[13]	
	shirt	
ó[13]	ò[14]	
done	book	
w̄[12]	ẃ[14]	
new	now	

Indeed, of all his contemporaries, it is perhaps Perry who takes the greatest care (despite the obvious complexities it adds to his system) to denote vowel duration:

> it must be particularly remarked, that there are many words which have *no* character over the Vowels; such as ăb'ba, salute', se-clūde', ĭn-dolĕnce, &c. These Vowels have the quality of sound as *ā, ē, ō,* &c. but are to be uttered quicker, that is, they are the long sounds of *ā, ē, ō,* &c contracted, and are in the same proportion to each other, as gòod is to fŏod or hòok, to rŏok, which have the same *quality* of sound, but different in *quantity* or *length* of time. (1776:ix)

Many schoolteachers recognised the inappropriateness and impracticality of such descriptive detail in a classroom context. The author of *The Instructor, An Introduction to Reading and Spelling the English Language,* published in Glasgow in 1798, while recognising Perry as 'pre-eminent' among contemporary grammarians, recognises that 'many of his observations, though in themselves very just and highly beneficial for persons of advanced years, cannot be comprehended by juvenile minds......An idea was once entertained of distinguishing the different sounds of the vowels, in every word, by visible marks; but after diliberate [sic:CJ] reflection this plan was wholly laid aside. The shades of difference in the variation of the vowel sounds are frequently so slight, and the marks necessary to discriminate them so numerous, that to instruct children in the knowledge of the one, by initiating them in the other, becomes a work of immense labour, and the greatest difficulty' (*Preface*:2-3). Such views are found in many English orthoepists of the period, notably Nares (1784:xx): 'Articulate sounds can be formed by imitation alone, and described only by similitude; This must be understood with limitation. The sounds of some letters may, with tolerable exactness, be ascertained by rules for the management of the organs of speech in pronouncing them. The consonants more readily admit of such description; but the nice discrimination of vowel sounds, on which the principle harmony of language depends, will generally elude the efforts of the most subtle definer'.

Matters are made more complex still, by Perry's introduction of a distinction between two different kinds of syllable type - the 'flat and slowly accented', to be marked with a grave accent, and the 'sharp and quickly accented' to be indicated by an acute accent; thus <bŏr`dér>, <wârn`ing>, <cē*i*l`ǐng>, <ī`cǐcl*e*> as against <bŏr'rōw>, <wăsh'ing>, <hē*i*f'ér> and <bĕt'tér> and so on. It is difficult to see what phonetic/phonological motivation lies behind such a 'slowly/quickly accented' syllable dichotomy, although the former might correlate with syllable structures where vowel length (either lexical or derived in homorganic cluster and other contexts) might be prominent and, as such, correspond (given the terminological similarity) to Sylvester Douglas' distinction between long and short syllables (*Of the Provincial Accentuation* (c1779): Jones (1992:16)):

> Let any one compare the three following words *foolish*, *fully* and *pully*. In each the accent is upon the first syllable and that syllable in each (as it seems to me and to others whom I have consulted) to be always, and necessarily uttered in a somewhat sharper tone than the other. But in *foolish* and *fully* the accented syllable is long, in *pully* short....(ff. 41-42)

3.3 Non-Symbolic Descriptive Taxonomies

Many of the Scotch linguists writing in the 18th century preferred a classificatory system for both vocalic and consonantal segments which eschewed numerical or accentual superscripts, relying instead upon metaphorical descriptive terms for the expression of quantitative and qualitative differences. The range of these terms was fairly constrained, with *long* and *short* the usual quantitative markers, notably with Buchanan (1757:1762), Telfair (1775), Adams (1799), Elphinston (1766:1786), and Geddes (1792), although we find *longer* and *shorter* in McIllquam (1781) as well. Qualitative contrasts are signalled with a much wider range of terminological flair, to include such characteristics as *broad, open, slender*, notably in *A Spelling-Book Upon a New Plan* (1796), Sylvester Douglas (1799) and Adams (1799), while more exotic terms such as *clear, sharp* and *foreign* are confined to writers such as Adams (1799), Elphinston (1766:1786) and McIllquam (1781).

James Buchanan (Emsley:1933) was the author of several grammar books in the mid 18th century, but is especially noted for three works which attempt to characterise matters phonetic and phonological: *Linguae Britannicae Vera Pronuntiatio* or *A New English Dictionary* (1757), *The British Grammar* (1762) and *An Essay towards Establishing a Standard for an Elegant Pronunciation of the English Language* (1766). The first is described in its fly-leaf as 'A Work intirely new, and designed for the Use of Schools, and of Foreigners, as well as Natives who would speak, read, and write English with Propriety and Accuracy', while the *Dictionary* is described as being intended to 'obviate a vicious provincial pronunciation, and to remove the complaints of foreign gentlemen, desirous of learning English' (1766:*Preface*:i). Buchanan seems to see his work as being aimed particularly at a Scottish audience, an audience which - were it to follow the precepts of his pronunciation guides - would not only benefit in terms of everyday social intercourse, but would find concomitant upon that a considerable political advantage, a theme taken up by many Scots linguistic commentators in the 18th century:

> With respect to the inhabitants of North Britain, as every word in the following work is presented to their view as it is actually pronounced by the best speakers, so that every one may become his own private teacher, it would be needless to say any thing to so sensible a people, farther than just to put persons of distinction there in mind, that it is highly consistent with their duty in their several districts, even for the sake of their own offspring, chearfully to lead the van towards a just and polished utterance. Let gentlemen at the bar, and those that minister in holy things, be especially exemplary, nor be diverted from such a gentleman-like accomplishment by any foolish names that low-breeding can suggest. And let both clergy and laity enjoin the school-masters over that part of the united kingdom, to acquire and teach a proper Pronunciation to the rising generation.....In fine, it will be joining them into one social family, and connecting them by much more benevolent and generous ties than that of a political union. (1766:*Preface*:xi-xii)

But what Buchanan had in mind by 'the best speakers' is perhaps not to be equated with Kenrick's views on the same subject, especially when we see, for instance in the *Essay*, renderings for items like <auxiliary> and <authenticity> such as *aukseĕlī-īrry* [ɒɒksilɩəɹɩ] and *authĕnteĕssītў* [ɒɒθɛntisɩɩɩ], with what might well have been interpreted as a stereotypical Scots stressed [i] vowel. However, as we shall discuss at length below, Buchanan (like Alexander Scot) may have been as much concerned to promote (at least certain aspects of) a Scottish as an English metropolitan standard form of contemporary pronunciation.

Buchanan's descriptive techniques are very different from those of Kenrick and his followers; he is hostile to what he sees as a confusion of superscripted numerals, seeing them principally as an impediment to the learning of pronunciation in the classroom: 'For a scholar to be obliged to comprehend and remember eighteen sounds when committed to the ear before he can understand three, is as absurd as if I number 1 2 3 4 5 6 7 8 9 10 11 12 13 14 15 16 17 18, and then tell him he must understand all these distinct numbers to be, or only mean three' (1757:4). What he puts in place of this for his analysis of 'the powers and various sounds of the vowels and consonants' is a system which relies principally upon descriptive terminology, notably a *short/long* dichotomy, but also on superscripted accent marks and some 're-spellings'. Yet he stresses that there are articulatory criteria (based upon cavity opening magnitude) for the vowel taxonomy he proposes (1762:7:footnote):

> The Vowels may be justly divided into three Classes, viz. guttural or Throat Vowels, palatal, or Vowels of the Palate, and labial or Lip vowels. The guttural Vowels are broad (a), short and obscure (o), and (u) and (e) Feminine. The palatal are long or slender (a), short or slender (i), and (e) Masculine. The labial are long (o) and (u), and (u) fat, i.e. when it is pronounced like *oo*. If we attend to the Formation of these Vowels, we shall find that there are three different Openings in each of these Seats for every Vowel, viz. a larger, a middle, and a less Opening.

In common with nearly all his contemporaries, Buchanan bases his vowel description on alphabetic symbols, assigning to each a set of sounds. Thus the letter <a> represents five separate sounds (Buchanan places phonetic entities in round brackets) one long (*cāme, fāme, māle)*, one short (*bӑd, bӑt, bӑnd, tӑllow, cӑllow, swӑllow)*, one broad (*all, call, bald)*, a sound more slender than long *a* ('like French (e) masculine, and is expressed in *late, plate rate*') and an open sound which 'approaches its broad sound' (*wrath, rather, father, glass*, 'and some others'). In the *Essay* (1766) this last sound is also described as 'acute' 'which seems to approach to *au*, but is really short *ӑ* twice, but rapidly pronounced, is denoted by a circumflex over it, thus *fâthīr, râthīr, ârmz* &c' (1766:*Preface:*xiv): a 'short ӑ twice', approaching a broad sound, might represent a segment like [ɑɑ]. However, Buchanan claims that the last two sounds 'occur but seldom', conflating them with slender long *a*, and the less open short *a* respectively. In the *Essay* too (*Preface*:xiv) Buchanan distinguishes yet another value for the <a> symbol, where it 'passes into the sound of short ĭ' in items such as *marshal, filial, human,* which he symbolically represents as *mărshĭl, fĭl-yĭl* and *heūmĭn.* As we shall explore further below, in addition to metaphorical descriptive terminology, Buchanan uses superscripted symbols and is especially given to 'respelling' - the first long sound of *a,* for instance, being described as 'like (ai)', with items like <came>, <fame> and <male> are to be pronounced 'as if written *caim, faim, mail'* (1762:8).

While, as we have already observed, it is commonplace for 18th century commentators to assign a long/short description to what in fact is a qualitative one: short *a* as [a] and long *a* as [e], Buchanan's use of such terminology may be more sophisticated. He goes out of his way to inform us that 'the short sound of (a) has the same opening as the long sound has, only it requires but half the time to pronounce it; as *fait, bait, baind* if pronounced quick, or in half the time that they naturally require, will be *fat, bat, band,* &c' (1757:8). Now, since he claims that the short *a* of the last examples 'differs but very little from short *e*' in contrasts such as *fet/fat, set/sat,* it might be the case that his long *a* represents some kind of [εε] (or even [εε˔]) segment, the [ee] reserved for those items he characterises as showing 'a sound more slender than long *a*', the quality of the vowels in the items *late, plate* and *rate.*

His <e> symbol represents three separate sounds, a long sound ('which is like (ee)') as in the items *hēre, Pēter, schēme;* a short sound 'which is free and open' (1762:8) in *bĕnd, sĕnd, fĕd, bĕt.* We have already observed how Buchanan (like Douglas:Jones:1992:118) sees this short *e* as somewhat similar to short *a;* <bad>, <bat> and <band> 'are pronounced but a little more open than *bĕd, bĕt* and *bĕnd',* an observation which may, in fact, reflect a more palatal, Scottish realisation of the low front vowel in [æ] or [ε˔]. The third segment this graph represents is 'a very obscure sound' which resembles 'the French *e* Feminine' (or 'passes into the sound of short ĭ (1766:xiv)), as in <liberty>, <liberal>, <property>. In the *Essay* (1766:*Preface*:xiv), Buchanan adds a fourth <e> type, 'an acute sound' which 'approaches to short ă, but as this sound has been disputed, it has no other mark to distinguish it but the short quantity. This acute sound, however, is warranted by the best speakers; it is heard before [r] followed by another consonant, such as rg, rj, rn, rs, rt, rv, as *sergeant, verjuice, discern, concern, perverse*....denoted *sĕrjĭnt, vĕrjooss, disĕrn..*'

An <i> graph is also used to represent three phonetic segments, a short sound, 'which is like (ee)', 'almost full (ee)', 'which approaches the diphthong (ee) or French (i)' (*Preface*:xiv) - apparently a segment more like [i] than [ι] - as in *dĭd, wĭll, cĭvĭlĭty* - 'Ee has the same Sound the French give to (i), i.e. very like our short (ĭ)' (1762:16); a sound 'like short (ŭ)', as in *first, shirt, bird,* 'pronounce *fŭrst, shŭrt, bŭrd'.* Buchanan (1762:10:footnote) is sceptical of the almost universal contemporary attempts to treat obscure vowels as reduced or otherwise mutated versions of the vowels in stressed syllables: 'Some Writers give the Sound of obscure (u) to (i) in *first, bird,* &c but I think it preposterous to represent the Obscure Sound of one Vowel by that of another, especially when we consider that these obscure Sounds can scarcely be communicated to, or distinguished by the Ear. For if we take, for Instance, the Word *Father,* and substitute *a, i, o, u* in the Place of (e), and still pronounce this Word with its proper Accent and Cadence, it will be difficult for the Ear to determine the Difference between *Fáthar, Fáther, Fáthir, Fáthor,* and *Fáthr* without the (e)'.

A third, Buchanan's long *i* appears to indicate a diphthongal contrast, perhaps [aɩ], since he equates it with the vowel sound in the pronoun <I> and states that it 'is expressed in *fīre, mīle, mīre, devīse,* &c' (1762:11); its precise phonetic value we shall discuss in more detail below. In the *Essay* (1766:*Preface*:xv) two more values are added, one where the sound 'passes into the sound of short ŭ' as in items such as *first* and *bird, fŭrst, bŭrd,* another where it 'passes into the liquid sound of the consonant [y], as in *collier, valiant..*' rendered *kŏl-yĭr, văl-yĭnt.*

Buchanan's short o, in items such as *rŏd, rŏt, gŏt* he claims to contrast with a long version in such words as *glōbe, rōbe, prōse* (a sound 'which makes the mouth of an orbicular form' (1757:9)) - some kind of high mid back [o] segment. But this seems to be a clear and rather typical case of inexact terminology, with a qualitative rather than a durational distinction intended, since his short *u* (some kind of [ʌ] segment) he describes as being 'very like short (o), only a little more guttural' (1757:13), suggesting an [ɔ] value for short *o* itself. Yet Buchanan (1757:8) stresses the fact that 'The short sounds of (o) and (u) are pretty similar; as *ŭnder, ŭnto; ŏnder, ŏnto;* and are so quick and obscure, as to make no motions in the parts of the mouth.' Indeed, in the *Essay* (*Preface*:xv), Buchanan adds to the long and short <o> variants, an 'acute sound', which he claims to be 'like (au) [possibly [ɒɒ] :CJ] rapidly pronounced'; illustrated by items such as *order, border, born, cordial,* which are to be represented as *ôrdĭr, bôrdĭr, bôrn, kôrd-yĭl. In* the *Essay,* the (au) digraph is characterised as 'broad *a'*, but when it 'passes into the acute sound of [a] as in *aunt, draught, jaundice, jaunt, laugh,* etc., it is denoted thus *ânt, drâft....*' (1766:*Preface*:xviii).

Under his description of purely orthographic diphthongs, Buchanan points to the fact that the sound represented by the digraph (oo) - 'the sound which most foreign Nations give to the Vowel (u), i.e. fat (u) - as in the items *hood, good, food, fool, Room, moor, prove* should be seen to contrast with the value for the same symbol, representing short *u* (a 'short guttural sound') in such words as *blood, foot, flood* and *soot* 'pronounce *blŭd, fŭt, flŭd, fŭt'* (1762:17). We might therefore tentatively assign values of [ʌ] and [ωω]/[uu] to his short and fat (u) sound respectively. However, again in the *Essay*'s more detailed descriptive mode, Buchanan makes a further, important distinction by introducing the category of 'acute and clear sound of *u*' (*Preface*:xvi). This sound, characterised as '[oo] rapidly pronounced' is to be found in the items *bull, bush, pull, full,* represented by the short diphthongal digraph: *boŏl, boŏsh, poŏl, foŏl.* Typical of other contemporary commentators, Buchanan's long *u* (much like his long *i*) has a clear diphthongal status, occurring as it does in items like *lūte, mūse, cūre, tūne,* to be realised by a diphthongal graph, as in *leut, meuz, teun* (1766:xvi). Buchanan also distinguishes two other values for the <u> symbol: one where its sound 'passes into' that represented by *ĕ,* as in the items *bury, burial;* the other where it 'passes into' the value for short *ĭ,* as in *busy, business* (*Essay*:*Preface*:xvi).

Perhaps the simplest descriptive system is to be found in Cortez Telfair's *A Town and Country Spelling Book,* claimed to be 'A comprehensive view of the pronunciation of the best speakers in London: designed more particularly for the use of Schools at a distance from London,' published in Edinburgh in 1775, and printed for Charles Elliot, Parliament Close. Its author also claims that his establishment 'cures Dumbness, Stammering and other Impediments in Speech, at his home in Barranger's Close, Edinburgh. In three weeks deaf and dumb persons are made capable of conversing in a plain and intelligent manner, and are taught reading, writing, arithmetic'. Telfair affects to be disillusioned by 'the number of good spelling-books now extant' which he sees as 'rather treatises on grammar than spelling, and that few, if any of them, contain a sufficient number of lessons for preparing the scholar for any other book' (1775:*Preface*:2). He despises the 'long and useless tables of words' contained in such works and their habit of 'arranging of single words into columns', even wishing to restrict his descriptive framework to a two term system: 'This division of sounds into long and short, it is hoped, is both more simple and more accurate than that commonly given of *slender, broad, open,* and such like.' (1775:150:footnote). However, although he resists the use of superscripted symbols, his classificatory technique still parallels the classical Sheridan/Kenrick model in the way in which it is standard orthography centred and sees sets of phonetic values for individual letter shapes, thus: '*A* has three long and a short sound: The first long in *age,* the second long in *all,* the third long in *star,* and the short in *hot*' (1775:149). Likewise, '*E* has one long and two short sounds: the long sound in *me;* the first short in *end,* and the second short in *nerve*' (1775:149). Yet the use of such a limited set of descriptive indicators brings with it the penalty of weak powers of differentiation and, especially, a gross lack of correlation between sound and symbol. Everywhere Telfair has to add footnotes and other comment to point out the homophony between phonetic segments he has labelled with identical terms or which are described with primary reference to their orthographic shapes: 'The first long *a* is the same with *ay* in *May,* and with *ai* in the French word *faire.* The second long *a* is the same with *aw* in *law*, and with *a* in the French words *grand*. The third long is the same with *ea* in *hearken*. The short is like *ea* in *wealth*, or *e* in the French word *elle*, and is the very same with the third long, only pronounced quicker' (1775:149). This combination of long/short and first, second, third terminology is perhaps seen at its most elaborate under his *U* entry (1775:153: and footnote):

> *U* has two long and two short sounds: First long in *muse*, second long in *rule*; first short in *cut*, second short in *full*. The first long *u* is a sound compounded of first short *i* and second long *o*; and is the same as *ew* in *few*: The second long *u* is the same with second long *o*, or with *oo* in *room*. The first short *u* is the only sound of all the vowels which cannot be pronounced but before a consonant; it approaches very nearly to the first short *o*: the second short *u* does not differ from the second long *u* but in the length of its sound

leading Telfair to conclude that there are twelve sounds capable of being distinguished 'nine of which are distinctly different, both in sound, and in time or length'. Nevertheless, for a set of words which he regards are exceptional, Telfair is forced to fall back on a 'respelling' technique: 'In the words *there, where, ere, women, bury, burial, busy* and *business* the vowels are quite irregular, deviating from all their sounds as above explained: they are pronounced *thair, wheir, air, wimen, berry, berrial, bizzy, bizziness*' (1775:150:footnote). Telfair's 'system' can be conveniently summarised as follows:

LONG

1	2	3
age	all	star
me		
my		
home	do	
muse	rule	

SHORT

1	2
hat	
end	nerve
in	mirtle
box	none
cut	full

typically showing the [ɑː] /[ɪ] contrast as one involving length and where, perhaps paradoxically, some pre-[r] segments (normally treated by most 18th century commentators as some kind of low, centralised vowel) are classified as 'short'.

Primarily a treatise on the rules of syntax, John Burn's *A Practical*

Grammar of the English Language, published in Glasgow in 1766 'For the Use of Schools', sets out to 'polish the writing, the conversation and minds of the young Ladies and Gentlemen of the town of Glasgow'. Burn's aims (*Preface*:xiii) were practical as well as purely intellectual: 'Were the English Grammar generally taught in English schools both in town and country, (which at a small expense of time and money might be done) what gracefulness would it not add to the conversation of the people in general! and what a tendency towards the polishing the minds of youth in the early part of life; as well as qualifying them for carrying on, to greater advantage, whatever branch of business they may follow.' His description of matters phonetic come in the form of question and answer (*Introduction*:3):

> How many sounds hath *e*?
> Five: short, as in *men*; shorter, as in *former*; long as in *betake*; longer as in *here*; long and sharp as in *there*.

and while his range of descriptive terminology is rather limited, it is not always used very consistently. Once again, long and short contrasts, for instance, cover not only duration but vowel quality. While the *e* in <former> may indeed be construed as a shorter version of that in <men>, and the stressed vowel of <here> a durationally extended version of the unstressed vowel in <betake>, the vowel contrast between <men> and <here> is clearly not one which primarily involves duration, although the long and sharp description of the vocalic segment in <there> could indeed be seen as a lengthened version of that in <men>. Likewise, Burn describes the vowels in items such as <note>, <roll>, <told> (as well as <lord>, <thought>) as long versions of the short vowel in <mop>, while his short, long, longer (or long and slender) contrast is a feature of the items <man>, <ma-ture> (perhaps a misprint for *na-ture*?) and <make>. Although in response to the question 'Where does the long sound of *a* generally take place?' there is the provocative response 'In the end of syllables unaccented; as *a-bout, ex-ta-cy*' (1766:2-3). Like almost all other commentators, Burn describes the vowel in <all> as long and broad, and once again a reliance upon an alphabetic descriptive base demands the mapping of identical phonetic segments against sets of disparate orthographic marks. Thus, 'like long slender *a* are *where, were, heir, feign*' and he provides extensive lists of orthographic diphthongs corresponding to the phonetic values of long *o*, long *e* and so on (1766:9-11).

It is not surprising that we should expect to find in what is undoubtedly the most detailed contemporary account of 18th century Scots pronunciation, a descriptive system of some sophistication. *A Treatise on the Provincial Dialect of Scotland* written by Sylvester Douglas (Lord Glenbervie) in 1799 (Jones:1992; Kohler:1966) provides, in essentially Pronouncing Dictionary format, an extremely detailed contrast between the Scotch and 'Pure' dialects of the late 18th century. Douglas' descriptive system is set out in detail in his *Observations on the Alphabet* (Jones: 1992:117-142), while its application is to be found in the extensive *Table of words improperly pronounced by the Scotch, showing their true English pronounciation* (Jones:1992:158-234). As the title of his *Observations on the Alphabet* suggests, Douglas - like Telfair and Burn - provides the phonetic equivalences of the orthographic system in terms with which we are now very familiar: the letter *A* has three sounds 'that in *father* has been called the open, that in *pare*, the close or slender, and that in *all* the *broad'* (Jones 1992:117). However, Douglas is not content with such a general level of description, and constantly adds detail and delicacy to his observations, enabling him to include a wide range of phonetic types. For instance, his first sound of *a*, the open sound, has a long and short version (illustrated by the items *father* and *hat* respectively) although Douglas stresses that the open sound in general is more likely to be short than long. Again, the close or slender variety of *a* (as in *pare, stare*) not only shows a long and short version (respectively in *glaze* and *race*), but the slender *a* itself can be divided into a thinner, feebler type versus a strong version (*grace, waste*) versus (*hare, care, tail*); even the feebler sound itself has long and short variants (as in *phrase, waste,* versus *race, pace*). But Douglas' attention to phonetic detail makes him suspicious of over-reliance upon descriptive criteria of this type: he is always conscious of 'shades' of difference between sounds which resist a crude classification like the one outlined above. His observations (by no means unique to this phonetic segment) on the broad and open *a*, with their emphasis on matters perceptual and premonition of recent phonological theories like Natural and Dependency Phonology (Donegan:1978; Anderson and Ewen:1987), seem startlingly modern and are worth citing at some length (Jones: 1992:118):

> But the broad and open are only to be considered as shades and gradations of the same sound like the lighter and darker shades of the same colour; and the same is true, in a still stronger degree, of the two sorts of the slender. Some philosophers think, notwithstanding the received opinion to the contrary, that there is an analogy between the laws of motion and communication of light, and of sound. There is certainly such an analogy in the manner in which they are perceived by our organs of hearing and of sight. For, as in the rainbow, although the pure middle part of each of the different stripes of colours is clearly distinguishable from the others, yet, while the eye gradually passes outwards, to the edge of each stripe, on either side, it seems to die away insensibly into the neighbouring tint, and is at length so like it, that it is impossible for the mind to draw the line, or fix the limit where the one ends, and the other begins; so the same thing is observable in our perception of vocal sounds. Thus we may consider the long open *a* in *father* as a sound placed between *o* and the strong slender *a*, or Scotch Eta (probably [εε]:CJ) But its sound in *all* gradually approaches

> and seems, in some measure, to confound and lose itself in that of *o*, as, on the other side, in *hat*, it approaches to the limits of, and begins to mix itself with, the short and strong slender sound in *better*.

While recognising an open ('usually short') and close ('usually long') version of *o*, as in <not>, <lost> and <bone>, <stone>, Douglas also claims to hear a long version of the former (seldom however represented by this single character) as the vowel in <bought>, <thought>. or <groat>, <broad>. But, typically and somewhat apologetically, he adds the qualifying comment: 'This sound, if not the same, is near the confines, or the external edge, if I may so speak, of the broad *a* in *all*. Some writers think them the same, I imagine I can perceive a difference' (Jones:1992:133). But it is perhaps in his description of the labial sounds represented by *u* that we find Douglas to be at his most observant. He recognises four different segments, a 'simple vocal sound' as in <pull>, <full>, a 'sort of smothered vocal' as in <Tully>, <scut>, <rut> and 'another shade of this second sound which approaches nearer the first in such words as *punk, hulk, rump, dub, mud*'. A third, diphthongal type, consists of 'the first sound of the *e* followed by the first of the *u*; but so as that the *e* is hurried over, and leaves the *u* to predominate' and he cites <pew>, <due> and <beauty> as instances (Jones 1992:139).

Yet, in the *Treatise*, Douglas never develops what he describes as a 'rational alphabet', even though he is prepared to set out in some detail its characteristics (essentially of the 'one sound, one symbol' variety not unlike the 'four rules' proposed by Sheridan: cf. page 52 above) (Jones 1992:107):

> It will appear evident, on an attentive consideration of the subject, that, to constitute a complete and rational alphabet, or series of written characters, in any language, there ought to be: 1. A distinct mark for every distinct vocal sound in the language, and the same for every simple consonant. 2. There should be no synonymous letters (if they may be so called) that is the same vocal sound, or consonant should never be represented in different words, sometime by one character, sometimes by another. 3. Single characters should in no case be used for a combination of two or more vocal sounds (which is what is properly called a diphthong). Or of two or more consonants. 4. A combination of two or more characters should never represent a simple vocal sound, or a single consonant. 5. There should be no characters in the written which correspond to nothing in the audible language; In other words, there should be no mute letters.

Ever the realist, Douglas is nevertheless quick to point out that 'there never has existed hitherto a language in which such an Alphabet, and such a plan of orthography, have been observed' and that there was little likelihood of its being achieved owing to 'the known caprice of mankind, in making continual variations in the pronounciation of words'

(Jones:1992:109). Indeed, Douglas appears to have major doubts about the feasibility of the entire prescriptive exercise: 'To regulate or restrain this caprice is beyond the efforts of any authority, were it to be thought, in any country, a proper subject for the exertion of authority. And if this caprice continue daily to operate, unless a society of scholars were appointed to alter and adapt the written to the changes introduced into the audible language, the sounds represented by the same characters must perpetually fluctuate and vary' (Jones:1992:109).

We shall, of course, have many opportunities to describe and discuss the finer points of Douglas' system in our sections dealing with the contemporary phonology itself. Douglas' views very much appear to echo those of Drummond (1767:5) who argues that 'Letters, being of themselves the simplest elements of speech, they ought therefore to be represented in the simplest manner, so that their several independent powers may appear, and that there may be as great a correspondence as possible between the eye and the ear; or, if you will, as great an unity between the sign and the sound as can be'. Yet, although he acknowledges that 'it may seem a very just maxim in theory, that each letter should always preserve an uniformity of sound, and that every sound should have a particular character to express it', he admits that 'this hath never been the case in any living language', going on to list what he considers to be the main agents of orthographic inconsistency (1767:19):

> Natural defects in the organs of speech, a misuse of them, an affectation of what may be called a fine or polite, or rather, as it well may be called, a finiken way of speaking - A provincial accent, a short and quick expression, or its opposite extreme, a heavy, drawling, whining, canting pronunciation; these and many other customs contribute to a change of sounds between the letters.

Beattie too (1788:40-44) (speaking out against 'the fashionable letters and syllables') abhors specialised, phonetic alphabets since, he argues, 'it may be doubted, whether there ever was an alphabet so perfect, as to contain characters adapted to all the elementary sounds of a language, and not one more or fewer', while redundancies and mis-matches in orthographic representations are to be expected rather than marvelled at since, 'There are not in Great Britain two provinces, which do not differ in some particulars of pronunciation; and in most countries the modes of speech, especially while literature is in its infancy, are vague and changeable.....Every thing deserves praise, which is done with a view to make language durable; for on the permanency of any tongue depends that of the literature conveyed in it. And if new words, new letters, or new modes of spelling, might be introduced at pleasure, language would soon be disfigured and altered; old authors would erelong be laid aside as unintelligible, and the new could be consigned to oblivion before their time'.

Two of the most forceful advocates of orthographic reform, James Elphinston and the Reverend James Adams, also utilise descriptive terminology of a type not entirely unlike that we have discussed above. Both writers centre their discussion of vowel types around an open/shut (in the case of Elphinston (Müller:1914; Rohlfing:1984), and a first (or free) versus a second position in Adams' scheme. Open or free vowels appear to be those occurring in monosyllables which are coda empty or in the peak position of 'open' syllables in disyllabic items. Elphinston in his *Miniature of English Orthography* of 1795 (a summation of the ideas he proposed in the first part of the 1786/87 *Propriety Ascertained in her Picture*) characterises as open in 'open syllable' contexts, the *a* slender vowel in such items as *pa-per, fa-vor, bra-ver,* while its equivalent in 'closed' syllables is to be witnessed in items such as *fain, fein,* the *e* vowel 'garded' from what would otherwise be a shutting syllable final nasal, by the presence of the <i> 'servile' which 'must gard dhe vowel from the consonant, hwich else wood shut it' (1795:14). The shut version of *a,* still described as slender, is to be found in such items as <fan>, <fanning>, while open/shut contrasts for '*a* braud', *e, i, o* and *u* can be summarised as follows:

	OPEN	SHUT
E	seize, mean, fiend	men, pen, fen
I	fine, dine, rime	fin, din, brim
O	po, pole, mode	polish, modest
U	unit, tune, punic	study, student, unabashed

with pre-sonorant vowels being treated as open; Elphinston (1795:16) summarises the distinction:

> *a,e,i,o,u* open; *ar, er, il, on, us,* shut; *may, me, my, vow, vew; mas, mes, mis, mos, must.* So *Mary, marry; even, sevven; ivy, Livvy; odor, odder; student, studdy.*

a set of vowel quality and monophthongal/diphthongal contrasts more familiarly seen under the long/short distinction in most of the writers we have so far considered.

James Adams' system is considerably more elaborate and he argues powerfully for spelling reform, not of the radical type we shall see espoused by Elphinston and Scot, but the more modest system using superscripted accents put forward by 'A learned and reverend Friend, native of Scotland, member of the honourable Scotch Society of Antiquaries' (1799:162), the Reverend Alexander Geddes, whose 'plan is a desideratum, and would at once proscribe the apparent inconsistency of the Scotch pronunciation, solely manifested by retaining our mode of spelling, and deviating from it in a manner not to be conceived by any powers of English combination of the letters. How, in the name of wonder, can Scotch Schoolmasters teach poor children to read their Bible printed the English way? They use no other. Hence every word is a stumbling block; and, from early youth, the Scotch are taught *that our pronunciation is anomalous and capricious' (The Pronunciation of the English Language* 1799:162). The use of the pronominal *our* by this English Jesuit from Saffron Walden points to the extent of his conversion to the Scotch cause.

Like Elphinston, Adams divides vocalic segments into two main kinds, free and 'second position'; the former again mainly stressed vowels in open syllables or syllables lacking a consonantal coda. However, his method is marked by a division of segment types according to their commonality, a notion he does not attempt anywhere to define: 'No. 1 is the general and common sound. No. 2 a frequent and secondary sound. No. 3 and 4 mark it to be accidental, potential and rare' (1799:22). In addition, Adams also characterises vowel segments according to whether they are foreign, clear, slender or broad. Thus, the vowel segments represented by the graph <a> have the following manifestations: common foreign clear *e*, as in *fa-tal, la-dy, a* (the indefinite article); common foreign slender as in *A-men, An-na*; common foreign clear, as in *ra-ther, fa-ther* and broad, as in *wâter* (where we note the use of the diacritic mark with *â*). He distinguishes two kinds of vowel segment represented by the graph <e>: in number one position the sound best represented by the graph <ee>, as in *be, he, she,* and a second *e* foreign 'in the compound of the Latin *de* and *re,* as in *de-fend, se-cond, re-sound, re-flect'*. While such a distinction may merely reflect a durational contrast between long and short [i], it is possible, as we shall discuss later, that the second segment may, in fact, represent a lowered version of the pure palatal: [i˕]. The two most common sounds to be represented by the <i> graph are the clearly diphthongal [aɩ], the 'EI, I pronoun' and '*i* foreign', as in *Chili, Brindi-si,* although he never specifies the relationship between this segment and that represented by the <ee> graph, nor with the *i* common foreign we shall discuss below.

His number one *o* vowel, described also as 'clear' (1799:87), is to be found in the items *go, lo, no, so,* while the number three Potential <o> graph corresponds to *ou* French, as in *mouv-oir* (*Rome* also sounds *ou* French, 'but *o* long prevails by use and rule') and is clearly some kind of [ʊ] or [ɷ] sound. Adams also provides a set of contrasting items illustrating this [ɷ]/[o] alternation: *do, to, who* versus *doe, toe, hoe* (1799:37), an orthographic contrast 'founded on reason' showing the language's ability to 'exclude bare and capricious exception'. Adams' description of the value of the <u> graph in its first position is interesting, 'having a twang and twist of voice peculiar to us' (1799:23), although 'Mr Sheridan seems to carry to affectation the mixture of the *i* and *ou*, in *Duke, diouk*' (1799:38). The second sound of this graph is 'bordering on the Italian *u*, or *ou* French: it also has a mixed sound of *u* French and Italian, losing the twang of *y, yu'* (1799:23). While we can only speculate on a possible phonetic value for such a description, evidence from other writers may seem to suggest, as we shall see, a value like [ɤ]. We might therefore suggest that Adams' set of 'first position', 'free' vowels is made up of segments such as [e], [a], [ɑ], [ɒ], [i], [o], [ɷ], and [ju].

In their second position, essentially in closed syllable contexts, Adams' vowels 'receive a foreign and contracted sound; and this is much more frequent than the long English sound'. In this area of the phonology Adams offers much more detailed description. For instance, sounds represented by the <a> graph are most commonly slender *a*, as in *bad, can, fan,* while in second position there are two separate entities, one 'clearer', and, with two consonants following, 'a little more open', thus *bank, cast, dart, fast.* It also represents a sound which is 'very open and broad *â'* especially when *w* precedes, as in *warm, war, ward.* Perhaps we are seeing here a description of segments such as [æ], [a], [ɑ] and [ɒ]/[ɔ], although the 'little more open' description may represent increased vowel length preceding such duration affecting clusters. <e> represents the common foreign <e> in this position, as in the items *bed, den, let,* while in its less common manifestation it undergoes the often observed lowering and centring in pre-[r] contexts (to *'u* rough'): 'the roughness of the letter *r*, totally absorbs and assimilates to itself *e, i,* and *y*...Hence *cler, der, mer,* sound *clar* and *clur, mar* and *mur,* in *clerk, Derby, merchant; servant, survant and sarvant,* &c' (1799:40). Drummond (1767:21) finds this lowering/centring 'injudicious' and characteristic of 'a country dialect': 'In *i*, as in *a*, many grammarians authorise a capricious custom, begun in some counties, of pronouncing u^2 [[ʌ]:CJ] for i^3 [[ɩ]:CJ] before *r*. - Even those who avow this practice, would start at hearing a *girl* pronounced *gurl*, and *gird, gurd*, &c. but their ears are grown familiar to *sur, thurd, furst,* &c. which are equally improper. Nay a late grammarian has gone still farther, and says *girl* ought to be pronounced *gal*, because some ridiculous coxcombs pronounce it so'.

Adams' <i> graph is described as *i* foreign, in items like *in, sin, bill,* while *o* short ('though it sounds long') resembles a kind of open *â*. But it is also described as being like (what is probably the synonymous) broad *a* 'before most consonants', thus *bog, God, on, rod.* The <o> graph also signifies 'short *u'*, especially in pre-nasal contexts, thus *son, com-ing, ton, hon-ey, Lon-don,* while Adams also identifies another 'common' or 'coarse' Flemish *u*, exemplified by *us, must, cur, fur run;* it is difficult to decide if he intends a genuine phonetic contrast between the two types, although the syllable terminations of the latter might suggest increased duration and hence lowering/centring. In general Adams' second position, closed syllable vowels appear to be [æ], [a], [ɑ], [ɒ]/[ɔ], [ɩ] and [ʌ], that is, principally the low mid, low and low central vowels in the inventory, the pure labial and palatal, high mid being the preserve of vowels in the 'free' position in his scheme.

The complex and often confusing picture given by phonetic representation based on metaphorical labelling is clear from the above brief description; a confusion compounded by the over reliance upon the standard orthography as a descriptive base, the conflation of diphthongal and monophthongal segments, and the use of terminology with quite different reference, as in the open nomenclature with its articulatory correlation in Douglas and syllable type implication in Elphinston.

3.4 Manipulation of the Standard Orthography

As we noted earlier, the 18th century was not a period which generally favoured the use of specialised phonetic alphabets involving specially adapted characters to achieve some 'one symbol one sound' goal. In this attitude it contrasts strongly with that of the previous two centuries where much of the basis for the modern *International Phonetic Alphabet* symbolic representation was set down. We commented that there was perhaps one exception to this general trend, the work of Thomas Spence of Newcastle, whose *New Alphabet* formed the descriptive base of his important, and much neglected, *The Grand Repository of the English Language* of 1775. A more modest attempt at orthographic reform utilising specialised characters was attempted by Abraham Tucker in his *Vocal Sounds* (1773:4-5): 'it seems necessary to rectify our alphabet, not that I mean to alter the common manner of writing but only to gratify the curiosity of such as may be desirous of analysing our language into its constituent elements, and to furnish them with a set of characters whereby they might express and distinguish every articulate sound that is current among us'. Yet his specialised additions are limited to six: <þ,ð, ﬁ, ŋ> plus the Greek ε and η.

When it came to the 'phonetic' representation of extended pieces of English text (and for an American attempt utilising super and subscripted numerals, see *A Plain, Rational Essay on English Grammar* by Duncan Mackintosh published at Boston in 1797, 'the main object of which is to point out a plain, rational and permanent standard pronunciation') the preferred alternative to the superscription of accents and numerals above a standard orthography, was the 'rescrambling' of that orthography in an attempt to make it more responsive to sound/symbol correlations. Spence himself attempted such a scheme in his *Crusonia: or Robinson Crusoe's Island* (A Supplement to the *History of Robinson Crusoe*) published in Newcastle in 1782. Spence was an unashamed improver of the lot of the uneducated populace and his works were aimed as much at heightening general literacy levels as imposing an upper class, London based standard on provincial speakers. He comes out too against the need for formal schools of grammar and pronunciation where 'Kŏnsĭstĭnsez' might be promoted. The *Crusonia* uses a mixture of a limited set of superscripted accent marks with some 'respelling' of the standard orthography, what Spence describes as the 'Kruzoneĭn Mănĭr' (1782:*Preface*):

> I Hav prĭntĭd this lĭtĭl Pes ĭn thĭ Kruzoneĭn Mănĭr (se thĭ Postscrĭpt) fŏr thĭ Ez ŏv Fŏrĭnĭrz ănd ŏrdĭnare Redĭrz. I tharfor ădjur aul Krĭtĭks and Skŏlĭrz nŏt too aprĭhĕnd thar Librarez ĭn Danjĭr, ŏr thĭngk I ĭntĕnd too kŏmpĕl ithĭr thĕm ŏr thar Chĭldrĭn intoo Kŏnsĭstĭnsez. No, I onle ĭntĕnd too fre thĭ Poor and thĭ Stranjĭr, thĭ 'Indŭstreŭs and thĭ 'Inĭsĭnt frŏm vĕksashŭs, tedeŭs, ănd rĭdĭkĭlĭs Absŭrdĭtez, : and aulso too mak Chărĭte Skoolz, and in a grat Mĕzhĭr, aul Skoolz fŏr techĭng 'Inglĭsh ŭnnĕsĭsare, thĭs Mĕ'thĭd beĭng so eze and răshĭnĭl.

The *Postskript* (1782:42-52) contains a key to the symbols used in the *Crusonia* ('We Crusonians [are:CJ] not only far above you in Politics but in Literature. Our Language is the best English, but you must not expect us to spell so absurdly as you do. It would be reckoned very barbarous indeed here, to beat Children for not comprehending the greatest Inconsistencies' (1782:42)). The vowels and diphthongs in the *Crusonian Alphabet* are characterised as :

Capitals	Named	Tentative value
A	a	[e(e)] <gratĭst>
'A	ă	[a] <ămŏng>
ˆA	â	[ɑ] <fâthĭr>
E	e	[i] <delit>
'E	ĕ	[ɛ] <ĕkspĕkt>
I	i	[ɑɩ] <delit>
'I	ĭ	[ɩ] <ĭz>
O	o	[o]<onle>
'O	ŏ	[ɔ] <nŏt>
U	u	[ju]<kŏntĭnuĭle>
AU	au	[ɒ] <aulmost>
OO	oo	[u] <too>
'U	ŭ	[ʌ]/[ɷ]<wŭd>:<stŭde>

However one commonly expressed argument against the whole concept of innovatory alphabetic systems was based upon the effect it would have on existing books written in traditional spelling. Buchanan (1762:6) makes the typical case *ante*: 'The same fate would attend the invention of a new Alphabet or introducing a Character for every simple sound, however useful and advantageous it might prove in rendering Reading and Spelling easy Tasks, and establishing a fixed and uniform Pronunciation: For few of any Nation would be prevailed upon to learn their Letters over again, or part with their Books in the present Character, which by such an Innovation would become altogether useless. It remains therefore, that we endeavour to exhibit as plain and conclusive Rules for the Powers and Properties of the Characters we now have, as the impetuous and prevailing Tides of Custom will admit'. Yet Sylvester Douglas is sceptical of such an argument (Jones:1992:109): 'To say that all old books would thereby be rendered useless, is to assert that the original manuscripts of Dante and Boccace, and the first editions of Corneille and Racine, are unintelligible, and of no value'.

3.5 James Elphinston and Alexander Scot

There can be little doubt that the greatest practitioners of the method of orthographic manipulation and management in the 18th century were the two Scots, James Elphinston and Alexander Scot. The author of several works on pronunciation, Elphinston's main contribution to orthographic 'reform' is to be found in his two volume *Propriety Ascertained in Her Picture, or Inglish Speech and Spelling Rendered Mutual Guides, Secure Alike from Distant, and from Domestic, Error*, published in 1786 and 1787 as well as in an abridged version of the same: *A Minniature ov Inglish Orthoggraphy* (1795). Elphinston (1786:xii) is uncompromising in his attempt to find an unambiguous symbolic method (*Inglish Truith*) for the representation of speech and to express a form of the spoken word which is some kind of immutable standard:

> It waz before barely possibel to' investigate INGLISH TRUITH: now it iz impossibel to' mistake her. Dhey, dhat for som time may be shy to' exhibbit her, wil at least approov dhe boldnes, dhat displays her here; dhat shows no shut vowel open, or open shut; and renders dhe very stres, an object ov intuiscion. Wo haz but to' read (if possibel) anny sentence, or cupplet, az hiddherto' writtten; and dhe same, according to' ORTHOGGRAPHY; to be struc not onely widh PROPRIETY, hware alone she can be found, but widh dhe sweet necissity ov ascertaining her in her picture. Ov dhis PROPRIETY dhe ear, not dhe eye, iz dhe judge: for dhe ear iz dhe eye ov dhe mind. Let us hear, to' write: dhen shal we see, to' speak. Let us first spel, az dhe best speakers speak; and dhen (but not til dhen) let us pretend to' speak, az we spel.

However, he is not so faithful to the 'one symbol one sound' criterion as he likes to make out. Arguing for a general representation of an [ɒ]-type vowel by <au>, as in his spellings <wrauth>, <squaudron>, he still allows spellings such as <halt>, <Bald>, <halter>, since the <u> symbol is 'still understood dho unseen' (1786:123). He sees in his reformed orthography a means of obtaining a 'harmonized Land' (1787:266) where a single standard will prevail, and as a method of preventing 'violacions' all too readily encouraged by a spelling system he regards as inadequate and conducive to further and continuing departure from standard 'Inglish Harmony', for 'shal even Scotch lowlanders be held lower dhan dhey ar, for dheir *Dezember*, insted of *December*?' (1787:267). Yet he cautions the reader of listening too readily to 'dhe lerned laffers ov London, hoo so duly decide in difficult cases' (1787:141). Nonetheless, his vision of 'Inglish Harmony' is a truly national one: 'Dhe dore ov our language dhus opened to' mankind, ov dhe Brittish Nacions iz a union so peciliarly effected; dhat widh won voice, az widh won spirrit; widh won pen, az widh won tung; dhey may glorify God, and enlighten men. EDINBURGH wil hencefoarth vy widh LONDON, in dhe nattural, az undouting excellence ov language; and in all dhe harmony, dhat can endear or empower dhe poolpit, dhe bar, and dhe pres' (1787:263-64). Yet Elphinston was clearly aware of the resistance the literary and linguistic establishment would raise against his proposed system (1786:x): 'Som wil say (for hwat wil not som say?) 'All chainges ar daingerous, dherfore non shood be made'. Dhis may, must, hav always been said; it iz obvious, by hoom. Yet chainges disgracefool, no les dhan daingerous, hav been insensibly, often absurdly, made dheze two centuries past; hwile dhe chainges, indispensabel to' Truith, hav continnued edher dredded, or unknown.'

Elphinston's reforms centre around the common 18th century distinction between proper and improper diphthongs (Jones:1992:89:footnote 62), the latter representing digraphs whose original purpose of marking vocalic transition has been overtaken by phonological processes involving monophthongisation, or which - notably the <ea> and <ie> graphs - were introduced by 16th and 17th century orthoepists for the purpose of differentiating monophthongal vowel values which had become conflated under single graphs; the <meet>/<meat> contrast being an obvious example. The major characteristic of Elphinston's reform, as we shall see, lies in the way in which it 'simplifies' and modifies this last group. To understand Elphinston's representational method we must first appreciate his (almost obsessional) concern for the distinction between *open* and *shut* vowels. The former (which generally occur as the peaks of syllables which are coda empty) he sees as having some kind of intrinsic length characteristic, while the latter, showing 'A stoppage ov vocallity, by clustering consonants; must retard, if it compres, dhe emmision ov dhe vocallity' (1787:117-18) appear to relate to vowel peaks whose codas are filled by a consonant or consonantal cluster. 'No vowel iz more different from anoddher, dhan dhe same vowel, open and shut; respectively, from its seeming self: dhus *a, an; me, men; I, in; O, on; u, un*; az in *unit, under* '(1787:117-18). Looking similar to an open/close syllable distinction, these [e]/[a], [i]/[ɛ], [ɑɪ]/[i], [o]/[ɒ], [jɷ]/[ʌ] contrasts are not at all unlike the First/free versus second position contrast we noted above under James Adams' scheme. Yet Elphinston's principals of syllable division can sometimes appear to have little consistent motivation: for while items like *paper* and *favour* are divided *pa-per* and *fa-vor,* the vowel in *fanning* is regarded as shut, on the analogy of *fan* (a syllable division like *fan-ing*), while the <l> in an item like *bawling* is seen as a marker of openness in syllable one, in *ballot,* where the phonetics of the vowel suggest that it is shut, Elphinston proposes a syllable division like *bal-lot* (1795:17); but see Chapter 9.1 below.

Central to Elphinston's reformed spelling system is the notion of marking open vowels in contexts where the standard orthography would suggest they are shut. That is, while a graphic combination <CV> would indicate one of the open vowel set at <V>, one like <(C)VC> would mark a closed version at the same spot. Clearly, however, there are many lexical items where the set of open vowels can appear with an orthographic consonantal mark immediately to their right; items, for instance, such as [miit] '*meat*' and [met] '*mate*'. It is cases like this that Elphinston's system brings into play a set of vowel graphs which act as 'distinguishers', 'associates', 'quiet friends' and, in his favoured terminology, 'serviles' rendering an 'essencial az vizzibel service, boath to' vowels and consonants. Hware such gards ar wanted, dhey doutles wil atend; and hwen dhey proov superfluous, az reddily widhdraw' (1795:3). Indeed, the over-riding principle of Elphinston's system is perhaps best summarised in his own maxim: *'Servants, wanted, must attend; unwanted, must widhdraw*' (1786:120). He spends considerable time setting out the serviles which, in his system, best show the open values for the vowels represented under the graphs <a>, <e>, <o> and <u>: the resulting 'preferred' combinations are <au> <ai>, <ei>, <oa> ('*o* loves *a*' (1786:138)) and <ui> (1786:117-160). These graphic combinations, together with the use of the 'final <e>' act to denote the set of open phonetic segments in stressed position in monosyllables. A typical statement is (1786:124):

> *E,* effectively (az in *Europe* and *few*) associating *u* and *w*; assumes evvery oddher vowel in dhe capacity ov a servile: *a*, az *heal* or *meat*; anoddher seeming self, az *heel* and *meet*; boath dhus occularly clear: *i*, in *receiv* and *receit*, widh dheir cognates (or cozzens); in *teil* dhe tree, not entangling *teal* dhe fowl: in certain Inglish surnames, identic widh oddhers, or widh common appellacions; az *Keil* widh *keel, Leigh* widh *Lee*, and *lea*; in dhe Scotch names, *Keir, Weir, Keith, Leith,* and dhe like: *O*, at least in dhe Inglish town ov *St. Neots.*

The importance of this quotation is that while it apparently shows a classic failure of a system like Elphinston's to mark one symbol with one sound, it is a deficiency of which he is fully aware, and one which he attempts to motivate. He freely admits that there are graphic correspondences for the same phonetic entity which are 'coincidents'. 'Vocal Substitution' is allowed: 'Dho won semblance may exhibbit, not onely two' senses, but two' sounds; won symbol must not pretend to paint anoddher, unles by distinctive substitution' (1795:8). While he allows *e* to be 'dhe lawfool substitute ov a, in...*weigh, wey, hwey, prey, dey*' (1795:9); '*e* cannot be *a*, widh dhe servile dhat distinguishes *e*: *tear* cannot be clas-mate, at wonce to' *fear* and *fair*' (1795:10). Elphinston's main motivation for permitting such 'vocal substitution' is his desire to see orthographic elements 'occularly clear'; '*Soll*, spirrit avoids occular union with *sole*, alike, and *soal*, by adopting the servile of *poll, boll, toll, roll* (widh *controll*) *scroll*, and *droll*' (1795:6). Thus such orthographic equivalents are set the task of visually differentiating otherwise homophonous items. As always, such concepts can receive Elphinston's wry comment (1786:138): 'Whore haz but to' drop dhe false iniscial, and turn onnest in (hore) dhe uncontamminating coincident ov hoar'.

As we have hinted above, what probably makes Elphinston's reformed orthography most distinctive is the way it treats many of the digraphs which surface in the standard spelling system as fossilisations of historical diphthongs or the efforts of earlier spelling reformers. He is particularly concerned to rectify those situations where a syllable peak showing a vowel of a quality he describes as shut, is expressed through a digraph shape or exists in an orthographic syllable terminated by a final *e*. The 'superfluous' second component of such digraphs, Elphinston calls 'falsifiers' or 'id'lers': 'If dhen no vowel can claim a servile, but to'gard its opennes; shal shut vowels be belied by pretended serviles?' (1786:162). He is particularly concerned by the role played by <a> as a falsifier (particularly when it is in a digraph combination with <e>), and he cites many instances of the 'fallacious..idel *a*' in items like *realm, earl, mearl, pearl, earn, yearn, learn* and several others (1786:162-23), preferring to see them rendered as *relm, erl, merl, perl*, etc. In the same way, he classifies <a> as a falsifier in items like <cease> *cese*, <lease> *lese*, <crease> *crese* and <peace> *pece*, where the servile *a* is redundant owing to the use of the final *e* which marks the open phonetic quality of the syllable peak, although he does allow for alternative representational solutions (1786:157): 'Dhe *i* or final *e* of *seize*, must vannish in *seiz* or *seze*', while 'preceding falsifiers' are to be strongly discouraged in shut vowel contexts, notable *friend* for *frend, heart* for *hart*, although he sees in the last a case for a 'spescial pleader' since it enables one to 'distinguish dhe *dear heart* ov man, oddher animal, or aught else; from dhe unfalsifying *hart*, dhe *deer*' (1786:170). Yet Elphinston is particularly outraged by the 'damage' he sees done to the speech habits - especially of the uneducated - by the presence of such falsifiers ('*Falsehood can doo notthing but evil*') especially in the items <either> and <neither>, the spelling of which with digraphs containing a falsifier 'tempted dhe untaught in Ingland, az dhe first dhoze ov dhe same clas in Scotland, to' open dhe subjunctive vowel, by a preceding servile: an inversion ov all litterary law, precluded (widhout dainger) by ...*edher* and *nedher*' (1786:171).

We shall, of course, investigate Elphinston's system in more detail when we come to examine what it tells us about contemporary Scots pronunciation; his own summary of his spelling method is provided at (1786:239) in a piece entitled 'Serviles Rectified' which sets out the principles his digraph representational method:

> Dhe vowels cood not be rectified, unles dheir serviles were so. Secured waz dhus: 1. A *Braud* in *braud* itself and *graut*; 2. A *Slender* open, in *grait, wair; peir, beir*; and dhe rest: 3. A *slender*-shut prolonged in *sahce*, and *sahsage*, better *sahcage*: 4. O *direct* in *soll, roll*, and *controll; dore, flore*, and *more*; or *doar, floar, moar*: in *foar, foarteen, soarce, coart, goard; coarse, coarce; moarn, boarn, foarm*: 5. O *depressive*, in *doo, shoo, canoo, Room; moov, proov, behoov, looz; yoo, yooth, uncooth, goold; in toor, amoor, acooter*; and in dhe shut or short *soop, groop; cood, shood, wood*; widh *pool, poot*, and dhe rest: dhus *e* no more attending the depressive, *o* the direct, *u* edher emission.

We might even here set out the bones of his descriptive system mapped against the tentative phonetic values they may have represented. Consider Table 3.3 below, where E represents a 'final <e>', usually in an open syllable context, C a 'closed' syllable with a consonantal coda and W, a lip rounded, semi-vowel syllable onset. It is important to bear in mind how seriously Elphinston valued his reforms not just as a means of representing the 'Truith' of current pronunciation ('dhe hoal System ov Inglish Harmony'), but also as a means of preventing 'error' as well as a mechanism for identifying the same in non-standard dialect forms:

> If writing dhen must repprezent utterance; prezerv it to' natives, and convey it to' straingers; if proze must be pure and melodious az verse; dho it cannot alike ascertain edher dhe quallity or dhe quantity ov sound; purity ov speech wil dictate purity ov picture, and dhe genuine picture wil reflect dhe genuine oridginal. Dhus dhe unvisciated ear furnishes rascional entertainment to' dhe eye, and dhe ubvisciated eye returns dhe mellody ov dhe ear. On dheir mutual dependance, depends human language; and, on dheir adjustment, dhe language ov Propriety. edher, erring, must injure dhe oddher; but dhe error ov dhe ear, dho striking for dhe moment, iz les consequencially, and les extendedly, fatal.

Possibly the only other extensive and significant bid to indicate pronunciation characteristics by means of some kind of 'scrambling' of the available alphabet set, is that attempted by Alexander Scot in his '*The*

TABLE 3.3
Elphinston's Vowel System

	Orthography: including 'co-incidents'	OPEN
A slender	<ai>, <ei>, <a>E	[e]
A broad	<au>, W<a>	[ɒɒ]
E	<ea>, <ie>, <ei>, <ee>, <e>E	[i]
O direct	<o># <o>E,<oa>	[o]
O depressive	<oo>	[u]/[ɷ]
U	<u>E	[ju]
I	<i>E	[ɑɩ]

	Orthography: including 'co-incidents'	SHUT
A slender	<a>C	[a]
A broad	<o>C	[ɒ]
E	<e>C	[ɛ]
O direct	<o>C	[ɔ]
O depressive	<oo>C	[ʌ]
U	<u>C	[ʌ]
I	<i>C	[ɩ]

Contrast: A Specimen of the Scotch Dialect, In Prose and Verse, According to the Latest Improvements; With an English Version of 1779. This document takes the form of a letter to a noble family, commenting upon the changes brought about by Scottish religious, political, economic and agricultural 'improvements' noted by Scot on his return to his native country after a sojourn abroad, in his case, most probably in France (Jones:1993). For the student of 18th century Scots phonology the main interest of this short letter arises from its claim to 'paint the present Caledonian English of the college, the pulpit and the bar' (1779:6). While *The Contrast* itself runs to only some six hundred and fifty eight words (see *Appendix One*), it presents us with a carefully worked out and, as we shall try to demonstrate below, phonetically detailed description not of the 'poalisht *lengo*' of London speech, but of the characteristics of late 18th century upper class, educated Scots pronunciation in Edinburgh:

> Oy haiv bin cradeblay enfoarmed, thaut noat lass auz foartay amenant samenaurays oaf lairnen enstruck cheldren en ainay laungage boot thaut whoch auloanne ez nidful, aund nurter tham en ainay haibet oonlass thaut oaf civeeletay. Oy haiv massalf tnoan dip-lairned profassours oaf fowr destengueshed oonavarsetays, caupable oaf coamoonicatten airts aund sheences* auss w-al auz laungages auncient oar moadarn, yet endefferent auboot, aund froam thance oonauquant woth thaut sengle laungage whoch ez auboov ainay laungage alz; aund en whoch auloanne thase maisters ware tow empairt tnoalege. Foar moy share, oy moast aunoalege oy caunnoat winder ev Cauladoneaun paurents sand cheldren tow Yoarksheir foar leeberaul adecatione, aund paurteekelarlay foar thaut poalisht *lengo,* whoch ez noat spoc en Scoatlaund.

Scot's system of vowel representation does not appear to be of the alphabetically based type underlying those using super/subscripted numerals or symbols, nor does it appear to owe much the efforts of Elphinston. Rather, it seems to be more of a genuine attempt to create a phonetic alphabet capable of reflecting subtle nuances in vowel (and especially, as we shall see, in diphthongal) variation. Indeed, Scot's representational system for vowels is remarkably simple and involves no complex manipulation of symbol combinations or orderings; a tentative value system for his orthography might be:

Orthography	**Phonetic Value**	**Examples**
<i>	[ii]	*mean, speak*
<ee>	[ɩ˔]	*visit, British*
<e>	[ɩ˕]	*sit, liberty*
<o>	[o]	*those, spoke*
<oa>	[ɔ]	*Scot, not*
<au>	[ɑ]/[æ]	*that, as, and*
<a>	[ɛ˕]	*education*
<ai>	[ɛ˔]	*many, learn*
<ee>/<é>	[e]	*paper, entertain*
<u>	[u]	*prove, book*
<oo>	[ɣ]	*could, would*

The phonetic values we have ascribed to Scot's symbols must be regarded at this point as highly speculative, although we shall attempt to justify them fully below; nevertheless, if we can for the moment accept them, they point to a system which is capable of connoting a wide range of phonetic values by means of a very efficient symbolic use. There is no reference in Scot's work to any attempt to use the second graph in digraphs as 'gards' or 'serviles' in Elphinston's sense, so we must look elsewhere for the motivations for his symbolism. It is interesting to observe that by and large Scot uses single graphs to denote the 'pure' palatal and labial [i] and [u] vowels. It is the 'mixed' vowels, the 'mid' vowels whose phonetic (notably acoustic) structure is definable in terms of combinations or mixtures of a restricted set of 'pure' segments (Jones:1990:5-8; Anderson and Ewen:1989:206ff) which in general attract a digraphic representation. <oa> and <ai> graphs are use to represent the low 'mid' front and back [ɔ]/[ɛ] segments both 'mixtures', respectively, of labial/sonorant and palatal/sonorant primary components, at least within the frameworks of non-linear phonological models such as Dependency and Natural Phonology which attempt to provide a more structured characterisation of the internal composition of what traditional Jakobson/Chomsky-Halle models characterise as relatively unordered 'bundles' of distinctive acoustic/articulatory features (Donegan:1978). If it is possible to see a segment like [ɛ] as a simultaneous expression of an internally complex combination comprising a sonorant and a palatal component, with the former preponderating - {i:a} - (Anderson and Ewen:1989:127; Anderson and Jones:1974:76; Jones:1990:5-7), then might it not seem plausible to orthographically represent this internal complex by means of the two graphs whose values themselves represent the internal components of the complex: <ai>? But we might object to a suggestion like this on the grounds that it is far too elaborate and imputes to 18th century phoneticians theoretical insights which are more properly associated with the late 20th century. But we should not rush into assuming either that modern theoretical speculations are more powerful or sophisticated than those current two hundred years ago, or that earlier phoneticians were incapable of viewing phonology from a very abstract standpoint.

Joshua Steele's *An Essay Towards Establishing the Melody and Measure of Speech* (1775) is one of the most sophisticated attempts in the 18th century at characterising suprasegmental phonological phenomena. Steele provides a rather unusual interpretation of the proper/improper diphthong distinction so beloved of 18th century orthoepists. Ordinarily seen as one which marks off orthographic diphthongs denoting monophthongal pronunciations (<ea> in *meat*), from those which represent vocalic transitions (the <ou> in *house*), Steele takes a rather more subtle view (1775: *Preface*:xi): 'I will define a *proper diphthong* to be made in speech, by the blending of *two vowel sounds* so intimately into *one*, that the ear shall hardly be able to distinguish more than one uniform sound; though, if produced for a longer time than usual, it will be found to continue in a sound different from that on which it began, or from its *diphthong sound*'. On the one hand, Steel wishes to distinguish those 'genuine' diphthongs which involve a transition from one monophthongal component to another: 'To try the like experiment on the English sound of I or Y, as in I in the first person, and in the words MY, EY, IDLE, and FINE, (both which letters are the marks of one and the same *diphthong sound* composed of the English sounds AU and EE) the voice begins on the sound AU, and immediately changes to EE on which it continues and ends'. On the other hand, he also recognises segments he controversially describes as *diphthong sounds* which, although they are perceived as monophthongs, nevertheless are made up of more than one vocalic component - internalised diphthongs, a theoretical stance not unlike that taken by the proponents of Dependency Phonology. For instance, for Steel (1775:*Preface*:ix): 'The English sound of E, in the words *met, let, get,* is a diphthong composed of the vocal sounds A and E....and pronounced very short'; while:

> The other English sound of U [as distinct from the U is *use*:CJ] as in the words UGLY, UNDONE, BUT and GUT, is composed of the English sounds AU and OO [[ɔ] and [ɷ]:CJ]; but they require to be pronounced so extremely short and close together, that, in the endeavour to prolong the sound for this experiment, the voice will be in a continual confused struggle between the two component sounds, without making either of them, or any other sound, distinct; so that the true English sound of this diphthong can never be expressed but by the aid of a short energetic aspiration, something like a short cough, which makes it very difficult to our Southern neighbours in Europe.

In a similar vein, we might cite Sylvester Douglas (Jones:1992:118):

> It might perhaps be called a whimsical refinement were I to carry the analogy still farther, and say that, although the sound of *a* in *all*, is certainly simple, and not diphthongal; yet it is, in a manner, formed of a mixture of the long open *a*, and the *o*; in like manner as green, one of the simple primitive colours, is formed by the mixture of blue, and yellow.

If contemporaries were coming to such conclusions concerning the complex internal structure of vowel segments, it might not be too improbable to suppose that Alexander Scot's orthographic method was based on similar kinds of principles. Particularly interesting is his distinction between the [e]/<ee> and [ɛ]/<ai>, [o]/<o> and [ɔ]/<oa> segments, where the second of each pair is orthographically characterised by the presence of the 'contaminating' sonorant [ɑ] segment. We shall leave to a later discussion the rationalisation for the <au> graphic value for a segment which may be either [ɑ] or [æ]/[a].

3.6 James Buchanan and Alexander Geddes

We mentioned earlier, in our discussion of Buchanan's descriptive methodology, how - although inclined to the use of a rather simple set of superscripted accentual marks - he experimented at the same time with a rather crude system of 're-spellings'. This system is at its most fully developed in his *An Essay towards Establishing a Standard for an Elegant Pronunciation of the English Language* (1766), although it also appears from time to time in his other works as well. The *Essay*, in addition to an extensive *Preface* in which Buchanan's aims and methods are set out in some detail, is essentially a Pronouncing Dictionary arranged in two columns, one containing an alphabetical list of 'orthographic words', which show the 'true orthography', the other a corresponding and matching set of 'pronouncing words', in turn reflecting what Buchanan describes as the 'true pronunciation'. The former also contain accentual marks for main stress placement: 'To avoid crowding or confusing the pronouncing words, I have placed the common accent, denoting the elevation or emphasis of the voice, over its proper symbol in the orthographic words' (1766:*Preface*:viii), giving representations like: *boíler, breákfast, avówedly* . The right hand, facing column containing the list of 'pronouncing words' is composed of a mixed system made up of diacritics and standard orthography manipulation, where sounds are to be 'properly represented in combination'. In the *Preface* to the *Essay* (1766:*Preface*:v-vi), Buchanan tells us how in his *Linguae Britannicae Vera Pronuntiatio* or *A New English Dictionary* (1757): 'I marked the long and short sounds of the vowels throughout the alphabetical words, distinguished every quiescent letter, pointed out the number of syllables each word consisted of where doubtful, and ascertained the various sounds of the vowels and diphthongs, and of the single and double consonants, &c'. Yet he appears to find an inherent fault in a system like this that it is somehow more difficult to read off without what he calls exemplification *viva voce*, and will not readily allow everyone to 'become his own private teacher'. Consequently, he attempts to represent stressed vowel quality by means of a set of digraphs, not unlike the system of 'serviles' and 'gards' to be employed later by Elphinston, combinations which, he claims, will enable a reader to come to an unambiguous conclusion about the phonetic value of the segment in question:

> For example, if I signify in writing, that (a) has five different sounds; and that, 1. it sounds long in *fame, fair, compare, profane*, &c. 2. broad, like German (a) in *call war, walk, bald, ward, water* &c whoever has not been taught these sounds *vivá voce*, or considered them abstractly, has received no instruction. But let these sounds be properly represented in combination, and a child that can read a little will readily pronounce them thus, *faim, fair, compair, profain, kaul, waur, wauk, bauld, waurd, wautir* &c. So if I signify that the diphthong (ea) has different sounds, and that 1. it sounds like (ee) in *arrear, appear, fear, dear*, &c. 2. like short (e) in *breast, head, deaf, sweat, ready*, &c. and, 3. like long (a) in *swear, bear, pear, great*, &c, I have conveyed little or no

> instruction to the generality of people: But when these different sounds are represented in combination, as in the pronouncing columns of this work, an indifferent reader wil easily express them thus, *arreer, appeer, feer, deer, brest, hed, def, swet, redy, swair, bair, pair, grait,* &c. (1766:*Preface*:vii).

While it is interesting to notice that it is the same set of 'long' vowels which attracts non-diacritic representation in Buchanan's scheme as in Elphinston's, and both writers use <ai> for [e], Buchanan makes little use of the 'final <e>' as a length marker, and eschews and <oa> representation for [oo]. Yet Buchanan does not provide us with either much motivation or empirical evidence for his claim that symbol 'combinations' provide readers with a more ready access to the phonetics behind the orthography, than does a system employing diacritic marks or using metaphorical terminology. We can only conclude that he prefers a system of representation as close as possible to the standard orthography, since although he comments on the fact that orthoepists such as Smith, Gil and Wilkins who introduced 'several new characters in order to rectify and fix our Orthography, which was formed by Chance in rude and illiterate Ages,' he stresses that their efforts met with a negative reaction. The invention of a new alphabet - 'a Character for every simple sound' - would undergo the same fate, he claims, 'For few of any Nation would be prevailed upon to learn their Letters over again' (1762:6:footnote). Buchanan's 'Scheme' is summarised at the beginning of the *Essay* as follows:

> In the following work, N. after a word stands for noun; V. for verb; Ad. or Adj. for adjective.
> The long a is denoted by ai; short a thus ă.
> The long e is denoted by ee; short e thus ĕ.
> The long i is denoted thus ī; the short thus ĭ.
> The long o thus ō; the short o thus ŏ.
> The long u is denoted by eu; the short thus ŭ.
> The long y is denoted by long ī or ȳ; the short by short ĭ or thus y̆
> A short quantity over ai, ee, oo, thus aĭ, eĕ, oŏ, denotes that they are to be rapidly pronounced, as only approaching to their diphthongal sound.
> Dieresis placed over the diphthongs ou and ow, thus, oü, öw, denotes the mixed sound of both words.

Although not on the same scale as either Elphinston or Alexander Scot, Alexander Geddes' *Epistle* (that paean in praise of Scots letters and language) is also clearly an attempt to use a 'non-standard' orthography for the purpose of connoting Scots linguistic characteristics. While he does not wish to use the system of superscripted accent marks ('this novel orthography') which characterises his 'translations into Scots verse' of the two classical pieces, not least because he possibly fears and anticipates a negative reaction from the Fellows of the Society of

Antiquaries whose company he so evidently wishes to join, Geddes nevertheless endeavours 'to make the orthography a little more uniform, and more agreeable to the Scottish idiom, than the orthography of the present day' (1792:438). Geddes' system is not particularly sophisticated, using <ai> graphs for [e] vowel segments, as in <mair> '*more*', <claith> '*cloth*'; <ee> and <ie> for palatal vowels, as in <ee> '*eye*', <wiel> '*well*', <weent> '*wont*'. His system is most developed, however, in the ways it attempts to represent the various kinds of labial vowels current in contemporary Scots, and we find manifestations such as <cuintry> '*country*'; <uther> '*other*'; <blude> '*blood*', <abeun> '*above*', <leugh> '*laugh*', <geud> '*good*' while, typically, he provides considerable descriptive comment on his system (1792:438-39):

> *ou* and *ow* are never confounded. The former is equivalent to the English *oo*, the latter to *ow* in *town*, or *ou* in *loud*. *Eu* and *ew* likewise express distinct sounds, *ew* is equivalent to the English *eu* or *ew*, but *ew* has a sound particular to Scotland, and which can hardly be represented in English characters; perhaps the combination *iow* pronounced smartly, will give some idea of it. The combination *ie* is always to be pronounced as *ee*, and *ea* like *e* short, or as the English pronounce *ea* in *death*.

3.7 Diphthongal Sounds

As we have hinted at several points in the above discussion, the 18th century linguistic materials are replete with attempts at definition for diphthongal elements, definitions bedevilled by a characteristic reliance upon a use of the symbols of the standard orthography as a vehicle for the expression of phonetic entities. Walker's (1791:25) attempt at a definition is typical: 'a double vowel, or the union or mixture of two vowels pronounced together, so as only to make one syllable. This is the general definition of a diphthong; but if we examine it closely, we shall find in it a want of precision and accuracy. If a diphthong be two vowel sounds in succession, they must necessarily form two syllables, and therefore, by its very definition, cannot be a diphthong; if it be such a mixture of two vowels as to form but one simple sound, it is very improperly called a diphthong, nor can any such simple mixture exist.' Sheridan sees diphthongs generally as merely the 'junction of two vowels' (1781:16), while Buchanan's definition (1762:14): 'What is a Diphthong? A Diphthong is the meeting of two vowels in one syllable' is immediately modified by: 'Some Writers absurdly define an English Diphthong to be the sounding of two Vowels in one Syllable; and make a bustle about dividing them into proper and improper, though they differ in the Method of their Division. They tell us a proper Diphthong is that which has a mixed or proper Sound of both the Vowels. According to this Definition there is not a proper Diphthong in the English Tongue, unless we allow (oi) to be one, to which some give the sound of the long (i)....It must be confessed that (oi) approaches the nearest of any combination in our Language to the Nature and Design of a Diphthong, as Diphthong imports the Coalition or Mixture of two Sounds in one.' Kenrick's scepticism for the descriptive powers of contemporary grammarians surfaces clearly in this area too: 'the very same Grammarians also tell us that *a diphthong or compound vowel, is the union of two or more vowels pronounced by a single impulse of the voice.* But how can there be *two simple articulate sounds* uttered by a *single impulse* of the *voice*? And that by *opening of the mouth only* in a particular manner? If the mouth be opened only in one particular manner, it will admit only one vowel, not two; and if two are emitted there must be some change effected in the manner of opening the mouth' (1784:38-9).

The Scotch grammarians in general add little to this debate, although it must be said that they tend to see through the inappropriateness of the 'proper'/'improper' distinction more regularly than some of their English counterparts. The writer of the *General View of English Pronunciation* (1784:4) confidently proclaims: 'A Diphthong is the union of two vowels, distinctly pronounced by a single impulse of the voice. Of all the combined letters usually called diphthongs, such as *oi, ou, au, eo, ie, oa, ui,* the only true ones are *oi,* made up of a^3e^3 in *noise, ou* of a^3o^3 in *thou*. As a proof of this, the word *author* is never sounded a^3-u^3thor; *people* pe^3-o^2ple, *field* fi^3-e^1ld, *load* lo^2-a^1d, guilt gu^2-i^1lt; but a^3-thur, pe^3ple, fi^3ld, lo^2d, gi^3lt' while he continues rather oddly 'To make up in part for this loss, it has of late been discovered that the i^2 in *fine, fire* &c and the u^3 in *cure*, are real diphthongs. The former is composed of a^3 and e^3, the mouth being opened as if about to sound the full a^3, and then suddenly closed upon the e^3. The latter is formed of the vowels e^3 and o^3, in the same manner as i^2'. The double significance of this 'meeting of two vowels in one syllable' is very clearly stated by John Drummond in his *A Grammatical Introduction* (1767:34-35) where he sees a diphthong as being, on the one hand, 'a transition from one vocal sound to another...produced by one, two, or more vowels, as *pine, fury, feud, lieu*' and, on the other, a circumstance where 'the meeting' is such that only one of the vowels is sounded 'hence the distinction of diphthongs into proper and improper', a distinction, he claims, which 'is of little consequence to young ones', views which are repeated, almost *verbatim*, by McIllquam, in his *A Comprehensive Grammar* (1781:12):

> *What is a Diphthong or double Vowel?*
> A transition from one vocal sound to another during the same impulse of breath, and may be produced by one, two, or three vowels; as *pine, fury, feud, lieu*; but, in the English language, there is a frequent meeting of two vowels in one syllable, one of which only is sounded. Hence diphthongs are commonly divided into proper and improper.

Not unlike this, the author of *A Spelling-Book upon a New Plan* (1766:131) treats diphthongs as the 'united sound of two vowels', or 'compounded sounds' (Cortez Telfair's 'compound sounds' (1775:153)), while Beattie's (1788:48) definition reflects his sophistication of phonetic analysis: 'the Diphthong...is formed, when two contiguous vowel sounds coalesce in such a manner, as that, though they form but one syllable, the sound of both, or at least a double sound, is distinctly heard; as *oy* in *joy*, *ow* in *cow*, *ui* in *juice*'. Dun (1766:44) concludes 'a *proper Diphthong* is that which is composed of any two Vowels in one Syllable, so distinctly pronounced, that such a Sound of both Vowels may be heard as Children learn at first in the Alphabet'. Burn too (1766:6-7) distinguishes proper double vowels, where we find 'a mixture of two vowels, making but one distinct sound', citing examples such as *neuter, jewel, abound, Caiphas,* while, on the other hand, 'improper double vowels' although meeting in the same syllable, are characterised by having one of the vowels 'always silent, or they have a sound distinct from that of either one or the other'. Thus '*i* is silent in *main* &c. where the *a* sounds like the long slender *a* in *care*.' In his typically flamboyant fashion, Adams (1799:68) using a what he claims is a 'free simile' describes diphthongs as 'the cavalry of our language: they have the combined force of a double vowel, which they frequently relinquish, and act as simple vowels'. Proper diphthongs he depicts as 'coalescing occurrence of vowels' with a 'double *mora* of tone' distinct from an improper, spurious and phantom variety which he nevertheless justifies on the basis that 'etymology, and the powers of this union, require the written form in order to discover the roots of words' (1799:73). Some of his arguments for treating diphthongs as either proper or improper are difficult to relate to: 'That *ai*, though it seems simply to sound long English *a*, is a proper diphthong, appears by the word *gay*; for if it were simple *e* foreign, *gay* by rule should be *djai*; therefore *ai, ay*, has the true property of a real diphthong' (1799:74). Barrie (1815) and Gray (1809) produce the usual proper/improper distinction, with 'two vowels meeting in one syllable' referring to digraphs and where 'both vowels sounded' suggests vocalic transition.

Buchanan adds a twist to the improper diphthong characterisation by suggesting that it applies not just to digraphs representing phonetic monophthongs, but that the type should be distinguished from the proper by purely formal orthographic means, by spelling them <ey>, <ay> (especially 'at the ends of words') rather than <ei>, <ai>, etc. But, typically, his pragmatic sense prevails: 'Thus we see how much the Invention of so many Diphthongs whose Sounds differ nothing in our Language (according to the present Pronunciation) from the long and short Sounds of the single Vowels tend to perplex our Orthography' (1762:15:footnote); sentiments echoed by McIllquam (1781:15): 'From these examples, it is evident that the vocal combinations, which are the chief difficulty in our Orthography, are mostly nothing else but the sound of single vowels differently represented: as, *day, fame, fair, where, heir,* etc.' Sylvester Douglas too, is equally scathing of the proper/improper distinction (1797:119):

> In the common grammars *ai, ea,* and *ei*, are generally treated as Diphthongs, which proceeds from that poverty of language, of which we have complained; namely, that there being but one set of names, for elementary sounds and elementary characters. For hence it happens that because a combination of two vocal sounds into one syllable is properly termed a diphthong; a combination of two vocal characters which is the regular way of representing such combined sound, is also termed a diphthong, even in cases where...the sound it represents is only a simple vowel. In this respect the Italian orthography is particularly superior to ours, for I believe there is not in that language a single example, where a combination of more than one vocal character does not represent a true diphthongal sound.

There can be little doubt that the most detailed account of the diphthongal space in the period is provided by the 'reformed' orthography of Alexander Scot's *The Contrast,* all the more felicitous for being an account of contemporary upper class Scottish usage. Scot provides no less than five separate symbols for diphthongal entities corresponding to what is usually referred to in the period as 'long i' and which is the ancestor of the modern [ɑι] diphthong. His variants are as follows: <oy> in '*my*', '*trying*, '*eyes*' (as well as '*boys*'); <oi> in '*desire*', '*five*', '*private*'; <ey> in '*why*'; <ei> in '*delighted*', '*quite*', '*write*' and <ai> in '*either*', '*neither*'. While a discussion of the possible phonetic realisation of these digraphs must wait till later, it is clear that Scot's system is capable of differentiating considerable phonetic detail, detail which, even at a cursory glance at the data, is conditioned by the shape of syllable final components, be they null, obstruent, voiced fricative or sonorant. However, Scot is clearly an exception in this matter, most writers providing little in the way of description as to what might constitute the surface phonetics of diphthongal forms. Walker's descriptive method (1791:14-15) is fairly typical of contemporary commentators: 'This letter [<I>:CJ] is a perfect diphthong, composed of the sound of the *a* in *father,* and *e* in *be,* pronounced as closely together as possible'. Buchanan's (1762:11) observation that 'Long (i) has a double Sound, and is compounded of *aw* and *ee,* pronounced very quick, thus *ăweĕ;* as *fire, desire,* &c. is pronounced as if written *faweĕr, desaweĕr;* though it is not always so very open, but in many Words resembles the Greek ε' was a definition which attracted the well attested venom of Kenrick (1784:65): 'this diphthong....has the appearance, when slowly pronounced, of being a compound of the *a* or *e* and *i*.....I have elsewhere observed that our Scottish linguists say it has the sound usually denoted by *awee,* but the errour of this is obvious to every Englishman'.

Most English commentators see the <house> diphthong as some kind of [ɑɷ] or even [ɒɷ] transition, Walker's 'composed of the *a* in *hall*, and the *oo* in *woo'* (1791:36), Sheridan's 'composed of the sounds a³ and o³' (1781:16), while even Elphinston, in his *The Principles of the English Language Digested for the Use of Schools* (1766:4) describes the transition as one where 'shuts broad *a* by the sound of *oo* or *w'*, and Telfair (1775:156-7) assigns a similar value with the 'second long A and W'. As we shall see below, it appears only to be Douglas and Buchanan who suggest a more 'Northern' value of [ou] for this diphthong, the latter stating: 'the first Sound is composed of both (o) and (uw), and if we sound *o-oo* extremely quick, it discovers this Sound exactly; as *louse, mouse, fowl, town,* &c. which are sounded quick, *lo-oos, mo-oos, fo-ool, to-oon*'(1762:17-18).

3.8 Consonantal Segments

The student of the major 18th century linguistic literature quickly comes to the conclusion that writers avoided any attempt to treat vocalic and consonantal segments as discrete, mutually exclusive phonological categories after the fashion of so many phonological models of the 20th century, notably the vocalic/consonantal dichotomy of the Chomsky-Halle model (1968) and its descendants. Rather, linguists such as Sheridan and Walker treated phonetic segments almost in a scalar fashion, seeing a progression between one type and the other. Such an approach equates well with recent classifications of phonetic segments in some non-linear phonological models, notably Dependency Phonology, where the notion of the phonological hierarchy, based on vocalic prominence inherent to segments - the *sonority scale* (Jones:1992:6; Anderson and Jones:1974) - ranks segments along a scale of increasing periodicity, a criterion of well defined and recognisable formant structure which might well be said to be equatable with notions such as 'prolongation'. Sheridan's main division of consonantal segments into mutes and semivowels is certainly based upon a 'prolongation' criterion, one which sees certain consonantal components as 'partaking in the nature of vowels' (1780:6-7); even his voiced/voiceless distinction is couched in terms like this, segments such as [b], [d] and [g] 'may be continued, though for a very short space'. Sheridan's system may be represented as in Table 3.4 below

Walker's system has a tripartite 'major class' division into *mutes, semivowels* and *liquids* (for Sheridan's *pure vocal semivowels*), where the first set is defined as being incapable of articulation in isolation ('no sound without the concurrence of a vowel'), the second 'emit sound without a vowel', while the third 'flow into' or 'unite easily with the mutes' (1791:4). Voiced and voiceless obstruents constitute the mute class, voiced and voiceless fricatives together with affricatives the second, and the sonorants [l], [m], [n], and [r] the third, liquid, class. Voiced and voiceless differences are listed under the nomenclature *flat* and *sharp* respectively, while affricatives like [š], [ʤ] and [ž] are treated as *aspirated* or *mixed* having 'sometimes a hiss or aspiration joined with them, which mingles with the letter, and alters its sound, as *t* in *motion*, *d* in *soldier*, *s* in *mission*, and *z* in *azure*' (1791:4). In his *On English Pronunciation* (1740), James Douglas describes the voiced/voiceless distinction in the following way: 'TH. *How are these Consonants Sounded?* These Consonants have two distinct ways of Pronunciation, the One like *t* a little soften'd by aspiration, the other Softer & Enclining to *D*. *When are the Consonants TH pronounc'd the Harder Way?* The Consonants *Th* are sounded the harder way, 1. In the Beginning of all Words, as THATCH, THISTLE, THEFT, THRIFT *Except* The following Words which are sounded the Softer Way, THAN, THAT, THE, THEE...' (Holmberg (1956:293).

TABLE 3.4

Sheridan's Consonantal Classification

MUTES cannot be prolonged		
PURE continued, for a very short space	IMPURE cannot be at all prolonged	
[k], [p], [t]	[b], [d], [g]	
SEMIVOWELS can be continued at pleasure		
VOCAL formed by the voice		ASPIRATED formed by the breath
PURE formed entirely by the voice	IMPURE mixture of breath with the voice	
[l], [m]. [n], [r], [ŋ]	[v], [z], [ð], [ʒ]	[f], [s], [θ], [š]

By this stage we might not be surprised to learn that it is Sylvester Douglas, of all the Scotch orthoepists, who gives the most detailed account of 'consonantal' structure. His scheme very much echoes that of Walker, with a division into mute (or perfect/pure consonant), semivowel and liquid. Vowels 'can be uttered by themselves', while consonants 'as the name imports, can only be pronounced along with vowells' (Jones:1992:106). Voiced and voiceless obstruents are grouped under the 'pure consonant' class and it is interesting to note how they are viewed by Douglas in terms of syllable terminations: 'The perfect consonants at the end of a syllable terminate the sound instantly. If we try to continue it the ear hears nothing farther, and the speaker perceives that in his ineffectual efforts he only retains by a certain muscular exertion, his lips, teeth, tongue, or throat, in a particular position, and forces his breath outwards, without suffering it to pass, so as to compleat the act of expiration' (Jones:1992:106).

Semivowels 'hold a middle place between the vowells and perfect consonants', are 'capable of solitary pronunciation' and 'may be protracted sensibly to the ear either in singing or in speaking for any length of time.' It is the case, he argues, that certain segments contain this quality of prolongation more than others, for which reason they accorded a separate class, the liquids ([l], [m], [n], [ŋ] and [r]). Yet, ever the pragmatist, Douglas nonetheless asserts that 'In the following pages it will be found convenient to speak of consonantal, as opposed to vocal sounds, and to lead the mind to contemplate (though the senses cannot perceive) the consonants in themselves abstracted from all accompanying vowells' (Jones:1992:106). For Drummond (1767:4) 'open-ness' is the distinctive characteristic of segments on some kind of vowel consonant scale: 'if the sounds of vowels are compared with those of consonants, no doubt the sounds of the first are more open and perfect than those of the latter, the same remark holds good with regard to the consonants, if compared with one another. The sound of *l, m, n,* is more vocal and perfect, than the sound of *b, p,* or *t* is but still the latter have sounds, though not so clamorous as the former'. Beattie (1788:30-34) distinguishes mutes (voiceless obstruents), semi-mutes (voiced obstruents), semi vowels (the nasal sonorants) and liquids ([l], [r]). His semi-mute distinction arises from the fact that such segments 'because without the assistance of any vowel....produce a faint sound, which continues for a little time, and seems partly to pass out by the nose, and partly to reverberate from the roof of the mouth. And hence, when the nose is shut, it is not easy for us to give them a distinct utterance'. As ever, following Wallis (1653), Beattie distinguishes open from compressed consonantal segments, the former being 'the aspirations of the mutes and the semivowels.....Thus, if, in pronouncing P, or rather *ip*, we permit the breath to pass out with some difficulty between our lips, we form that sound of F which is heard in *off*'(1788:32). This perception of an interconnection between segment types distinguished only by gesture contrast, is a strong characteristic of Beattie's descriptive work, notably in the class of 'liquids': 'we know that R is one of the last letters which European infants learn to pronounce, and that they are apt to use L in its stead. From all which we may gather, that the liquids N, L, and R, bear a close affinity one with another' (1788:33-34), and Elphinston (1786:30) is careful to point to the affinity between labials and vowel segments: 'If dhe licquids be also named *half-vowels*, az variously approaching to' vocallity; no won so approaches it, az does *l*, hwich dhe Itallian set dhe French dhe exampel ov exchainging widh *i*'.

Definitions of consonantal segments by other Scotch orthoepists and grammarians are considerably less sophisticated, centring round the concept that consonants are incapable of isolative utterance, thus Buchanan (1762:19): 'What is a consonant? A Consonant is a Letter which cannot make a perfect Sound without adding some single or double Vowel either before or after it'. Likewise, McIllquam isolates a class of sounds called 'Consonants, or modes of Articulation, because they do not make a perfect sound of themselves; but only serve to modify the Articulation of the Vowels either preceding or succeeding them (1781:10); Burn (1766:1): 'A consonant is a letter that cannot make a perfect sound of itself, without the help of a vowel'. Although Drummond (1767:4-5) produces the standard: 'consonants can have no sounds without a vowel', he also provides an insightful articulatory vowel/consonant definition: 'In the articulation of the vowels, the breath and sound are freely emitted from the lungs and breast, as in *care, be, mine, more, pure, try, win*....In the formation of consonants, the breath and sound are intercepted in their passage, with a greater or less compression'. In this context too it is worth noting Beattie's (1788:29) observations that 'When the voice, in its passage through the mouth, is totally intercepted, or strongly compressed, there is formed a certain modification of articulate sound, which, as expressed by a character in writing, is called a *Consonant*', while differences in place of articulation are to be explained with reference to the point where the speech sound is 'intercepted' in the oral cavity (1788:30):

> The human voice, in passing through the mouth, may be intercepted by the lips, or by the tongue and palate, or by the tongue and throat: and each of these interceptions may happen, when the voice is directed to go out by the mouth only; or through the nostrils only; or partly through the mouth, and partly through the nose.

There appear to be five main techniques used for consonantal description among linguists in the period, sometimes in isolation at other times in a combined fashion: 1. perhaps most commonly are simple substitution description of the type: 'c before e, i, or y is sounded like s', 'ch sounds sh', 'c before i and another vowel sounds sh', a technique favoured especially by Warden, McIllquam and to a lesser extent by Buchanan and even Sylvester Douglas; 2. descriptive terminology is employed to characterise consonantal characteristics such as voicing, continuancy, obstruency and even delayed release. Most commonly, the terms *hard* and *soft* are utilised to describe voiceless and voiced segments respectively (notably by Perry, McIllquam, Barrie and Buchanan), although there is not always consistency in usage, as Douglas comments:

> In English the z has always the second or soft sound of *s*. As in *gaze, baize, zeal*. The Scotch, at the beginning of words, as *zeal, zone, zenith,* pronounce it with the combined sound of *d*, and the soft *s*. This is its most common sound in Italian. It may be proper to remark that Dr Johnson calls the sound of *z*, or the second of *s*. the hard *s* Whereas I have applied the epithet soft to that sound, and have called the other hard. It matters little which is used. Both expressions are metaphorical. But according to my ear and to the ears of those whom I have consulted on the subject, there is more propriety in calling the *s* in *praise*; soft, than that in *past*.

Paradoxically, although *b* and *d* are classified on occasion as *soft mutes*, Sylvester Douglas (like Burn and occasionally Buchanan) often contrasts with a *hard* categorisation, a *soft* (sometimes *mellow*) configuration which refers to continuancy, affricativeness, rather than any voicing co-efficient. Thus the soft version of his *hard g,* is an item composed of a complex of *d* and *z,* as in *azure*. Perry introduces a *sharp/flat* contrast between [gz] and [gs] complexes in items such as *example, expect,* while Buchanan introduces a *smooth* category to distinguish delayed release segments like [ʧ] in items like *bench* and *wench* as well as [š] in *share, shame,* 'to be pronounced like (ish) *whispered* '(1762:25).

The use of specialised symbols and other identifying orthographic marks, such as super/subscripted accents or symbols, is less common a feature of consonantal than it is of vowel representation in the period. Although Elphinston's voiced interdental <dh> symbol is perhaps the most obvious consonantal marker in his scheme (his *bath/badhs* contrast), he also endeavours to find a symbolisation for affricatives and other voicing contrasts as well; recall his *az tutching dhe madjesty ov relidgion* (1795:21), Buchanan too is given on occasion to such consonantal 're-spellings', with his <paidsh> '*page*', <waidsh> '*wage*' and <măsheen> '*machine*' representations. So to Sheridan utilises <zh>, <etħ> and <j>/<edzh> for what are possibly [ʒ], [ð] and [ʤ], Barrie <zh> for [ʒ], while Telfair shows the items '*medium*' and '*Indian*' as <meed-yum>, <Ind-yun>.

Only Perry (1766:11) seems to use subscripted symbols, when for his hard and soft *g* , we respectively find representations such as <g,> and <g>. But on the whole there is a noticeable lack of consonantal marking by diacritic in the period, especially in comparison to a system such as Hodges' (1644). However, Scott, Perry and Barrie, extensively use a typographical roman/italic contrast to indicate various consonantal values (often potentially ambiguously) as in the recto/verso headings in Scott (1793; 1807): ra*g*e, ro*s*e, na*t*ion, e*x*alt and pun*ch*, where voicing contrasts, affricativeness and complex orthography are all signalled by the italic device. It appears only to be Drummond (1767:22) among the

Scotch orthoepists, who extensively uses superscripted numerals to signal consonantal characteristics: c^{123}, g^{12}, s^{1234}, t^{123}, x^{1234}, z^{12}, ch^{1234}, gh^{123}, ng^{12}, th^{123}, wh^{12}. For instance, x^{1234} is described as '*x* sounds *ks,* in *box*^{1}, sounds *gx* in *ex*^{2}*act, ksh* in *flux*^{3}*ion, z* in *X*^{4}*erxes,* although the <th> graph is not treated in this way, but as : *th* sounds *th,* in *thin,* harder *th,* in *then, t* in *thyme;* we have also noted above how Warden, Drummond's possible model, also uses numerical diacritics to denote consonantal variations.

Almost all the above linguists provide detailed mechanistic articulatory description for the consonantal segments they highlight, none more so than Sheridan and Buchanan, although while there is a general recognition of the single 'voice' characteristic distinguishing otherwise identical segments like [d]/[t] etc., the laryngeal nature of voicing itself never seems to be grasped consistently; Douglas, for instance, confidently asserting that [p] differs from [b] by being 'pronounced only by a more forceful exertion of..the pressure of the lips' (Jones:1992:119;133). The voicing difference together with syllable initial and final variation between obstruent consonantal segments is one which he pontificates upon, if not very lucidly (*Of the Provincial Accentuation,* ff 31-34):

> The difference which takes place in point of muscular exertion between the pronounciation of the same consonant in one syllable and in another has not been in general so much attended to, but that such a difference may take place, any one may discover by trying the experiment with his own voice, and that it really occurs in the usual pronounciation of languages may be perceived by one who will attend to the phenomenon of speech. On the stage, in the pulpit, at the bar, and in the senate, we may observe some speakers who in uttering certain words, to which they mean to draw the particular attention of their hearers, use a very marked effort of the muscles in forming the beginning of consonants of those words, and the concluding consonants of certain syllables are by all speakers pronounced with a more forcible exertion of the muscles than the same consonants are in others. This is particularly observable in our language where the same consonantal character is doubled at the end of a syllable. Thus the single *t* before *e* in the first [sic:CJ] syllable of the word *appetite* and the *tt* in *petty* represent exactly the same consonantal modification, and the only difference is that in the word *petty* there is a more vigourous and forcible pressure of the tongue against the upper part of the mouth. Here again I find that I was hampered in a former part of this work by the sterility of language of which I have more than once taken notice, for I have there described the *d* as differing from *t* only in the degree of muscular exertion, but this diversity between the *tt* and the *t* in such words as *petty* and *appetite,* being of a nature very different from the difference between either and *d,* it should seem that I ought to have described the exertions in forming the *d* and *t* as differing in kind as well as degree, and agreeing exactly only in the same position of the organs.

It is Beattie who typically provides what is a remarkably modern and mechanistic description of the voicing mechanism and its production in the laryngeal space (1788:21-22):

> Galen, and many other philosophers, affirm, that both the larynx and the wind pipe co-operate in rendering the breath vocal. But later authors have determined, and I think on good grounds, that the human voice is produced by two semicircular membranes in the middle of the larynx, which form by their separation the aperture that is termed the Glottis. The space between them is not wider than one tenth of an inch; through which the breath transmitted from the lungs needs pass with considerable velocity. In its passage, it is supposed to give a brisk vibratory motion to the membranous lips of the glottis, and so to form the sound which we call voice: by an operation, similar to that of the two lips of the reed of a hautboy, when one takes them in one's mouth, and blows into them.

Indeed, Beattie's mechanistic, articulatory based description relating to the production of speech itself, is a one which would not be out of place in a modern textbook dealing with the anatomy of the production of speech (1788:20 ff): 'Human voice is air sent out from the lungs, and so agitated, or modified, in its passage through the windpipe and larynx, as to become distinctly audible. The windpipe, wezard, or rough artery, is that tube, which, on touching the forepart of our throat externally, we feel hard and uneven. It conveys air into the lungs for the purpose of respiration and speech. It consists of cartilages, circular before, that they may the better resist external injury; but soft and flattish on the opposite side, that they may not hurt the gullet, or esophagus; which lies close behind, and is the tube whereby what we eat and drink is conveyed in to the stomach'. The following from Drummond (1767:6-7) are fairly typical in the kind of detail that can be provided by observers in the period: '*B* - is formed by pressing the lips hard together, and forcing a sound inwards, nearly at the time of bursting them asunder, as *babe*; *TH* - is formed by placing the point of the tongue between the teeth, and sending forth a gentle aspiration, as in *thin*. It has another sound formed by drawing in the tongue a little, and making it vibrate gently against the teeth, as *that*; *N* - is formed by placing the tongue nearly in L, only a little flatter, and forming a sound through the nose, as *drone*'. The level of both description and abstract correlation in this area of the phonology can be high and often strikes us as remarkably modern, especially when several observers (notably Sheridan, Beattie and Sylvester Douglas) see the phonological inter-relationship between the sets of mutes and semivowels in their inventory. Douglas notes how:

> *B*, and *p* are pronounced by the same position of the organs of speech, and are as much entitled to be considered as one letter as the two sounds of *s* or of *th* are. The same is true of the hard *g* and *k*. And of *d* and *t*. Now each of

these has a corresponding semivowel, which have the same sort of affinity together as the co-relative mutes. The semivowel of *b* is *v*; of *p*, *f*; of the hard *g*, the Dutch and German *g*; of *k*, the Scotch and German *ch*; of *d*, the soft *th*. It is to this affinity between these different sets of consonants that we are to ascribe the frequent changes from one of them to another, in words which have been transplanted out of one language into another.

4

THE SCOTS LINGUISTS' VIEW OF 18TH CENTURY PHONOLOGY: PALATAL VOWEL SEGMENTS

4.1 Vowel Sounds: the Descriptive Model

The descriptive framework within which we shall operate throughout the following sections will be as far as possible a pragmatic one. Vowel and consonantal segments will be represented in classical IPA terms and standard articulatory and acoustic distinctive feature terminology will be evoked. However, from time to time we shall find it necessary to make reference to more highly structured phonological models to enable us to deal with and explain concepts of and motivations for phonological change which might otherwise elude us. In particular, we shall refer to those models of phonological representation which see the vowel inventory as composed of various combinations of primary components, the Jackobsonian palatal, labial and sonorant types. These show the well known diffuse-compact spectral contrast, with palatal and labial segments characterised by a 'skewing' of the frequency concentration to one or other end of the energy level spectrum; 'pure' palatals in general showing high F_1 and F_2 frequency values (and with a well defined 'gap' between F_2 and F_3), while 'pure' labials show clustering of periodicity around relatively low Hz values. Sonorant segments like [ɑ] manifest a relatively even distribution of energy concentrations across the frequency range, coupled with a tendency to show a raised F_1 above the baseline (Lieberman and Blumstein:1993:241ff). Corresponding to this palatal, labial and sonorant typology are the English vowels [i]. [u] and [ɑ] respectively. 'Mid' front and back vowels are interpreted as mixtures of these primary values (or 'colours' (Donegan:1978)); vowels such as [e] and [ɛ], for example, we shall interpret as consisting of compounds of palatal and sonorant primary characteristics, the palatal 'colour' dominant in the [e] type, the sonorant value in the [ɛ] output. Likewise, the mid back vowels [o] and [ɔ] are complexes of labial and sonorant primary types, each in turn weighted towards a higher value on either the labial or sonority component. In this way front and back vowel sets are seen as points on a continuum between extreme values of sonority-palatality and sonority-labiality (Anderson and Ewen;1987:Chapter 6; Jones:1989:7)

Central to our description of phonetic segments too will be the notion that they exist on a scale or cline of relative vowel-ness, or the relative degree of structured distribution of acoustic energy (periodicity). Thus, at one end of such a scale would be the maximum vowel valued components, the vowels themselves, at the other those segments which show no traces of vocalic/laryngeal activity (characterised by spectral *zeros*), the voiceless obstruents. At various points along such a scale are to be found those phonetic segments whose internal structure is a complex or mix of vowel-like and consonantal-like segments, the more predominant the vowel component in the mix, the higher up the sonority hierarchy (Giegerich:1994:132ff) will a given segment be. Thus, segments such as [r] and [l] are heavily vocalic and low in consonantalness in their mixture, with segments like voiced fricatives showing a more or less equal weighting of the two primary components. For a formalism for expressing such a concept, see Anderson and Ewen (1987:171-177); Jones (1989:5-7).

4.2 Vowel Sounds: Palatal Segments

This is an area of the phonology/phonetics where there is not only considerable discussion among the Scotch linguists concerning the quality of the relevant vowels in their 'standard' manifestations, but there occurs too an exceptional level of comment concerning the idiosyncrasies of contemporary Scots outputs. Indeed, this is a context where native and non-Scottish observers alike see highly salient instances of peculiarly Scots regional (and, we shall argue Scots standard) dialect. Recall as an example Walker's perception in the 'Rules to be Observed by the Natives of Scotland for attaining a just Pronunciation of English' in his *A Critical Pronouncing Dictionary* (1791:xi-xii): 'With respect to quantity, it may be observed that the Scotch pronounce almost all their accented vowels long. Thus, if I am not mistaken, they would pronounce *habit, hay-bit; tepid, tee-pid; sinner, see-ner; conscious, cone-shus;* and *subject, soob-ject.*' While we must question his assessment that the *tepid/teepid* alternation is one which is primarily concerned with vowel duration rather than the relative distribution of F_1 and F_2 in the stressed vowel configurations, nevertheless his observation that Scots speakers appear to alternate an [i] segment with some kind of [ɩ], is one which is mentioned, as we shall see below, by several contemporary observers.

4.2.1 Pure Palatals: [i] and [ii] Segments

From the evidence provided by a wide range of sources, there would appear to be at least two different phonetic manifestations of the pure palatal [i] segment in the Scots of the 18th century. The first, usually described in terms of its alphabetic reference as 'the first sound of *e*' (Sylvester Douglas (Jones:1992:123)), is also the 'proper' E1, Ea1 and Ee1 of James Douglas (Holmberg:1956:47), and 'the original true sound of *i*, and the only one the Italians, Spaniards and Germans know' of Alexander Geddes (1776:432). The 'very same' with the last is Sylvester Douglas' second sound of *i* 'the universal sound in Italian' (Jones: 1992:129). It is also Buchanan's (1757) 'long *e*' ('the same sound the French give to (i)') and the acute sound of *i*, both spelt (ee): *măgăzeen, mărreen;* it is Warden's e^1 (1753) and it may also be what Robertson tantalisingly describes as 'the sound of (i) as taught in Scotland' (1722:6). Items provided as exemplifying this segment include: *scene, he, she,* the most comprehensive list appearing under the APPEAR and EAT entries of Sylvester Douglas' *Treatise on the Provincial Dialect of Scotland,* where items such as *east, beast, feast, least, yeast, beat, cheat, defeat* and many others are listed. It is Sylvester Douglas too who provides the bulk of the evidence for the durational characteristics of this segment in the contemporary language, especially where he records the existence of 'protracted' palatal sounds principally to be found in the context of syllable and word final voiced palatal fricative [z]: 'In *thief* the *ie* has the first sound of the *e* shortened. Add the *e* at the end and as in *thieve* (where indeed the consonant is also altered) and the *ie* retains the same sound but protracted' (Jones:1992:124). A more detailed statement of this fact is to be found under his (curiously erased from the first MS version) EASE entry: 'The *ea* as in *appear* the *s* soft as in *please*....pronounce in the same manner, *appease, disease, please, tease, lease* verb synonymous to *glean*. In the following words the *ea* has the same sound but shortened and the *s* is hard: *cease, decease, surcease, lease* verb and noun...*release, crease,...decrease,...increase'* (Jones:1992:190). While we shall see in several places below that we must be on our guard against treating 18th century grammarians' statements about the 'long' and 'short' quantity of vowels as one unambiguously reflecting simple durational differences, it does seem that, like Douglas, Burn (1766:3) also perceives some genuine length contrast for this segment in certain phonological contexts: 'How many sounds hath *e*? Five: short, as in *men;* shorter, as in *former;* long, as in *betake;* longer, as in *here;* long and sharp, as in *there*'. The 'longer' sound of *e* is said to occur 'in the end of syllables, and when silent *e* follows it in the same syllable, and also at the end of monosyllables; 'as *E-den, fe-male, here, mete, these, blaspheme, complete, extreme, he, she, we*.' On the other hand, the 'long sound' of *e* is said to occur 'in the end of syllables unaccented; as *be-stir, male-factor, mainte-nance*.' But we might wish to treat some of these observations with caution in the light of John Drummond's observation in his *A Grammatical Introduction to the Modern Pronunciation and Spelling of the English Tongue, for Private Perusal and for Public Schools* (1767:21) where he points to the difficulty Scots themselves seem to have in ascertaining vowel length:

> The sound of every vowel may be made long or short, either by continuing to emit the breath for a longer or shorter time, preserving the articulation of the vowel unchanged; or we may change the articulation, while the breath continues to pass; and this change may be made sooner or later. But to ascertain the time of pronouncing them is the greatest difficulty to the Scots, in the English Tongue.

4.2.2 Scotch Peculiarities of the Pure Palatal Segment: Vowel Shift Discrepancies

Much in the way they do today, non-standard pure palatal vowel realisations in 18th century Scots centre around differential application of the de-sonorizing effect of the *English Vowel Shift*. Essentially we find three divergent usages: (1) where the *English Vowel Shift* appears with an 'advanced' manifestation, etymologically durationally long vowel segments 'leapfrogging' over their standard position (4.2.2a). (2) where the *English Vowel Shift* appears unapplied to long palatal vowel segments, with no resultant diphthongisation to something like [aɩ] (4.2.2.b/c). (3) where the *English Vowel Shift* appears to be operative in etymologically *short* vowel contexts (4.2.5.a).

4.2.2.a Advanced Vowel Shift Types: [i]/[e]/[ɛ] Alternants

Several observers of 18th century Scots record instances (which may well be lexical item specific) where the mixed palatal/sonorant [e]/[ɛ] segments appear to undergo additional palatalisation to [i]. Perhaps the most extensive evidence for this tendency occurs in Sylvester Douglas, who records <bear>, <chair>, <e'er>, <mare>, <ne'er> <pear> with rhyming exemplars for the Scots pronunciation given as <beer>, <cheer>, <ear>/<appear>, <mere>/<here>, <near>, <appear> (Jones:1992:27-28). Likewise, Elphinston (1787:2) decries the fact that the Scotch pronounce <mare> as <mere>, <blaze> as <bleze>, <complain> as <compleen>, <entertain> as <enterteen>, while Adams (1799:152) records as Scotch pronunciations like <dee> '*day*' and <see> '*say*' (although he also observes that such items may be represented with whatever he means by the 'more open *dâi, sâi*', perhaps some kind of [e̞]). Telfair assigns the '*e* in *me*' to items like <Beard>, <Break> and <weasand>, and although in such cases it is often difficult to determine which is the 'model' form in the contrast, Robertson gives as 'similar in sound' pairs such as <Bleed/Blade> and <Beat/Bait>. Under his BEAR entry Sylvester Douglas points out that 'This word, to the ear, is, in both senses, exactly the same with *bare*. The Scotch generally pronounce it like *beer* ' (Jones 1993: 172; 28-29). For Douglas the vowel in *bear* in the Pure dialect is almost certainly the long low mid [ɛɛ] and his remarks relating to the item BEAR are worth quoting in some detail:

> Now looking downwards just as grieved *appears*
> To want the strength of bulls, the fur of *bears*.

> This rhyme is perfect according to the Scotch pronounciation [sic:CJ], but according to the English, it is as little so, as *steers* and *mares* would be. Of these two sounds of the *ea*, the Irish, and the inhabitants of the west of England, use that in *bear*, in almost every word. I remember to have seen a book advertised in an Irish paper, wherein the author, who

> was a native and inhabitant of Dublin, undertook to prove that in this respect the Irish, was the true English pronounciation. I must question whether he made any prosylites to his opinion on this side of the water. The Scotch almost as generally use the other sound of the *ea*. Many who correct themselves in some words, retain the improper sound in others, and, as there is no rule to go by, they often in trying to shun their vernacular sound, where it is improper, introduce the other, in words in which (like *spear*) the English sound the *ea* in the Scotch manner.

Again, under MARE he comments that the rhyme is with *pare, stair,* and *fair* although 'The Scotch make it, to the ear, the same word with *mere*', while 'In many parts of Scotland, and by some vulgar persons in England' *chair* is 'pronounced *cheer*'. He records too that: 'The Scotch often make [ne'er:CJ), to the ear, the same with *near*', while the LEIZURE, LEIZURELY entry hints at some uncertainty of usage and lexical diffusion (Jones:1992:205): 'The Scotch who aim at the proper sound, either pronounce these words as if written *leezure, leezurely,* or so as to rhyme to *pleasure, measure.* But the *ei* ought to be sounded as *ay* in *say, day, pay;* or *eigh* in *weigh*. The first syllable is long'.

4.2.2.b Retarded Vowel Shift Types

The failure in 18th century Scots of the *English Vowel Shift* of pure palatal [i]/[ii] to realise some kind of [aɩ] diphthong is manifested in Geddes' Edinburgh dialect Vergilian translation in such spellings as: <èn> '*eyes*' (Jones:1994:90). This 'retarded' version of the vowel shift process is also well documented for Scots of the period by other commentators; recall, for instance, Sylvester Douglas' entry under the item TWILIGHT (Jones 1993: 230): 'The first *i,* (as the second,) has the diphthongal sound. The Scotch pronounce the first, as *ee* in *tweezer*' and that for IDEA, where 'The *i* has its diphthongal sound, as in *tide, wide.* The Scotch often give it its long vocal sound as in *caprice, magazine*' (Jones:1992:203). Much after the same fashion, Alexander Scot records the monophthongal <adefeeing> '*edifying*', <leecence> '*licence*' and <sheences> '*sciences*' (Jones:1993:115). In this context too we find Geddes using what he describes as the '*i* Italian, or English *ee;* This is the true original sound of *i,* and the only one the Italians, Spaniards, and Germans know. It is often used by the northern Scots, where the English pronounce it *y,* as in *write, rival, skill*' (1792:431;434). Geddes (1792:423), commenting upon the 'more harmonious' nature of the Scots sound system, points to the use of this '*Italian i*':

> Neither will it be denied, I think by any, but perhaps an Englishman, that the Italian *i,* equivalent to our *ee,* is a more harmonious sound than the English *i* long [perhaps an [aɩ] diphthong:CJ]. The Scots, accordingly, preferred the former, as in the words *admire, retire, live, survive, require,* &c. which they pronounced, as if they were written *admeer, reteer, leeve, surveeve, requeer* .

It is interesting to notice how Geddes reserves this *i* Italian for the majority of failed *English Vowel Shift* [ii] → [aɩ] types, notably the Buchan <dìan> '*dying*', <lìbashon> '*libation*', <nìcht> '*night*', only the <èn> for '*eyes*' being recorded as showing an <è> symbol, a fact which - as we shall see below - suggests that he perceived a distinct qualitative difference between palatal vowels in this context from others arising through different etymological and phonological processes. Geddes' observations are supported by those of Buchanan (1770:49) who, in his long discussion on stress placement, inadvertently provides exemplification of a Scots 'failure' to realise long pure palatal segments in stressed positions in words as his 'long ī' (possibly some kind of [aɩ] diphthong), although he suggests that it is a characteristic of speakers of 'broad' dialectal habits: 'To put it beyond controversy, that accent is not pronunciation, numberless examples might be produced; such as *frīar, clīent, impīety, īdolīze, agonīze,* &c. which the people of North-Britain accent the same way as those of South-Britain, but the former (I mean all those who retain the dialect called broad Scotch) do not pronounce the same way; for they say *free-ar, clee-ent, impee-ety, socee-ety, eedoleeze, agoneeze,* &c'. Recall, too, Buchanan's (1770:45) comments under what he interprets as examples of 'how North-Britons destroy just quantity, by expressing the long sound for the short, and the short for the long' where speakers realise '*sympatheeze* for *sympathīze, eetem* for *ītem, eer* for *īre, leer* for *lȳre, breer* for *brīar*'. Although it is difficult to place a precise phonetic value on the orthography, Elphinston's <grep>/<gripe>, <strep>/<stripe>, <smet>/<smite>, <clem>/<climb> and <blend>/<blind> might just bear witness to a similar 'failure' of an etymological high mid front segment (perhaps subsequently lowered and centralised in Scots to some kind of [ë]) to undergo raising/diphthongisation. Telfair (1775:54), under his discussion of the <ei> improper diphthong, which he suggests is normally to be pronounced 'as the *a* in *same*' even records this high mid segment in items like <height> and <sleight> where a 'double' application of the vowel shift to some diphthongal form has subsequently occurred, although it is difficult to tell whether he sees this vowel shift failure as typical of purely Scots contexts. Robertson (1722) includes a large number of 'equal in Sound' items which at least appear to show failure of [ii] to [ɑɩ] vowel shifting (although the 'direction' of the discrepancy is, in fact, not clear): <find/fined/fiend>; <kin/kine>; <nice/niece>; <wield/wild>; <lice/least/lest>; <peal> '*a thunder*'/<pile> '*an heap*'; <steal> '*a hard mettal*'/<steel> '*a Sirname*'/<style> '*of language*' and <teal/tile>, as well as Fisher (1762:20) who equates <niece>/<Nice>. Indeed, the relative advanced/retarded nature of vowel shifting among different social groups in Scotland during our period is best attested under

Sylvester Douglas' WEIGH entry (Jones:1992:231-32):

> The vernacular Scotch pronounciation makes this word rhyme to *eye, try, high*. Those who endeavour to speak with more propriety make it rhyme to *see, pea*. But the true pronounciation is with the thin slender sound of *a* or *ay*, in *pay*. Or as the second sound of *ne*, or *nae*, in the vulgar Scotch dialect, when used instead of *no*. Both the following rhymes are perfect.
>
> One self-applausing hour, whole years *outweighs*
> Of stupid starers, and of loud *huzzas*.
>
> Where is nice balance, truth with gold she *weighs*
> And solid pudding against empty *praise*.

Here there is interesting sociophonetic evidence for an advanced, diphthongal realisation of the 'true' [e] vowel among those Douglas categorises as vernacular speakers, a pronunciation perhaps seen as too marked for the group who 'endeavour to speak with more propriety' where the vowel shift is advanced only as far as a pure palatal [i] type vowel. Robertson too seems to suggest an [e]/[ɑɩ] alternation in 'near alikes' such as <fry/fray> and <neigh/nay/nigh> '*near*', while Adams (1799:152) records as Scotch <heed> '*hide*'; <creed> '*cried*'; <bee> '*by*'; <skee> '*sky*'; <chil> '*child*'; <meeld> '*mild*' and <weeld> '*wild*'.

4.2.2.c Diphthongal Discrepancies: Scots [ɑɩ] for [ii].
While the extensive discussion of 'long-*i*' in Walker (1791:14-18) points to considerable contemporary 'uncertainty' (especially in the light of Sheridan's comments) concerning the [ii]/[aɩ] *English Vowel Shift* application, there is also some evidence that 18th century Scots pronunciation showed some distinctive variation in this area of the phonology/phonetics as well, although it is clear that much lexical specification is involved in the process. Many instances are cited for 18th century Scots of a situation where one could see the production of an [aɩ]-type diphthong in environments where a 'pure' metropolitan dialect would realise [ii]. An excellent example appears in the list of 'those words in which the Natives of North Britain are most apt to err, in order that the teacher may be particularly on his guard to prevent the children from falling into these common errors' which is set out in *A Spelling-Book upon a New Plan* (1796:*Preface* vii). There we see the items <reprieve> and <retrieve> rendered for 'Common' and 'True' pronunciations as follows: reprîv*e*/repreev*e*; retrîv/retreev*e*, with what looks like diphthongal stressed vowels in the 'commonly pronounced' context and the pure palatal under the 'True'. In this context too we might include Elphinston's (1786:7) observation that the vowels in <rip> and <sip>

'open Scottishly' as <ripe>, <sipe> (together with his <Aprile>/<April> and <fifeteen>/<fifteen> contrasts) as well as the claim by McIllquam in his *A Comprehensive Grammar* (1781:13) that items terminating in <-sieve> are 'sounded' as long *i*, a claim born out by Sylvester Douglas (Jones:1992:219) under his REPRIEVE entry:

> The *ie* here, as in *field, mien*, &c has the long vocal sound of *e*, or *ee*, or the second sound of *i*, or that of *ea* in *appear*; which are all one and the same. The Scotch in this word give it the diphthongal sound of *i*, so as to make *reprieve*, and *thrive* form a perfect rhyme.

However, under BEDIZEN he shows how Scots speakers are just as likely to resist diphthongisation, perhaps because of the different phonetic value they give to the palatal vowel:

> In this word, and its original (*dizen*) the Scotch pronounce the *i* short, and as in *phiz, mizzen*. In both it should have its long diphthongal sound, as in *wise, miser*.

Again under BEHIND we are informed that 'The *I* has its diphthongal sound as in *Mind*. The Scotch are apt to pronounce it as *rescind*', although there is clearly sociophonetic variation even in the pure dialect: 'Pronounce as *rescind, Abscind, wind*. (Subst). At least this last word is so pronounced in conversation. Some great speakers, in solemn discourse, or on the stage sound it as *mind*' (Jones:1992:174). Douglas' observations on the Scotch pronunciation of VICAR seem to suggest that Scots speakers emulating the most propitious pronunciation, are liable to realise the diphthongal pronunciation:

> The short obscure *i* as in *victory*. The Scotch, when they aim at the English pronounciation, are apt to give it the diphthongal sound as in *vice*.

Yet Douglas (Jones 1992:149) is still somewhat sceptical of some 'advanced' vowel shift changes in this area of the phonology, even when they are apparently attested by authoritative sources: 'If Pope does not scruple to make *bears* rhyme with *appears, care* with *war*, and *vice* with *caprice*, it cannot be a conclusive inference in any case because the two words are found rhyming together in *his* writings.'

Robertson (1722:10) comments on the fact that '*i* is always long when it ends a Syllable by itself, as in *i-mage, i-ni-qui-ty*, and where the silent *e* is at the end of a word, if there be but one or two consonants betwixt them, the *i* is long, as in *Bridle, Mitre*', while his 'sounding alike' lists includes <Peal> '*a Thunderclap*': <Pile> '*an heap*'; <Rhyme> '*verse*': <Ream> '*of paper*'; <Wield> '*to manage*': <Wild> 'not tame'; <Steel>

'a Sirname': <Style> *'of language'*; and even <Toil> *'labour'*: <Teal> *'a Bird'*: <Tile> *'Brick'*; <Wheat> *'a grain'*: <White> *'colour'*: <Wight> *'an island'*; <Tithe> *'a tenth'*: <Teeth> *'in your head'*; <Tip> *'the End'*: <Type> *'or Figure'*: <Tup> *'a Ram'*. Angus's (1800:29) <bïtumen> may also bear witness to some kind of [ii]/[aɪ] alternation. In his *Analysis of the Scotch Dialect*, Adams (1799:152) observes that it is a Scotch characteristic to pronounce items like *hide, cried, by,* and *sky* as *Heed, cree'd, bee,* and *skee,* claiming (1799:153) that he does not know 'a more striking opposition than that of short and long, and the change of our characteristic *i; prì-mat, preemat; víc-ar, vì-car; exer-cìse, exer-cèese'*, suggesting a possible Scotch output of [vaɪkʌr]; he observes too (1799:59) that '*i* long, in *mist,* &c. is the Scotch dialect'.

4.2.3 Almost Pure Palatal Sounds and their Variants

In addition to pure palatal long and short segments (the 'long *ee*' and other related types), late 18th century Scots commentators also identify several other phonetic segments in what might be loosely called the palatal area (periodic segments with relatively high Hertz F_2 characteristics). At least one of these might be characterised as some kind of Scottish 'standard' type, while the others appear to represent usage of a more 'broad' or 'vulgar' kind. The level of phonetic differentiation between all these types is relatively delicate and its characterisation taxes the ingenuity of both the descriptive as well as the representational ingenuity of contemporary commentators. In this section (and 4.2.3a) we shall investigate in some detail the possible values which might be assigned to the low level phonetics in this area, both in Scots and English, all the while being conscious of the danger of assigning too much significance to the orthography and the descriptive terminology of the commentators.

Almost all observers agree that the Scots 'short *i*' resembles some kind of pure palatal segment like [i], rather than some lowered and centralised [ɪ], possibly like its metropolitan standard equivalent:

> Grammarians have usually annexed two sounds to the *i*, which they have called the long and the short; but the sound given to the short *i*, for instance in *fit, give,* etc. is by no means a mere contraction of the sound given to the long *i* in mine, *life,* &c. It is a sound of very different quality; being a contraction of the long sound of *e* or *ee*, in *me* or *meet*. This is plain by repeating the words *fit* and *feet, pit* and *peat, mit* and *meat*; in which the similarity of sound is very perceptible (Kenrick:1784:61).

So too Buchanan (1757:9) when he states that the short sound of (i) 'which is like (ee) [his [ii]:CJ] is expressed in *did, will, in, which, bid,* &c'; 'which is almost full (ee)' (1762:10) and which 'approaches the diphthong (ee) or French (i), is denoted by short quantity *dĭd, wĭll, bĭd, fĭt*' (1766:xiv). At the same time, the anonymous author of *A Spelling*

Book upon a New Plan lists under a 'long sound, like *ee*' a restricted set of lexical items which includes: *click, crick, drill, drip, gig, king, pig, pill* (1796:9).

This raised-fronted characteristic of the [ɩ] segment appears to have been a peculiarly salient characteristic of 18th century Scots pronunciation, a feature we have already seen commented upon in citing Walker's 'Rules to be Observed by the Natives of Scotland for attaining a just Pronunciation of English' in his *A Critical Pronouncing Dictionary* (1791:xi-xii): 'if I am not mistaken, they would pronounce.... *sinner, see-ner*.' Recall too how Buchanan (1770:45) criticises Scots pronunciation in the way that it 'confuses' short for long, and vice versa: 'I shall adduce but a few examples, out of a multitude, to shew how North-Britons destroy just quantity, by expressing the long sound for the short, and the short for the long;....as *ceevil* for *cĭvil*'. Sylvester Douglas' HIS entry (Jones:1992:202) suggests a similar close to pure palatal realisation of the item's vowel space: 'At Edinburgh, and in the adjoining counties, this pronoun instead of being made to rhyme to *is*, is pronounced as if written *hees*'. The [i]/[ɩ] alternation is one of the most common Scotticisms observed by Douglas, although it is often characterised as 'vernacular' rather than 'vulgar'. Again, his LIBERTY entry recommends an '*i* short', with 'The Scotch are apt to give it the long vocal sound of *e*, or *ee* as in *leer, leave*'; *sieve* 'rhymes to *give*. This is the vernacular Scotch pronounciation [sic:CJ]; but many people make it rhyme to *receive*'. So too under SICK: 'The *i* has its short obscure sound as in *thick*. The Scotch make this the same word, to the ear, with *seek*'; WHIM: 'In this word and in *swim*, the Scotch give the *i* its long vocal sound like the *ee* in *seem*. But it should be pronounced short as in *him*'; WICK: 'pronounce like *lick*. The Scotch make this, to the ear, the same word with *week*'. The repeated use of 'to the ear' may possibly imply near, rather than total homophony.

Elphinston too (*English Orthoggraphy Epittomized* 1790:11) seems to see the palatal sounds in items like <indivizibility> as closer to the pure palatal [i] than the modern [ɩ] shape: 'Hwile the shutting dhus shortens evvery vocal sound, it guivs to *a, e,* and *u* new sounds, az different in quality az in quantity; but to *i*, dhat of *e* short'. His description is of a much less explicit type than that characteristic of Sylvester Douglas, and he merely states that while the shortened versions of [u] and [ɑ] are different in quality from their long congeners, [ii] (his *e open*) when shortened is [i]. Again, in his list of 'words of the same sound, though widely different in their Sense and Signification', George Fisher (1762:21) includes as homophones <sheep> '*a beast*' and <ship> '*for the sea*' and Robertson's (1722:40ff) list includes such pairs as <deep/dip>; <itch/each>; <pick/pique> and <green/grin>. William Angus is particularly instructive in the way he treats palatal segments. In his *Key to the Sounds* in his *English Spelling and Pronouncing Vocabulary on a New Plan* (1814:7), he includes among 'Vowel sounds, *similar* in Quality but *different* in Quantity' *ē, ė, i, y,* where *ē* and *ė* are exemplified by the vocalic segments in <revere> and *i* by that in the item <fin>. Telfair (1775:149), commenting on the *short i* in items such as *hymn* and *in*, states that this segment is 'the same with *e* long, only pronounced quicker', where his '*E* long is the same with *ee* in *need*'. Also, in his *Pronouncing Vocabulary* of 1800, Angus ascribes full palatal status to the *ė* marked vowels in items like <ėconomėcal>, <ėconomė>, <fė-nans>, <mėnorėtė>, <attrėbut> and many others where some less palatal [ɩ] segment might be expected to surface. Likewise Geddes assigns a value of *i* Italian, probably some pure palatal [i] value to items like <citizens>, <Britan>, <imaj>, <citi> and <admirashon>, while in such a context we might mention Sylvester Douglas' BURIAL entry (Jones:1991:179):

> **BURIAL BURY** (a verb, and the name of a town.)
> These words are great stumbling blocks to many a Scotchman. The true provincial sound of the *u* in the southern counties, both in these and a great many others, is like the French *u*; And in the north of Scotland, they are pronounced *Beerial, beery*. Scotchmen soon discover that their vernacular pronounciation is wrong. But then they generally adopt the diphthongal *u*, and make *bury* and *fury*; *Burial* and *Escurial* rhyme together. This is equally wrong. When this is also discovered they recur to *beerial*, and *beery*. The true pronounciation is like the short *e* in *merry* with which word *bury* forms a perfect rhyme. Chaucer writes it *bery* or *berie*.

Yet Buchanan (1770:106) appears to argue against the propriety of at least some of the [i] for [ɩ] pronunciations under his discussion of the value of rhymes as models for pronunciation norms: 'We must not at all favour the rhyme, by which both accent and pronunciation are destroyed. For example, *Whose mind unmov'd, the bribes of court can see/Their glittering baits, and purple slavery*. Here, if we pronounce *slaverée*, to rhyme with *see*, we remove the accent from the proper syllable, and spoil the pronunciation, which should be *sláverў*; the same as in prose. So, *Through gen'ral life, behold the scale arise/Of sensual and of mental faculties*. Here we should pronounce *facultўs*, and not *facultis*'. We recall too in this context Thomas Batchelor's (1809:Zettersten:1973:75) reservations in this area: 'If the unaccented *e* ought, in any case, to take the long sound of double *ee*, this must happen when it forms the first syllable of a word, as in *electricity*; but no degree of solemnity in pronunciation will authorise the use of the same sound at the end of a word, and still less in any other situation. How would Mr Walker pronounce '*thee deegree of thee veeloseetee of eelecktriseetee*' yet these words are spelled according to that gentleman's description of the sound of *e*, when it ends a syllable'. It should be noted that the Scot James Douglas (describing a London standard usage) treats the vowels (his *I2*) in items like <bib>, <crib>, <big>, <din>, <pip> as 'short and aspirate' (Holmberg: 1956: 157), 'a small sound very Short and Aspirate' and 'as if it were written *ih*' (Holmberg: 1956: 60), in contradistinction to his *I Improper 1*, the stressed vowel in *caprice, machine*. While Holmberg's notational usage is confusing in this area, it would appear that this 'aspirate' *i* corresponds to [ɩ] rather than [i].

Once more, though, it is Sylvester Douglas who provides the most detailed description of pure palatal and close-to-palatal segments both in the usage of upper class London speech and in whatever he means by provincial Scotch. Commenting on the close-to-pure-palatal types, Douglas (Jones:1992:129ff) recognises for the 'pure' dialect two separate types of what he calls the *short close sound* of the <i> graph. One of these (and we shall discuss this phonetic context in more detail below) is where whatever is meant by the *short close sound* appears when its syllable termination is rhotic; the other 'approaches the first sound of the *e* shortened' and is 'most generally perceived before a semivowel', as in the items *fin, sin, will, is, his, lizard*. He makes the general comment that speakers of provincial Scotch are liable to substitute the segment which occurs in pre-[r] contexts (whatever he means by *short u*) for the short close vowel before semivowel syllable terminations: i.e. a segment which is lower and more central for one which approximates to a pure palatal. However, especially under his FILL entry (Jones 1991:193-94), he goes on to make an important further distinction between two different 'shades' of short close sounds in non-rhotic contexts. He claims that in the 'pure' dialect there is a special type of palatal vowel (his *obscure short i*) to be found in those cases where syllables terminate in voiced obstruents and voiced fricatives, i.e. in items like <is>, <big>, <live>, <crib>, <smithy>, while another type surfaces in syllable final voiceless and dental lateral sonorant and the dental nasal positions: <kick>, <kill>, <ship>, <Liffy>, <skim>, <kin>. He notes that 'In *is*, which the Scotch pronounce in the same manner with the English pronunciation of *fit, wit, fin*, something nearer the *i* in *caprice*. But this I believe is owing to a property common to all the softer semivowels and mutes (viz. this soft *s*, *v*, the soft *th*, the *b*, the *d* and the *g*) by which they reflect back, as it were, a sort of hollowness on a preceding obscure and short vowel'. He goes on to make the important observation that 'As there is only a slight shade, or gradation, between the Scotch method of sounding the *i*, in *fill, fit, wit* &c and the English, the difference generally escapes the attention of Scotchmen who are endeavouring to mend their pronounciation [sic:CJ]. It is however so sensible to the English, that when they mean to ridicule the Scotch dialect they frequently lay hold of this circumstance....Indeed, as caricature adds to the ridicule in all sorts of mimicry the English in their imitation exaggerate the Scotch pronounciation of the short *i*, and turn it into the obscure *u* or *a*. '*What's your wull?' 'You have a great deal of wat'* (Jones:1991:194). Clearly in this *obscure/hollow* alternation we are dealing with a phonetic opposition which for Scottish speakers was phonetically 'conditioned' but apparently involved only a slight acoustic contrast, but a contrast significantly different from the corresponding English 'standard' shape to make it, for southern speakers, a major salient characteristic of Scots speech habits. That this was indeed the case is evident from the 'Commonly Pronounced' <hum>, <hus>, <un>, <uz> and <ut> respellings for the 'True' <hīm>, <hīz>, <īn>, <īz> and <īt> in the list of 'those words in which the Natives of North Britain are most apt to err' in *A Spelling Book Upon a New Plan* (1796:vii), and perhaps too in Elphinston's almost despairing comment on the vagaries of Scotch 'interchainge' (1786:3): 'Evvery sound becoms dhus anoddher (almoast anny oddher) sound: *hwip* hwop; *lodge* ludge; *trudge*, trodge; *joggel*, juggel or shuggel; *jostel*, justel; *rustel*, ristel; *summer* and *winter*, semmer and wonter...'; with Adams (1799:152) noting Scotch *'Hell, mell, tell*; and *hull, mull, tull...fust'* matching English short i^2 types such as *'still, mill...mist, fist'*. Perhaps here too belongs Robertson's (1742:41ff) near homophonous group: <Tip> *'the End'*: <Type> *'Figure'*: <Tup> *'a Ram'*.

We are left with two questions: 1. what is the nature of the phonetic difference, if indeed there was one, between etymologically pure palatal sounds and those 'near' pure palatals which have subsequently surfaced as more central and lower vowels approximating to [ɩ] - the *civil/ceevil* types - and 2. what is the phonetic value for the segment described by Douglas as the 'obscure short *i*', the segment viewed as such a marked characteristic of Scots speech. The answer to the first question is perhaps to be found in an examination of the orthographic systems of Alexander Geddes and Alexander Scot, both of whom appear to differentiate between segments which are close to the pure palatal vowel space. Geddes (1792:431;434) perceives a contrast between what are apparently recognisable palatal alternations: His '*e* long as in *scene*: The sound of this letter is hardly distinguishable from that of *i* or English *ee*' he represents by the <è> graph and exemplifies in items such as <apèr> *'appear'*, <bèch> *'beech'*, <drèkhli> *'dreichly'*, <très> *'trees'* etc. (Jones 1994:79). At the same time he appears to distinguish (by means of an <ì> graph) the '*i* Italian, or English *ee;* this is the true original sound of *i*, and the only one the Italians, Spaniards and Germans know' (1792:423). This sound, he claims, is 'equivalent to our *ee*'. However, the set of items he indicates as showing this '*i* Italian' are not, in general, characterised by showing an etymological pure palatal: <cìty> *'city'*, <cìtizens> *'citizens'*, <cìvil> *'civil'*, <Brìtain> *'Britain'*, except in those instances where the *English Vowel Shift* has failed to apply: <inspìran> *'inspiring'*. We might be tempted, nevertheless, to treat Geddes' observation that <è> and <ì> are 'hardly distinguishable' as an admission of homophony, were it not for the evidence provided by his contemporary, Alexander Scot.

We have already observed the extent of the use of what would appear to be the pure palatal vowel in contexts where [ɩ] might be expected in the phonology of 18th century. For the modern language too, Grant and Dixon (1921: 40-41) record this vowel (using an <ee> orthography) in <ceevil> '*civil*'; <peety> '*pity*' and <poseetion> '*position*', observing (somewhat contentiously) that the palatal vowel is retained in 'words of Romance origin'. Recall too in this context, Kenrick's parodying <wheetsh> '*which*' and <transpozeeshun> (1784:2) and Buchanan's (1766) renderings such as <aukseĕlĭ-ĭrry>, <authĕnteĕssĭtў>. It is important to stress, however, that Alexander Scot (Jones:1993:109-11) differentiates <ee> spelt words such as <mischeevous>, <civeeletays>, <veezet>, <leeberaul>, <ooteeletay>, <eemaugenatione> and <Breetish> from those (mainly with lexical [ii]) spelt with <i>, such as <min> '*mean*', <spic> '*speak*', <rid> '*read*', <swit> '*sweet*', etc., and the orthographic methods of such a careful observer of phonetic distinction as Scot, must surely suggest that Geddes' <è> and <ì> symbols represent a genuinely perceived and perceivable phonetic vowel quality contrast. Certainly Scot's representations involving such close proximity of the two symbols within a single lexical item such as <civeeletays> '*civilities*' and in items in close physical proximity <swit freendshep> '*sweet friendship*' suggest that some kind of qualitative distinction was indeed observable. That some 'intermediate' palatal segment between [i] and [ɩ] in fact existed in the phonetic inventory of late 18th century Scots speakers is implicit in Sylvester Douglas' observation (Jones:1991:193) that:

> In *is*, which the Scotch pronounce in the same manner with the English pronunciation of *fit*, *wit*, *fin*, something nearer the *i* in *caprice*.

Although Sylvester Douglas is notorious for the use of a descriptive nomenclature dependent upon such phrases as 'a shade of', 'close to' 'nearly', we would be rash to dismiss his 'something nearer' attribute as insignificant. Indeed our reluctance to treat etymological pure palatals as phonetically identical with those palatals in 18th century Scots which subsequently surface in a more sonorant ([ɩ]-type) shape is strengthened in the light of the fact that the latter appear confined in the period to specific phonetic and phonological contexts. For instance, the <ì> spellings of Geddes and the <ee>'s of Scot - the <cìvil>/<leeberal> types - appear mainly in contexts where (a) *English Vowel Shift* diphthongisation fails to occur, (b) in 'weak' vowel lengthening environments (i.e. pre-homorganic [nd] clusters), (c) in polysyllabic lexical items where stressed vowel length may be 'curtailed' (Lehiste: 1970:40) and (d) are almost everywhere subsequently realised as [ɩ]. We might therefore perhaps tentatively treat such segments as 'not quite so palatal' as [i], and consequently as some kind of F_2 lowered, centralised [i˕] or even [ɨ] vowel shape.

The provision of a precise phonetic value for Sylvester Douglas' *obscure short* or *short close i* is a more difficult matter. We recall that for the pure dialect he makes, in his *Observations on the Alphabet*, a binary distinction in this sound which he claims to be easily observable by the 'attentive ear' and which is peculiar to the English language : items he cites showing the vowel in stressed position are <picture>, <fixture> and <sin>. This 'short close' sound is divisible into two 'shades', the one in pre-[r], the other in all other contexts. The pre-[r] palatal type *i* sound in items such as <first> and <thirst> approaches, for Douglas' ear, 'nearly to but seems not exactly the same with, the short *u*' (Jones:1991:129): not a particularly helpful description in view of the fact that, as we shall discuss below, 'short' *u* for Douglas could apparently range from [u] through [ɤ]. His statement that a <burst>/<first> contrast will illustrate the difference between the two shades is also not particularly useful, since in his descriptions of pure labial sounds, Douglas does not distinguish pre-[r] developments, except to list <bur> under 'obscure *u*' in contrast with the more 'hollow' *u* under his FILL entry. This might point to a pre-[r] value of [ʌ] rather than [ɤ]. So the vowel in <first> is 'nearly, but not exactly the same with' [ʌ]. Such a conclusion is reinforced by Douglas' FIR entry, where he says that the '*i* is sounded nearly like the short obscure *u* in *burst*.' Such a vowel, we might tentatively suggest, could be the half close, upper mid, central vowel [ɘ]. But we shall have more to add to this discussion when we come to consider the CLERGY item (Valk:1980; Gabrielson:1913). At the same time, there would appear to be considerable evidence of lexical diffusion, from the observations of most grammarians in the period, affecting relatively central vowel shapes in the pre-[r] context; the Scotsman Gray (1809:9-14) for instance listing the items <sir> and <her> as sharing the pronunciation of <tun>, <done>, <touch>, <work>, <love>, with <first> and <gird> represented as <furst> and <gerd>.

The second shade of the *short close i* Douglas asserts to be a version of the *first sound of e shortened* - where the *first sound of e* is some kind of [ii], illustrated be the items *scene, he, the, she* (Jones:1991:123). Claimed to be 'most sensibly perceived before a semivowel' this sound is evidenced in the stressed vowel spot in items like <fin>, <sin>, <will>, <ill>, <his>, <women>, <Lizard>. But before we speculate upon a phonetic value for this segment, it is important to realise that Douglas makes a further sub-division of it. Under the important FILL entry he observes that there is a contrast between *i* pronunciations which is a function of the shape of the segments terminating their syllable. When the syllable coda is of the 'class' voiced fricative or voiced obstruent, an 'obscure' *i* is realised, contrasting with what is described as a more 'hollow' version, where the syllable is terminated by 'the softer semivowels and mutes (viz. the soft *s*, the *v*, the soft *th* the *b* the *d* and the *g*)' and where the vowel is perhaps a low central [ʌ] or even [ɣ]. Such a contrast is lexically exemplified as follows:

OBSCURE SHORT *I*	MORE 'HOLLOW'
<fit>	<big>
<wit>	<bid>
<fin>	<crib>
<is>	<smithy>
<skim>	<live>
<Liffy>	
<Lizard>	
<women>	
<kick>	
<kill>	
<kit>	
<ship>	
<pith>	

Items under the first column show syllables terminated by the (rather odd) set voiceless obstruent ([t], [k], [p]), non-[r] sonorants ([l], [m], [n]), voiceless continuants ([f], [θ]) and the voiced fricative continuant ([z]). Although 'most sensibly perceived before a semivowel' (the sonorants and voiced/voiceless continuants) this set manifests, Douglas claims, stressed vowels showing a 'shade' of *i* sound which 'approaches..to the first sound of *e* shortened'. We might therefore speculate that in the pure dialect we are dealing in the column one items with a vowel space which, while palatal, is not so palatal as [i], and might therefore be treated as [ɨ]. The items under column two manifest stressed syllable codas which are either voiced fricatives or voiced obstruents. In such contexts (as we shall see for the labial vowel segments as well - see p. 149), the syllable space is perceived as more 'hollow', where the codas 'reflect back as it were, a sort of hollowness on a preceding obscure and short vowel', a 'hollowness' illustrated by Douglas as typical of the stressed vowel space in items like <drum>, <sullen>, <dub> and <tub>. The column two stressed vowel might therefore be interpreted as a more sonorant (more central and lower) segment than [ɨ], perhaps [ι] , the retracted front unrounded vowel.

4.2.3.a Scotch Forms of the Short Obscure i

We have, however tentatively, come to the conclusion that in the pure dialect Sylvester Douglas appears to distinguish three kinds of near palatal sound: one in [r] contexts which we suggested might represent an upper mid central [ɘ]-type segment; the second 'approaches to the first sound of *e* shortened', a segment we speculated which might be represented by [ɨ]; the third a more 'hollow' version of the last, whose value we might place somewhere near [ɩ]. Douglas claims that one of the most salient features of the Scotch dialect lies in the way it is 'apt to substitute' an [ɘ]-like segment in those items like <fin>, <will>, <ill>, <is>, <his> in which the pure dialect realises an [ɨ] vowel. Indeed, we can recall his assertion that 'before *n*, *l* and *t* [Scottish speakers:CJ] scarcely ever hit this exactly. Hence the English in caricaturing their pronunciation will say *wull, full, spull,* for *will,* &c'. But Douglas gives us no more precise information as to what this 'Scotch *i*' might have been like phonetically other than that it is somewhat more sonorant than [ɨ]. Indeed his terminological descriptions of the sound (assuming they all refer to it) are quite varied: *short obscure i, short i, obscure i, short smothered i, short close i.* The Scotch examples and their English counterparts for these descriptions are as follows:

DOUGLAS' DESCRIPTION	ENGLISH EXAMPLE
SHORT OBSCURE	
<Venice>	<fin>, <winning>
SHORT	
<weather>	<wither>
<whether>	<wither>
<tremble>	<thimble>
<bedizen>	<phiz>, <mizzen>
<behind>	<rescind>
OBSCURE	
<rem*e*mber>	<timber>, <window>
SHORT SMOTHERED	
<rem*ai*nder>	<wind>, <sin>, <fin>
SHORT CLOSE	
<*p*iracy>	<*p*irate>

while the Scotch *i* vowels in the items <pencil> and <clever> are given no descriptive name by Douglas, but are merely said to be pronounced 'as if written *Pincil*' or made to 'rhyme to *liver*' (cf Adams' (1799:152-3) <pincil> '*pencil*', <wist> '*west*' and <till> '*tell*'). Perhaps we are looking here at a sound not so palatal as [ɨ] and yet not so sonorant as [ɘ], some more central [ɨ̞] or perhaps even [ə], a mid central unrounded vowel. Alternatively, some kind of [ɛ̈] segment may be is what is being suggested. This Scots tendency to lower/centralise palatal vowels is perhaps reflected too in Robertson's (1722:62) <Bill>/<Bell>/<Bull> and <Big>/<Beg> 'equal in sound' pairs.

Some support for an interpretation like this comes from Geddes who identifies (using an <i> graph) a segment he calls '*i* short, as in *sin;* This letter has often so nearly the sound of short *a*, that it may be used for it' (1792:431;434). Edinburgh dialect examples he cites (many of which, but far from all, are in Douglas' 'semivowel' context) include: absint; Amarillis; apils; apin't; bami; banis't; blastit; blist '*blessed*'; brink; chin; contentit; disturbit; divyn; drink; fatlins; fattist; firs; first; funtins; gentil; gin '*begin*'; happi; hikhts '*heights*'; hils; hir; his; hit; hivi '*heavy*'; hivir; hizils '*hazels*'; hori; huilk '*which*'; humbil; ilke; ill; in; inhabit; inokulat; into; invy '*envy*'; ivir '*ever*'; katchist; kiddan' '*cudding*'; klift; kushi-du '*cushet dove*'; ladin; langir; list '*please*'; mikil; mirri; motif; nikht; oni; prunirs; rarli; reinstatit; responsif; rigs; rustik; Scytia's; shadit; shephirds; silvan; sin; sith '*since*'; sitst; sivir't '*cut*'; still; t'uthir; tempils; this; till; tis; tuins '*twins*'; turtil; unhappi; uthir; wi; wundir't; yit. Geddes (1792:431-432) describes his short *a* in the following terms:

> *a* short, as in *hand*, or nearly so. This is not entirely the English *a* short, as in *hand*, a sound not known in Scotland, till very lately; but the shortest and most indistinct of all vocal sounds, and which might be almost equally well expressed by a very short *i*, and even by *e* or *u*. Sir William Jones informs us, that, in all the Indian dialects, 'this vowel is considered *inherent* in every consonant'; and so it seems evidently to have been by the Hebrews, Chaldees, Syrians, and Arabs. I have retained it particularly in all active participles: as *doand, writand,* &c. where it is plain, that *i, e,* or *u*, if rapidly pronounced, might be readily substituted for it.

A literal interpretation of these remarks might lead us to an interpretation of Geddes' 'short *a*' as some kind of [ə] segment, although the fact that he assigns it to items like <lang>, <was> and <huat> where modern standard Scots realises an [ɔ] output, might just suggest that the segment he hears is the more open, central [ɐ]. It is interesting too that there appear to be only two instances where Geddes cites the existence of a low central vowel for an etymological [ɩ]: cf. his Buchan <wun> '*win*' and Edinburgh <wullan> '*willing*'. While we might interpret his <u> symbol in these cases literally as [ʌ], it is just possible that it symbolises some kind of mid central [ë] vowel, a segment prominent in the phonology of Modern Standard Scots (Wells 1982:129; Abercrombie 197974-75). In this context too we might see Adams' remarks (1799:121) concerning the *busy/bizzy* contrast, which he ascribes to 'affinity of letters: so in Latin *u* and *i* are often placed one for the other, *op-ti-mus* and *op-tu-mus*. *Buzzy*, per *u*, is true Scotch, very expressive of the bustle, hurry, and buzzing noise of a *buzzy* or busy crowd, resembling the buzzing of bees, verified daily at the Royal Exchange at London, &c. however, use has preferred the short *i*'.

4.2.4 Mixed Palatal/Sonorant Segments: Mid Front [e] and [ɛ] Types: the [ɛ] Vowel

Most commentators in the period (notably Dun, Robertson, Telfair and the two Douglases) refer to this segment as the short version of *e*, the vowel to be heard in items such as *hed, bread, head*. For others, such as Adams, it is 'free and open' or, for Dun, 'a more obscure sort of a sound of *e*'. Burn sees a three fold distinction in the segment: 'short, as in *men;* shorter, as in *former*...long and sharp, as in *there*' (1776:3). A great many writers are careful to distinguish this segment's manifestation in pre-rhotic contexts, Angus' 'occasional' sound of *e*, Buchanan's acute, with Telfair's description of the sound in this environment as 'the same with *u* in *run*' being fairly typical. The diacritic school generally mark this mid, front vowel as e^2 or ê (Perry, McIllquam, Warden and William Scott in particular) while some observers provide further contrastive detail, such as 'short *e*, free and open, differs little from short *a*' (Buchanan:1757:8), and there is considerable information concerning the segment's phonetic value to be gleaned from several of the many 'near alike' lists. But once more, the most sophisticated and detailed descriptions are to be found in Sylvester Douglas, Alexander Scot and Alexander Geddes.

Sylvester Douglas equates the sound with his *strong slender a* exemplified in *pare, stare, bear, pear* and the contemporary Scotch pronunciation of the Greek η or the 'French *e* open' in items such as *bête,père* and *ferme* (Jones:1992:32:123), and he states that the segment has a long variant in items (mainly syllable final in [r]) such as *pare, share, bare, hare, bear* and *wear,* while it shows a durationally short form in *stem, rest, fell, rest* and *pen*. Typically too, he recognises in some pre-rhotic contexts 'a sort of obscure and smothered sound not unlike that of the French *e* in *le, ce, que, le*vez-vous &c. Examples of this sound we have in the English method of pronouncing *clergy, earth, impertinent*' (Jones:1992:123).

Alexander Scot uses five symbolic representations for vocalic elements which in Modern Standard Scots are realised as either [e] or [ɛ]: <au> in <caupable> '*capable*'; <a> in <trad> '*trade*', <tham> '*them*'; <ee> in <antarteen> '*entertain*'; <é> in <péper> '*paper*' and <ai> in <mainy> '*many*'. The data from *The Contrast* suggest that he uses two distinct symbols for stressed vowels which are realised in Modern Standard Scots as some kind of [ɛ] vowel: <a> and <ai>. With the former we find <sartan> '*certain*', <ware> '*were*', <tham> '*them*' and <mat> '*met*', with the latter <mainy> '*many*', <lairnen> '*learning*', <airlayest> '*earliest*' and <aicsap> '*except*', and there can be little doubt that Scot's system was one where a 'one symbol/one sound' principle operated wherever possible. The <a>/<ai> contrast does not fit neatly with any rhotic character of syllable termination, while <a> is to be found regularly with items such as <trad> '*trade*', <laddy> '*lady*' and <favor> '*favour*' where we might expect some kind of [e] to surface and with <haibit> '*habit*', <pairts> '*parts*' and <chaipel> '*chapel*', where [a] or [æ] would seem a probable historical English development.

Alexander Geddes' description of mid front vowels is particularly detailed in that it utilises four separate characters for what appear to be vowels composed of various internal weightings of palatality and sonority (1791:431-434):

1. <ei> digraph: '*ei* German and Italian, nearly English *ay*: The combination *ei* is not known in England, at least in the Metropolis. It is the Italian *ei*, and nearly the English *ay*.'
2. <â> graph: '*a* slender, as in *fate, nation*. This is plainly a simple sound, and would better be represented by the Greek η. I believe the Scots have but lately adopted it from the English. It approximates to é [e middle, as in *send*:CJ], but is longer.'
3. <e> graph: '*e* short, as in *element*. E short is less common in Scots than in English; the next letter [*e* middle, <é>: CJ] commonly taking its place.' (1792:431:433)
4. <é> graph: '*e* middle, as in *send*: The mean sound of *e*, though not mentioned by grammarians, is more or less an English sound; for surely it is not pronounced exactly in the same manner in *elegy* and *lend*. But the difference is much more apparent in Scots.'

However, the fact that some low mid [ɛ] segments in Scots are associated with subsequent pure palatal and etymological [a] types might lead us to the conclusion that in late 18th century Scots there were, in fact, two different types of low mid front vowel to be distinguished in the phonetic inventory. The evidence from some writers that the 'standard' Scots of the late 18th century showed two such distinguishable low mid vowel types seems to be quite clear. Under his CLERGY entry (Jones:1991:183-184), Sylvester Douglas observes:

> The short close *e* as in *berry, merry*. The Scotch pronounce it long and like their sound of the Greek η or the *a* in *bare*. The proper sound approaches near that of the *i* in *fir, stir*, but it is not the same. It is a shade between that sound, and the *e* in *pen*. The Scotch *merry, ever, never, every*, sound it exactly as the *i* in *fir*.

Douglas' Greek <η> seems most likely to stand for an [ɛɛ] segment, while 'the *i* in *fir* is sounded like the short obscure *u* in *burst, fur*. But not exactly so' (Jones 1991:194). Although Douglas' terminology is especially inconsistent in this area of the phonology, the short obscure (or *smothered*) *u* seems to represent some kind of [ʌ] or [ə] vowel, yet what value we should assign to it under the constraint that 'it is not the same', is difficult to decide. It is interesting to note too that in *The Contrast*, Alexander Scot's orthography also seems to suggest just such a double low mid front vowel division. While his <ee> symbol seems unambiguously to point to [e(e)] values in <antarteen> '*entertain*', his <a> in <sartan> '*certain*'; <ware> '*were*' versus the <ai> digraph used in items like <mainy> '*many*' and <lairnen> '*learning*' shows a contrast which may well represent a palatality variation between [ε˕] and [ε˔] (Jones 1993:109-110).

Geddes distinguishes between an '*a* slender' (<â>), an '*e* middle' (<é>), and an '*e* short' (<e>), the distinction between the last two being 'much more apparent in Scots' than in English (1792:433). Almost all the items in both regional dialects (Edinburgh and Buchan) which Geddes cites as containing the *e* middle vowel show a low mid [ε] in their subsequent development, (perhaps with the exception of <é> '*eye*', which may just be a misprint for <è>):

> ascénd; bést; confés; conténtit; é '*eye*'; égernis '*eagerness*'; éxyls; frémit '*thirsty*'; Gérman; hédj '*hedge*'; héns '*hence*'; léft; péndan' '*hanging*'; poséshon; proténd; réfréshan '*refreshing*'; ségs '*weeds*'; sént; témpils; téndir; thém; thér '*their*'; tuél '*twelve*'; wér '*were*'.

Geddes observes that the *a* slender (<â>) - 'I believe the Scots have but lately adopted it from the English' - is a longer version of *e* middle and, importantly, is 'represented by the Greek η' (1792:433). Sylvester Douglas is careful to distinguish the relative phonetic values of the Greek η and ε:

> The sound in *pare, stare,* and *tail* is exactly the same with that given to the Greek η in Scotland, and to the *e* in *bête, père*; or *oi* and *ai,* in *vouloit, pâitre,* by the French. The other in *waste, grace, tale* is the Scotch sound of the ε and the French sound of their *e* in *portér*, and *extrait* in which last word the two sounds are contrasted' (Jones 1991:118).

Douglas' value for Greek η is clearly [εε], a shortened version of which is probably the value of Geddes' *e* middle. However, it is important to notice how he specifically says that *a* slender 'approximates' to *e* middle and that '*e* middle, as in *send*: The mean sound of *e*, though not mentioned by grammarians, is more or less an English sound; for surely it is not pronounced exactly in the same manner in *elegy* and *lend*. But the difference is much more apparent in Scots'. *a* slender and *e* middle would therefore appear to involve a qualitative as well as a quantitative difference for Geddes, especially in the Scots phonetic inventory.

On the other hand, it is interesting to notice that while many of Geddes *e* short examples occur with low mid front etymons - *brest, gentil, tenement* - and might therefore seem appropriately designated as [ɛ], many others are found with this graph which are historically pure palatal in their configuration or which subsequently vowel shift to this value: *he, besyd, brethan, rep.* It might be appropriate therefore to consider segments represented with this graph (since they are systematically kept distinct from his <è> ([i])), as some kind of palatality heightened version of [ɛ], such as [ɛ˔] or [e˕].

Given that Geddes' <ei> graph, witnessed in items such as <deis> '*days*', <grei> '*gray*' and <preis> '*praise*' seems unequivocally to represent some kind of [e(e)] segment, we might characterise his system as follows:

<ei> [e(e)]
<â> slender [ɛɛ]
<è> middle [ɛ˕]
<e> short [ɛ˔]

a system apparently showing a similar three height front low mid vowel split as that attested by Alexander Scot:

<é> <péper> [e(e)]
<ai> <mainy> [ɛ˔]
<a> <sartan> [ɛ˕]

4.2.4.a The [e] Vowel

Sylvester Douglas recognises a long and short version of what he chooses to call the *thinner, feeble, slender a* (Jones 1992:117), exemplified in *phrase, waste* and *race, pace* respectively and which corresponds to 'the Scotch sound of the ɛ and the French sound of their *e* in *portér,* and *extrait*' (Jones:1992:118). Indeed, the most common nomenclature for the [e] segment is related to the <a> graph, most commentators (notably Dun, Burn and Buchanan) describing it synonymously as 'the sound of *a* in *Cane*', marking it <ā> or <a^1> (Warden, Barrie and William Scott) or equating it with 'improper' diphthongs such as <ai>, <ay> (Dun, Warden). For Angus it is one of his 'name sounds' <ā> or <á> as in <vācáte>, A1 and Ai1 for James Douglas, while Adams indulges in his customary idiosyncrasies by describing the segment as '*a* common foreign; 'clear *e*' and '*e* foreign long'. It is Elphinston's *a* slender open.

4.2.5 Scotch Peculiarities of the Mixed Sonorant/Palatal Segments

This is a complex area of the phonology of 18th century Scots and there is much evidence of mid front vowels alternating with low front [a] and pure sonorant [ɑ] vowels (4.2.8/9), failing to undergo the *English Vowel Shift* to [ii] (4.2.6), as well as alternating with one another (4.2.7). At the same time, several commentators supply through their descriptive methodologies sufficient phonetic detail to cause us to suspect that a simple 'mid' vowel [e]/[ɛ] type contrast is too weak a description of the phonetic inventory of the period.

Our discussion of the front mid vowel types in Scottish English in the late 18th century will centre largely around the ways in which they are manifested in that dialect *vis à vis* their behaviour with respect to the 'classical' interpretation of the *English Vowel Shift* process. We shall, however, repeatedly come up against the problem of deciding how to interpret these segments as regards the length characteristic they display in Scots in the period, and it will quickly become evident that - unlike the claim made in the standard *English Vowel Shift* model - input to the process in Scots appears not to be confined to segments which show either etymological or derived durational extension; short vowels would appear to be just as ready to undergo palatalisation and labialisation as those which are historically long. At any rate, it is often extremely difficult to tell from the nature of the evidence available to us the distribution of vowel length characteristics in the 18th century, although Sylvester Douglas probably makes the most systematic attempt to do so (Jones:1992:32-33). We have already seen, for instance, that there is evidence to show how (in defiance of traditional interpretations of the event) the vowel shift could apparently involve *short* vowels as input - recall the [hɛd]/[hid] *'head'* alternation noted above. At the same time, we observed in the last section too how the evidence provided by Sylvester Douglas for both the Scotch and the Pure dialect points to a manifestation of long vowel English vowel shifting which is at once 'retarded' and advanced' in relation to the 'standard' and stereotypical interpretation of this phonological process.

4.2.5.a The Short Front Mid/Pure Palatal Alternation in Scots

Geddes provides what seem to be unambiguous instances of the 'advanced' nature of the vowel shift process in Scots showing mixed palatal/sonorant (front, mid) vowels undergoing palatalisation as far as [i]/[ii] even in contexts where the affected vowel is etymologically short in duration, suggested by spellings such as <frènd> *'friend'*; <drèd> *'dread'*; <hèld> *'held'*; <plèsant> *'pleasant'* and others: here too we might include Adams' Scotch *bread, head,* and *death* with '*E* long' (his [ii]) contrasting with the same English items with *E* short, or [ɛ]. The phenomenon is certainly well recorded throughout the period, Robertson assigning an *e* long value to the vowel in *earth*; Warden marking with *e*[1] (the vowel in *be, me*) the italicised vowels in <altogether>, <general>, <never>, <second>, <very>, <necessary>; Burn showing *e* long in the stressed vowels in <lecherous>, <pleasant> and <weapon> (although he suggests short *e* ([ɛ]) in <peach> and <yeast>) while Angus is extremely prone to recommending the pure palatal, his <ė>, in items like <dė-kȯ'rus> 'decorous', <ė-nig'ma> '*enigma*' and <ė-skwir'> '*esquire*'. Sylvester Douglas likewise points to many instances of this Scotch habit, noting for example that the stressed vowel in an item like <bread> is 'as in *bear*, but short. The Scotch pronounce it as *breed*' (Jones:1993:177), although the majority of instances he cites for this increased level of palatality involve items associated at some point in their etymological history with long vowel space. His [ɛ]/[ii] alternation in SUPREMACY, however, may be the result of some concern for 'analogy':

> The *u* as in *sublime*. The Scotch aiming at the English pronounciation, sound the *e* as in *decent*. It should be pronounced as in *pen, stem*. In *supreme* it ought to be sounded as in *decent*.

Here too we might include Elphinston's (1786:8) remarks that 'So poor *next, jest* (and even *joist*), *arrest* and *stretch*, becom *neest, jeest, arreest* and *streech*'. But perhaps the most sustained evidence for this phenomenon is to be found in the 'Table of Words, equal in Sound, but very much differing in Sense and Spelling' provided by James Robertson in his 1722 *The Ladies Help to Spelling*, a work (perhaps because of its early date) replete with 'Scotticisms' or, perhaps, with pronunciations which were acceptable as some kind of local Glasgow standard Scots of the period: <Leaper/leper>; <league/leg>; <well/wheel/weal>; <lead> '*a heavy mettal*'/<lead> '*as a Captain doth*'; <beast/best>; <ear/err>; <heel/hell>; <Easter/Esther> as well as several others.

4.2.6 Retarded Vowel Shifts

There is considerable evidence in the period of Scottish (as well as English) speakers manifesting [e(e)] stressed vowel shapes in a 'retarded' *English Vowel Shift* manner, in contexts where the pure dialect realises the chronologically earlier mid vowels as the pure palatal [ii] - consider the following data provided by Sylvester Douglas:

PURE DIALECT	SCOTCH
[ii]	[e]/[ee]
<recent>	[resənt]
<cream>	[kreem]
<tea>	[tee]

although Douglas claims that the [kreem] pronunciation only occurs 'sometimes', while the [tee] version is specifically associated with 'the North of Scotland' (Jones:1992:226), suggesting that the 'unshifted' [ee] for pure [ii] was infrequent in Scottish English at the close of the 18th century (Jones:1992:226-27):

> TEA
> In the North of Scotland, they pronounce the *ea* as the English do the *ay*, in *day, Tay*, the *ey* in *obey*, or the *a* in *tale*. That is, with the second, or thin sound of the slender *a*. According to the English pronounciation of *obey* and the Scotch pronounciation of *tea*, the following is a perfect rhyme.
>
> Here thou, great Anna! whom three realms *obey*
> Dost sometimes counsel take, and sometimes *tea*.
>
> But the English now (whatever may have been the case when the *Rape of the Lock* was written) pronounce *tea* as in *appear* .

Several examples are also cited by Adams (17999:152-3), who represents as Scotch the pronunciation of the items *decent, thee, me, be* by <dai-cent>, <thai>, <mai>, <bai>, where his <ai> can mean an [e]-type vowel; Robertson has <earth> with some kind of pure palatal and shows <beat/bait>; <chair/cheer>; <shave/sheaf>; <bleed/blade>; <vail/veal> and <spare/spear> among several others, as 'sounding alike'.

At the same time, Sylvester Douglas' description of Scottish vernacular [ɛ]/[ɛɛ] stressed vowel shapes suggests that for some lexical items at least the result of the vowel shift was for these too a 'retarded' one:

PURE	SCOTCH
[ii]	[ɛ]/[ɛɛ]
<neat>	BEAR
<retreat>	BEAR
<spear>	BEAR
<deal>	BREAST
<idea>	PEN
[ɨ]	[ɛ]
<dinner>	<denner> 'as if written'

In the Scottish vernacular the <neat>, <retreat> etc. items have not undergone the 'expected' English vowel shifting of [ɛɛ] to the more palatal [ee]/[ii]. At the same time, the vernacular Scottish situation may even reveal lexical diffusion and socio-phonetic alternation of some sort: Douglas emends his DEAL entry (Jones:1992:187) from 'The Scotch often pronounce *all* or *some* of these words as *breast* is sounded in the pure dialect' to 'Many Scotch people pronounce *all* and most [people:CJ] some of these words as *breast* is sounded in the pure dialect.' Again, under

SPEAR (Jones:1992:224) he comments: 'The *ea* as in *appear*. The Scotch often sound it as in *bear*. Tho' the other is their vernacular pronounciation', suggesting a polite vernacular [spiir] pronunciation with a less acceptable, vowel shift retarded [spɛɛr] variant. While we might speculate that Douglas' recording of the fact that although <dinner> 'rhymes to *sinner*, in Scotland it is often pronounced as if written *denner*' (Jones:1992:187) indicates a 'retarded' state of some short vowel shift of [ɛ] → [ɩ]/[ɨ], it is perhaps more probable that what we are witnessing here is an instance of pre-nasal lowering (Ohala 1974). Note however, Adams' (1799:152-3) contention that, in the Scotch dialect, a palatalisation of [ɛ] to some kind of [i] occurs in pre-nasal contexts, thus he represents '*send*' and '*end*' by <seend> and <eend>.

Retarded vowel shifting may also underlie Telfair's recommendation of a low mid front vowel (*e* as in *end*) in items such as <clearly>, <leap>, <seamstress>, <yeast> and <lieve>, while Dun also recommends *e* short in <fierce>, <tierce>, <piece>, <pierce>. Nevertheless, we should always bear in mind the possibility, suggested by Scot's description, that '*e* short' vowel types may represent some kind of palatality heightened version of [ɛ], such as [ɛ˔] or [e˕], thus making their 'conflation' with pure palatals something of a near rather than a complete merger (Harris:1985; Jones:1989:288).

4.2.7 The [ɛ]/[e] Alternation in Scots

Instances of the two way [ɛɛ]/[(ee)] alternation abound in late 18th century Scots. Some of the instances Geddes cites for the Edinburgh dialect as showing <â> ('*a* slender, as in *fate, nation*. This is plainly a simple sound, and would better be represented by the Greek η. I believe the Scots have but lately adopted it from the English') are as follows:

> admirâshon; agân; bâr '*bare*' ; domân '*domain*'; fâr '*fair*'; fâr '*fare*'; gâ '*gave*'; kâr '*care*' ; kâr't '*cared*' ; mâd '*made*'; nât '*native*' (but note <náti'> '*native*' (461/7)); plân '*plain*'; râril '*rarely*'; remân '*remain*'; shâdan '*shading*'; suâin '*swain*'; suzurâshons; tânt '*taint*'; ungrâtfu' '*ungrateful*'.

This [ɛɛ] value appears to be assigned by Geddes to stressed vowel space which we might expect to be realised in contemporary polite London English by [ee]; Indeed, Geddes shows more instances of this [ɛɛ] value with standard [e(e)] shapes than he does with those derived from low mid values. We only have to recall too the <adecation> '*education*', <trad> '*trade*', <laddy> '*lady*' spellings of Alexander Scot where <a> appears to represent some kind of [ɛ˕] segment (Jones 1993:119) and Douglas' entry for *Thames*:

> The *th* has the sound of *t*. The Scotch, following the analogy of other words spelt in this manner, as *lame, same, blames*, pronounce the *a* long and

> slender ([ee]:CJ). They make *thames,* and *tames, (Mansue facit)* the same word, to the ear. But in England the *a* is short, and has the same sound with *e* in *ten, hem, pen* (Jones: 1991:227) .

Even the anonymous author of *A Spelling-Book Upon a New Plan* (1796:7:14) describes the first sound of *e* (as in <beck>, <bell>, <bet>), as 'an open sound similar to *ai*' with <ai> itself characterised as 'like slender *a*' in items like <aid, ail, hay>, perhaps suggesting that we are not always dealing with a straightforward [e]/[ɛ] contrast but perhaps one between [e] and [ɛ˔] or between [e˕] and [ɛ]. It is in his CLEMENCY entry that Sylvester Douglas shows most forthrightly the salience of the Scotch [e] vowel in contexts where low mid vowels might be expected:

> The *e* is short, and as in *pen, hen, Pembroke.* The Scotch pronounce it long, and like their sound to the Greek ε; or like the English pronounciation of *ay,* in *pay, say, a* in *phrase,* and *eigh* in *weigh.* In *delicate, delicacy, indelicacy,* &c there is the same difference between the Scotch and English pronounciations of the *e.* This particularity, like the Scotch manner of pronouncing *bought, sought,* &c, is among the things which are most striking to an English ear, and are generally laid hold of in 'taking off the Scotch dialect,' as the phrase is.

The fact that Douglas sets aside such a long entry for this word itself attests to the 'Scotchness' of the stressed high mid vowel in this item, as does the fact that he equates it - as a marker of regional salientness - with the Scotch high mid [o] in *bought* and, indeed, the peculiar Scotch 'short obscure *i*' in '*will*', '*ill*' (perhaps some kind of [ɛ̈] segment) in reference to which he writes (Jones:1992:26): 'It is, however, so sensible to the English, that when they mean to ridicule the Scotch dialect they frequently lay hold of this circumstance, at the same time with the provincial sound of the *ou* in *bought* and *sought,* and of the *e* in *clemency, memory, echo* &c'. Other items Douglas records with an [e]-type vowel, or one which we may speculate is nearer [ɛ˔], include *Helen, jealousy, pedant.* The JEALOUSY entry is particularly interesting, since Douglas observes that 'The Scotch pronounce it as they often do in *death* and as they sound the *e* in *clemency*' (Jones:1992:203). We have noted a palatal type pronunciation for *death* in the Scotch vernacular (perhaps something in the region of [e˔] or [i˕] rather than a pure palatal) which might suggest that Douglas hears the *e* in *clemency* contexts to be some kind of more palatal version of [e]. The sociophonetic implications of this Scotch high mid usage are hard to assess with certainty from Douglas' comments; while the fact that English speakers find them such a characteristic of Scotch might lead us to believe that they are low status, vulgar outputs, Douglas rather pointedly comments under his HELEN entry that 'the Scotch do not sound the *h.* And are apt, when they mean to speak correctly to sound the *e* as they do in *clemency*'

(Jones:1992:201). However, the phrase 'when they mean to speak correctly' may be interpreted in a number of different ways, and we must not rush to assume that it refers to some kind of Scottish standard in every instance, a point we shall return to below. In all the other instances mentioned above, Douglas merely refers to the Scotch use of [e˔] for [ɛ] as 'Scotch'. This mid front vowel alternation may also be attested in James Robertson's 'sounding alike' list in his *The Ladies Help to Spelling* (1722), where we find pairs such as <age/edge>, <abate/abett> and <bacon/beckon>, while Elphinston (1786:3) comments 'Hwile *defference* retained dhe false face ov *deference,* no wonder dhe Scots, insted of opening dhe apparently open Inglish *e,* (hwich dhey knew not) called in the (sic) French *é* to' dheir *déference*'.

Two further points about the Scottish vernacular [ɛ] are perhaps at this juncture worth noting - firstly, Douglas observes (Jones:1992:218) that in the southern counties of Scotland:

> the *e* of *question* is commonly pronounced very broad, like the sound of *a* in *bare,* or the Scotch sound of the η. This peculiarity has been often remarked in the House of Commons when the gentlemen of Scotland have happen'd to unite in calling for the *question*.

Although it is difficult to guess what Douglas means by 'broad' in this context, we might assume that it points to yet another instance of the highly salient [ee]/[ɛ] contrast in Scotch/pure dialect mixed palatal/sonorant vowels. Secondly, and more puzzling is the record of the Scottish pronunciation of <launch> (in the pure as AUNT, and therefore perhaps [ɔ] or [ɒ]) as 'if written *lench*'. Perhaps we should mention here too the [e(e)] Scotch version for the stressed vowel in <caution> said to rhyme to that in PATIENCE and often used specifically in a technical legal context (Jones:1992:181). But we shall return to these matters under our discussion below of the 'broad *a*' (see pp. 175-177).

4.2.8 The [ɛ]/[a] Alternation in Scots

Consider the following data (Table 4.1) from *A Treatise on the Provincial Dialect of Scotland,* where we contrast what Douglas considers to be the pure dialect stressed vowel form against its Scotch counterpart, with upper cased items representing perfect rhyme congeners in the pure dialect. These data would seem to suggest that what for the pure dialect are (long as well as short) low vowels - i.e. either pure sonorant or more sonorant than palatal in their mix - are realised in the Scotch dialect as relatively more palatal ('raised'), a perception perhaps heightened by Sylvester Douglas' APPLE entry: 'The *a* must be pronounced short and open as in *tap, rap, happen.* By the common Scotch pronounciation this word should rhyme to *Kepple.* According to the

TABLE 4.1

Sylvester Douglas' [ɛ]/[a] Alternation

PURE DIALECT	SCOTCH
[æ]/[ɑ]	[ɛ]/[ɛɛ]
<apple>	KEPPEL
<chariot>	CARE, STARE
<rather>	FEATHER, LEATHER
<master>	MESS
<napkin>	NEPTUNE
<saffron>	SHARE
<yard>	AIRED, SPARED
<Saturday>	SHARE
<Harry>	PARE
<harvest>	PARE
<large>	CLARE, WARE, STARE

proper sound it rhymes to *grapple*' (Jones:1992:164). The Scotch forms show what we might therefore metaphorically describe as an 'advanced' state of the *English Vowel Shift* process for the particular lexical items in question. Indeed, several observers in the period comment upon the fact that there is a close phonetic likeness between [a] and [ɛ] segments: the observation by Walker (1791:xi) that in the Scottish dialect 'the short *e* in *bed, fed, red,* &c borders too much upon the English sound of *a* in *bad, mad, lad* &c' might suggest that the Scottish vernacular pronunciation, as we have already argued, was some kind of [ɛ˕] rather than simply an [ɛ] shape. Buchanan (1757:8) comments that 'The short sound of (e) differs but very little from short *a*; as *fet, set, bed* &c differ but little in their sounds from *fat, sat, bad*; only these with (a) have a little more opening', while his acute sound of *e* 'approaches to short *a*, but as this sound has been disputed, it has no other mark to distinguish it but the short quantity. This acute sound, however, is warranted by the best speakers; it is heard before (r) followed by another consonant, such as *rg, rj, rn, rs, rt, rr,* as *sergeant, verjuice, discern, concern, perverse...*' (1757:xiii). Likewise Sylvester Douglas claims that the sound in *hat* 'approaches to the limits of, and begins to mix itself with, the short and strong slender sound in *better* (Jones:1992:118). Cortez Telfair (1775) describes his 'first short *e* in *end*' to be 'the same with *a* short' a sound he represents in the item *'star'*, while Elphinston (1786:4) records 'broad' and 'true Scotch' <sax>, <stap>, <wat> for *'step* and *'wet'*, with his <sax> for <sex> appearing to show a subsequent 'lowering' of the common Scots [ɛ̈] vowel to some kind of [a]. An [a]/[ɛ] alternation is also suggested in many 'sounding alike' lists, notably Warden's where we find equated <catch/ketch>, <lattice/lettuce>, <rack/wreck>, <vassal/vessel>, while Robertson (1722:41ff) shows <Reddish> *'inclining to that colour'*:

<rhaddish> '*a root*'; <ketch> '*a ship*': <catch> '*to lay hold*'; <said> '*spoke*'; <sad> '*melancholy*'. Geddes' uses his *a* slender, possibly [ɛɛ], with items such as <apils> '*apples*', <banist> '*banished*' and <shados> '*shadows*'. Scot too records this Scots tendency in his renderings like <haibit> '*habit*', <pairts> '*parts*', <airts> '*arts*' - where his <ai> represents [ɛɹ] - but as instances of the 'present Caledonian English of the college, the pulpit and the bar' (Jones 1992:102). Other writers regard the usage as vulgar, notably Sylvester Douglas under his entry for ART, ARTIST (Jones 1992:164-65):

> Pronounce the *a* short and open, as in *start*. The Scotch commonly give it its long slender sound ([ɛɛ]:CJ) As in *fared, pared*. They commit the same error in most other words of this sort; as *cart, dart, hart, part, party, smart*. In avoiding this false pronounciation [sic:CJ], care must be taken not to substitute the long open *a* as the inhabitants of the north of England particularly do, in the word *cart*.

In much the same fashion, the anonymous author of *A Spelling-Book Upon a New Plan* (1796) records <ărt> '*art*' and <cārd> '*card*' with possible [ee] or [ɛɛ] as 'Commonly Pronounced', with Adams (1799:152) acknowledging, although without sociolinguistic comment, the Scotch forms <airt>, <airms> <faither>, <hait> '*hat*', even registering Scotch <waiter>, '*water*'; <wais> '*was*'; <waint>, '*want*'; <wair>, '*war*' and <wairm> '*warm*' against English items characterised by the 'broad a', possible [ɔ] or [ɒ].

That items such as <apple> and <napkin> show 'raised' Scotch vowels might lead us to conclude that here again we have an instance of the *English Vowel Shift* affecting short stressed vowel segments, a view reinforced by Douglas' remark that although <Harry> as well as <parry> and <tarry> show a short open *a* ([a]): 'The Scotch generally pronounce it in these words with the slender *a* as in *pare*, but shorter' (Jones:1992:200) - some kind of [hɛrɪ] pronunciation.

4.2.9 The [e]/[a] Alternation in Scots

There is evidence too from Sylvester Douglas' *Treatise* to suggest that the vowel shifting of [æ]/[ɑ] segments in the Scotch dialect was more 'advanced' still, since it seems to be the case that Douglas records even more palatal [e]/[ee] values for such low vowel inputs. For instance, although the stressed vowel in <saffron> is said to rhyme to '*share*' and thus show [ɛɛ], rhyming analogues like '*paper*', '*wafer*' are also proposed suggesting a [seefrən] pronunciation. In the same way, although <Saturday> and <Saturn> are likewise said to rhyme to that in '*share*', i.e. with an [ɛɛ] vowel, they too are compared to '*state*', pointing to realisations like [setərn] and [setərde]. But Douglas' uncertainty over the 'raised' value of the pure [æ]/[ɑ] stressed vowels (whether to [ɛɛ] or to

[ee]) as they appear in Scotch can be sensed in his NAPKIN entry where, although the rhyme model is given as '*Neptune*' (possibly with [ɛ]), Douglas in his Signet Library revision of the Advocates Library version of the *Treatise,* has scored through rhyming model entries like '*nape*', '*cape*', '*rape*', the last unambiguously marked as [ee] (under STAPLE) in the *Table*. Consider data like the following from Douglas' *Treatise:*

PURE DIALECT	**SCOTCH**
[ɑ]/[æ]	[e]/[ee]
<dragon>	PLAGUE
*<Danish>	FAME
*<famine>	FAME, GAME, TAME
*<have>	SAVE
<pageant>	PAGE
<camel>	FAME
<patent>	PATE
*<plaid>	PLAY'D
<rather>	RATE
<ravish>	PAPE, RAVE
*<statue>	STATE
<talent>	TALE
<drama>	SAME
<garden>	CAVE

where items marked * represent those specifically referred to as long in the *Table* with items in upper case denoting rhyming exemplars. It is important to observe how Douglas describes many of the Scottish vernacular [e]/[ee] versions notably <dragon>, <Danish>, <camel>, <famine> and <drama> as characteristic of the usage of those Scottish speakers who 'aim at propriety', 'try to catch the right pronounciation' or are 'aiming at the improvement of their pronounciation'. Elphinston's (1786:14) record of Scotch <mak>, <tak>, <brak>, <mappel>, <apel>, <craddel> and <sadel> forms against English <make>, <take>, <mapel>, <appel>, <cradle> and <saddel>, also seems to point to some kind of low/mid vowel alternation, as do his <garden>/<gairden>, <yard>/<yaird>, <dazzel>/<dazel>, <stag>/<staig> and <nag>/<naig> contrasts, among others. John Warden's *A Spelling Book* (1753) probably contains the greatest number of instances of what appear to be [e] for [a] stressed and unstressed vowel forms. His long list of words in Section VI of his *Preface* contain many instances of his three kinds of *a* sound, his sub and superscripted a^1, a^2 and a^3, stereotypically exemplified by <place>, <and> and <all> respectively. Listed with a^1 we find <era$_1$dicate>, <ta^{1}lents>, <a$_1$bundance>, <va$_1$lue>, <a$_1$re>, <na^{1}tional>, <necessa$_1$ry>, <a^{1}bsurd>. <a^{1}mong>, <era$_1$dicate>. An [e] (or occasionally [ɛ])/[a] alternation may be what supports some of James Robertson's (very Scots) 'sounding alikes' in his *The Ladies Help to Spelling* (1722), especially <add/aid>, <babel/babble>, <bar/bare/bear>, <barely/barely>, <mad/made>, <lamb/lame>, <plane/plain/plan>, <quack/quake> <cattle/kettle>, <said/sad>, <stair/star> and <rack/rake>, while in this context also we should note Telfair's <waistcoat> and <plaintif> with a recommended [a] pronunciation.

Such 'advanced' English vowel shift manifestations of [e(e)] for [ɛ] and [æ]/[ɑ] are frequently associated by Sylvester Douglas with hypercorrections or accommodation characteristics, suggesting perhaps that Scots speakers perceived the pure dialect palatal/sonorant mixed inventory as weighted towards the palatal end of the spectrum, hearing [æ] and [ɛ] as [æ˔] and [ɛ˔] respectively. Yet the [a]/[e] alternation can apparently work the other way, with several examples recorded of 'vowel shift resistant' [a] vowels. Under his CRADLE entry, for instance, Sylvester Douglas asserts that 'The Scotch (*endeavouring to speak properly*) [italics:CJ] are apt to pronounce the *a* short as in *bad, addle, paddle.* But it should be pronounced as in *shade, glade.* Or as *ladle*'. He recommends as Scotch usage too [a] vowels in items like <apron>, <dative>, <David>, <came>, <acorn> and <implacable>, yet in relation to these he makes no comment as to the propitiousness of these pronunciations, merely recording that they are Scotch or 'apt to be pronounced by the Scotch' in this fashion, although under his HAVE, HAVING entry, he asserts: 'The *a* has its short open sound as in *hat, hard.* The ill educated among the Londoners, and many of the Scotch, make it long and slender as in *save.* This is to be avoided' (Jones 1992:200). This recommendation to 'avoid' [e] for [a]-type vowel segments is perhaps to be witnessed as well in the evidence provided by Alexander Scot's *The Contrast.* There we find specialised spellings for <habit>, <pairt> and <airt> for '*habit*', '*part*' and '*art*' where <ai> we claimed to be some kind of [ɛ˔] segment (when we might have perhaps expected [e]); also <trad>, <laddy>, <paurent> and <auncient>, again where we might have expected an *English Vowel Shift* produced high mid vowel to surface, showing instead what we interpreted Scot's spelling system to be representing [ɛ˔] and [ɑ]. While we can only speculate as to the reasons why there should be a vowel shift 'failure' in these instances, it may just be connected to the remarks Sylvester Douglas makes so forcibly under his CLEMENCY entry, to the effect theat the 'raised' [e] shape is so saliently a Scots characteristic. Perhaps, we might tentatively suggest, [e] was 'too Scotch' for those (notably Scot) who wished to represent a more propitious type of pronunciation with the effect that there was 'hypercorrection' away from [e] towards lower front vowel outputs in at least some sets of lexical items, a suggestion perhaps given some support too from Adams' Scotch *Lâ-dy, fâ-tal, tâke, wâke* for English *Là-dy, fà-*

tal, tàke and *wàke,* where his <â> seems to represent some kind of [ɔ] segment (1799:152).

But clearly variation existed in the extent to which palatalisation of the pure dialect [a/ɑ] type segments could occur in Scottish English, as can be seen from Sylvester Douglas' description of the Scotch pronunciation of RATHER:

> The Scotch either sound it like the *ea* in *feather, leather,* so as to form a perfect rhyme with those words; and this is the vernacular pronounciation; or they make it like *a* in *rate.*

But in general, Douglas is often uncertain as to the extent of the raising of [a]-type vowels in the Scottish vernacular; commenting on the fact that the pure dialect realisation of the item NAPKIN is a stressed short and open [æ], while the Scotch make it the [ɛ] of the highlighted vowel in <Neptune>, Douglas has nevertheless had to erase from the Signet Library version (f 234) his intuition that the 'Scotch pronounce it as in *nape, cape, rape,* but short' - some kind of [e] vowel. On the whole, the Scotch [ee]/[e] for the pure [æ]/[ɑ] is viewed by Douglas as either a hypercorrection or simply 'Scotch' without judgmental comment.

5

LABIAL VOWEL SEGMENTS

5.1 Descriptive Techniques

Once again we can rely upon a wide range of observers and sources for the various manifestations of the [ʊ]-type, labial monophthong in the phonology of both the pure and Scotch dialects of the late 18th century. Commentaries are often detailed and revealing, yet it has to be admitted that in some respects they are also tantalizingly complex and often difficult to interpret with any degree of precision. Almost every observer recognises some kind of three fold division in this phonetic segment, two of them monophthongal, a third diphthongal; there appears to be a general recognition of the existence of of what at the moment we might characterise as the segments [ʊ], [ʌ] and [jʊ], although - as we shall see - it is possible to add considerable phonetic detail to these crude realisations. Typical of labial vowel characterisation is Barrie (1794:v) who lists as labial types *do*^{3}, *bu*^{3}*sh*, *cu*^{1}*be*, *do*^{4}*ne*, *few*^{2}, and Perry (1777) who distinguishes *u duke*, *u*^{2} *buck*, *û/w bush*, *w̄ new*, *ò book*, *ô prove*, *ó done*, while Drummond (1777:20) describes *u* sounds as :

> his first sound in *music*
> his second sound in *murder*
> his third sound in *figure*
> his fourth sound in *bush*

with the diphthong in the first syllable of *music* categorised as 'a transition from *e*^{1} to *w*'. However, this is supplemented with some contextual detail (1777:24):

> *U* - sound his third sound, always in the last syllable of words ending in *re*, if the accent falls not on him; - his fourth is used sometimes for the first, as easier to the organs, particularly after *r*. - It is often used before *l*, *sh*, &c. But this sound is so arbitrary and irregular, that we have placed it last in order; and dare not be positive in our rules, concerning a sound best learned by practice. - He sounds *i*^{2} in the Saxon *busy*, and *e*^{2} in *bury* with their compounds. In these, custom has got the better of analogy.

Descriptions of the [ʊ] type segment are mainly orthographically based, commentators utilising <oo>, <w>, <ŭ>, <ô>, <ò>, <ou> and <ow> representations among several others for this class of sound. Only occasionally do we find descriptions such as *Italian u* or *French ou*, and only Buchanan uses terms like *acute* and *clear* and even *fat u* (1757:11) for this labial. [ʌ]- type vowels are mainly described as *short*, but (in typically flamboyant fashion) Adams characterises them as *a* clear, *u* rough, common Flemish, coarse Flemish, hard *u*. On the whole, however, orthographic and diacritic descriptions are used, in particular <u^{2}>, <o>, <ó>, <ò>, <ō> and <ŭ>. On the other hand, [jʊ] diphthongs are almost everywhere characterised as '*u* long' and orthographically through <eu>, <ew>, <yu>, <ui>, <û>, <ū> and <ù>. However, some observers, notably in *A Spelling-Book Upon a New Plan* use the description '*u* long' for segments which may not be diphthongal at all, but more appropriately described through <oo> or <u>. Once more Adams (1799:38-39) has an idiosyncratic description:

> *U*, No. 1. *yu*, no English word terminates in *u*: we find its sound in the word *use*. Mr Sheridan seems to carry to affectation the mixture of the *i* and *ou*, in *Duke*, *diouk*, &c. No. 2. as *u* before the combination with the final consonant loses the twang of *iu*, so the long *u* often seems to lose it: no one ever sounded *us* by *ious*, *give oius this day* &c., so *true*, *blue*, &c. lose that twang.

The commentators who provide the most detailed phonetic descriptions of labial segments - Alexander Geddes and Sylvester Douglas - reinforce the interpretation of a tripartite division between the labial sounds in their phonetic inventory. Geddes uses three principal graphs to differentiate what appear to be separate pure labial and near pure labial sounds. Their description occurs mainly in the *Table* and his *Observations* upon the same (1792: 431-438) and can be summarised as follows:

> 1. <ù> graph: '*oo*, or *u*, Italian; This is the genuine sound of *u*. How we came to express it by *oo*, it is not easily conceived. The Scottish combination *ou* was much nearer the sound.'
> 2. <u> graph: '*u* short, as in *shut*. This short sound of *u* is peculiar I think to the Scots and English.'
> 3. <û> graph: '*u* English, as in *pure*; This is really a compound of *e* and *u*. It is, however, to be observed, that it is not sounded exactly in the same manner by the Scots and English. In the mouths of the latter it seems to be composed of *i* and *eù*; while the former pronounce it more like the French *u* or *eu*, in the word *peur*.'

Yet, Alexander Scot's orthographic method appears to distinguish only two types of labial vowel <u>, [ʊ] and <oo>, [ʏ] (Jones 1993:112-13) although there may be special sociophonetic reasons for this, as we shall discuss below. Perhaps needless to say, it is Sylvester Douglas who provides the most extensive discussion of the nature of this vowel sound, its spelling shapes as well as the idiosyncracies of the details of its pronunciation in regional and social contexts in his *Observations on the Alphabet* (Jones:1992:138-140), while there is also to be found explicit and sometimes contradictory information under individual lexical items in his *Table of Words*, notably under the entries for ABOVE, BURIAL, FILL, FULL, MOURN, FORTH and PULL. The discussion presented in the *Observations on the Alphabet* suggests that in the pure dialect three distinctive varieties of labial-type monophthong could be distinguished at this period. The first of these Douglas describes as a *simple vocal* variety, a sound characterised by whatever is intended by the orthographic marks <u> and <ou> in Italian and French respectively. Items specifically associated with this sound (possibly the labial [ʊ]) in the pure dialect are cited as: <prove>, <tomb>, <two>, <pulpit>, <pull>, <full>, <stool>, <good>, <brood>, <move> (Whitehall and Fein:1941).

Under the second labial type Douglas, in fact, describes what are two separate vowel qualities used in the pure dialect: the one, a *smothered vocal*, characteristic of what seems to be a deliberately small lexical set made up of <Tully>, <scut> and <rut>. The other, in terminology typical of Douglas, is depicted as 'another shade of the former', and is apparently peculiar to items such as <flood>, <blood>, <love>, <dove>, <glove>, <come>, <couplet>, <punt>, <hulk>, <rump>, <dub> and <mud>. This labial (sub) type, Douglas is at pains to emphasise, 'approaches nearer to the first' (i.e. to the *simple vocal* [ʊ]) (Jones:1992:138). Walker (1791:21:§165) notes too that the vowel in such items is associated with a segment which is more, rather than less, labial:

> The fourth sound of this vowel [*o*:CJ] is that which is found in *love, dove,* &c. and the long sound which seems the nearest relation to it, is the first sound of the *o* in *note, tone, rove,* &c.

If we are to give any significance to the numerical size of the sets of lexical items said by Douglas to manifest each labial vowel type, then we might conclude that the first and third are the commonest in the pure dialect, while the second (the *smothered vocal*) is constrained to occur with an extremely restricted lexical set. At the same time, if it is indeed the case that the other two types are perceived as being close to each other in the vowel space, i.e. both are relatively 'pure' in their labiality signature, then as a first approximation we might suggest that the most common labial sounds in the standard dialect in Douglas' time were (1) [ʊ] and (2) [ɤ] or perhaps, as we shall suggest below, [ɷ] or [ɵ]. The third, *smothered*, sound (the *Tully, scut,* and *rut* type) might well be interpreted as a more central and sonorant [ʌ] or [ə] shape, but these possibilities too we shall investigate in more detail as we proceed.

5.2 Labial Vowel Types: The [ʊ]Vowel and its Variants

Compared with the remarks of say Elphinston and Walker, Sylvester Douglas presents us with what is a rather unusual interpretation of the manifestations of the pure labial vowel in the standard English dialect. Like them, he sees what is essentially a length differential in the vowel space in items like <full> and <fool>, a distinction he sets out in some detail under the entry for PULL :

> The *u* as in *full, bull*. The *u* in *pull*, and *full* has the same sound, in quality with that of the *oo* in *pool*, and *fool*, and they are one long syllable. Yet every body perceives, that *fool* and *full*, and *pool* and *pull*, are not, to the ear, the same words. They differ in two respects. First, the vocal part in *pull*, and *full* is short; in *pool*, and *fool*, long. Secondly, *pull* and *full* are long syllables by means of a protracted stress of the voice on *ll;* which does not take place in the pronounciation of *pool*, and *fool*.

Again, under the entry for FULL, we find that 'the *u* has its distinct vocal sound like *oo* in *foot, fool*', added to which in Douglas' own hand is the insertion 'but shorter' (Jones 1992:198). Elphinston distinguishes just such a long/short distinction for a similar set of lexical items, those with [ʊʊ] (his *o depressive open*) including <fool>, <soup>, <lose>, <move>, <prove>, <whom> and <two>; those in [ʊ] (his *o depressive shut*) embracing <book>, <put>, <cushion>, <full>, <put>, <book>, <good>, <wood>, <could>, <should> (Rohlfing 1984: 372). Walker (1791:22-3) too sees a distinction like this, although for him there appears to be a qualitative difference as well. Long [ʊʊ] items are, he claims, rare in the lexical inventory, restricted to <prove>, <pool>, <move>, <lose>, <do>, <who>, <whom>, <wood>, <tomb>. In contrast, items like <bull>, <full>, <pull> are on the one hand like the [ʊ] in words like <tube> and <cube>, minus their glide initial [j] component, but not so long as the <oo> in <pool>. At first sight this would suggest some kind of [ʊ] segment, but Walker goes on to state that the vowel in the <bull>, <full> items is an 'obscure' sound, a 'middle sound' between the [ʊʊ] of <pool> and what we shall for the moment see as the [ʌ] in <dull>. Such a segment might be interpreted as [ɷ] or [ɤ]. Kendrick (1784:55-60) seems to recognise three labial vowel types, a long *ou, oo, o*, in items like *soup, noon, who, boot, fool, food*; a short *o* in *stood, wood, wool, bull, could* and *good*; and an 'indistinct' sound (perhaps [ʌ] or [ə]) in *cur, blood* and *scourge*: 'The short *u* ...as in *bull, could, good*...is not of the same quality as the former number [[ʌ]-type vowels in *cur, blood*:CJ]: *bull* and *trull, could* and *cud, good* and *blood*, being no rimes in London; where they have a very different and distinct quality of sound. I have said that this is only a contraction of the former long sound.' He goes on to tell us, however, that the Irish, the inhabitants of Yorkshire and 'many provincials' frequently substitute the 'indistinct' sound for the short sound [ʊ] in the items *blood, rut* and *rush*. On the other hand, Sheridan (1781: 26, 49) appears to see only a [u]/[ʌ] contrast in this area of the phonology: 'This vowel (*U*) has always its first sound as in the words *lull, pluck, hurl* &c; except in the following words, where it has the sound of u²; *bull, full, pull, bush, push.*' Nares (1784:75-77) differentiates [ɯ]/[ʊ], the former in *cool, moon, doom,* the latter in *good, hood, wood, stood, foot, book, cook, bull, bullet, full, pull, bush, cushion, push, pulpit* and *put.* He also admits of a *u* short (1781:35ff) which 'has an obscurer sound' and is characteristic of *but, number, ultimate, blood, flood* and *foot.*

The Scot Buchanan (1757:8-11) seems only to differentiate some kind of [ʊ] sound in items like *move, prove, do, who, womb, tomb* (with no indication as to length differential) and what he calls a 'short or obscure' *u* sound (possibly [ʌ] or [ə]] in a long list of items which includes *but, cut, gun, rub, come, some, conjure, conduit, Monday, honey.* In the light of the variety and complexity of description associated with the labial vowel segment, it is not surprising to read Walker (1791:173) caution us about the difficulties of interpreting the vowel space in the <bull>, <full> items which is: 'sufficient to puzzle Englishmen who reside at any distance from the capital, and to make the inhabitants of Scotland and Ireland, (who, it is highly probable, received a much more regular pronunciation from our ancestors) not infrequently the jest of fools'.

5.3 Length Contrasts

Among the most salient features of vernacular Scottish English recorded by 18th century observers is the failure in that dialect then, as now (Wells 1982:401-402), to realise length differentials in <full>~<fool> type contrasts. Walker (1791:xi) comments under his *Rules to be observed by the Natives of Scotland for attaining a just Pronounciation of English*: 'In addition to what has been said, it may be observed, that *oo* in *food, mood, moon, soon,* &c. which ought always to have a long sound, is generally shortened in Scotland to that middle sound of the *u* in *bull;* and it must be remembered, that *wool, wood, good, hood, stood, foot,* are the only words where this sound of *oo* ought to take place.' It is worth recalling that the Scot Drummond (1767:21) points to what he sees as one of the major observational deficiencies of his countrymen: 'The sound of every vowel may be made long or short, either by continuing to emit the breath for a longer or shorter time, presenting the articulation of the vowel unchanged; or we may change the articulation, while the breath continues to pass; and this change may be sooner or later. But to ascertain the time of pronouncing them is the greatest difficulty to the Scots, in the English tongue'. Sylvester Douglas records the following items with stresses [ɯ]~[ʊ] contrasts in the pure dialect: showing [ɯ] are: <fool>; <foot>; <pool>; <boot>, while with [ʊ] he has <full>; <bull>; <pull>; <put> and <pulpit>, claiming that all these lexical items are characterised as showing a short, 'unsustained' [ɣ] or [ʌ] in the Scottish vernacular.

Angus (1800:7) notes that <û>, <ŭ> and <w> 'are similar in Quality but different in Quantity' appearing to suggest some kind of [ʊ]/[ɯ] contrast; likewise Perry (1777:ix) when he observes that those vowel sounds his system marks *without diacritics* 'are to be uttered quicker, that is, they are the long sounds of *a, e, o* &c contracted, and are in the same proportion to each other, as *gòod* is to *fŏod* or *hòok,* to *rŏok,* which have the same *quality* of sound, but differ in *quantity* or *length* of time.' Adams (1799:76) too appears to suggest a length contrast under his discussion of the 'false diphthong' <oo>:

> *oo,* No,1. *oo* French - *food, fool, moon, ooze,* &c. No. 2. *oo* is a little shorter before *d* and *l,* formerly doubled in the words - *good, hood, stood, wood, wool*: and before *k,* - *book, cook, rook,*

Buchanan's observations (1762:13) on length are sparse indeed, restricted to comments to the effect that while the <oo> in items such as <hood>, <fool>, <food> is 'like German *u*....when a short quantity is over it, thus *oŏ*, it must be rapidly pronounced', marking as short the respelled items *bull* (boŏl), *bush* (boŏsh), *pull* (poŏl) and *full* (foŏl). William Scott (1796:vi footnote) lists under his vowel 13 items such as *full, bull, bush, push, food, full,* while 'in *hood, good, wood, stood, wool* the vowel sound is quite short'. These observations are not unlike those provided by contemporary English writers such as Kenrick (1784:58) who observes: 'The sound at present in question [the *long ou, oo, o*:CJ] is generally expressed in English writing by the double *oo,* as in *boot, fool, food,* where it is long, and also in *stood, wood, wool,* where it is short'.

The situation as regards labial vowels as represented by James Douglas (Holmberg 1956:185-92:214-215) is a complex and somewhat idiosyncratically expressed one. While he argues for the existence of 'The Vowel *U* Sounded Long like its Common Name which may be call'd the true English *ū*, as *union, curious*', that is, some type of [jʊ] diphthong, he also argues that it has a value 'sounded like its Common Name but Short, as *calcŭlate, corpŭlent*', suggesting a [jʊʊ]/[jʊ] contrast, an interpretation supported by Holmberg (1956:77-78). However, we shall discuss this interpretation in more detail below. James Douglas also identifies a *short obscure lingual u,* his *Scotch u,* exemplified by items such as <udder>, <urge>. He claims too to see a distinction in items with <oo> vowel spellings, where the vowel is like *u* short, 'but broader', thus <book>, <crook>, <cook>, <foot>. Again, he records another labial vowel output which is 'intermediate between Scotch *u* and short English *u*' (Holmberg's [jʊ]) or is 'a mixed sound between the English and Scotch *u* short', as in the items <bull>, <bush>, <full>, <pull>, <puss>, <bullet>, <bully>, etc., where the <u> graph is marked as <ŭ>. A segment composed of a 'mixture' of [jʊ] and his vowel in <up> is difficult to imagine, and must cast doubt on the interpretation of *u* short as a diphthongal element. That the <bull>, <bush> vowels are meant to contain some kind of [ʊ] vowel is suggested (not merely by their subsequent historical development and the comments of other contemporary observers) by the fact that James Douglas also records a *u* long, represented by the <oo> digraph, in items such as <canoo>, <cuckoo>, <shoo>, <too>, <boot>, <broom>, where (despite the terminology usually reserved for diphthongal elements) Douglas appears to intend some kind of durationally extended [ʊʊ]. Beattie (1788:28:footnote) claims that the vowels in *Bull, Wolf* and *Push* and those in *Pool* and *Troop* are 'the same in the sound, and different only in the quantity; the former short, and the latter long'.

Yet Sylvester Douglas typically paints a more complex picture, seeing some relationship between the lack of durational extension of the vowel in <full>, <pull> as in some way connected to 'syllable length', manifested by 'protracted stress of the voice on the *ll*'. Consider his entries for PULL and PULLY (Jones:1992:217)

> PULL
> The *u* as in *full, bull* (vide supra) The *u* in *pull,* and *full* has the same sound, in quality with that of the *oo,* in *pool,* and *fool,* and they are all four long syllables. Yet every body perceives, that *fool* and *full,* and *pool* and *pull,* are not, to the ear, the same words. They differ in two respects. First, the vocal part in *pull,* and *full,* is short; in *pool,* and *fool,* long. Secondly, *pull* and *full* are long syllables by means of a protracted stress of the voice on the *ll*; which does not take place in the pronounciation of *pool,* and *fool.*
>
> PULLY (One of the mechanical powers)
> Here the *u* is to be sounded both in quality, and quantity as in *pull, full.* But this word does not rhyme exactly to *fully.* In *fully* the same stress is laid on the *ll,* as in *full,* and accordingly the first syllable is long; in *pully* there is no such stress laid on the double liquid. The voice hurries over the *ll* and the first syllable is short. *Bully* rhymes exactly to *pully.*

while again in *Of the Provincial Accentuation* (ff. 41-2), he claims:

> Let any one compare the three following words *foolish, fully* and *pully.* In each the accent is upon the first syllable and that syllable in each (as it seems to me and to others whom I have consulted) to be always, and necessarily uttered in a somewhat sharper tone than the other. But in *foolish* and *fully* the accented syllable is long, in *pully* short. Again in *foolish* the length of the accented syllable arises from our protracting the vocal part, in *fully* we hasten over the *u* and rest upon and protract the *ll* which being a liquid is capable of being lengthened, but in *pully,* no such stress is laid on the *ll* nor is there any difference between the manner of sounding this consonantal termination of the syllable single *l* in *foolish...*

Douglas appears to argue that while there is a long/short difference in the pure dialect in items like [pʊʊ l] <pool> versus [pʊl] <pull>, that contrast is not simply one of stressed vowel duration: items such as <full> and <pully>, while they have short vocalic segments nevertheless manifest, he argues, long syllable characteristics, realised through the temporal extension of the highly sonorant labial coda (although - as we shall see below - there is some evidence that this characteristic is, in fact, a Scotticism). Thus in his eyes, the phonetic contrast between <full> and <fool> is one of [fʊ ll]~[fʊʊ l]. Indeed, Douglas claims to observe a rather complex situation where, with morphological accretion, we can find variants such as:

Morphologically Complex

Long Accented Syllable	
<full>	[fʊll]
<fully>	[fʊllɩ]
<fool>	[fʊʊl]
<foolish>	[fʊʊlɩʃ]
<pull>	[pu ll]
<fool>	[fʊʊl]

Morphologically Simple

Short Accented Syllable	
<bull>	[bʊ l]
<bully>	[bʊlɩ]
<pully>	[pʊlɩ]

These data raise a number of interesting points. As Kohler (1966:39) observes, the long versus short accented syllable dichotomy in disyllabic items is a function of the productive versus the non-productive morphological status of the unstressed syllable; the <fully> and <foolish> cases with their meaningful accretions correlate with long accented syllables, while items like <pully> and <bully> - showing no productive morphological relationship with <pull> and <bull> - are associated with the short accented syllable. Such a relationship is apparently observed too by Elphinston (Rohlfing 1984:144):

> Dhe shut vowel keeps distinct from dhe open, by shortnes and shutting: *fool* (filled) *foolling*, from *fool* (unwize) *fooling*; *foollish* from *foolish*, and dhe like.' (1790:49)

> Dhis *oo* shut and short, must questionles, hware possibel, appear so. Sense wil secure dhe short *pool* and *fool* from dhe long; *poolling* and *foolling*, like *pootting* and *footting*, wil secure dhemselves. (1786:236)

But what is perhaps more interesting is Sylvester Douglas' observation that there are, as it were, two stratagems where long accented syllable status can be achieved, especially in those items terminated by 'liquid' consonants like [l] ('*oo* is always long before a liquid:' Elphinston *The Principles of the English Language* 1765:70). Both 'stratagems' involve an increase in vocalic weight (periodicity) in the peak or post peak area of the syllable. In the one case, the peak or central syllabic element shows its vowel with durational increase, thus [pʊʊ l] <pool>, [fʊʊ l] <fool>. In the other, the vocalic increase is arrived at (perhaps in a 'weaker' fashion) by the highlighting of the sonorant coda with its durational increase - [fʊ ll]. Both stratagems result in a more periodic rhyme component in the syllable.

Kenrick's (1781:95-6) observations on the duration of consonantal segments (under his *Rules to be observed in sounding the Consonants*) are worth recalling here: 'None of them are to be prolonged except when the accent is upon them; which can only happen when they are preceded by a short sounding vowel: as *tell, can, love.* When a long sound precedes, the voice must dwell upon the vowel, and take the consonant into the syllable in its shortest sound; otherwise, were they both dwelt upon, the syllable would take up the time of two long sounds, and would therefore seem to be two: as *vā-le, raī-n, brā-ve, dāy-s.* This is an article very necessary to be attended to by the natives of Scotland, who are apt to prolong the sound of a semivowel after a long vowel. On the other hand, the people of England are to be cautioned against running the sound of the vowel too quickly into the following consonant, which is too generally the practice, to the great diminution of the number of our long syllables.'

Yet we might speculate that Sylvester Douglas' observations concerning syllable length may bear some relation to what he sees as vocalic length proper. We might just suggest that contrasts such as [pʊʊl]/[fʊʊl] versus [fʊll]/[fʊllɩ] versus [bʊl]/[bʊlɩ] have something to tell us about relative stressed vowel length, such that (metaphorically);

[pʊʊl] represents full vowel length
[pʊll] represents relatively full vowel length
[bʊl] represents relatively short vowel length

The <pool>/<pull> length contrast is based, of course, on the etymological history of the items themselves, stemming as they do from [oo] and [u] sources (Luick 1921:§281); but if it is the case that some items showing historically short vowel origins were coming to be merged with those with a long vowel ancestry, and where that merger was incomplete, then a form such as [fʊll] <full> as an 'approximation' to [fʊʊ l] might result. Certainly, it would appear from Douglas' evidence, that lexical diffusion was prevalent in the pure dialect in this area of the phonology: some historically short vowel items like <full> being merged (perhaps only partially) with <fool> types, others like <bull> retaining their short vowel characteristic.

5.4 The [ʌ] Vowel and its Variants

The evidence from the vast majority of the kinds of commentator we are discussing in this book would suggest that there existed in English and Scots some kind of *short u* variety of sound, exemplified in items such as <run>, <cut>, <us>, <buck>, <done>, pointing to its interpretation as a segment like [ʌ]. Most of our observers make no comment on this *u* sound other than to say that it is short and whatever is meant by Angus' *shut* with little or nothing in the way of phonetic or contextual detail. Otherwise, observations are not particularly enlightening : '*u* short, as in *shut*. This short sound of *u* is peculiar I think to the Scots and English' (Geddes 1792:437). Yet, when detailed comment does exist, and there are at least two sources which provide considerable amounts of it, it is often difficult to interpret and sometimes contradictory. What it does appear to suggest, however, is that there is certainly more than one phonetic value both in the standard and Scots versions of English in the late 18th century. Buchanan (1777:8) , for instance, confidently assures us that 'The short sounds of (o) [his [ɔ]/[ɒ]:CJ] and (u) are pretty similar; as *ŭnder, ŭnto*: *ŏnder, ŏnto*; and are so quick and obscure, as to make no motions in the parts of the mouth,' while in the *British Grammar* (1762:13) he tells us that the short sound of *u* 'is very like short (o), only a little more guttural...expressed in *Bŭt, cŭt, gŭn, rŭb, sŭp, drŭb*'. Cortez Telfair (1775:151:footnote) describing the pronunciation of 'the best speakers in London' asserts that his 'second short *o* is the same with *ou* in *double*; and is a sound approaching very near to the first short one' where the first short is exemplified by *box;* it is interesting to note too how Telfair lists under '*U* in *Nun*' items like *cough* and *Knowledge*. Dun too asserts, under his *o* discussion, that the sound 'is sometimes sounded *almost* [italics: CJ] as a short *u*, as in *Dove, love, dost*...pronounced *Duve, luve, dust*', where his short *u* is exemplified in the item *Cur*. James Robertson's (1772:41ff) 'pronounced alike' lists include as 'similarly pronounced' the items <Hot> '*with heat*' and <Hut> '*a little house*'. John Drummond's assertion (1722:29) that 'o^1 [his [o]:CJ] in some words must be pronounced 'nearly as quick as *u* in *run*' might point to the fact that his high mid vowels were, in fact, somewhat and Scottishly lowered to a value nearer [ɔ] (see pp 168-172 below). However, spellings like the following from such a careful observer as Alexander Scot (Jones:1993:113) suggest that we are dealing in this area of the phonetics with a rather complex problem: <shud> '*should*'; <wood> '*would*'; <boot> '*but*'; <rabook> '*rebuke*'. James Douglas recognises a *short obscure lingual u* in items such as <urn>, <us>, a segment he specifically labels the '*Scotch u*' (Holmberg:1956:185-86): 'It is sounded Short, Obscure & Lingual like the Sound of *ŏo* Short which may be call'd the Scotch *U*, as *ŭlcer, ŭnkind. What are the*

Improper Sounds of the Vowel U? 1. It has a kind of intermediate sound between the Scotch *U* & the Short English *U*, as , *bŭll, pŭll.*' Holmberg (1956:80) concludes that 'It is true that [ʌ] seems to have been dominant early in Scotland, but still this 'name' is not of decisive importance'. James Douglas' <ŏo> short is equated with his *ŭ* short and exemplified by items like <blood>, <flood>, <forsooth> and <soot>, while items like <book>, <crook>, <wool> and <stool> - which we might associate with a durationally extended [ʊʊ] - are described as 'like *U* short...tho' something Broader than the Foregoing [*blood, bloody, flood, forsooth, soot*:CJ] (Holmberg:1956:214-15). It is, of course, extremely difficult to ascribe a definite phonetic value to a term like 'broader' in this context, but at the very least we might conclude that James Douglas hears the vocalic segment in items like <blood>, <flood> <up> <udder> on a scale somewhere between a low unrounded and central [ʌ] and a rounded close back [ʊ] - perhaps a segment like [ɤ] or [ɷ]/[ɵ].

It is when we turn to the evidence provided by Sylvester Douglas that we see the variation in this area of the contemporary phonetics in the greatest detail. We have already observed how Sylvester Douglas identifies 'smothered' (and sometimes 'obscure') labial vowels exemplified in items like <rut>, <dub>, <love>, <luck> and many others. However, he is careful to provide both lexical and phonetically contextualised information which he sees as distinguishing at least two sub types of this *smothered u* vowel type. We must, of course, always bear in mind the fact that Sylvester Douglas' use of descriptive terminology is rarely completely consistent; indeed, the number of items described as showing a 'smothered' or even 'obscure' *u* in the pronouncing dictionary proper (his *Table of Words Improperly pronounced by the Scotch, showing their True English Pronunciation* (Jones: 1992:158ff)) is extremely small; likewise (as we have already indicated) the specific lexical items proposed in the *Observations on the Alphabet* section as showing this vowel shape are confined to <Tully>, <scut> and <rut>. It is most difficult to ascribe any precise phonetic value to this 'smothered vocal' labial, mainly as a result of the problems which arise from the uncertainties involved in the interpretation of what Douglas means by the term 'smothered' and 'obscure' with which he sometimes appears to equate it. He uses this terminology in a variety of contexts: for instance, the Scotch pronunciation of the second syllable in <Sunday> is described as showing an 'obscure *a*' (Jones:1992:226); unaccented syllables 'are always pronounced in an obscure, indistinct manner, so as to be scarcely distinguishable' (Jones:1992:140); there is a version of an *e* sound 'which has a sort of obscure and smothered sound not unlike that of the French *e* in *le, ce, que*' (Jones:1992:123); the obscure *j* or *y* in the pure dialect pronunciation of <calf> ([kjæ(l)f]:CJ) is said to be a 'smothered sort of *y*' (Jones 1992: 180). Under his FILL entry too we are invited to contrast an 'obscure *u*' in the pure dialect in items like <luck>, <skull>, <bur>,

<but>, <buss>, <sup>, <scum> and <bun> with the 'hollowness' characteristic of the *u* sound in <tug>, <bud>, <tub>, <buzz>. Scottish speakers are said to substitute this obscure *u* for the palatal [ɩ] in items like <fill> and <will> and Southern English speakers, conscious of the salientness of this Scottish characteristic, mimic it by producing the obscure *u* or obscure *a* in expressions like '*What's your wull*' for '*What's your will*' (Jones:1992:194). And we might recall here Robertson's (1722) 'near alikes' such as *Bill*, *Bell* and *Bull*.

While none of this points to any unambiguous or obvious value for Douglas' 'smothered vocal' *u* sound, his tendency to equate it with some kind of highly sonorant [ɑ], the suggestion that it has a 'more hollow' version and (less obviously, perhaps) its likeness to the French unstressed vowel in <le>, <ce>, may indicate a vowel with a low F_2 feature, one which is rather sonorant and perhaps even central: obvious candidates would be [ʌ] or [ə] with the more 'hollow' version in the not quite fully open, central unrounded [ɐ] vowel (Holmberg:1956:78-83). Sylvester Douglas also identifies what he describes as 'another shade' of the smothered *u* vowel. From the number of lexical items Douglas associates with this labial, it would appear to be for him the most common type in this area of the vowel space in the pure dialect. The only clue we have to the phonetics of this segment is Douglas' statement in his *Observations on the Alphabet* to the effect that it 'approaches nearer to the first [sound of *u*:CJ] in such words as *punt, hulk, rump, dub, mud*' (Jones:1992:139). If our observation is correct that the first vocal *u* represents a relatively pure labial [ʊ] sound, while the 'smothered' *u* is a relatively sonorant [ʌ] or [ə], then a *u* type vowel 'approaching nearer' the pure labial than the latter, perhaps suggests a segment mixed for both sonority and labiality with the latter predominating; perhaps some kind of [ɤ] (a back upper mid unrounded vowel) or [ɯ] (high back unrounded) vowel space - corresponding to James Douglas' 'Broader' version of *u* short in <blood>, <bloody>. And it is interesting to note that Sylvester Douglas specifically mentions that 'in the North of England' <oo> is always heard as this 'second shade' of *u*, in items such as <stood>, <good>, <flood>, <blood> as well as <scull>, <Tully> and <rut>. The difficulty with Douglas' methodology is that he rarely (if ever) distinguishes in the *Table* these two 'shades' of the second sound of *u*, so that it is extremely difficult to decide whether he is referring to [ʌ] or [ɤ] type vowels in those items showing the second *u* vowel. However, it is perhaps reasonable to interpret all his references to the second sound of *u* (unless they are actually accompanied by terms like 'obscure', 'smothered' or 'hollow') as if they are the latter, a stance also prompted by the small lexical set accorded the smothered type in Douglas' *Observations on the Alphabet* section.

We have already suggested that these two 'shades' of the *smothered u* are also in Douglas' mind in his discussion under his important FILL entry (Jones:1992:193):

> But this I believe is owing to a property common to all the softer semivowels and mutes (viz. this soft *s*, the *v*, the soft *th*, the *b*, the *d* and the *g*) by which they reflect back, as it were, a sort of hollowness on a preceding obscure and short vowel. What I mean will be manifest by attending successively to the sound of the obscure *u* first in *luck, skull, bur, but, buss, sup, scum, bun*; and then in *tug, bud, tub, buzz.*

Just how 'manifest' the distinction is a matter for some reflection, but in the context in which Douglas is writing, namely where he is describing the salient Scotch [ɩ]/[ɛ̈] variable (see pp 109-110 above), it might just be possible to interpret his comments as suggesting a more centralised and sonorant segment to be present in pre voiced obstruent and non-sonorant continuant contexts.

The problem is typically seen under the ABOVE entry (Jones:1992:159) where the *o* 'has the second or short sound of *u*' (Douglas introducing a new *short* descriptive term for the first time with this item) characteristic of words like <love>, <dove>, <glove> and contrasted against a long version in <groove>. Some of these are realised by Scottish speakers with [ʊ], others with [oo], again just perhaps suggesting a pure dialect [ɤ]/[ɷ] rather than a more sonorant [ʌ], [ə] or [ɐ}. Such a description of a labial vowel with three main phonetic manifestations ([ʊ]/[ʌ]/[ɤ]) as observed by Douglas perhaps adds some support to Luick's (1921: 529-30) view that the original Middle English [u] vowel developed between the late 16th and early 18th centuries into a slightly unrounded [o] sound, before becoming completely unrounded to [ʌ], a view it seems accepted by Wells (1982:197):

> The split of the old short /u/ into two distinct qualities seems to have been established by the middle of the 17th century. It may well have originated as an allophonic alternation, with unrounded [ɤ], the forerunner of the modern /ʌ/, in most environments, but a rounded quality (modern /ʊ/), retained after labials.

If Douglas' observation of a triple development for Middle English [u] is a correct and accurate one, the existence of some 'intermediate' [ɤ] stage is attested by him at a date later than most other observers.

5.5 The [jʊ] Diphthong or 'Long *u*'

Most handbooks suggest that the modern British English standard [ju] complex mainly derives from two historical sources: the [iu] diphthong and the [uu] vowel; in both instances it appears that some kind of syllabicity shifting has occurred, making the 'right hand side' vowel the more prominent and, in consequence, bringing about a vowel level reduction in the 'left hand' half of the vowel space to some kind of semivocalic (energy reduced) [j] segment (Jones 1989:180-2). Many of the commentators writing in Scotland in the 18th century attempt, with varying degrees of success, to provide phonetic descriptions for this diphthong, Sylvester Douglas' being perhaps the most attractive to the modern phonetician, in its attempt to capture his intuitions concerning the relative prominence between the vocalic items which go to make up the complex vowel space, as well as pointing to the fact that the highlighting of one element brings about a concomitant reduction in vowel-ness in the other (Jones:1992:139):

> The third sound of *u*, and that from which it takes its name in England, is diphthongal; consisting of the first sound of the *e* followed by the first of the *u*; but so that the *e* is hurried over, and leaves the *u* to predominate. Of this we have examples in *usage* (which some old authors have written *yeusage*) *curious*, *unity*, *pure*.

Sheridan's (1791:20) definition of the diphthong is very similar : 'To form it properly therefore, a foreigner is to be told that it is composed of the sounds e^3 [[i]:CJ] and o^3 [[ʊ]:CJ], the first sound not completed but rapidly running into the last,' although Walker (1791:22) is less precise: 'The first sound of *u*, heard in *tube*, or ending in an unaccented syllable, as in *cubic*, is a diphthongal sound, as if *e* were prefixed, and these words were spelt *tewbe* and *kewbic*.' Nares (1784:35) observes that: 'This sound certainly is a compounded one; it is the very same as is also expressed by the combination of three letters in the words *you* and *yew*. Yet that this is the regular long sound of the *u* with us is evident, by the manner in which we pronounce the vowel when we mean to name it alone, *u*. Dr Wallis says that this sound is compounded of *i* and *w*; but since, in English, the proper representative of the simple sound of *u* is the reduplication or false diphthong *oo*, I should rather say that it is compounded of *y* and *oo*.' Elphinston (1765:14) is his usual enigmatic self, with 'The diphthongs inverted make *liquefactions*, where *y* and *w* become prepositive, and melt into vocal articulators of the subjunctive vowel. The former thus virtually articulates *oo* in *u*, equal to *you* for *yoo*, as also to *yew* the tree.'

Telfair's 'first long *u* is a sound compounded of first short *i* [as in *in*:CJ] and second long *o* [his *oo* in *doom*:CJ]; and is the same as *ew* in *few*' (1775:152); Barrie (1815:14) represents the item <scripture> as *scrĭp'tȳŭr*. Perhaps emulating Dun's (1766:25) description of these improper diphthongs as 'the united sound of *e* and *u*', the anonymous author of *A Spelling-Book Upon a New Plan* comments upon the diphthong that, in words such as *blew*, *dew*, *mew*, *pew* '*Eu* and *ew* have the united sound of both vowels' (1796:17) - a not very helpful distinction since he lists three different phonetic values for the *e* symbol. However, he goes on to claim that 'The vowel *u*, in the terminations *ure* and *ute*, though marked with a circumflex accent, has not exactly the sound of *ew*: - It sounds rather like *yŭ*, as *creature*, (creatyŭr); *leisure*, (leisyŭr) &c.' (1796:26:footnote), where his <ŭ> symbol, *u* short, is manifested in *adult*, and might represent some kind of centralised [ʌ] segment and is perhaps the product of a process of pre-[r] lowering and centring.

James Douglas' comments on this segment are not always straightforwardly interpretable either. He distinguishes a 'Vowel *U*' which 'is sounded Long like its Common Name which may be called the true English *ū*, as *ūnion, cūrious* '(Holmberg:1956:185) - although he also describes a sound called *u* Long to be found in items like *boot, broom, brood, cuckoo, shoo* (Holmberg:1956:214). Nevertheless, it would seem clear that the stressed vowel in *union* is some kind of [ju] segment. However James Douglas describes a 'Vowel *U*..sounded short like its Common Name' in items such as *absolŭtion, constitŭtion, infŭsion, exclŭsion, altitŭde, amplitŭde, creatŭre, natŭre, pictŭre* (Holmberg:1956:189-190), a segment Holmberg interprets as [ju] contrasting with the [juu] of the Long Vowel *U* (1956:76-77). Indeed, some justification for the recognition of a length distinction in this diphthong might be produced from Sylvester Douglas EXCUSE entry: 'The *u* has its diphthongal sound, but is short, and the *s* hard [voiceless:CJ]. So that this word rhymes to *use* a noun, or *Bruce, spruce, truce*' (Jones:1992:192). But the general voiceless nature of the 'short' diphthongal terminations would argue against perceived vowel length at the syllable peak. We shall return to this matter below and investigate the possibility that the short diphthongal [ju] may indeed be some kind of fronted labial like [ü].

5.6 Scottish and other Regional and Social Variants : Centralised and Lowered Alternants to [ʊ]/[ɣ]

Perhaps the most commonly commented upon Scotticism in this area of the phonology is the tendency of Scots speakers to alternate an [ʌ] or [ɣ] type segment for a 'pure' or standard English [ʊ]. Kenrick (1784:56) discussing the 'indistinct' vowel in items like *blood* and *cur* comments that 'it is further observable of this sound, that the people of Ireland, Yorkshire and many other provincials mistake its use; applying it to words which in London are pronounced with the *u* full, as in No. 17 [his 'short *u*, as in *búll, coúld, góod*':CJ] ....as *bull, wool, put, push*: all which they pronounce as the inhabitants of the Metropolis do, *trull, blood, rut, rush*'. Yet Buchanan (1762:15:footnote) observes 'Fat (u) [probably [ʊ] :CJ] is scarcely used now by the English, its sound being expressed by (oo); yet it is in use among the Scots, who pronounce *unrighteous, understood, university*; thus, *oonrighteous, oonderstood, ooniversity*'.

Sylvester Douglas' ABOVE entry perhaps gives us the greatest insight into the contemporary situation regarding polite Scotch usage for labial-type vowel space. Under this entry Douglas (Jones 1992:159) says that Scottish speakers generally 'confound' vowel sounds like [ɣ], [ʊ] and he takes pains to provide detailed exemplification of pure and Scotch vernacular practise. The entry is worth citing in full:

> The *o* has the second or short sound of *u*, exactly as in *rub, sunk*. The Scotch are very often apt to sound it like the long vocal *u* or *oo*; so as to make *above*, rhyme to *groove*. There are a considerable number of words of this termination, and they are pronounced in three different ways. Some of them in the manner we have just described. In some, as *strove, rove, grove*, the *o* has its long close sound as in *abode*. And in some, as *move, prove*, it is sounded in the manner in which the Scotch pronounce it in *above*. As these 3 sounds are generally confounded in Scotland, so that the words pronounced in England in one way, are, in that country, pronounced in an other, it will be useful to attend to the following lists, where they are arranged according to their true pronounciation. *Love* which they sound properly, and which rhymes to the true pronounciation of *above* will serve as the leading word in the first list. *Move* which rhymes to *groove* in the second. And *Jove* (which is also properly pronounced by the Scotch) in the third.
>
> 1. *Love, above* (pronounced by the Scotch like *move*) *dove* (by the Scotch like *Jove*) *shove*, noun and verb (by the Scotch like *Jove*) *glove, True-love*.
> 2. *Move, amove, approve, behoove, disapprove, improve, prove*, (*remove, reprove*). All often pronounced by the Scotch like *love*.
> 3. *Jove, alcove, cove, clove* (verb and noun,) *drove* (verb and noun,) *grove, hove, rove, strove* verb and noun, *throve, wove*. The following is a perfect rhyme
>
> O! witness earth beneath, and heav'n above;
> For can I hide it? I am sick of love.

The pure dialect, he claims, contains both [ɤ] (his second and - now for the first time - the *short* sound of *u*) and [ʊʊ] (the long vocal) lexically distributed as set out in Table 5.1 below. All those in the second column, Sylvester Douglas claims, the Scottish speaker 'often' realises with an [ɤ] as in the 'target' word <love>, and from the body of the *Table* we can deduce that [ɤ] stressed vowels are a feature of Scots in items like <duck>, <word>, <budge>, <trudge>, <gulph>, <pulp>, <but>, <dub>, <shut>, <hut>, and <cut>. From those in the first column he claims that Scottish speakers produce a long vocal [ʊʊ] in only the items <above> [əbʊʊv] (to rhyme to <groove>), <dove> [dʊʊv] and <shove> [šʊʊv]. This long vocal [ʊʊ] sound Scottish speakers can also use where the pure dialect generally has the long close [oo] sound in what might be the single item <door> (as do 'some few English persons aiming at peculiar propriety' (Jones:1992:188)). The centralising tendency of Scots speakers Douglas records in many places, notably under FOOT where 'The Scotch, Irish, and Northern English, pronounce the *oo* like the *u* in *shut, hut, cut*. It should be pronounced as in *fool*, and so the *oo* is to be sounded in all other words of

TABLE 5.1

Labials in the Pure and Scotch Dialects

PURE DIALECT	
[ʏ]	[ʊʊ]
<love>	<move>
<above>	<amove>
<dove>	<approve>
<shove>	<behove>
<glove>	<disapprove>
	<prove>
	<remove>
	<reprove>
SCOTCH	
[ʊʊ]	[ʏ]

this termination. Some few English people who speak well pronounce it in *soot* as the *u* in *shut*' (Jones:1992:197). Under FULL too we find: 'The *u* has its distinct vocal sound like *oo* in *foot, fool* but shorter. In Scotland and in the North of England it is pronounced as in *dull*' (Jones:1992:198) while we see similar comments under the PULPIT and PULL entries. Indeed, the salientness of the centralised vowel realisation for Scots speakers is highlighted by Douglas in his BUSINESS, BUSY entry where, despite the idiosyncratic [ɪ] stressed vowel realisation so assiduously recorded by almost all 18th century observers, Douglas is careful to point out that although the Scots too 'in their vernacular pronounciation.....sound it nearly in this manner, but they often when they *aim at speaking well* [italics:CJ] give the *u* the sound it has in *guzzle, puzzle*' (Jones 1992:179). The Scotch centralised version of the pure labial is perhaps also reflected in the word lists of James Robertson (1722:41ff) where we find described as 'equal in sound' the following sets: *look/luck*; *pulls/pulse*; *ruff/roof/rough*; *sun/soon*; *sucker/sugar*; *shout/shut/shoot*; *could/cool'd/cud*; *cruse/cruise/crush* and *dove* (a pidgeon)/*do* (to act).

5.7 The [jʊ] Diphthong and the French *u*

The contemporary social, regional and lexical alternation between [uu] and [ju] vowel space is commented upon by almost all observers in the 18th century; Walker (1791:§§462:178), for instance, noting the [t] → [tʃ] change in [ju] contexts, comments that:

> Though it is evident.....that as the *u* is under the accent, the preceding *t* is preserved pure, and that the words ought to be pronounced as if written *tewtor, tewmult, tewmour*, &c. and neither *tshootur, tshoomult, tshoomour*, as Mr Sheridan writes them, nor *tootor, toomult, toomour*, as they are often pronounced by vulgar speakers.

Walker (1791:§335) lists with [ju] the items: *clue, cue, due, blue, glue, hue, flue, rue, sue, true, mue, accrue, ensue, argue, imbue, imbrue, pursue, subdue, perdue, residue, avenue, revenue, continue, retinue, construe, statue, tissue, issue, virtue, value, argue.* Sheridan (1781:22) includes *cube, few, new, clue, view, beauty.* Nares (1784:62-3) lists dew, *ewer, new, pew, deuce, Deuteronomy, feud,* while Perry (1777:29) shows: *brute, flute, lute, mute, crude, rude, cube, tube, cure, lure, pure, sure, duke, Luke, puke, dupe, stupe, plume, spume, lune, prune, tune, luce, spruce, truce, mule, rule, Ruth, truth.* Most of the Scots observers comment on the [jʊ]/[ʊ] alternation as well, although there is some evidence of lexical contrast, Robertson (1722) for instance including with the diphthong such items as *blew, brew, shrewd, bruit, fruit,* and Elphinston (1776:9) muses 'Evverihware indeed hav untutored (raddher untuned or untoned) organs ben in dainger ov interchainging dhe due prezzence, and dhe due absence, ov licquefaccion. Dhe vulgar Inglish drop it, not onely in dhe provvinces: in dhe cappital doo we hear *Look, bloo, rool, trooth, noo, toon, doo, dook, soo;* for *Luke, blue, rule, truith, new, tune, due* and *dew, duke, sue;* and dhe like'. Items cited by Sylvester Douglas in his *Table* as showing [ju] in the pure dialect are not numerous, but include such items as: *excuse, use, profuse, humility, Hume, humane, curious, unity, pure, pew, dew* and *hue,* and there appear to be a few showing [ju] which have not survived into the modern British English standard, notably *Bruce, spruce, truce, recluse.* In this context we should recall the nickname *Jackboot* applied to the unpopular Lord Bute in the 18th century.

Walker (1791:§178) notes as characteristic of Scottish English a tendency to generalise the [jʊ] diphthong in certain lexical items: 'But the strangest deviation of this letter [*u*:CJ] from its regular sound is in the words *busy, business,* and *bury.* We laugh at the Scotch for pronouncing these words *bewsy, bewsiness,* and *bewry;* but we ought rather to blush for ourselves in departing so wantonly from the general rule as to pronounce them *bizzy, bizness,* and *berry.*' Sylvester Douglas' comments under his BUSINESS, BUSY entry (Jones:1992:179), would appear to suggest that Scots speakers are conscious of the social disadvantage of a diphthongal pronunciation in this item, and hypercorrect to their 'standard' [ʏ]:

> The *us* is sounded like the *izz* in *mizzen, dizzy;* or like *is* in *his.* The Scotch, in their vernacular pronounciation, sound it nearly in this manner; but they often when they aim at speaking well give the *u* the sound it has in *guzzle, puzzle*.....The Scotch commonly make *business* (as it is written) a word of three syllables. But the English always suppress the *i*, not only in verse, but in prose, and in public speaking, as well, as familiar conversation.

But before we proceed to examine the sociophonetic and lexical distribution of this diphthongal element, it is important to realise that many of the Scotch observers include under its discussion evidence for the existence of a peculiarly salient Scotch labial - the *French u*. We have already commented upon the detailed discussion provided by Sylvester Douglas on the characteristics of labial [ʊ] sounds in the polite (most probably Edinburgh) Scottish English of his day. Indeed, at the beginning of his *Treatise*, in the *Observations on the Alphabet*, he observes that while the pure dialect manifests (as we have just seen) a threefold [ʊ]~[ʌ]~[ɣ] alternation:

> In the northern counties of England *oo* is always pronounced in this latter manner [i.e. as the shade of the second *u*: [[ɣ]:CJ] as much as in *stood* and *good*, as in *flood* and *blood*. And so is the *u* in words like *scull, Tully, rut* when it has the first shade of the second sound [[ʌ]:CJ] in the pure dialect

suggesting a merger of [ʊ], [ʌ] and [ɣ] in whatever Douglas means by 'the Northern counties of England'. But it is almost by chance and in passing that Douglas comments upon what he perceives to be its standard shape in the southern Scottish vernacular in those instances where in the pure dialect some kind of [jʊ] diphthong might be expected to surface. Under his discussion of BURIAL, BURY, he observes that while 'these words are a great stumbling block to many a Scotchman...The true provincial sound of the *u* in the southern counties [of Scotland:CJ], both in these and a great many others, is like the French *u*' by which he perhaps intends a [ʉ] or [ɯ], a high central rounded or high back unrounded vowel shape. These observations appear to be an echo of those of Buchanan (1788:29) who quite confidently states that 'In other tongues there may be simple vowel sounds quite different from ours. Such is that of the French *u*; which is not heard in England, or in the North of Scotland; but in all the lowland provinces of North Britain, from the Grampian mountains to the Tweed, is still in very frequent use'. Elphinston too makes a similar observation: 'Against the English *oo*....dhe Soddhern Scots hav garded dheir dialect widh *u*....French; hwich dhe nordhern [Scots] found as forrain, az did the Inglish' (1786:4;10), commenting that '*duke* retains dhe licquid in *dyuc*; hwen he plays not hiz parent, dhe French *duc*. Dhus ar dhe Inglish *duke* and *duc* Scottishly interchainged....Dhe Scots, naming dhe vowel forrainly *oo*, nevver prefix dhe licquefier, but hware dhey shood not. Hence *book* iz *byook*, *byuc*, or (Frenchly) *buc*; and *rebuke*, *rebook*, *rebyuc*, or (French-like) *rebuc*. No wonder dhe soddhern Scots adopt dhe French vowel in *cure* and *curious*, if so manny Inglish provincials drop dhe licquefaccion in dhe blunt *coor* and *coorious*, or even *coorous*. If dhe Inglish hav hiddherto' expected *coosshon* or *coossion*, from *cushion*; dheir neighbors may az wel (but alas! no better) think to' bring dhe town ov *Coopar*, from *Cupar*...'

Again under his important BURIAL entry, Sylvester Douglas tells us that speakers in the north of Scotland realise the vowel by what Douglas represents as <beerial>, <beery>, perhaps a pure palatal [i]/[ii] sound or a high central unrounded [ɨ] vowel. Both pronunciations are recorded by Elphinston who tells us that in Edinburgh <shoe> is '*chu* 'Frenchly'' and <rude> '*rude* French'; on the other hand for Aberdeen speakers he cites *shee* for <shoe> and *rid* or *reed* for <rude> (1786:4). Perhaps something like this [ɨ]-type vowel is referred to by Adams in his description of the *Scotch Dialect* (1799:152) when he suggests as Scotch variants of *soon* and *moon* realisations rendered as <sain>, <main>, where he uses <ei> as a symbol for [e], perhaps perceived by him as being phonetically close to [ɨ].

As we have already seen, Alexander Geddes recognises three types of labial vowel, his '*u* short, as in *shut*', '*ù*, *oo*, or *u*, Italian' and a *û* '*u* English as in *pure*' (1792:432); his observations on the last are worth repeating:

> This is really a compound of *e* and *u*. It is, however, to be observed, that it is not sounded exactly in the same manner by the Scots and English. In the mouths of the latter it seems to be composed of *i* and *eù*; while the former pronounce it more like the French *u* or *eu*, in the word *peur*

appearing to suggest that for standard English speakers there exists a genuine [ju] diphthongal segment, which some speakers of Scots are liable to interpret, at least on occasion, as monophthongal and approximating to a 'French' probably fronted labial segment of the type we have tentatively suggested immediately above. Robertson too describes <eu> and <ew> as having the 'long sound of *u* as is taught in *England*' (1722:16) seeming to infer that the diphthong is not a salient Scots feature. That speakers should perceive [ju] as something approximating to [ʊ̈] is not altogether surprising or phonetically unnatural. Rather than interpret the [ju] signal as comprising a palatal/labial *sequence*, listeners hear it as a complex or internally mixed phonetic segment comprised simultaneously of a labial (prominent) and (subordinate) palatal segment, the surface manifestation of such a mixture perceived as [ʊ̈] or [ɯ] (Anderson and Ewen:1987:212-214). This 're-interpretation' of linear segments in terms of simultaneously expressed internal components of a single, complex segment also appears to lie behind the well-known English and Scots diphthongal [au] to monophthongal [ɔ] change in the history of words such as <law> and <bought>, where linear sonorant/labial sequences are interpreted as the simultaneous internal components of a mixed segment like [ɔ] (Jones:1989:260). It is perhaps a process like this which lies behind the observations of James Douglas relating to his classification of a long and short 'proper *u*' (Holmberg:1956:185ff). The 'long' version is 'like its Common Name which may be call'd the true English *U*, as ŪNION CŪRIOUS'. However, he also identifies a version which is 'sounded like its Common Name but Short, as, CALCǓLATE, CORPǓLENT'; items listed with the short diphthong version including, *circulate, conjurer, certitude, fortitude, picture, treasure, prelude,* among others. The implication is that James Douglas hears a [jʊ]/[jʊʊ] contrast in his contemporary phonetics, an alternation not readily re-inforced by other observers of the period, with the exception, as we have seen, of Sylvester Douglas (Jones:1992:192). However, it may be just possible to argue that what James Douglas describes as a short version of 'the proper *u*' is, in fact, some kind of palatalised [ʊ̈] or [ɯ] monophthongal shape.

Although he readily admits that in this area of the phonology even 'good speakers among the English differ' (Jones 1992:139), Sylvester Douglas almost everywhere treats as either accommodations or as grave errors in taste, the Scottish [ju] substitute for pure [ʊ], [ʏ] and [ɨ] shapes in items such as <blue> and <pursue> where the '*ue* represents the first sound of *u* where the Scotch give it the diphthongal sound'; while under BUILD he informs us that 'Many Scotch people sound the *ui* like the diphthongal *u* in *mule*', while the others sound it 'like the long first sound of *e*, or *ee*; so as to make *build* and *steel'd* or *wield* rhyme together. Both these methods are erroneous' (Jones:1992:178). Again, under LUXURY we are told pointedly that 'the second *u* has not the diphthongal sound which some Scotch people give it; but the same short, close vocal sound, as the first, or as it has in the words *stuck, luck,* but more obscure' (Jones 1992:207). Perhaps Douglas' most strenuous injunction against [ju] pronunciations appears under the BURIAL item, that great 'stumbling block' in Scotch vernacular speech. Scotch speakers, he suggests, realising that their production of an [ii] stressed vowel in the item is highly stigmatised, then 'generally adopt the diphthongal *u*, and make *bury* and *fury*...rhyme together'; this accommodation is 'equally wrong'. In all, it would seem that in general Douglas regards the contemporary Scotch [ju] vernacular pronunciation for the pure [ʊ], [ʏ] or [ɨ] as an unacceptable hypercorrection. Viewed in the context of Elphinston's remarks above that '*duke* retains dhe licquid in *dyuc;* hwen he plays not hiz parent, dhe French *duc.* Dhus ar dhe Inglish *duke* and *duc* Scottishly interchainged', Walter Scott's observation in *Heart of Midlothian* (1818;Parker:1971:207:footnote) is perhaps based on the perception that for certain Scots speakers in the late 18th century the stressed vowel in an item like <duck> would show a centralised [ʏ] shape, which under conditions of hyper-correction might well appear realised as [jʊ]:

> The Magistrates were closely interrogated before the House of Peers, concerning the particulars of the Mob, and the *patois* in which these functionaries made their answers, sounded strange in the ears of the Southern nobles. The Duke of Newcastle having demanded to know with what kind of shot the guard which Porteous commanded had loaded their muskets, was answered naively: 'Ow, just sic as ane shoots *dukes* and *fools* with.' This reply was considered as a contempt of the House of Lords, and

> the Provost would have suffered accordingly, but that the Duke of Argyle explained, that the expression, properly rendered into English, meant *ducks and water-fowl.*

We might mention in this context too the 'near alikes' <duc> '*a fowl*'/<duke> '*a prince*' and <mouse>/<Muse>, <power>/<pure> recorded by Robertson (1722), while the social status of the apparently undiphthongised vowel in <fowl> , <mouse> and <power> in Scots of the period we shall comment upon below.

However, it is worth noting here as well the widespread tendency in the Buchan dialect, as recorded mainly by Geddes, to see etymologically pure labial forms realised as what are possibly pure palatals, expressed by Geddes by <è>. Commenting upon *Burial* and *Bury*, Sylvester Douglas (Jones 1991:20:179) observes that in these words 'in the north of Scotland, they are pronounced *Beerial, beery*.' Likewise Elphinston (1787:vol 2:4):

> Against dhe Inglish *oo* (hweddher simpel, or licquidly articculated in *u*) and *a* slender, dhe soddhern Scots hav garded dheir dialect widh *u* and *é* , equally French; dhe former of hwich dhe nordhern sound az forrain, az did dhe Inglish. Hwile Eddinburrough, dherfore, uttered boath *shoo* and *she*, Frenchly *chu*; Abberdeen joined Ingland to' prezerv dhem; dho vulgarly emitting boath, *shee*: won pronouncing dhus, *rood* and *rude*, alike *rude* French; dhe oddher, like *rid* or *reed* Inglish.

There are many instances in Geddes' (Buchan dialect) translation of the Theokritus passage where pure palatal stressed vowels are found where a pure labial would be appropriate in the Edinburgh dialect:

> bèth '*both*'; brèm-hill '*broom-hill*'; fèls '*fools*'; flèds '*floods*'; frèt '*fruit*'; ghè '*you*'; lè-lorn '*love lorn*'; lèv '*love*'; Mèses '*Muses*'; nèn '*noon*'; sèn '*soon*'; sèth '*sooth*'; shèt '*shoot*'; snèd '*snood*'; unmèvt '*unmoved*'

even the single <abèn> '*above*' instance in the Edinburgh materials might represent an unconscious intrusion from Geddes' native Buchan speech.

We recall that Alexander Geddes' third labial sound is represented by a <û> graph: '*u* English, as in *pure*; This is really a compound of *e* and *u*. It is, however, to be observed, that it is not sounded exactly in the same manner by the Scots and English. In the mouths of the latter it seems to be composed of *i* and *eù*; while the former pronounce it more like the French *u* or *eu*, in the word *peur*.' Examples Geddes cites for the Edinburgh dialect include:

> abûn '*above*'; attûn '*attune*'; brûz (461/22); brûzan '*browsing*'; bûs '*bows*'; dû '*due*'; enûkh '*enough*'; fûl '*fool*' (458/16); imbû '*imbue*'; lûk't '*looked*'; mûs '*muse*'; nû '*new*'; refûs; sûner '*sooner*'; tûn '*tune*'.

Despite this, Geddes, through his use of an <iou> trigraph, seems to admit to the existence of an actual Scots [ju] diphthong, a trigraph which he describes in his *Table* (1792:431) and *Observations* (1792:435) as representing 'a sound peculiar to the Scots and Northern English, and might in English be written *you;* or it might be expressed by some diacritic mark over the preceding consonant, like the Spanish *n*.' Again, under his description of *l*, which he characterises as 'the softest of all the liquids' and which 'the Scots make..still more liquid than the English by retaining its Gaelic or Celtic sound; which is also common in Spanish, and expressed by *ll*. It is nearly the *ll* in French, and exactly the *gl* in Italian. It might in my alphabet have been denoted by a diacritic point - but as other three liquids are liable to a similar modification, and as one combination of vowels, namely *iou* after the single consonant, suits all the four, I thought it better to use that combination, than, without necessity, to multiply symbols.' Yet, despite this lengthy description, we see only one instance of the trigraph in the Edinburgh dialect - <Thy prègnant ious> (460/1/7) - and one in the Buchan (464/31):

> A ritsh akánthus, shèdan frum aniou
> Its cirklan' lèvs, sèms, wunnirfu! to grou!

There is a real difficulty in interpreting the significance of Geddes' <ou> digraph, but if we take it (as he suggests) as equivalent to <*oo*> or '*u* Italian', then the <iou> trigraph might seem to indicate a value like [ju]. This interpretation is reinforced by the fact that Geddes regularly renders '*ewe*' as <ghou>, where <gh> is described as '*y* consonant' and which 'is still aspirated..in some parts of Scotland' (1792:434).

It is interesting to note, however, the fact that one of the 18th century's most careful observers of Scots usage, Alexander Scot, appears to deny the existence of [ju] diphthongal types in the phonology of his (apparently prestigious) contemporary Scots (Jones:1993:102):

> That Caledonians can think, nay, that Caledonians can write, is no secret to the learned world. But that any nation should write a language, which it can neither read nor speak, was a paradox reserved for the ingenuity of modern times. Certain it is however, that our Country, amidst the many improvements which daily more distinguish her, has within these fifty years made considerable alteration in her language. The Scottish dialect of this day is no more that of Allan Ramsay than of Gawin Douglas; but that the language of Edinburgh is not nearer the language of London than it was a century ago, whether in idiom or in utterance, will irrefagably appear from the following letter, which fairly paints the present Caledonian English of the college, the pulpit, and the bar.

Table 5.2 below sets out the items he records against a simple orthographic contrast between <u> and <oo>:

TABLE 5.2

Scot's Labial Vowels

Modern Standard Scots	Scott's Spelling		18th Century Scottish Standard
SHOULD/BUT [ʉ]/[ʉʉ]/[ʌ]	<u>		[u]/[uu]
	<shud>	*should*	
	<buke>	*book*	
	<ful>	*full*	
	<much>	*much*	
NEW [jʉ]	<u>		[u]
	<graitetud>	*gratitude*	
	<curaoozetays>	*curiosities*	
	<excuze>	*excuse*	
	<oapoartunetay>	*opportunity*	
SHOULD/BUT [ʉ]/[ʌ]	<oo>		[ɤ]
	<wood>	*would*	
	<boot>	*but*	
	<cood>	*could*	
	<auboov>	*above*	
	<oonless>	*unless*	
NEW [jʉ]	<oo>		[ɤ]
	<rabook>	*rebuke*	
	<oonavarsetays>	*universities*	
	<coamoonicatten>	*communicating*	
	<maunoofaucters>	*manufactures*	
	<amoolatione>	*emulation*	

The absence of [ju] diphthongal types is puzzling, but in the light of Sylvester Douglas'injunctions against the use of the diphthong in provincial Scotch, we might interpret Alexander Scot's reticence to record it as a signal of its stigmatised status with the users of 'the present

Caledonian English of the college, the pulpit, and the bar.' Yet Adams (although possibly describing a more 'broad' version of Scots) uses the [ú] symbol , his *yu* as in *Duke*, <diuuk>, for the Scotch rendering of '*poor*', '*door*' and '*moor*'.

5.8 Mixed Labial/Sonorant Segments: Mid Back [o] and [ɔ] Types

The descriptive terminology accorded by Scottish observers to whatever sound is represented by graphs such as <o>, <oa>, <ou>, <ow> and <oe> is usually limited to the appellations *long* and *short* (Telfair, Dun, Burn) or the symbolic o^1, o^2, a^3 (Perry) and <ō>, <ŏ>, <â> (McIllquam, *A Spelling-Book Upon a New Plan*). While Adams refers to a *long clear* version, Buchanan idiosyncratically has an *acute* type in addition to his *long* and *short*. The question immediately arises as to whether the use of a tripartite descriptive nomenclature infers three distinguishable phonetic outputs, such that Adams' <ò>, <ó> and <â> might correspond to a phonetic contrast such as [o], [ɔ], [ɒ]. Buchanan, for example suggests three sounds for <o>, the long 'which makes the mouth of an orbicular form', represented in items like <globe>, respelled <glōbe>, the short, as in <lot>, <got>, respelled <lŏt>, and the acute, which is '*au* rapidly pronounced' (mainly in pre-[r] contexts) as in <order> (ôrdir) and <border> (bôrdir). His *au* appears to be synonymous with his *a broad*, exemplified in items such as <bald>, <walls>, although he also states that the 'acute sound, which seems to approach to *au*, but is really short *a* twice, but rapidly pronounced, is denoted by a circumflex over it, thus *fâthĭr*, *râthĭr*, *ârmz* &c'(1766:4). Short *a* is exemplified through items such as *fat*, *bat* and *band*, suggesting some kind of [aa] or [ɑɑ] realisation, although the fact that it 'seems to approach to *au*' might just suggest [ɒɒ]. Alexander Barrie's representational system recognises four different *o* sounds, as in <hâll>, <nōte>, <nŏt> and <störm>. Confined to his edition of 1796 the <ö> types all appear in pre-[r] contexts which may suggest some more sonorant segment such as [ɒɒ], although we must always be prepared to accept the diacritic as merely a marker of increased vowel duration, thus [ɔɔ]. His 1794 version which uses superscripted numerals, only shows o^1 as in <hoe>, <low>, o^2 as in <fox>, <for>, o^3 as in <law>, <ball>; the fact that <nought> shows o^2, while <naught> has a^3 just suggesting that he hears a quality contrast, perhaps of an [ɔ]/[ɒ] type. However, we should bear in mind in this context the observations by Walker (1791:21) that 'The second sound of this letter is called its short sound, and is found in *not, got, lot,* &c, though this, as in the other short vowels, is by no means the short sound of the former long one [his *long open o* as in <prove>:CJ], but corresponds exactly to that of *a* in *what*, with which the words *not, got, lot,* are perfect rhymes. The long sound to which the *o* in *not* and *sot* are short ones, is found under the diphthong *au* in *naught*, and the *ou* in *sought*; corresponding exactly to the *a* in *hall, ball,* &c'. But in most instances descriptions are too inexact for us to come to certain conclusions about the precise vowel qualities referred to.

Length contrasts for the back mid segments are relatively rarely specified, although Telfair (1799:152) contrasts what appear to be durational differences in his first short *o* in items like *fond, odd,* where it is short, and *fawn'd, aw'd* where it is long, and John Burn (1756:3) distinguishes *long and broad a* (particularly in pre-[l] plus consonant cluster and [w] environments) in items like <talk>, <calm>, <malt>, <warm> and <ward> from a *broad a* in <all>. There seems little doubt too that (certainly by the 1813 edition) William Angus' *An English Spelling and Pronouncing Vocabulary* indicates length differential versions of a low mid back segment through Â and Ă when he includes them under his heading of 'Vowel Sounds *similar* in QUALITY, but *different* in QUANTITY', as in items such as *wĂsh-bÂll.* Perry (1776:16) seems to equate the short *o* in *loft* with 'the sound of â in *hall*', while 'the â in *wash* sounds *o* as in *not*', hinting at a conflation between what his use of discrete *â* and *ŏ* symbols might suggest was a contrast between low and lower back mid vowel segments. Yet he is careful to indicate that words he asterisks are 'variously pronounced'. For instance, while he classifies *wan* under words which have a vowel sounding 'like *o* in *not,* which is the short sound of *â*', he nevertheless notes an alternative for the item 'which is also classed under the third sound of *a*', his *â* in *ball,* thus perhaps suggesting a durational rather than a qualitative distinction. The sociophonetics of the length contrast are clearly stated by Walker (1791:22:§170): 'What was observed of the *a,* when followed by a liquid and a mute, may be observed of the *o* with equal justness. This letter, like *a,* has a tendency to lengthen, when followed by a liquid and another consonant, or by *s, ss,* or *s* and a mute. But this length of *o,* in this situation, seems every day growing more and more vulgar: and, as it would be gross to a degree to sound the *a* in *castle, mask,* and *plant,* like the *a* in *palm, psalm,* &c, so it would be equally exceptionable to pronounce the *o* in *moss, dross* and *frost,* as if written *mauwse, drawse,* and *frawst.* The *o* in the compounds of *solve,* as *dissolve, absolve, resolve,* seem the only words where a somewhat longer sound of the *o* is agreeable to polite pronunciation.'

The potential quality and quantity contrasts for back mid vowels in the late 18th century prestige London standard are perhaps best encapsulated in the entry under *O* by Sylvester Douglas (Jones:1992:133), which is worth quoting in full:

> This letter has two distinct sounds differing in quality from each other. The one is open and commonly short, as in *not, lost, cross, horse.* The other close, and usually long, as in *bone, stone, post, hoarse, toll.* The first we give to the Greek *ο,* and the other to the *ϖ.* It is evident that the sounds we give to those two vowels differ in quality, and we have mentioned under the letter *e* a reason for supposing that such a difference subsisted in the living

> pronounciation of Greece. There is in our language a long sound of the open *o*, as in *Corn, Horn.* It is seldom however represented by this single character, But sometimes by *ou* as in *bought, thought;* or by *oa*, as in *groat, broad.* This sound, if not the same, is near the confines, or the external edge, if I may so speak, of the broad *a* in *all*. Some writers think them the same. I imagine I can perceive a difference.
>
> The close *o* which verges towards the vowel represented by *oo*, is, in like manner, sometimes short: especially before the soft mutes *b, d,* & *g,* as in *sob, pod, log.* The long close *o* is often represented by *ow*, as *bowl, sow,* or also by *ou* as in *soul, though,* or *oa*, as in *road.* or *oe* as in *woe, toe, foe,* By *eau*, in *beau;* and, in one instance, by *ew* viz *shew.*

From this and the information in his *Table*, we can deduce that he assigns length and quality values something as in Table 5.3:

TABLE 5.3

Sylvester Douglas' Mid Back Vowel Values

OPEN	**Commonly Short**
LONG	**SHORT**
<corn>	<hot>
<horn>	<lost>
<bought>	<cross>
<thought>	<horse>
<groat>	
<broad>	
[ɔɔ]	[ɔ]
CLOSE	**Commonly Long**
LONG	**SHORT**
<bone>	<sob>
<stone>	<pod>
<post>	<log>
<hoarse>	
<bowl>	
<sow>	
<soul>	
<though>	
<road>	
<woe>	
<toe>	
<foe>	
[oo]	[o]

That Douglas hears the *open o* to be 'near the confines, or the external edge, if I may so speak, of the broad *a* in *all*. Some writers think them the same. I imagine I can perceive a difference', might suggest some kind of [ɔɔ˕]/[ɒɒ] contrast between items such as *broad* and *all*, while the fact that he hears the *close o* to 'verge towards *oo*' suggests for items such as *stone* and *post* some kind of relatively raised [oo˔] vowel space value. Yet in general Douglas' four *o* types and the lexical items with which he associates them bear a close resemblance to the shape of the vowel space in their standard modern British English analogucs, with thc cxccption that there many [oo] vowels have taken on (since the beginning of the 19th century) a diphthongal ([ou], [oə] etc.) configuration (Wells 1982: §4.2.4). Yet while his assignation of open, short values to items like <not>, <lost>, cross>, <horse>, and close (and usually) long values to <bone>, <stone>, <post>, <hoarse> is as we might expect, his claim that items such as <sob>, <pod> and <log> show stressed high mid vowel types might strike us as unusual. That such an [o] value for these items is what he genuinely seems to intend is supported by his comments under the OF, OFF, OAF entry (Jones:1992:45):

> These three words afford examples, of three, out of the four sounds of *o*. In the first it is short, and close; in the second short, and open; and in the third, the *ou* has, as in other cases, the long close sound of the *o*.

James Douglas as well appears to see an [oo]/[o] distinction in his contemporary phonology, noting under his discussion of the letter O (Holmberg:1956:164/65):

> *How is the Vowel O Sounded?*
>
> The Vowel O has two Proper Sounds, and Seven Improper, in some words it is transpos'd and in others not pronounc'd.
>
> *What are the Proper Sounds of the Vowel O?*
> I. The Vowel O is Sounded Long, Like its Common name in the Alphabet, as, ŌMEN ŌCEAN
>
> II. It has the Same Sound only Pronounc'd Short, as,
>
> ABRŎGATE

Holmberg (1956:69) comments that 'As far as I know D[ouglas] is the first to have distinguished this short sound from [ɔ]'.

Yet we are never left with a completely clear or satisfying picture of the phonetic values for mid back vowels as perceived by 18th century observers. Alexander Geddes (Jones:1994:100) seems to distinguish between two types. His <o> graph corresponds, he claims, to '*o* short, as in *hot*: It has been observed, that this sound when rapidly pronounced, coincides nearly with short *a*'. As we have already noted, his short *a* is characterised as like the vowel in *hand* 'or nearly so. This is not entirely the English *a* short, as in *hand,* a sound not known in Scotland, till very lately; but the shortest and most indistinct of all vocal sounds, and which might be almost equally well expressed by a very short *i,* and even by *e* or *u*. Sir William Jones informs us, that, in all the Indian dialects, 'this vowel is considered *inherent* in every consonant; and so it seems evidently to have been by the Hebrews, Chaldees, Syrians, and Arabs'. I have retained it particularly in all active participles: as *doand, writand,* &c. where it is plain, that *i, e,* or *u,* if rapidly pronounced, might be readily substituted for it.' It is very difficult to decide anything like a precise value for this 'short *a*' in Geddes scheme of things, but it is worth noting that there are a few cases where this graph is used to represent vowels which have, in current Received Standard, come to be realised as [ɑ]: <pas> *'pass'* and <ar> *'are'*. At the same time, Geddes shows this graph with items which are monosyllabic and syllabically 'short' <had>, <huat>, <as>, <ar>, etc., and in several instances the graph appears in syllables which lack prominence: <forran>, <plesant>. In the light of these cases, it might be tempting to interpret Geddes' descriptive remarks quite literally, and assign a phonetic value of [ə] to this 'most indistinct of all vocal sounds'. However, the propensity for the graph to be used with vowels which surface in the modern language as [ɔ], might just tempt us to treat it (when 'rapidly pronounced') as the central, half open vowel [ɐ]. But to see 'the *o* long, as in *bone*' as 'only a protraction of *o* short' requires some dexterity. We have already commented upon the fact that Sylvester Douglas interprets the *long o* of the 'pure' dialect, if anything, as a more labial [oo˔]; Geddes seems to suggest that it approximates to [ɔɔ˕] or even [ɒɒ]. It is possible that Geddes' interpretation is based not upon a close observation of London usage, but on more Scottish standard models. Given the propensity, as we shall see immediately below, for Scots speakers to alternate high and low mid back vowels (recall Elphinston's (1776:4) comment: 'But dhe Scottish sound, dhat swallows all dhe rest, open or shut, iz (*au*) the universal *a* braud, and first ov all vowels in oddher tungs....oppozite borderers interchainge *aw* and *ow*; dhe Scots making *slow slaw,* and dhe Cumbrians *law low*' - the Scots habit justified by 'But iz not *a* braud dhe vowel, dhat moast natturally opens dhe human mouth?'). We might therefore just see Geddes' [ɔɔ] for *long o* as some kind of hyper-correction in the direction of increased sonority, away from the too saliently Scotch tendency to treat etymologically low mid back vowels as high mid.

It is worth pointing out too that it is not only in Scots usage that there appears to be a discrepancy in the lexical distribution of high and low mid back vowels; there appears to be much evidence from the Scottish materials to show a similar alternation in what is claimed to be the contemporary standard language of the metropolis. Sylvester Douglas, for instance assigns low mid values to items such as *revolt, oat meal, Trojan, groat, ford* and *form*, while for *knowledge* a high mid value appears: of the [ɔ] in the first syllable of <oat meal>, he tells us (Jones:1992:45):

> In this (I believe single instance) the English pronounce the *oa*, like the short open *o*, in *not*, in so much that to make it long and close (although in the primitive word *oat*, the *oa* is sounded as in *oath*) would appear pedantic and affected.

Walker (1791) shows an [o] value for *revolt, oats. ford*, [ɔ] for *oatmeal, pod, log, sob* and [ɔɔ] for *groat, form*. For *knowledge* he provides an [o]/[ɔ] alternative, while Kenrick informs us concerning the sound associated with the <ou>, <ow> graph that: 'This sound is variously applied to particular words in different parts of Great Britain and Ireland. Mr Ward gives us the words *foul, sound, grow, knowledge*, as being all of the same sound; whereas the two first only are alike in the sound: the two last differing not only from the first, but from each other, both in quality and quantity. Thus, *grow* is the long sound....as in the words, *no, toe, though*, &c. whereas the first syllable in *knowledge* is the short sound...as in *not, what*, and the like; which is not the same quality with either ..*no, toe*, or ...*how, thou*, &c'. While Adams (1799:16) comments: 'Some modern variations, arising from simple combinations and analogy of rule, and sounds differently uttered and supported by the authority of practice of our Universities, are respectable and optional, as *Rome* per o long [[u]:CJ]. So most Cambridgians pronounce *know-ledge, kno-ledge*, others *knól-edge*, both by rule; *kno*, from the radical words to *know; knol* is guided by the shifting accent, which seizes the sound of simple *o* (found in *ow*) and unites it to the double consonant.'

Such a lexical item specific identification of pronunciation is clear as well from Douglas' observation on the items covered under FORM (Jones:1992:196-97):

> This word in the ordinary acceptation (and its compounds) are pronounced with the long open *o*, as *fork, corn*. When it signifies a class in a school, or a bench, the *o* has the long close sound. To acquire a clear idea of the distinction between these two sounds of the *o*, I cannot recommend a better method, than to get an English man who speaks well, to pronounce *form*, first, as used in the one sense, and then, as in the other.

Again, although he describes <revolt> as showing an [ɔ] stressed vowel, items like <colt>, <dolt> and <jolt> are specifically excepted and show [oo]. That the [o]/[ɔ] alternation was, for the pure dialect, one of some considerable sociophonetic significance can be seen from Douglas' observations under the item KNOWLEDGE whose stressed vowel, he claims (Jones:1992:204), is generally pronounced in both England and Scotland as [ɔ], yet 'some English people affect to give it the long close sound, as in *flow, know*.' Walker (1791:37) observes:

> This diphthong, in the word *knowledge*, has of late years undergone a considerable revolution. Some speakers, who had the regularity of their language at heart, were grieved to see the compound depart so far from the sound of the simple, and with heroic fortitude have opposed the multitude by pronouncing the first syllable of this word as it is heard in the verb to *know*. The pulpit and the bar have for some years given a sanction to this pronunciation; but the senate and the stage hold out inflexibly against it; and the nation at large seem insensible of the improvement. They still continue to pronounce, as in the old ludicrous rhymes - 'Among the mighty men of knowledge,/That are professors at Gresham College.'

5.9 Scotch Peculiarities of the Mixed Sonorant/Labial Segments

The alternation between high and low mid back vowels is without doubt one of the most salient phonetic and sociophonetic characteristics of the phonology of 18th century Scots, as it is of the modern language, a salientness reflected in the ready supply of anecdotal observation on the phenomenon. The following from Sylvester Douglas (Jones:1992:185) and James Adams (1794:21) are fairly typical:

> COAST, COAT, COAX
> The *oa* as in *boat*. Not long ago, a Scotch Gentleman, in a debate in the House of Commons upon the Affairs of America, began a speech, in which he proposed to examine whether it would be more advisable to adopt compulsive, or soothing measures towards the colonies. Unfortunately instead of *soothe*, *coax* was the word that had presented itself to his mind. And he pronounced it as if written *cox*. This, added to several other peculiarities of manner and dialect, tickled the House extremely, and produced a general laugh. The Gentleman was unconscious of the false pronounciation into which he had fallen. His speech had been premeditated, and *coax* was, it seems, a sort of cue, or catch word. Every time therefore that the silence of his hearers permitted him to resume his harangue, he began by repeating this unlucky word. But every fresh repetition of it occasioning a louder burst of laughter, he was obliged at last fairly to give the matter up. And break off his oration in the middle.

> In 1775 I lived in the Scotch College of Doway in Flanders, having learnt as good English and Latin as St Omers afforded to moderate proficients. The old Scotch gentlemen soon began to fear I should spoil the accent of their pupils, who endeavoured to imitate my pronunciation. Our table wanted not the better store and seasoning of instructive reading during meals. A young reader (Chearly Câmeron) lighting on these words, *the body of his father*,

> read them according to the English way, upon which the presiding old Gentleman's ears being shocked, he cleared his mouth as fast as possible, and dropping his spoon and hands on the table, made him repeat the words several times, and spell them again and again. Still the youth read *bâddy*; then the old gentleman ordered each letter to be named and counted, which being done, and repeated again and again, he fixed his eyes on me, and with triumphant smile, mixed with a good Scotch grin, rebuked the reader sharply for spoiling the *a*, and introducing a second *d*, then ordered him to sound it *bô-dy*

We recall too Buchanan's list of eminent Scotticisms which include 'confusions' of long and short vowels, such that 'North-Britons destroy just quantity, by expressing the long sound for the short, and the short for the long; as *abhōr* for *abhŏr*, *abhōrrence* for *abhŏrrence*, *abōlish* for *abŏlish*, *thrōn* for *thrōne*' [sic:CJ], while William Scott (1807:xxvi:footnote) - under his 'list of words in which the Natives of Scotland are very apt to err' - tells us that 'These two sounds of the vowel [represented by <o> and probably his [o] and [ɔ]/[ɒ] :CJ] are particularly difficult to North Britons when occurring in the same word or near one another; as in *post-office, coach-box, a long story, I thought so, not only, go on*, &c'. Sylvester Douglas (Jones:1992:47) (under his BOUGHT entry) perhaps paints the clearest picture of all his contemporaries of the significance of this variable:

> In this and similar words, as *sought, thought, fought, drought*. The *ough* has the long open sound of the *o* in *corn*, or of *oa* in *broad*. This sound, if at all, is but just distinguishable from the long broad *a* in *all*, *malt* or *au* in *Paul*. Some writers on pronounciation consider them as entirely the same. They are generally made to rhyme with such words as *taught*, and *fraught*, but that is no proof that their sound is exactly the same.
>
> If e'er one vision touch'd thy infant thought
> Of all the nurse, and all the priest e'er taught.
>
> The Scotch, after they get rid of the more barbarous pronounciation in which the *gh* is pronounced as a strong guttural, generally fall into the mistake of using the long close sound of *o*, and making (for instance) *bought*, and *boat*, the same word to the ear. And this they do so generally that in endeavouring to mimic the Scotch pronounciation I have observed that the English are apt to hit upon this particular way of sounding this class of words. Yet this, in truth, is not part of the vernacular pronunciation of Scotland.

It is interesting to observe that Douglas (under his BROAD entry) is careful to exclude the [oo] variant from the 'vernacular pronunciation of Scotland' (Jones:1992:178): 'In this word and in *groat*, the *oa* has the same long open sound approaching to the *a* in *all*, which we have described under the word *bought*. These two words are the only instances I believe where the *oa* has this sound. In *road, goad, toad, float* &c the *oa* has the long close sound as in *boat*. If there is any simple vocal sound in the pure English dialect, not to be found in the Scotch, it is this long open *o*. or *oa*'.

While it is difficult to decide what he means by the term 'vernacular' in this context, it is interesting to note that while he contrasts it with the 'true pronunciation' (see his EITHER and PRIVY entries especially), he also sets it against the 'vulgar' used by 'low people' in both England and Scotland. We have already observed how he is states quite categorically in his *Treatise* that 'it is by no means my intention to observe upon all the grosser barbarisms of the vulgar Scotch jargon. This would be an useless and an endless labour. I only mean to treat expressly of the impurities which generally stick with those whose language has already been in a great degree refined from the provincial dross, by frequenting English company, and studying the great masters of the English tongue in their writings: Of those *vestigia ruris* which are apt to remain so long; which scarce any of our most admired authors are entirely free from in their compositions; which, after the age of manhood, only one person in my experience has so got rid of in speech that the most critical ear cannot discover his country from his expression or pronounciation' (Jones:1992:101). He regrets that fact that 'a provincial phrase sullies the lustre of the brightest eloquence' and bemoans the 'awkwardness of a provincial dress'. Perhaps we can best interpret his 'vernacular' as some kind of regional Scots (perhaps Edinburgh) standard or even an 18th century version of some type of 'Standard' Scots; that such a 'standard' might include what today might appear to be marked 'Scotticisms' such as [hid] <head> and [ərʊn] <around> need not affect such an interpretation (Jones:1993). However, despite his protestations, Sylvester Douglas is often given to outbursts against the 'vulgar Scotch' usage: describing the pronunciation of the sound *A*, he comments: 'It has besides these a third sound in the words *call, all, salt, malt,* which is also a sound very frequent in the south of Scotland; and is what the vulgar inhabitants of Edinburgh give to it in those very words *salt*, and *malt*' (Jones:1993:117).

The evidence provided by Alexander Scot's *The Contrast*, which, we recall, attempts to portray the presumably prestigious language of 'the present Caledonian English of the college, the pulpit and the bar' (Jones:1993:102) seems to offer information regarding the sociophonetic significance of the Scots [ɔ]/[o] alternation. Using the <oa> digraph to characterise [ɔ]-type pronunciations, we find Scot realising: <poalesh> '*polish*', <proaper> '*proper*', <Scoat> '*Scot*', <foar> '*for*', <noat> '*not*' <bayoand> '*beyond*', <aupoastles> '*apostles*', <foarty> '*forty*', <oad> '*odd*', <oar> '*or*', <poands> '*ponds*', <poassebly> '*possibly*', <froam>

'from'. Using <o> for [o(o)], he includes: <those>, <notted> *'noted'*, <spoc> *'spoke'*, <premoted> *'promoted'*, <hopful>, <pronunsatione>, <obadiant>. However, there are four (and only four) instances where <oa> is used where etymologically a high mid vowel might be expected: <soajurner> *'sojourner'*, <auloanne> *'alone'*, <tnoan> *'known'* and <prevoack> *'provoke'*. While there is nowhere evidence in the text of *The Contrast* for Scottish [o]/[oo] forms for etymological [ɔ], the presence of the opposite phenomenon, albeit in only a few items, suggests that, for speakers of the kind of language Scot is describing, so stigmatised was the substitution of [o] for [ɔ], that a limited 'hypercorrect' accommodation to stressed [ɔ] vowels in some items with etymological [o] is to be found. But the Scots evidence is not always easy to interpret and observers do not always appear to be able to distinguish high and low back mid segments; The entry under *O* in James Robertson's *The Ladies Help to Spelling* (1722:12) is not untypical:

> Lady: What's the Sound of (o)?
> Master: O, generally right pronounc'd, has less variation in its sound, than any other Vowel; being short before all double consonants, as in *oblige, Colt, most*, &c, but before *ld*, it sounds like *ou*, as in *cold, hold, fold*; see how the silent *e*, lengthens it, in these Examples, *I will not rob you of your Robe; He gave me a note, I will not deny; he beat with a rod, while he rode on his way*...it's alwise long if there be but one Consonant betwixt it and another Vowel, as in *Open, Onion, Olive.*

There can surely be little doubt that the norm of pronunciation being recommended by Robertson is not that of a contemporary London metropolitan standard, a conclusion borne out by some of the examples from his 'Table of Words, equal in Sound, but very much differing in Sense and Spelling' (1722:41ff): <God> *'Almighty'*: <Goad> *'a long sting'*; <Horse> *'to ride upon'*: <Hoarse> *'with cold'*; <Coast> *'the Sea-shore'*; <Cost> *'a great price'*; <Note> *'a mark'*; <Not> *'at all'*; <Knot> *'tying'*. Under his *Analysis of the Scotch Dialect*, Adams (1799:152) points clearly to the Scotch/English high/low back mid alternation. For the English *ode, rose* and *go* (with his o^1, *ò*, or *o long*) he describes as Scotch *ôdd, rôz* and *gâ*, where the vowel 'deemed short, though it sounds long, and resembles a kind of open *â*' (1799:24:152). Indeed, his comment on the *o long* in items like *bord, ford, hord* 'auntiently written per *oa* sounded *o*. This still appears by the modern spelling of many such words, *and our Northern mode of pronouncing*' [italics:CJ] and his assertion that '*Old, Ord, Ost* when sounded long by us, or vice versa, Are sounded short in Scotch, & vice versa' points clearly to a Scotch [o(o)] for [ɔ(ɔ)] substitution. It is surely Geddes (1792:423) who most strikingly illustrates the Scots tendency to favour low mid over high mid back vowel varieties:

> Fourthly, it is my opinion, that even the vowel sounds that predominate in the Scottish dialect, are of themselves more harmonious than those which are the most prevalent in English. That the open or broad *a*, for example is one of the most harmonious vocal sounds, is clear both from its being the most common, in almost all known languages, European or Asiatic, from the Italian to the Hindoo. Yet this sound very rarely occurs in English, but in Scots is extremely common, even now, and was formerly still more so. Not only did it take place of the English open short *a*, as in *grass, hand, man, mass*, &c but even of the long slender *a* as in *same, dame, spake, awake, brake, take, nation, consideration*, &c. It was also retained in a number of Saxon words, in which we have gradually changed it into *o* long, as *snaw, knaw, craw, blaw, thraw* for *snow, know, crow, blow, throw*, &c.

Although we cannot always assume that they represent current Scots usage, several of the Scottish observers assign values to <o>, <ou>, <ow> and <oa> which are often difficult to equate with 'standard' practice: Angus (1800) assigns [oo] values to <o> in items like: *chronology, decorate, comedian, coquetry, disoluble, solemn*; Warden (1753) shows [oo] in *solemnity, solid, monument, moderate, constant, provident*; Barrie has [oo] for *corn, cord, sort, cost, sloth*; Burn shows [oo] in *acknowledgement, fought, brought, George, Georgics, lord* with [ɔ(ɔ)] for <ow> in *fellow, follow, meadow*. The anonymous author of *A Spelling-Book Upon a New Plan* has [oo] in items like *glossary, florid, homage, oven, evolve, resolve, border*, as well as in the first <o> in *colonnade, colossus, columnar*, while low mid values are assigned to *arrogant, revolt, brocade* and *glorify*.

One of the most surprising features of the 18th century record, is the scarcity of its evidence for what is probably now seen as one of the most salient features of Scots phonology, the fronting and unrounding of [o] vowels to [e], as in *ane* for *own, stane* for *stone*, the classically Northern 'route' for long sonorant vowels to take under the *English Vowel Shift*. It is really only Adams (1799:152-53) who shows such a development in his record of <more>/<maire>, <own>/<ain>, <grown>/<grain>, <oak>/<aik>, <oats>/<aits> and <oath>/<aits> alternants and it is interesting to note that written in hand in the Edinburgh University Library copy of *The Pronunciation of English*, are <bone>/<bain> and <stone>/<stain>. Elphinston claims that 'Hence hear we, in colloquial Scotch....*sloe* slae; *more* mare, *home* hame; *cave* cove, *rave* rove' (1786:2). However, it is interesting to note how Geddes represents what for him is one of the main Scottish characteristics of the use of a pure palatal vowel [i]. He cites its regular appearance in items where a Southern English etymological [oo] and a Northern [ee] would be expected. Spellings such as <mèr> '*more*'; <Rèm> '*Rome*'; <rèm> '*roam*' and <stèns> '*stones*', point to a 're-application' of the *English Vowel Shift* of the typically Northern [aa] → [ee] to one where a further increase in palatality takes place such that [ee] → [ii]. We might be tempted to treat such <è>

spellings as printer's errors for Geddes' <e> which seems to represent an [e(e)] segment, but this would involve an acceptance of an otherwise unjustifiably high level of printing or proofing incompetence. The lack of [stiin] '*stone*' types in Douglas and Scot may well be a reflection of the fact that they appear to be attempting to represent some kind of 'standard' - certainly educated - Scots, while Geddes' forms might well represent something somewhat closer to a lower social level vernacular.

6

SONORANT VOWEL SEGMENTS

6.1. The [ɑ]/[a] Contrast

This is the area of 18th century phonology where contemporary observers are perhaps at their most ambiguous and where they are clearly finding difficulty with a recognition of the phonetic facts as well as with a suitable descriptive framework within which to set them. The main problem for the modern observer mainly centres around ascertaining whether the 18th century commentators recognise in their contemporary phonetics/phonology any contrast between pure sonorants like [ɑ] and those near pure sonorants (such as [a]) showing a lowered F_2 with an F_1 less raised above the baseline than is typical for pure sonorants. At the same time, it is also somewhat difficult to determine the extent to which they differentiate more rounded (close-to-pure) sonorant types such as [ɒ] as separate phonetic entries from both [ɑ] and [ɔ]. The statements these commentators make concerning the precise phonetic value of such vowels are often intriguingly imprecise. Of the English observers it is perhaps Walker (1791:10-11) who gives the clearest picture of the elements characteristic of the phonology in this area. Walker identifies what he calls an open or middle *a* sound, which is 'nearly' the Italian *a* in items like *Romana* or the final *a* in *mama, papa*. Its phonetic value he defines negatively, stating that the vowel sound in *all, ball* is 'still more open' and is 'deeper' than the *a* middle. However, he is careful to point out that this segment - possible [ɑ] - (and which he claims to be long) is rare in the contemporary phonology, restricted to appear in monosyllabic rhyme codas terminating in [r], [lf], [nt/s], [s], and [θ], as in *far, calf, grant, glance, glass* and *bath*, as well as 'in the word *father*'. He comments unfavourably too on the fact that 'this pronunciation of *a* seems to have been for some years advancing to the short sound of this letter, as heard in *hand, land, grand,* &c, and pronouncing the *a* in *after, answer, basket, plant, mast,* &c as long as in *half, calf,* &c borders very closely on vulgarity' (1791:10-11). There is, what he claims to be a 'short' version of the *long a middle* manifested in items like *man, pan, tan, hat,* a sound which is 'generally...found before any two successive consonants', throwing up vowel length contrasts in such items as *mar/marry*. However, the short sound of this middle *a* seems to show a quality distinction as well, since it 'is generally confounded with the short sound of the slender *a*...the sound of this vowel in *man, pan, tan, hat*'. His slender *a* is the high mid front [e] vowel in *rage*, and Walker makes the not untypical claim that its short version is the vowel in *met*. While this may simply be the result of the usual contemporary confusion between quantitative and qualitative descriptive terminology, it might also just suggest that the low mid vowel could have been perceived as showing a raised characteristic like [ɛ˔]. A 'short' version of [ɑ] corresponding to the vowel in *met*, suggests an [a], [æ] or even [ɛ] value for this segment; Mather Flint (1740:74) observing : '*A* suivi d'une seule consonne est bref, & se prononce comme un *e* français ouvert & bref'.

The position taken on this issue by Sylvester Douglas is interesting from a number of different points of view. For both the pure and the Scotch dialects he distinguishes : (1) the *long open a* as in <father>, (2) the *short open a* as in <hat> and (3) the *broad a* characterised by the vowel in the item <all>. Interestingly, Douglas' description of these segments is a relativistic one. The broad and open *a* sounds are, he claims, 'only to be considered as shades and gradations of the same sound', and - as we have already noted (page 74) - the kind of description he proposes where phonetic segments are non-discrete, analogous to the continuum of the colour spectrum, is not unlike that put forward by many modern proponents of phonological description (notably Donegan 1978; Stampe 1972):

> For, as in the rainbow, although the pure middle part of each of the different stripes of colours is clearly distinguishable from the others, yet, while the eye gradually passes outwards, to the edge of such stripes on either side, it seems to die away insensibly into the neighbouring tint, and is at length so like it, that it is impossible for the mind to draw the line, or fix the limit where the one ends, and the other begins; so the same thing is observable in our perception of vocal sounds. Thus we may consider the long open *a* in *father* as a sound placed between *o* and the strong slender *a*, or Scotch Eta (Jones:1992:52).

Such a use of colour terminology to express the non-discrete character of sound segments perhaps stems from a similar remark of Kenrick's (1784:54): 'By the addition of several distinctions, introduced by a multiplication of the vowels, it is true, that mankind have acquired a greater diversity in the matter of speech: but these vocal distinctions are by no means so forcible and precise as consonants. As in the mixture of colours in painting, there are many artificial varieties to be made, sufficiently distinguishable from each other by connoisseurs and artists; but the strongest and most precise distinctions of coloured lights and shades, do not come up to the full partition of black and white, or the divisions marked out by the primary colours of light. Thus, although there be more clearness and precision in the articulation of polished tongues, not withstanding their increase of vowels, than in the imperfect general languages; yet the nicer vocal distinctions, affected by fine speakers, tend not only to render their language enervate but indistinct.' Sylvester Douglas' description of the *long open a* characteristic of the stressed vowel in <father> is not easy to interpret unambiguously. While it is difficult to assess what he means by *o* in this context, we might surmise that since his *long close o* ([oo]) is such a common feature of the pure dialect as he records it, this high mid segment rather than some [ɔ] type is intended here. The strong slender *a*, we have already suggested, represents [εε] (see above, pp. 123). A low sound 'placed between' a long high back rounded and a long front unrounded segment we might see literally as referring to a long unrounded central(ised) shape like [ä]. On the other hand, if Douglas intends us to envisage a low segment with the backness characteristic of [oo] and the unrounded feature of [εε], then some low back unrounded [ɑ] segment may be what he means us to understand by this description.

Yet lexical items unambiguously marked with this vowel specification appear to be relatively rare in Douglas' *Table*, only PATRICK showing a clear analogue to the *father* model, although even here Douglas shows some uncertainty concerning phonetic value, deleting in the *A* version of the manuscript of the *Treatise* the description of the vowel as *short* and open for one in the *S* version where it is described as *long* and open. That the pure dialect realised short versions of what might be a long [ɑɑ] vowel seems to be inferred from a comparison between the FATHER item and its immediately preceding FAMINE entry. The stressed vowel in *father* is described as 'the *a* as in the foregoing word but longer'. If the *a* in *father* is indeed [ɑɑ], then *famine* would seem to show an [ɑ] stressed vowel space, analogues to which are given as *ham, swam* and *ram*. Likewise, the vowel in *lather* is described as 'the *a* short. In other respects as in *father*'. *Rather* too is cited as a pure dialect analogue of *lather*.

Like Walker, what Sylvester Douglas intends by the much more frequently exemplified *short open a* is clearly not merely a durationally curtailed version of [ɑɑ]. The vowel sound in *hat* 'approaches to the limits of, and begins to mix itself with, the short and strong slender sound in *better*' (Jones:1992:117) reminding us of Buchanan's (1762:8) description which also suggests a more palatal possibility for the *short a* vowel:

> The short sound of (a) is expressed in *băd, băt, bănd, hănd, mănner, bătter,* &c. which Words are pronounced but a little more open than *bĕt, bĕd, bĕnd, hĕnd, mĕnner, bĕtter*.

and again (1757:8):

> The short sound of (e) differs but very little from short *a*; as *fet, set, bed* &c differ but little in their sounds from *fat, sad, bad,* only those with (a) have a little more opening.

Such a description might fit a phonetic entity with a palatal/sonorant mix, where the sonority component was more prominent that the palatal, a segment like [æ], rather than [a]. Kenrick too observes (1784:62-3): 'Expressed in letters by *a, au, ua,* short, as in *hand, barr'd,* and long as in *hard, guard, laugh,* is a sound common to most languages.....It is somewhat surprising, that men of letters, and some of them even residing in the Metropolis, should mistake the simple and genuine applications of this sound. "The native sound of *a,* says Dr Bailey, is broad, deep, and long, as in *all, aw, war, daub;* but it hath generally a mixed sound, as in *man, Bath, Mary, fair,* which are sounded as if written *maen, baeth,* &c." But who, except flirting females and affected fops, pronounce *man,* and *Bath,* as if they were written *maen, baeth,* or like *Mary, fair,* &c.' Yet Cortez Telfair (1775:149) assures us that the *short a* in items like *hat* is like the <ea> in *wealth* or *e* in the French word *elle;* indeed 'it is the very same with the third long [the vowel in *star*:CJ] only pronounced quicker'. The *star* vowel probably corresponds to Sylvester Douglas' *strong slender a,* commonly found in rhotic syllable rhymes, showing a value of [εε].

Although the items most commonly cited by Sylvester Douglas for this low front vowel are those whose stressed rhyme peaks terminate in [r] codas, (a context which we might expect to produce stressed vowel length) he nevertheless repeatedly refers to these as *short* open, thus <art>, <start>, <cart>, <dart>, <car>, <claret> and so on. Perhaps echoing Walker's concerns about the spread of [ɑ] types, Douglas - under the ART entry (Jones:1992:164-65) - warns Scotch speakers who, we recall, regularly use [εε] in such words, against falling into the error of substituting for that sound 'the long open *a* as the inhabitants of the north of England particularly do, in the word *cart*'.

6.2 the [ɑ]/[ɒ] Contrast

We have already attempted to address the difficult and vexed question as to what might be the precise phonetic value of the *father* stressed vowel, the *long open a.* Our assignment of an [ɑɑ] value (rather than, say, [aa]) to Sylvester Douglas' *long open a,* might at least in part be justified by looking at his comments relating to *broad open a,* the vowel he hears in <all>, <alter>, etc., and one he clearly sees as close in value to *long open a.* The identifying feature of this (usually durationally extended) *broad* sound can be gauged from Douglas' observation that it is 'a mixture of the long open *a* and the *o*' - see page 74-75 above. While such a description might equally well point to a mixed labial/sonorant [ɔ] or [ɒ] shape, it is worth recalling Douglas' claim concerning the [ɔɔ] (the long sound of the open *o*) in items like <corn>, <horn> when compared with the vowel (broad open long) in <all>:

> This sound if not the same, is near the confines, or the extended edge, if I may so speak, of the broad *a* in *all.* Some writers think them the same. I imagine I can perceive a difference.

Therefore, if the broad *a* shows clear evidence of being the relatively highly sonorant [ɒ], then it would not seem implausible to suggest that the long open *a*, which is claimed to be one of its component parts, should be the pure sonorant [ɑ], rather than the palatality contaminated [a]. The English grammarians comment extensively on this area of the vowel space. Walker (1791:11:§ 77) recognises long and short versions of a 'deeper sound and still more open than *father*', the former in items like *fall, ball, gall, all, wall, call, salt, bald, false* (with 'the long sound of the deep broad German *a*'); short versions he claims occur in syllable initial [w] contexts like *wallow, swallow, want, wasp, was, what* and since he also gives the same value for items like *not, got* and *lot*, sees it as homophonous with his second sound of the *o*, which is 'called its short sound, and is found in *not, got, lot,* &c'. This sound in turn 'corresponds exactly to that of the *a* in *what*, with which the words *not, got, lot,* are perfect rhymes. The long sound, to which the *o* in *not* and *sot* are short ones, is found under the diphthong *au* in *naught*, and the *ou* in *fought*; corresponding exactly to the *a* in *hall, ball,* &c.' (1791:§ 163) Sheridan too seems to see no difference between the short *o* and broad *a* types, listing all the following items under his a^3: *call, talk, laud, taught, claw, broad, George, form, ought*. (1781:25). However Buchanan's (1762) short *o* vowel in *got, rod, George,* is kept distinct from the 'guttural or broad sound' of *a* in *all, call, bald, ward, walk,* etc., and Nares (1784:31), under his discussion of Broad A, comments: 'though this sound is very like that of the short *o*, it is yet distinguishable from it; *moss* and *dross* are not the same as *cross* and *loss*.'

What appears to be a refinement of the [ɑɑ] /[ɒɒ] contrast is brought to our attention by Sylvester Douglas in his detailed description under the AUNT item (Jones:1992:165): 'In this word *aunt*, and several others, [the stressed vowel:CJ] has the long open sound of *a* - yet less open than that in *father*', which, if we are to take it at its face value, appears to suggest the existence of some kind of segment intermediate between [ɑ] and [ɒ], although we might wish to doubt a level of observation of such delicacy. Sylvester Douglas points too to the fact that among the vernacular Scotch 'those who try to catch the English method sound it [*'aunt'*:CJ] long and broad, like the *a* in *all*, or as the English pronounce it in *haunt*.' Unlike for the [ɑɑ] vowel, Douglas lists many items which show the broad open *a* sound, both in his *Observations on the Alphabet* and in the *Table* proper, e.g. <all>, <also>, <altar>, <halt>, <halter>, <hall>, and many others, and he seems to suggest as well that in the pure dialect a short [ɒ] version of the sound was also to be found; for instance, under the CAUSEWAY entry (Jones:1992:181) he describes the '*au* as in *cause* or *Paul*, but short', while under WANT (Jones:1992:231) we find 'The broad *a* as in *all*, but not quite so long'.

Buchanan (1757:7) recognises a sound which is 'broad like *aw*...as most foreigners pronounce it'; this 'guttural or broad sound' is exemplified by the usual items like *all, call*. However, he distinguishes an 'open sound, which approaches to its broad sound, and is expressed in *Wrath, Rather, Father, Glass* and some others'. Indeed in *An Essay* (1766:66) he goes so far as to label an 'acute sound, which seems to approach to *au*, but is really short *a*, twice, but rapidly pronounced, as denoted by a circumflex over it, thus *fâthir, râthir, ârms*, &c.' However, as we have seen, Buchanan's *short a* approaches some kind of [ɛ], suggesting that his *father* stressed vowel is [aa] rather than [ɑɑ] , whatever 'rapidly pronounced' means. He is quick to assure us though that the *open* and *acute* sounds occur 'but rarely', and in his Dictionary, both sounds are conflated under the 'less open short' *ǎ*. James Douglas too seems to provide some evidence that the sonorant vowel in his inventory was [aa]. His A2 in *mad, bad, sirrah*, is described as short, acute and guttural, and Holmberg interprets it as [æ] (Holmberg:1956:32ff). A4, however, 'has a kind of Middle Sound between the broad Scotch *A* & the short guttural *A* which may be call'd the Scotch *A* Short, as CHAFF, CHANCE' (Holmberg:1956:121). But it is not easy to provide a precise phonetic value for Douglas' 'broad Scotch *A*' from his description: 'The Vowel *A* is sounded after the Scotch manner, Broad, full, & open, in the Beginning of Monosyllables before *LL*, as ĀLL'. While we shall look in more detail at Scots sonorant manifestations in the next section, it would seem not unreasonable even now to interpret James Douglas' *broad Scotch a* as something approaching [ɑ] or even [ɒ]. A sound between this and the *short guttural A*, is as likely to be [a] as anything else: 'We can state without any hesitation that A4 was a short vowel that had an *a*-quality and was not [æ] as so many of its equivalents in contemporary sources. It seems probable that this *a*-quality was something like [a] but it is a hopeless task to try and find out exactly what sort of a front or neutral *a* it was' (Holmberg:1956:45).

6.3 Scotch Retraction and Rounding

Many of the Scotch observers provide little in the way of information concerning the phonetic value of the broadly sonorant vowels in their inventories. Some, like Warden, McIllquam and Burn, refer only to a single *a* vowel for which they provide little or no interesting phonetic detail. Others, notably Robertson, Scott, Gray, Telfair and Perry, distinguish short and long *a* vowels but shy away from stipulating whether the latter is [a] or [ɑ] or whatever, notably Barrie with *ǎ* for *hat, at, an* and *à* for pre-[r] *are, pardon, far*. Angus' (1814) tripartite symbolic distinction of *a, â* and *ǎ* is difficult to interpret, although his *shut a* as in *bad, cab, tram, ram, bat, fat*, might just suggest an [æ]-type segment, while his 'name sounds' *â* and *ǎ* (exemplified through *arms, bar, card, barber, jar, star, harm, vaunt, haunt* as against *pass, lass, past, task, craft, France, lance, vast*) may merely serve to signify a durational distinction, perhaps [a]/[aa], and he does stress that *â* and *ǎ* are 'vowels similar in Quality but different in quantity'. Other commentators show what appears to be a genuine phonetically distinct tri-partite system of representation for low vowels, especially Adams under his *Second Position* description (1799:39):

> *A*, No.1. *a* slender, *at, bad, can, fan, man, mad*. No. 2. two consonants render it a little more open, as *bank, cast, dart, fast,* &c.; and the *r* alone, or followed by consonants, still more, as *bar, car, far, star, arms, art, cart, dart, bard,* &c.: if *w* precedes, then by rule of *w* alone...a is very broad, *war, warm, ward, want, wan*, &c.

where the *Second Position* is defined as one where 'our vowels receive a foreign and contracted sound; and thus is much more frequent than the long English sound' and where 1. refers to 'the general and common sound', with 2. 'a frequent and secondary sound'. The *slender/little more open/still more open* and *very broad* might be interpreted as some kind of [æ]/[a]:[ɑ]/[ɒ] alternation. Perhaps closest in spirit to this system is that of the anonymous author of *A Spelling-Book Upon a New Plan* (1796:6ff) who in some parts of the work distinguishes merely a *broad* (*bald, fall*), *slender* (*base, lame*) and *open* (*band, bank, aunt*) distinction, nevertheless in his SCHEME and in his word lists uses a more complex diacritic classification under five heads: *â ā á ắ à*. - where â is the vowel in <all>, and *ā* the vowel in <waste>. The following table lists some of the items to be found under the symbols *ắ* and *à*, as well as *á*, the last having no descriptive label and only appearing exemplified in the SCHEME and notably in the lists of words (which are arranged according to both syllable number and stress pattern):

á	*ắ*,	*à*
patrol;	hắrăss;	lànguáge;
faction;	quắdrănt,;	patron; păpà;
càrnáge;	adrift;	castle; castor;
lappet	adrift; abode;	father; pathos;
	acute; adult;	plaster; Eclat;
	away; afloat;	almond;
	wry;	arbour,
	ărrănt;	ardent; argue;
	arrow; ătlắs;	army; bargain;
	many; raven;	candour;
	vapour	farther;
		farthing;
		garden

The values attached to such symbols are difficult to determine. The propensity for column three items to show rhymes which are rhotic or continuant might suggest vowel length and, in the light of subsequent development in some dialects, [ɑɑ]. The column one items are very rarely attested, and their identification in the SCHEME with French terminations in *age* might suggest [aa], while column two items seem to show a low front [æ], or in the light of the *many* instance, a slightly raised [æ⊥] or even [ɛᴛ], while the <răven> and <văpour> instances might just be Scotticisms. But that there was recognised by some contemporary observers a genuine phonetic contrast between low vowels in the inventory is perhaps best illustrated by looking once again at Sylvester Douglas' AUNT entry:

> In the vernacular Scotch pronounciation of this word, the *au* is sounded like the open *a* but short. Nearly as the *a* in *ant*; but more open. Those who try to catch the English method sound it long and broad, like the *a* in *all*, or, as the English pronounce it in *haunt*. But in this word *aunt*, and several others, it has the long open sound of *a* - yet, less open, than in *father*. Indeed it appears to my ear, that not only this long open sound of the *au* differs from that of the *a* in *father*; but that the short open *a*, as in *ant*, *scant*, *scar*, *cant*, *fast*, &c is not only, not the same in quantity, but also differs in quality, from the long open *a* in *father*. That it is, in short, a shade lying between that last-mentioned sound, and the slender *a*. This, I think, will be manifest to any one who will carefully attend to the English and Scotch modes of pronouncing the word *ant*. The difference between them will be very perceptible, and in the latter the sound of the *a*, seems exactly the same in quality, but shorter, than in *father*.
>
> Pronounce the *au* as in *aunt*, in *haunch*, *launch*, *paunch*, *staunch*. All these words, make a perfect rhyme with *blanch*. In most other words as *paunch*, *haunt*, *daunt*, *sauce*, the *au* is sounded like the broad *a*, or like *aw*.

Here we see a sound in *aunt* which is less open than the *a* in *father*, which in its turn is different in both quality and quantity from the *a* in *ant*. Such an observation would perhaps suggest respectively values like [fɑɑð-], [aant] and [ænt]. Again, while the vowel in <wax> should, in the pure dialect be 'sounded something between the *a* in *wafer*, and that in *father*', [some kind of [a] sound:CJ] the Scotch pronounce it '*too* open' (where Douglas underscores *too* in the Signet version) probably as [ɑ] or [ɑɑ]. Yet the lists in the *Spelling Book upon New Plan* appear to show a considerable amount of what is probably lexical diffusion (although we cannot always discount typological error) in that we see both *ǎ* and *à* in rhotic rhyme position, as in *dǎrling* and *àrmour*, and even alternative manifestations like *cǎndle*/*càndle* and *càrnáge*/*cǎbbáge*.

For William Adie (1769) there appears to have been a complete conflation of[ɑɑ] under something like [ɒɒ]. Under his *Rule 1* word list, where 'A Vowel is short in a Syllable which ends with a Consonant' he notes that the reader should 'Pronounce *a* and *a* marked thus ^, chiefly before *r* and another Consonant, like *aŭ*' (1769:3). His *au* is exemplified by such items as *lawn, pawn, daub, claw* and *draw* - although also *heart, learn* and *groat* - and he notes too that '*A* sounds *au* before *ll, ld, lk, lt,* and between *w* and *r,* and in the termination *lk*' (1769:9). Among the many items he lists showing *â* are: *hard, hart, yard, garb, cart, harm, papâ, father, alarm, charm, chant, carve, large, gardens, harness, slander, darling, asylum* and a great many others. However, it might just be the case that for him the vowel in items like *corn, sport, cloth, froth, border, short,* etc., - all marked with <ô> - represented some more labial (rounder) version such as [ɔɔ].

In sections 4.2.8 and 4.2.9 we pointed out the tendency in late 18th century Scots, especially on the evidence provided by Sylvester Douglas, to alternate [a]/[æ]/[ɑ] with [ɛ] and [e] segments. Douglas generally stigmatises mid vowel realisations in words like *art, cart, dart,* calling them 'errors' and 'false pronounciations', and in so doing reflecting the value judgements of many of his contemporaries in this area of the phonology. However, the situation is clearly a rather complex one since under DRAGON he states quite categorically that 'The *a* as in *drag, brag, wagon.* The Scotch, when they aim at propriety of pronounciation are apt to sound it as in *plague*' (Jones:1992:189). He also records mid to low substitutions as well, notably *apron* produced by Scotch speakers with the vowel in *father*, denounced as 'vulgar Scotch', yet in *cradle* 'The Scotch (endeavouring to speak properly) are apt to pronounce the *a* short & as in *bad, addle, paddle*'. We can only speculate on the reasons behind this apparently contradictory behaviour. Perhaps we need to see his expressions 'aiming at propriety' and 'endeavouring to speak properly' in terms of the type of 'standard' at which speakers were aiming. [e] pronunciations for items like <art> (recall Buchanan's (1770:45) examples of 'how North Britons destroy just quantity....in *mairy* for *marry...maijesty* for *majesty*') and <clemency> were regarded as equally 'Scottish' and 'generally laid hold of in 'taking off the Scotch dialect' and 'among the things which are most striking to an English ear', but the former may have represented a stigmatised pronunciation in a *Scottish* standard context, while the latter did not. We should recall in this context too Alexander Scot's spellings for items such as *capable, ancient, parent, regaled, initiatory* as <caupable>, <Auncient>, <paurent>, <ragauled>, <eeneetiautoray> where <au> is normally used to present some kind of low back or low front vowel as in the items <aund>, <thaut> and <auz>. These spellings, we recall, are an attempt to represent the 'present Caledonian English of the college, the pulpit and the bar' (Jones:1993:114) suggesting perhaps that [a] for [e] substitution was a prestigious characteristic in Scotland in the period.

In perhaps much the same way, Adams' (1799:152) summary of English/Scotch contrasts (see Table 6.1. below) seems to point to much [e]/[a]/[ɒ] alternation (his A1, A2 and A3 respectively in *Free* position (cf. Adams:1799:34)). We pointed out above too how William Adie (1769:3) lists items such as *hard, hart, yard, garb, cart, harm* with *â*, some kind of

TABLE 6.1

Adams' Sonorant Vowel Contrasts

	ENGLISH	SCOTCH
A1, ai	Làdy, fàtal,	Lâdy, fâtal,
	tàke, wàke	tâke, wâke
A2. á		A.1
	Art, arms,	airt, airms,
	father,	faither,
		fâther,
	hat	hait, hât
A3. â	Anna,	Awnnâ,
		ainnai,
	waggon,	wâgon,
	wax,	wâx,
	(wàfer).	wâfer.
	Wâter,	Waiter,
		wáter, wais,
	wâs,	wus,
	wâant,	waint,
	war,	weir, wàr,
	wârm	wairm

[ɒɒ], and this may well tie in with Geddes' (1792:423) observation that 'Not only did it [the *broad a* as in *law*:CJ] take place of the English open short *a*, as in *grass, hand, man, mass*, &c but even of the long slender *a* as in *same, dame, spake, awake, brake, take, nation, consideration*, &c.' - reminding us of the *Commonly Pronounced* <cânle> and <âgent> for the *True Pronunciation* <căndle> and <āgent> from the list of items 'in which the Natives of North Britain are most apt to err' in the *Spelling Book upon a New Plan* (1796:vii), where <ă>, <ā> and <â> represent something like [a], [e] and [ɒ]. Perhaps this tendency is what Elphinston (1786:8) refers to when he states that 'Boath sides dhe Tweed hav been misled, howevver differently, by dhe appearance ov *quality*; dhe Inglish into' wrong *quallity*, often slendering dhe braud shut vowel; dhe Scots, into' false *quantity*, opening and extending dhe braud sound. *Water* (for *wauter*) haz drawn all Scotland into' *watter* (won ov dhe Teutonnic emissions)'. The tendency for Geddes' 'Edinburgh dialect' to show rounded manifestations for sonorants like [a] and [ɑ] is clear from the lexical distribution of his <à> graph which appears to represent [ɒ]: à' '*all*'; àll; àromátick '*aromatic*'; awà '*away*'; bàd '*bade*'; bàmi '*balmy*'; bárbàrian; behàd '*behold*'; dàn'd '*dawned*'; glàmor '*light*' ; hà' '*had*' ;

kàtchist *'catchest'*; krà *'crow'* ; lànd; làrd *'lord'*; sà *'saw'*; sà' *'say'*; sàl *'soul'*; tàld *'told'*; wel-fàhkt *'well-made'*; whà's *'who's'* (Jones 1994:98).

Geddes describes his <á> graph as: '*a* Italian, as in *father*. The Scots seem formerly to have known no other sound of this letter, which is indeed the general sound all over the world, except in England' and shows it in 'Edinburgh dialect' items such a: ábsint; admárâshon; áft *'oft'*; ál; áltar; àromátick; árun *'around'*; bárbàrian; bárran *'barren'*; blástit *'blasted'*; dáms *'ewes'*; drág; fár; fátlins; fáttist láms *'fattest lambs'*; fávrán' *'favouring'*; Gálátea; gáng *'go'*; gráff *'graft'*; háng; háppi; huáre'r; huát; inhábit; invád *'invade'*; kám *'came'*; kráp *'crop'* vb; láms; láng *'long'*; Iángan *'longing'*; lángir *'longer'*; lást; mán; márkat; náti' *'native'*; Oáxis; Párthians; plánt; prolång; quáff; rápid; sákred *'sacred'*; sáng *'song'*; shál; táp *'top'*; thrádom; tráks *'tracks'*; unháppi; wárld; wát *'know'*. Data like these tend to suggest a (still prestigious?) Scots preference for low back over fronted back sonorant segments. Even the Scots *a* short in *hand* is only 'nearly so'. This is not entirely the English *a* short, as in *hand*, a sound not known in Scotland, till very lately'. Indeed, Geddes describes the '*i* short as in *sin*' as 'so often so nearly the sound of short *a*, that it may be used for it' (1792:432-35). We have suggested in section 4.2.5 that this description might fit some kind of centralised [ë] vowel, perhaps once more suggesting a Scots preference for more sonorant, low and centralised vowels.

7

DIPHTHONGAL SOUNDS

7.1 The [ɑɩ] Diphthong

We have already seen the controversy in the period surrounding 'true' and 'false' diphthongs' and the set of descriptive techniques employed to characterise the complex nature of the former. What we may at this stage loosely characterise as the [ɑɩ] diphthong is variously described in both English and Scottish sources. 'This letter [<i>:CJ] is the perfect diphthong, composed of the sound of *a* in *father*, and *e* in *he*, pronounced as closely together as possible' (Walker:1791:14) or Steele's (1775:*Preface*:ix-x): 'To try the like experiment on the English sound of I or Y, as in I in the first person, and in the words MY, EYE, IDLE, and FINE, (both which letters are the marks of one and the same *diphthong sound* composed of the English sounds AU and EE,) the voice begins on the sound AU, and immediately changes to EE on which it continues and ends' compared with the more obscure: 'Dhe vowels ov a dipthong, being boath effective, lend mutual aid; and, needing no servile, admit non...Dhis *ty* and *toy*, *coy* and *cow*, *oil* and *owl*, *coit* and *gout*. Dhis accounts for dhe unshut vowel, or open dipthong, ov *Crist* (wonce *Chryst*): also ov *Wyche* and *Dyche*. Az dhe Inglish *Hydhe* or *Hidhe*, so dhe Scotch *Forsydhe* or *Forsidhe*, and *Kilsythe* or *Kilsithe*, cannot now be known widhout dhe servile' (Elphinston 1786:152). Referring to Buchanan's (1762:11) observation that: 'Long (i) has a double Sound, and is compounded of *aw* and *ee*, pronounced very quick thus *ăweĕ*; as *fire, desire*, &c. is pronounced as if written *făweĕr, desăweĕr*; though it not always so very open, but in many Words resembles the Greek *E*', Kenrick (1784:65), in his usual anti-Scottish vein comments: 'This sound is typified by *i* or *y*, *ui*, or *ie*, as in *I*, *why, nigh, guide, fie*. As at present uttered by the best speakers in the Metropolis, it is the sharpest, shrillest, and clearest vowel in our language; altho' it has the appearance, when slowly pronounced, of being a compound of the *a* or *e* and *i*. I do not know that any other language has it equally clear, single and distinct. I have elsewhere observed that our Scottish linguists say it has the sound usually donoted by *awee*, but the errour of this is obvious to every Englishman.'

Yet most other Scottish commentators are pretty unhelpful in describing this diphthong merely as *i long* or i^1, illustrating it through items such as *mile, devise, hight, night, bridel, mitre, child*. In view of the current Scots double realisation of the *English Vowel Shift* effect on historically long pure palatal vowels in such items as *Fife* and *five*, with [ʌɩ] and [ɑe] respectively (Abercrombie 1979:68-84); Catford:1957:110), it might not be too surprising to find in those late 18th century observers who were themselves Scots some feeling for a contextually driven alternation like this. Sylvester Douglas (Jones:1992:108) describes the complex vowel space in an item like *sigh* as one where 'the vocal part is a compound sound, consisting of a combination....of the two simple vowels, commonly represented by the characters *a* and *e*.' Under his discussion of the phonetic value of the orthographic <i>, he includes 'what I would call its diphthongal sound (Jones:1992:129):

> being in truth a diphthong composed of the short open *a*, and the first sound of *e*. Although a diphthong, this sound is sometimes short, as in *dice*, often long, as in *wise*. When it is long the ear can with the greatest facility discriminate the two vocal sounds, of which it is composed. When short, this cannot be done without a considerable effort of attention.

His long/short contrast (sensitive, as we shall see, to the voicing coefficient of the syllable final segment) is perhaps best interpreted as referring to diphthongal complexes with different starting and finishing points rather than to any inherent durational characteristics of their composite vowels. The fact that the 'long' diphthong is the more audibly perceptible might just suggest that its 'degree of travel' or steepness of its F2 transition, is greater than its 'short' equivalent. That Douglas describes the first element of the 'long' version as 'short open *a*'. i.e. [æ], infers that the complex is [æɩ], while the short version, with the lesser degree of travel, may represent some kind of [ɛɩ] (or even [eɩ]) shape. In his *Table*, Douglas only occasionally describes pure dialect samples as showing the long diphthong (e.g. <precise>, <privateer>, <short lived>) generally characterising [æɩ] simply as 'diphthongal *i*' or as the 'diphthongal sound of *i*', thus <direct>, <dizen>, <Friday>, <idea>, <oblige>, <scite> and some others. In the pure dialect he lists <ice>, <nice>, <precise>, <twice> and <entice> as 'short' [ɛɩ] types. From the evidence he cites, there appears also to be some pure/Scotch alternation between the two diphthongal types: in general the pure [ɛɩ] items with syllable final [s] (<ice>, <nice>, <twice>, <thrice>, <entice>, <precise>) are realised in the Scotch dialect with [æɩ]; however, in the context of preceding a syllable final voiced segment, the Scotch <precise> rhymes to <wise>. Douglas notes too (Jones:1992:130) the similar German diphthong in items like <eis>, <Rhein> but where the diphthong is 'composed of the short slender, instead of the open, *a*, and the first sound of *e*. Many Scotch people pronounce the diphthongal *i*, exactly like the German *ei*', arguing for a Scotch realisation like [ɛɩ] or [æ̝ɩ]. But whatever their exact phonetic characteristics, Douglas' short and long diphthongal types seem to correspond well both in contextual preference and F2 transition curve with their modern [ɑe] and [ʌɩ] congeners.

Even more detailed support for a non-homogenous interpretation of the *long i* in late 18th century Scots comes from the elaborate and sensitive orthographic representations found in Alexander Scot's *The*

Contrast (Jones:1993:103-106). Scot uses no less than five digraph representations - <oy>, <oi>, <ey>, <ei>, <ai> - for what generally passes for *long i* among other observers at the time. Scot's lexical distribution of these digraphs is as in Table 7.1:

TABLE 7.1
Scot's [ɑɪ] Diphthong

	Modern Standard Scots FIVE [ɑɛ]	
Scot's Spelling		
<oy>	**<oi>**	**<ey>**
oy *'I'*	dasoir *'desire'*	whey *'why'*
moy *'my'*	enspoir *'inspire'*	
troying *'trying'*	foive *'five'*	
troyal *'trial'*	auroival *'arrival'*	
oys *'eyes'*	proivat *'private'*	
reloy *'rely'*	foiray *'fiery'*	
	poious *'pious'*	
	serproize *'surprise'*	
18th Century Scots Standard [ɑɛ]	**[ɑʌ]/[ɑə]**	**[ɛɪ]**
1	**2**	**3**

	Modern Standard Scots FIFE [ʌɪ]	
Scot's Spelling		
<ei>		**<ai>**
daleited *'delighted'*		aither *'either'*
queit *'quite'*		naither *'neither'*
steil *'style'*		
dazein *'design'*		
baseids *'besides'*		
mein *'mine'*		
wreit *'write'*		
Yoarksheir *'Yorkshire'*		
leik *'like'*		
Cleid *'Clyde'*		
feind *'find'*		
lein *'line'*		
18th Century Scots Standard [ɛ̆ɪ]		**[ɑɪ]**
4		**5**

While the 18th century Scots standard values we have entered for the items in columns one through five must be seen as highly speculative, it is clear that Scot's orthographic contrasts are not without phonetic, phonological and morphological foundation. Column 1 items show a stressed vowel in a syllable, morpheme and word boundary context, those in column 2 a stressed vowel mainly in syllables terminated by voiced sonorant and fricative segments, segments associated with low F_2 and, in consequence, having a 'lowering' effect on vocalic elements at the syllable peak, suggesting diphthongal shapes like [ɑʌ] or [ɑə]. The <vauroietay> and <poious> types show the diphthong in morpheme boundary contexts where the interface is vocalic. Column 4 types show syllables terminated by palato-alveolar obstruent and sonorant segments sympathetic to high F_1 vowel configurations in their vicinity (although note <Yoarksheir>), suggesting a second diphthongal element of a palatal sympathetic type, such as [ɩ] or [i]. The lexical item specific examples of column 5 are usually accorded separate comment by contemporary observers.

However, the most obvious phonetic and morphological contexts differentiating column 1/2 and column 4 types correspond almost exactly with the environment affecting stressed vowel and diphthongal length and quality in Modern Standard Scots, known as the *Scots Vowel Length Rule* (Aitken 1981; McMahon 1991; Wells 1982:400-402; Ewen 1977). This rule attempts to capture the fact that contemporary Scots diphthongs will have a durationally extended first element before voiced fricatives, [r] (the <oi> cases) and word boundaries (as in *rise, ties, tie, tire*), while a short and qualitatively different transition (usually [ʌɩ]) will be manifested before voiced obstruents and [l], thus, *ride, tide, tile*; a similar alternation is sensitive to morpheme and word boundary contexts (the <oy> types), as in [tʰɑˑed]/[tʰʌɩd] *tied/tide* (Anderson and Ewen:1987:62). We recall the argument in section 4.2.5 that Alexander Scot and others may have used an <e> vowel symbol in items such as <his> and <hit>, not to represent some near palatal [ɩ] segment, but rather to denote the fact that Scots speakers generally lowered and centralised this vowel (as they still do) to some value like [ɛ̈]. This interpretation might enable us to treat Scot's <ei> spellings as some kind of 'long transition' diphthong, such as [ɛ̈ɩ], the antecedent, perhaps, of the modern Scots [ʌɩ].

It is interesting too that Scot should treat separately column 5 - the lexically specific <aither>, <naither> - since many observers in the period record alternative pronunciations for these words. Sylvester Douglas' EITHER entry (Jones 1992:191) is enlightening in this respect:

> There are two ways of pronouncing the *ei* in this word, and in *neither*. 1 with the diphthongal sound of *i* or *y*. As in *blithe, Scythe*. 2 as *ay* in *pay, day, lay,* or *ei* in *weigh*, that is with the sound of the Scotch sound

> of ε. This last pronunciation is, I believe, the most approved. The common vernacular pronunciation of Scotland differs from it only in making the first syllable short. But in endeavouring to catch the true English sound most Scotch people (who do not adopt the first method) pronounce the *ei* like *ee* in *Steel*, or like the *e* in *ether*.

But whatever the precise phonetic realisation of these diphthongs might have been for speakers of the 'present Caledonian English of the college, the pulpit, and the bar', Scot's differential orthography at least shows that he appears to have heard some kind of contrast between these sets of items, a contrast which Scot was sufficiently acute as an observer of pronunciation habits to record, and a fact which therefore might lead us to treat with great respect the observations we have seen him make in other areas of his contemporary phonetics/phonology.

McIllquam (1781:14) records that the *long i* diphthong in items like *guide, guile, guileful* and *buy* is a composite of his short *i* (as in *fin*) and the long *i* (as in *fine*). Such an apparently triphthongal [jɑɩ] vowel space is well attested in the period (and is to be found in some Modern English varieties); Walker (1791:13) records among his 'Irregular and unaccented sounds' of *A* the fact that 'When the *a* is preceded by the gutturals, hard *g* or *c*, it is, in polite pronunciation, softened by the intervention of a sound like *e*, so that *card, cart, guard, regard,* are pronounced like *ke-ard, ke-art, ghe-ard, re-ghe-ard*'. Elphinston's (1786:10) attitude to this tendency is hardly enthusiastic:

> after a pallatal (*c* or *g*) articculating *a* shut, *ir* for *ur*, or *i* open: az in *card, gard; skirt, guird; kind sky*; hwich must be duly herd (dho not seen) *kyard*, and so on. From dhe same clas, of (if possibel) a lower, may be evvery day herd dhe no les nauseating insertion: in *tyoo, dyoo; kyow, kyount*, and *gyound* (g keeping hard), for *two, do, cow, count, gown*, and dhe like. But dheze vulgarrities nevver hav reached Scotland; dho dhare az in Yorkshere, *gang* or *gyang* (for *go*) ar not quite expelled dhe colloquial

while a very similar observation is made by Sylvester Douglas under his CALF entry (Jones:1992:180):

> The *l* is mute in this word and in *half*. The *a* has the same sound as in *art*, but with this difference that a sort of obscure *i* or *y* is prefixed to it. It is only in that circumstance that the pure English and the Scotch pronounciations of the word disagree. In general wherever the hard *c*, or *k*, or the hard *g* is followed either by the short open *a*, as in this word, or by the diphthongal sound of *i*, or *y*; as in *kind, sky*, the smothered sort of *y* just mentioned is introduced in the pure dialect of the English. It is so in *cart, carriage, casuist, garden, gadso*, &c. I call it smothered *y*, because the voice hastens over it to the *a*, or diphthongal *y*. Yet it is almost as much heard as the *i* in the Italian word *chiaro, chiedere, cuchiaio*. Indeed the *chiar*, in *chiaro*, has in every

> respect the same sound with our word *car*. To illustrate this matter still farther, this unwritten *y* before the *a* or *y*, is exactly the same with that, which makes the first part of the diphthongal sound of *u* in *use*, *abuse*......In the pronounciation of the northern provinces of England, the unwritten *y* we have been describing is not used. And few natives of those provinces who leave them after their early youth, ever acquire that characteristic of the pure dialect.

Beattie (1788:49) too recognises such 'triphthongs...the sounds annexed to the vowels in the words *sky* and *kind*: in which the diphthong expressed by the *y* in the one, and the *i* in another (his 'springy separation of the tongue from the palate') is apparently introduced, in pronunciation, with something of the sound of the English *e* as heard in the words *he, she. be*', and so too Barrie (1796:3) 'Italic *i* before a consonant and *y* take the sound of initial *y* before them, as in g*u*ide, sk*y*; pronounced gy̆ȳd, sky̆ȳ'. However Nares (1784:138) argues that the phenomenon is *passé*: 'It is observed by Dr Wallis, that the sounds of *w* and *y* creep in upon us unawares after the guttural consonants: thus, *can*, he says, is pronounced *cyan*; *get*, *gyet*, *begin*, *begyin*; and even *pot*, *pwot*; *boy*, *bwoy*; *boile*, *bwoile*. This strange corruption is now, however, quite abolished, except in some instances already noticed'.

7.2 The [ɑʊ] Diphthong

Although many commentators are content to describe this diphthong simplistically as the 'sound of the diphthong <ou> and <ow>' others try to capture its phonetic shape by attempting to describe its starting and finishing points. Although he views the 'improper' version of this diphthong as appearing in 'the most irregular assemblage of words in our language', Walker describes the first of what he sees as its seven sounds as: 'the proper sound of this diphthong is composed of the *a* in *ball*, and the *oo* in *woo*, or rather the *u* in *bull*, and is equivalent to the *ow* in *down*, *frown*, &c.' (1791:36). The *bull* vowel is his 'middle' sound of *u* and seems to be a durationally reduced version of the *oo* in *wool*, some kind of [ʊ] segment. His 'third long sound' of *a* 'is that which we most immediately derive from our maternal language the Saxon, but which at present we use less than any other' (1791:11), is almost certainly a durationally extended vowel closer to [ɒɒ] than to [aa] or [ɑɑ]. We might therefore tentatively represent his *down* diphthong, the *English Vowel Shifted* version of Middle English long [uu], as [ɒʊ]. This description follows very much along the lines of that proposed a decade earlier by Sheridan (1780:10): 'The diphthong *ou* or *ow* is composed of the sounds a^3 [the *hall* vowel:CJ] and o^3 [the *noose* vowel:CJ]; and is formed much in the same manner as i^2 [the *fight* diphthong:CJ] the mouth being at first in the position of sounding a^3, but before that sound is perfected, by a motion of the under jaw and lips to the position of sounding o^3, from which results the diphthong *ou* or *ow*, as in *thou, now*'. Kenrick's remark (1784:58) to the effect that this diphthong 'greatly resembles the barking of a full mouthed mastiff, and is perhaps so clearly and distinctly pronounced by no nation as by the English and Low-Dutch' is not particularly helpful.

Sylvester Douglas' treatment of this diphthong in the pure dialect is rather different and perhaps reflects the characteristics of the diphthong in his own Scottish usage: 'The combinations of *o* and *u*, and *o* and *w* very frequently represent a proper diphthong (as in *foul, howl, now*) composed of the close *o*, and the simple vowel sound of the *u* in *full, pull*.' (Jones:1992:133). This apparently northern [ou] diphthong is commonly attested by Douglas as being characteristic of the pure dialect in items like the following: <bough>, <how>, <allow>, <avow>, <enow>, <now>, <vow>, <owl>, <cowl>, <fowl>, <growl>, <howl>, and many others. Adams (1799:77-8) gives us little information about the phonetic value of the *ou* ('the most variable and difficult') diphthong other than that it resembles the 'coarse Dutch'. He does, however, provide a table of minimal pairs contrasting whatever is meant by this 'coarse Dutch' sound and [o]/[oo], which include <Bow> '*reverence*'/'*instrument*'; <Bowl> '*globe*'/'*cup*'; <Crowd> '*numbers*'/'*crowing of fowl*'; <Grows> '*a bird*'/'*he grows old*'; <Enough> '*for number*'/<enuff> '*quantity*', etc. In his *The Principles of the English Language, Digested for the Use of Schools* (1766:4) Elphinston describes the '*ou* or *ow*' combination as one 'where shuts *a* broad by the sound of *oo* or *w*', some kind of [ɒu] value (Rohlfing:1984:166-8). Perhaps not unexpectedly, it is Buchanan (1762:17-18: Meyer:1940) who provides a description of the diphthong, like Douglas', with some kind of [o] (or perhaps [ɔ]) first element:

> How many sounds have *ou* and *ow*? *Ou* and *ow* have four; the first Sound is composed of both (*o*) and (*uw*), and if we Sound *o-oo* extremely quick, it discovers this Sound exactly; as *louse, mouse, fowl, town,* &c. which are sounded quick, *lo-oos, mo-oos, fo-ool, to-oon*.

and again in his *An Essay* (1776:xviii) he describes <ou/ow> as 'a mixed sound, composed of both (o) and (uw), and if we sound (o-oo) extremely quick, it discovers this mixed sound exactly, as *louse, mouse, fowl, town* rapidly pronounced as one syllable, *lo-ooss, mo-ooss, fo-ool, to-oon* &c; this sound is denoted by a diaerisis thus, *loüs, moüs, föwl, töwn* &c'. Despite his claim that this technique describes the sound of the diphthong 'exactly', we are still left with the problem of the phonetic nature of the diphthong's starting point. It may be that Buchanan means the (o) to be his *short o,* and we recall that he confidently assures us (1777:8) that: 'The short sounds of (o) [his [ɔ]/[ɒ] :CJ] and (u) are pretty similar; as *ŭnder, ŭnto*: *ŏnder, ŏnto;* and are so quick and obscure, as to make no motions in the parts of the mouth' while in the *British Grammar*

(1762:13) he once more asserts that the short sound of *u* 'is very like short (o), only a little more guttural..expressed in *Bŭt, cŭt, gŭn, rŭb, sŭp, drŭb*'. If this is indeed the case, his <ou>/<ow> diphthong might be interpreted as showing some kind of [ʌʊ]/[ɔʊ] transition. Cortes Telfair seems to see <ou> diphthongs as having a low first element, comprised of what he describes as the 'second long *A* and *W*' (1775:156-7), where the 'second long *A*' in his system is the vowel sound in items like <all>, <ball> and <stall> and therefore, presumably, some type of [ɔ] or [ɒ] shape. Items he includes as showing this diphthong are: *aloud, about, howlet, youngster*. Burn (1766:10) cites *poulterer, poultice, poultry, uncouth,* and Dun (1766:8) *shoulder, grown* and *growth*. Warden (1753: *Preface* xi) describing 'diphthongs where both the vowels are pronounced; the sound of each vowel is expressed by the figure denoting that sound. Thus in so^2u^2nd, *o* marked o^2, being the same name it is expressed by in so^2t; and *u* is marked u^2, being the name it is expressed by in tru^2e'. Such an [ɔʊ] or [ɒʊ] transition he sees characteristic of items like *out, foul, fountain, without, ground* as well as *soul, would*. Robertson (1722:17) includes *pour* among his <ou>/<ow> 'true' diphthongal examples.

Sylvester Douglas (like many of his contemporaries) also lists a few pure dialect instances which, in comparison at any rate with modern British standard usage, appear anomalous. For instance, items such as <cucumber>, <pronounciation>, <wound> '*lesion*', <mow> '*of barley*' and <low> ('*as a cow*'), seem to appear with [ou]/[ɔu] stressed vowel space. There are also a few instances of a 'retarded' application of the vowel shifting process, manifested in [proo] '*prow*' and [droot] '*drought*', although Douglas observes that 'Formerly perhaps this word (<drought>) was pronounced in England as in Scotland, with the diphthongal sound of the *ou*' (Jones:1992:189), perhaps attesting the survival of the 13th to 15th century Middle English diphthongisation ('*Breaking*') of [o] → [oʊ] in pre [xt] syllable final contexts (Jones 1989:146-7). Douglas also records the Scottish dialect as showing a diphthongal stressed vowel space in the item SHOULDER (an item with the long close *o* sound in the pure dialect): 'The Scotch are apt (when they aim at propriety) to give it the diphthongal sound as in *foul*' (Jones:1992:223). On the other hand, Scots speakers are claimed to make the item <frown> rhyme to <shown>, i.e. with [oo] stressed vowel space, where the pure dialect 'has its diphthongal sound as in *cow, vow*' (Jones:1992:176-177). However (with the exception of the items we are about to discuss immediately below) pure and vernacular Scotch dialectal differences, as regards contrasts between diphthongal and steady state vowel shapes, are for Douglas not particularly marked in this area of the phonology and discrepancies are worthy of comment, as for the item TOUCH (Jones:1992:229):

> The Scotch in general, pronounce this word properly, so as to rhyme to *such, much,* But I know a Scotchman who from the rule of analogy has persuaded himself that it should be pronounced so as to rhyme to *crouch, pouch*: and constantly did pronounce it in that manner. The reader will judge of the ridicule this necessarily brought upon him.

But perhaps some of the most interesting observations Douglas makes in this area of the phonology relate to items such as <bow>, <row>, <bowl> and <sow>, items which even in the 17th century were appearing in homophone lists and 'near alike' lists (with either [oo] or [ʊʊ]) despite being etymologically diversely derived (Dobson:1968:161-172). The <bow> item, lexically representing '*arcus*' (OE <bōga>) or '*to bend*' (OE <būgan>) shows, according to Douglas, both [boʊ] and [boo] manifestations in the pure dialect. However, the [bou] pronunciation is restricted, he claims, to the '*to bend*' interpretation, the [boo] to the '*arcus*' (Jones:1992:177):

> But Scotchmen, who have acquired a good and ready pronounciation in other respects, often find themselves puzzled and confounded between the different pronounciations of this word.

The 'true provincial' pronunciation, he asserts, is [bʊʊ], to which if the Scotch speaker does not aspire, then [boʊ] is the favoured alternative, with [boo] the least preferred (and by implication the least prestigious) in the Scotch vernacular.

This tendency in the pure dialect to differentiate phonetically between lexical contrasts is also noted by Douglas for the item SOW; when referring to a female pig, the pure dialect realises an [oʊ] vowel, the '*act of sowing*' with [oo], Scotch speakers pronouncing the latter as [sʊʊ] (to rhyme to *shoe*), but they 'often pronounce it with the diphthongal sound so as to rhyme to *Now, cow.*' In the same way, <bowl> '*a basin*' and <bowl> '*ball in the game of bowling*' are distinguished as [bool] and [boʊl] respectively - only the Scotch pronunciation of the former as [boul] is recorded by Douglas. Yet both the pure and the Scottish vernacular dialect treat the two lexical specifications of <row> ('*a line*', '*to paddle*') as homophones, the former dialect in [roo], the latter in [roʊ]. But it seems in general that the Scotch vernacular treats <row>, <bow> and <sow> items homophonously, generally under [ou] and does not reflect the lexical/phonological matching that Douglas claims to exist in the pure dialect. Recall here too Kenrick's observation (1784:59):

> Mr Ward says this sound [the [aʊ] in <town>:CJ] may be made more or less, close and deep, by making the mouth more or less hollow, and directing the breath more or less towards the palate. To instance this he falls into the errour countenanced by Johnson's Dictionary; saying, that 'a *bowl,* meaning

an orbicular body, requires a close sound; but a *bowl,* meaning a vessel, requires a more open sound.'

The people of Ireland, and perhaps those of some counties of England, do indeed pronounce *bowl,* meaning a vessel, in the same manner as we in London pronounce the words *howl, scrowl,* &c. but polite speakers in the metropolis pronounce the word *bowl,* whether meaning an orbicular body or vessel, exactly in the same manner; both long and open, as in the words *toll, hole, roll,* &c.

Considering the salientness of the modern Northumbrian and Scots labial vowel failure to undergo the *English Vowel Shift* to some kind of diphthong, there is remarkably little comment on the phenomenon in the 18th century record and what there is is not always what we might expect. For instance, one surprising feature of Alexander Scot's characterisation of prestigious Scottish English pronunciation - 'the present Caledonian English of the college, the pulpit and the bar' - is his representation of the items '*round*', '*about*' and '*however*' as <roond>, <aboot>, <whoever>, all showing a non-*English Vowel Shift* monophthongal [u] stressed vowel shape, rather than some expected [ɑu] type (Jones:1993:115). On the other hand, and as we might expect, the *Spelling Book upon a New Plan* assigns <oor> and <oot> realisations of '*our*' and '*out*' to the 'Commonly Pronounced' category (1796:*Preface*:vii) under its list of 'those words in which the Natives of North Britain are most apt to err, in order that the teacher may be particularly on his guard to prevent the children from falling into these common errors'. Yet it would seem that for Alexander Scot such undiphthongised vowels were not - *for polite Scots speakers* - examples of any kind of 'barbaric' usage, but part and parcel of a local prestige standard, perhaps the kind of 'vestigia ruris' characterised by Sylvester Douglas. The picture painted by Alexander Geddes is a more complex one. In addition to a centralised [ʌ/ə] vowel and a diphthongal [jʊ] complex, Geddes recognises among his labial sounds, through his <ù> graph, a vowel he designates: '*oo*, or *u*, Italian; This is the genuine sound of *u*. How we came to express it by *oo*, it is not easily conceived. The Scottish combination *ou* was much nearer the sound' (1792:438). Instances showing this <ù> graph are plentiful in Geddes' materials, and appear to represent some type of pure labial [ʊ] sound. The following represent some of the occurrences he cites from his Edinburgh dialect:

arùn '*around*'; brùk '*brook*'; bùr '*bower*'; devùrs '*devours*'; dù '*do*'; dù '*dove*'; flùr '*flower*'; flùrs '*flowers*'; ghù; ghùr '*your*'; ghùth '*youth*'; hù '*how*'; krùds '*curds*'; kùrs '*course*'; lù-lorn *love-lorn*'; nù '*now*'; prùn '*prune*'; prùnirs; rùth '*grief*; thù '*thou*'; tùn '*tune*'; tùns '*towns*'; unpù'd '*unpulled*'; wù '*woo*'.

The <arùn>, <bùr>, <devùrs> and <flùr> types show retarded *English*

Vowel Shift characteristics with no subsequent diphthongisation to some kind of [aʊ] vowel space. There is a tendency, of course, on the basis of modern usage (Macaulay 1991:41-44) to associate pure labial vowels in such items as instances of stigmatised or 'broad' usage, and it is difficult to know precisely the speech of which socio-economic class Geddes intends under his 'Edinburgh dialect' label. There is a further problem arising from the fact that Geddes also uses a <ou> digraph in contexts where *English Vowel Shift* diphthongs might be expected to surface. On the whole he confines the use of this particular digraph to the *Epistle* (where there is nowhere near the same degree of symbol differentiation found in his translation pieces) although there are a few Edinburgh and Buchan dialect instances as well. Commenting on his choice of spelling forms in the *Epistle,* he tells us that 'I have ventured, however, to make the orthography a little more uniform, and more agreeable to the Scottish idiom, than the orthography of the present day. Thus *ou* and *ow* are never confounded, the former is equivalent to the English *oo,* the latter to *ow* in *town,* or *ou* in *loud*' (1792:438). While it is difficult to know precisely what Geddes means by 'the Scottish idiom' in this context, the fact that his *Epistle* is addressed to 'the President, Vice-Presidents, and Members of the Scottish Society of Antiquaries (1792:441) might suggest that it is not some kind of 'gutter Scots' close to the 'broad' end of the sociophonetic scale, but perhaps a variety closer to Scot's 'present Caledonian English of the college, the pulpit and the bar'. That he sees the <ou> graph as equivalent to *oo* is reinforced by his description in the *Observations* of *u* Italian as *oo*: 'How we came to express it by *u* is not easily conceived. the Scottish combination *ou* was much nearer the sound' (1792:437). Although this digraph is used in the *Epistle* with segments which would appear to be unequivocally pure labial: <you>, <boussom> '*buxom*'; <routh>, its principal occurrence is with vowel space which has in most other English dialects, *English Vowel Shift*-ed to a diphthongal [ɑʊ]: <outlandics> '*outlandish*'; <hou> '*how*'; <around>; <flours> '*flowers*'; <poudert> '*powdered*'; <ours> '*ours*'; <nou> '*now*', suggesting perhaps once more that these undiphthongised varieties were not seen as stigmatised in certain Scots social contexts.

In his dialectal pieces, the translations into 'Skottis vers', Geddes' use of the <ou> digraph seems to be rather different: while the Edinburgh dialect piece alone shows it used with items showing etymological pure labial vowel space: <ghou> '*ewe*'; <throu> '*through*' and <routan>'*rutting*', both pieces show the digraph confined to three principal contexts. Two of these appear to represent vocalisations, one of [ʊ]/[w], the other of [l]: <flouan> '*flowing*', <grou> '*grow*', <our> '*over*', <tou> '*tow*', <goudin> '*golden*', <fouk> '*folk*'. While we might treat the former type as Geddes simply using a <u> graph to denote lip rounding, and thus meaning to represent [flo^{w}-], etc, the <goudin> types would appear to point to a pronunciation like [goud-], the <ou> digraph, contrary to Geddes' use of it in the *Epistle*, representing a diphthongal element. That such an interpretation is possible is suggested by the *Epistle* spellings in <ow> for the items <gowd> '*gold*', <ow'r> '*over*' and the <down>/<renoun> rhyme at 1792:453/-1,2. The third set of items with this digraph are apparently genuine labial [u]/[ɷ] types, showing advanced *English Vowel Shift* manifestations of etymological [oo], <nout> '*note*', <stoun> '*stone*', <vousit> '*boasted*', <rous> '*rose*', corresponding to the <kurs> '*course*' type. Yet we have to note too the alternate <nouther>/<nowther> '*neither*' spelling forms and the juxtaposition of the <ou> and <ow> graphs in the lexical item <outowr> '*beyond*', '*outside*'. But the situation is full of apparent inconsistencies, since in the *Epistle* Geddes uses <ow> graphs in items like <owns> '*owns*', rhymes <grow>/<low> '*fire*', as well as <shown>/<alone>, suggesting that (while a diphthongal output in Scots is not an impossibility in such items) he perhaps occasionally uses <ow> with its 'normal' orthographic expression.

Elphinston too records many instances of undiphthongised labial sounds, although it is difficult to decide from the context in which he presents them whether they represent stigmatised or prestige usage in his contemporary Scots; under his description of *Dhe interchainge ov open vowels* (1786:2) we find loose, *louse*, and louse *loose*; brew *brow*, and brow *broo*, like dhou *dhoo*, or foul and fowl, *fool*....chew (Scottishly *chow* widh dhe dipthong'; rendering of the 'French *dur* hard, hard-harted, sends *door*' (1786:167); the Scots 'equivalent' of the English phrase *Hwen yoo doo com into' dhe garden, I hope yoo wil remember to' pluc (or, pic) nedher fruit nor flowers* Elphinston (1786:124) claims to be: *Hwan ye doo com into' dhe yaird, I houp ye wol meind, ta poo nadher froot* (*u* French) *nor flooers;* and for *Yoo know wel how to' dres insinnuacion* as *Ye ken weel hoo to' butter a hwiting* (1786:122); *Syne drivv'n frae hoose and hald* representing *Driven from house and hold* (1786:83); *I thenk ye'r oot o' yer judgement* for *I think yoo ar out ov yoor mind* (1786:119); under a section dealing with 'Scottish idioms' we find too: *From dhe time ov dispensing, dhe eleven-oors (elevven-ours) or twal-oors (twelv ours) after dhe French iddiom for 11 and 12 o'cloc, iz named dhe Scottish luncheon; so dhe four-oors (foar-ours) dhe afternooning or bever: dhe former and latter collacion or refreshment*' (1786:207) and many others (Rohlfing:1984:172).

7.3 The [ɔɩ] Diphthong

> Boath master and scollar had herd, no les dhan seen, dhe difference between *oil* and *isle*, az boath doutles painted our *ile*: for dhe good rezon, dhat French (our parents and parragons) had not entirely cesed so to' paint dheir *île*. Yet nedher harmonist had conceived dhe suspiscion dhat won dipthong might not chime widh anoddher, compozed ov so cognate partikels.

In this observation, Elphinston (1786:279) succinctly captures some of the most discussed characteristics of 18th century diphthongal phonology - the apparent conflation of [ɔɩ] and [ɑɩ] diphthongs and the nature of the former transition's terminal points. Indeed, for many observers <oi> is the only 'true' diphthong in their inventory: 'Some writers absurdly define an English Diphthong to be the sounding of two Vowels in one Syllable; and make a bustle about dividing them into proper and improper, though they differ in the Method of their Division. They tell us a proper Diphthong is that which has a mixed or proper Sound of both the Vowels. According to this Definition there is not a proper Diphthong in the English Tongue, unless we allow (oi) to be one, to which some give the Sound of long (i); and indeed (oi) resembles that Sound, as *foil, fīle, boil, bīle, toil, tīle,* &c. It must be confessed that (oi) approaches the nearest of any Combination in our Language to the Nature and Design of a Diphthong, as Diphthong imports the Coalition or Mixture of two Sounds in one' (Buchanan:1762:14:footnote). In Walker's (1791:35) view, the component parts of this diphthong are: '*a* in *water* (his a^3; possibly [ɔ] or [ɒ]:CJ), and the first *e* in *me-tre.* This double sound is very distinguishable in *boil, toil, spoil, point, anoint,* &c. which sound ought to be carefully preserved, as there is a very prevalent practice among the vulgar of dropping the *o*, and pronouncing these words as if written *bile, tile, spile,* &c.', while Sheridan (1781;16) sees this diphthong composed of the same elements as that in <time>, <mine>, etc, but with a discrepancy in the duration of the first component: 'The diphthong *oi* or *oy* is formed by a union of the same vowels as of i^2; that is a^3 (the vowel in *hall*:CJ) and e^3 (the vowel in *beer*:CJ); with this difference, that the first vowel a^3, being dwelt upon, is distinctly heard before its sound is changed by its junction with the latter vowel e^3; as *oi, noise.*' All commentators note, and usually lament the fact that this diphthong is being merged with that in items like *my, night,* especially Nares (1784:73-4): 'This diphthong (oi) has a full, rich, and masculine sound, peculiar to itself, and its substitute *oy*. It is distinctly heard in *noise, voice, rejoice,* &c. Those who are zealous for the harmony of our language, have lamented that this sound has been in danger of being lost, by a corrupt and vicious mode of pronunciation. It has been, indeed, the custom to give to this diphthong, in several words, the improper sound of the *i* long; as *boil, broil, choir, join, joint, point, poison, spoil.* The banished diphthong seems at length to be upon its return; for there are many who are now hardy enough to pronounce *boil* exactly as they do *toil,* and *join* like *coin,* &c.' And again, Kenrick (1784:61) '*oil, toil,* are frequently pronounced exactly like *isle, tile.* This is a fault which the Poets are inexcusable for promoting, by making such words rhime to each other. And yet there are some words so written, which by long use, have almost lost their true sound, such are *boil, join,* and many others; which it would not appear affectation to pronounce otherwise than *bile, jine*. We find, indeed, that this mode of pronunciation becomes every day more general; a striking proof, among others, of the antipathy, if I may so call it, of speech to the use of diphthongs, or the utterance of the two sounds of different qualities, with one impulse of the voice.'

The Scotch observers share these concerns and attempt to provide their own definitions of the phonetic parameters of the diphthong. While McIllquam describes the diphthong as 'sounds ŏĭ' where ŏ is as in *not* and ĭ as in *fin*, it would appear that Sylvester Douglas saw the value of this diphthong as [oi] rather than [ɔi]. This emerges from his description in the *Observations on the Alphabet* (Jones:1992:133) where he contends that 'The combinations of *o* and *u*, and *o* and *w* very frequently represent a proper diphthong (as in *foul, how, now*) composed of the close *o*, and the simple vowel sound of the *u* in *full, pull*. *O* and *i* also form a proper diphthong composed of the same sound of the *o*, and the first sound of *e*, as in *boil, foil*.' His *close o* ('usually long') sound we noted earlier to be some kind of [oo] segment, so that the *boil* diphthong would appear to represent [oi]. Under his BOIL entry (Jones:1972:175), Douglas stresses that 'there are great disputes among the English about the proper method of pronouncing the *oi* in this and many other words, *foil, oil, anoint, point, void*':

> The vulgar pronounciation makes the sound the same as that of the *i*, in *bile, file, pint*. Those who are admirers of a full and solemn manner of speaking sound the *o* long, and very distinctly; and hurry over the *i*, as is always done in the word *noise*, or as the *oy* is pronounced in *boy, employs*. But this method is generally thought too stiff and formal. There is a middle way which is practised by some of the best speakers, in which the *o* in the diphthong is sufficiently uttered to be distinguishable from *a* but yet the two vowels are compressed together, if I may so speak, in the same manner as the sounds of *a* and *e* or *i* are in the diphthongal *i*.

It is difficult to determine precisely what Douglas intends by 'the two vowels are compressed together' and for the 'middle way' pronunciation we can only hazard something like [ɒɩ], and what is probably the hypercorrect pronunciation of those 'admirers of a full and solemn manner of speaking, (who:CJ) sound the *o* long, and very distinctly: and hurry over the *i*', suggests pronunciations like [noojz] '*noise*' and [boojz] '*boys*': 'But this method is generally thought too stiff and formal'. Alexander Scot's evidence is not of much help either, since there are not sufficient data in *The Contrast* text to enable us to come to any certain conclusion as to the behaviour of this diphthong in any late 18th century Scottish Standard. Scot's spelling system distinguishes between items such as <rajoayz'd> '*rejoiced*', <joayful> '*joyful*' as against <sebjine> '*subjoin*'. We recall how Scot utilises <oa> digraphs to represent what are in all likelihood [ɔ] outputs, as in <Scoat> '*Scot*', <oad> '*odd*' and so on. An

<oay> cluster might therefore be taken to signify [ɔɩ]; however, it is the <subjine> stressed vowel <i> which is the more difficult to interpret within the terms of Scot's overall spelling representations. As we have already seen, Scot uses the <i> graph, to denote [i] or [ii], as in <mit> '*meat*', <spik> '*speak*', and it would seem unlikely that this is the value he expects to be read for the graph in <subjine>; perhaps, for once, Scot is using the traditional <i> for *long i*: [ɑɩ]. It is just possible, however, that - if there has been indeed been an [ɑɩ]/[ɔɩ] merger, then Scot's use of a pure palatal might represent the kind of retarded *English Vowel Shift* phenomenon he illustrates with items like <adefeeing> '*edifying*', <leecence> '*licence*' and <sheences> '*sciences*' (Jones:1993:115). It is worth noting that Scot includes the item <boy> alongside others with the <oy> digraph, such as <moy> '*my*', <oys> '*eyes*' etc., showing a value which we suggested might be [ɑɛ]. With such a low first element for the <oy> diphthong in this item, it is perhaps not surprising that a merger with diphthongs in items like <boy> might have occurred. Perhaps too the existence in late 18th century Scots of an [oɩ]/[ɑɛ] alternation is hinted at by Elphinston - for whom the <oi> diphthong is 'dhe seccond *a braud* long, to' *e*' (1790:49): 'But *Ay*, not being now (az it wonce waz) a substitute ov dhe interjeccion *Yes*; cannot picture *Oy*, its prezzent varriacion' (1786:156) and again 'So dhe interjeccion *Oy*! haz, in spite ov Nature and dhe Greek, too long assumed dhe semblance ov *Ay*, dhe true picture ov *A* slender, in dhe old acceptation ov *always*'. While Adams' (1797:153) description of the diphthong itself is not very helpful: '*oi, oy*, No. 1 open and broad *a-i*. - *Coil, foil, toil*. No. 3 it is sounded softer by some, - in *boil* (*bile*), *quoir, quire* or *kire*', he categorically states that *kìle* and *file* - where his *ì* is an [aɩ] type diphthong - are specifically Scotch variants of the English *coil* and *foil*. For James Douglas however, the [ɔɩ]/[ɒɩ] alternation appears to have become lexicalised (Holmberg:1956:213-214):

> Oi
>
> How is this double Vowel Sounded?
>
> 1. This double Vowel is a true diphthong uniting part of the Sound of both Letters into one, in the Beginning & middle of Words, as,
>
> OISTER NOISE MOI-ETY COIN CLOISTER
>
> 2. In the following Words it is sounded like *I* Long, or *Ei*,
>
> BOILE BROILE TOILE ANOINT JOIN JOINT JOICE OINTMENT POISON JOINTURE OIL POINT

Perhaps of all the Scots commentators, it is Robertson (1727:10-18) who sees the <oi> and *long i* diphthongs as merged. In response to the Lady's question: 'What Sound hath (i)?' the Master responds 'This Letter and (y) have both one sound, and what's said of one, may be said of both....*my, by, duly, mighty.*' When asked about the value of *oi* and *oy,* the response is 'They have the Sound of *y,* pronounced long, as in *Joy, Joint, Choice, Voice, Oy, Spoil, Foil*'. This identity, or near identity if we are to give any significance to the distinction hinted at in 'pronounced long', is highlighted in the many instances cited in his list of words 'sounding alike', such as <High> '*lofty*': <Hoy> '*a ship*'; <Kind> '*discreet or civil*': <Coyned> '*as money*'; <Line> '*to fish with*': <Loyn> '*of a Man*': <Lyon> '*a ravenous Beast*'; <Mighty> '*powerful*': <Moiety> '*a Sum paid by Parcels*'; <Viol> '*for Musick*': <Viol> '*a Glass*' and others. However, the extent to which Robertson's examples are taken from some local (?standard) source is clear from his inclusion as homophones of <Boil> '*in a Pot*' and <Bile> '*a Sore*' (a homophonous pair also found in the lists in *A Spelling-Book Upon a New Plan*), while his <Joyst> '*a Beam*': <Jest> '*a merry Tale*' pair we might very tentatively suggest points to some kind of some kind of [ʤɪst] realisation for both words.

8

NON-VOWEL SEGMENTS

We have seen in Chapter Two how elaborate and sophisticated was the theoretical framework within which the extensive and detailed description of non-vowel segments was couched in 18th century treatises on pronunciation. Such segments were regularly described in non-autonomous terms, being related to vowel segments along a kind of sonority trajectory involving mutes and semi-vowels. Beattie's (1788:31) description of nasal sonorants is worth considering from this point of view: 'while the voice is passing out by the nostrils chiefly, if the lips be closed, we hear the sound of M; if the forepart of the tongue be applied to the palate, N is formed; and if the tongue be drawn a little backward towards the throat, we produce the final sound of the words *sing, ring, long*, &c. These are called *Semi-vowels;* because of themselves, and without the aid of any vowel, they make a sound which is not very indistinct, and may be continued as long as we please. If, while we are sounding them, we suddenly shut our nose, the sound ceases entirely; which is a proof, that it goes out by the nostrils. And if we attempt to articulate them, after having first shut our nose, the sound produced will resemble B, D, and G, more than M, N, and ING; a proof, that, in these two classes of consonants, the mode of interception is almost, if not altogether, the same'. We saw too how the descriptive mechanism used in the depiction of consonantal segments was often extremely 'modern', involving close observation of the mechanisms of the musculature and other anatomical components of the speech producing mechanisms. While on the whole the 18th century Scotch grammarians and spelling book writers confined their observations to consonantal phenomena in the prestigious dialects of their time, there are nevertheless both explicit and indirect observations of characteristically Scots features to be found in many of their writings. These centre around a number of quite distinct phonological and phonetic contrasts between the prestigious English and Scotch phonologies, notably: (1) voicing differentials; (2) the voiced and voiceless palatal and velar fricatives; (3) [l] vocalisation; (4) [r] segments; (5) nasal segments; (6) consonantal cluster simplifications; (7) *h* dropping and adding; (8) continuancy adjustments and substitutions and (9) metathesis phenomena.

8.1 Voicing Contrasts

We have already seen in Chapter Two how relatively rare it is to find among 18th century observers any perceived relationship between voiced and voiceless segments and laryngeal centred activity. Beattie (1788:21-22) is untypical in describing the 'two semicircular membranes in the middle of the larynx...through which the breath transmitted from the lungs needs pass...to give a brisk vibratory motion to the membranous lips of the glottis, and so to form the sound which we call voice'. Discussing the voicing contrast between obstruents like [b]/[p], [d]/[t] etc. Walker too seems to recognise some kind of force-related laryngeal activity (1791:§41): 'It is certain the difference between them is very nice; the upper letters [the voiceless set:CJ] seeming only to have a smarter, brisker appulse of the organs than the latter; which may not improperly be distinguished by sharp and flat. The most marking distinction between them will be found to be a sort of guttural murmur, which precedes the latter letters [the voiced set:CJ] when we wish to pronounce them forcibly, but not the former. Thus, if we close the lips, and put the fingers on them to keep them shut, and strive to pronounce the *p*, no sound at all will be heard; but in striving to pronounce the *b* we shall find a murmuring sound from the throat, which seems the commencement of the letter'.

However, in the descriptions of most commentators in the period 'hard' and 'soft', 'sharp' and 'flat' consonants are ascribed to the effects of other kinds of phenomena, notably the 'force' or 'exertion' of the air passing across the articulators. Sylvester Douglas, for instance, never appears to relate [s]/[z] and [p]/[b] alternations to anything connected with laryngeal activity, far less vocal fold agitation; his explanation for the physics of the difference within such sets hinges on rather ill-defined references to the 'particular exertion of the organs of speech' (Jones:1992:122). In this light, voiced [g] is 'a single consonant formed by the organs of speech in the very same manner with *k*; except that the last mentioned requires a stronger exertion' (Jones:1992:127). After the same fashion, [p] 'has but one uniform sound, being formed in the same manner with *b*, but with a more forceful exertion of the lips' (Jones:1992:133) and '*t* is formed in the same manner with *d*, and only differs from it by being uttered with more energy, as *k* does from the hard *g*, and *p* from *b* (Jones:1992:138). Voiceless forms appear, under this model, to be differentiated from their voiced congeners purely in terms of some additional degree of aspiration or ejectiveness. Preceding his *Table ov Affinity* (1786:2-3) Elphinston sees the voice contrast in terms which are not dissimilar: 'Dhe consonants ar signifficantly divided into' *licquids* and *mutes*; az wel az into' dhe classes ov dhe organs, dhat emit dhem. Nor iz articulacion, simple or aspirate, les natturally divizzibel into' *direct* and *depressive*; according to' dhe emission ov dhe breth. A divizzion, hwich aroze from experriment, wil be justified by it; in dhe utterance ov *p, b; f, v*; or anny fellow-pair ov oppozite identicals, radher dhan cognates'. Again, in his *Principles of the English Language* (1766:7) obstruent pairs like [t]/[d], [p]/[b] are characterised by the one 'uttered by a direct and forceful emission of the breath, and the other by one indirect or depressed'. Perhaps it is criteria like these which underpin Sheridan's characterisation (1781:35) of non-standard aspirated obstruent pronunciation: 'In pronouncing this letter [*t*:CJ] the Irish and other provincials thicken the sound....for *better,* they say *betther;* for *utter, utther,* and so on in all words of that structure.' Sylvester Douglas too (*Of the Provincial Accentuation,* ff. 31-34) seems to appeal to criteria of this kind:

> The difference which takes place in point of muscular exertion between the pronounciation of the same consonant in one syllable and in another has not been in general so much attended to, but that such a difference may take place, any one may discover by trying the experiment with his own voice, and that it really occurs in the usual pronounciation of languages may be perceived by one who will attend to the phenomenon of speech. On the stage, in the pulpit, at the bar, and in the senate, we may observe some speakers who in uttering certain words, to which they mean to draw the particular attention of their hearers, use a very marked effort of the muscles in forming the beginning of consonants of those words, and the concluding consonants of certain syllables are by all speakers pronounced with a more forcible exertion of the muscles than the same consonants are in others. This is particularly observable in our language where the same consonantal character is doubled at the end of a syllable. Thus the single *t* before *e* in the first [sic:CJ] syllable of the word *appetite* and the *tt* in *petty* represent exactly the same consonantal modification, and the only difference is that in the word *petty* there is a more vigorous and forcible pressure of the tongue against the upper part of the mouth. Here again I find that I was hampered in a former part of this work by the sterility of language of which I have more than once taken notice, for I have there described the *d* as differing from *t* only in the degree of muscular exertion, but this diversity between the *tt* and the *t* in such words as *petty* and *appetite,* being of a nature very different from the difference between either and *d,* it should seem that I ought to have described the exertions in forming the *d* and *t* as differing in kind as well as degree, and agreeing exactly only in the same position of the organs.

8.1.a [s]/[z] Alternations

While detailed lists of [s]/[z] contrasts in nominal and verbal pairs are provided by Nares (1784:121ff) and Walker (1791:§437), the former seeing [z] as 'the duller sound of *z*', the latter the [s] as 'sharp and hissing', it is undoubtedly Sylvester Douglas who provides the most detailed description of the lexical distribution of this contrast in contemporary Scots. While he indicates that the pure dialect differentiates nominal/verbal usage in lexical items such as *excuse* and *grease* with stressed syllable final [s] and [z] respectively, we have to conclude from his general observations that speakers of Scots make no such phonetically signalled contrast, realising [z] for both. As is clear from the following data, there appear to be several lexical items where there is a direct pure/Scotch voiced determined contrast:

PURE [s]	SCOTCH [z]
debase, rase, erase, place, base	base
precise	precise rhyming with *wise*
profuse	profuse
design	design
nuisance	nuisance

PURE [z]	SCOTCH [s]
damsel	damsel
resign	resign
possess	possess
preside	preside
president	president rhyming with *precedent*
reside	reside rhyming with *precede recede*
residence	residence

Douglas also records a [ʃ]/[ʒ] contrast under his discussion of the ASIA item, where the pure dialect is said to realise the former, as in <nation> and <Dacia>, the Scotch producing [ʒ] as in <pleasure> or as the French <j> in <ajouter>. Walker (1791:54) condemns contemporary voiceless pronunciations of the intervocalic fricative in *Asia* 'when...it ought undoubtedly to be pronounced *Azhia*...This is the Scotch pronunciation of this word, and unquestionably the true one: but if I mistake not, *Persia* is pronounced in Scotland with the same aspiration of *s*, and as if written *Perzhia*'. While recognising the relationship between the voicing contrast and grammaticality in the prestige dialect: 'Inglish verbs and dheir accions, hwen coincident in all else, ar butifooly apt to discriminate final sibbilacion. Verb assumes dhe genial depressive, noun dherfore dhe oppozite power, thus *abuse*, noun; *abuze*, verb; *close*, noun; *cloze*, verb' (1786:82), Elphinston too makes much of voicing alternations in his *Anallysis ov dhe Scottish Dialect*, seeing in them examples of his 'interchainges' (Rohlfing:1984:280ff): 'Notthing can be more dialectally incident, dhan dhe interchainge ov direct and depressive. If, from unmodelled, or unmoddulated moudhs, may be stil herd ar London *padrole, pardner, prizes,* for *patrole, partner, prices,* and dhe like; it cannot surprize, if dhe same rank in Scotland guiv *blash, barley, cabtain, luvtennant, steve, boddom, gowk, baggabag; Zion, uz, elz, caze, baze, rize, doze, excuze, moroze, precize* (if not *preceze*) *dezign; choiz, rejoiz, Nanzy, Dezember, Prezentor, egzit;* for *plash, parley, captain, lieftennant, stif, bottom, coocoo, buccabac; Sion, us, else, case, base, rise, dose, excuse, morose, precise, design; choice, rejoice, Nancy, December,* Precentor, *exit,* dhat is *ecsit.* But dhe direct sinks not oftener into' dhe depressive, dhan dhe depressive rizes into' dhe direct, particcularly in Scotland az in Wales, in dhe Celtic or Gaulic manner. Az *Taffy Etwarts,* and *TonnelTingwall,* for *Davy Edwards,* and *Donnald* (or *Donnel*) *Dingwal'.*

The *Spelling Book upon a New Plan* cites *Baze* as being 'Commonly Pronounced' against the standard *Base;* George Fisher's list of *Words of the Same Sound* in his *The Instructor* (1789:12-22) includes *muscle/muzzle, news/noose, his/hiss, baze/base, devices/Devizes,* although it is not certain whether we should treat these as Scotticisms, while Burn's (1766:15) extensive list of items showing 'soft *c*' includes *jocose, nauseate, nauseous, operose, reside, residence, resign, resignation, resiliency, resolute, resonant, transact, us.* William Scott (1807:ix) includes *us* and *Asia* among items showing voiceless [s] segments. Alexander Scot's *The Contrast* illustrates what would appear to be non-London standard, but polite Scots contemporary usage in : <curaozetays> *curiosities,* <rajoazy'd> *rejoiced,* <wicket> *wicked,* <alz> *else* and <oaf> *of* (Jones:1993:124).

8.1.b [θ]/[ð] alternations

'TH, La Gloire, et L'Opprobre de Notre Alphabet' (Adams:1794:81). Many 18th century observers comment upon the uniquely English language status of the inter-dental fricative, a 'lisping aspirate....which the English alone have practised and preserved' (Elphinston (1765:141)) who also notes the difficulty it produces for the non-native speaker: 'This double Consonant [*th*:CJ] and our manner of pronouncing *ch, j,* or soft (*g*), makes the Pronunciation of our Language very difficult to Foreigners; all the Difficulty is contained in these Words, *What think the chosen Judges*? which Foreigners pronounce, *What dink de shosen shudges*?' (1762:27:footnote); 'the simple pronunciation of any English word is easy to all foreigners, except the French, with the sole exclusion of the hard *th,* which is difficult to most nations: but that *th* should prove too rough for the powerful organs of our brethren the Irish, is surprising, as English is their adopted language' Adams (1799:17); see too Adams (1799:64-65). It is perhaps this 'difficulty' which explains the considerable effort devoted to the description of this segment and the conditions for the appearance of its voiced or voiceless shape: 'In the beginning of the words, *th* has always its aspirated sound, or is formed wholly by the breath...it always has its vocal sound when followed by a final mute *e* in the same syllable; as in *bathe, breathe*' (Sheridan:1781:39); see too Nares (1784:131ff); Walker (1791:§467). James Adams' description is, as usual, rather imaginative (1799:65): 'TH, No.1. is soft *dh*, in all pronouns, adverbs, and particles; as *thy, they, that, this, them, these, there, then, though, the*, and before *e* syllabic - *fath-er, weth-er, broth-er*, &c. TH, DZH. This harsh *th* resembles the Hebrew *thau*, the Egyptian *thoth*, and Greek *theta*, which sound is expressed by an hieroglyphic or emblem of the figure and hissing of the serpent, initiated by darting the tip of the tongue beyond the teeth, and then hissing, which will throw open the lips with an undulating kind of vibration, and often produce a titillating sensation on the upper lip, *dzh*, as *thump*.'

Sylvester Douglas records [θ] voiceless fricative shapes in the pure dialect ('To our ear accustomed to it there is something peculiarly mellow in its softer sound (for it has two) as in *thou*, and *though*' (Jones:1992:122)) for items such as <thought>, <breath>, <death>, <sheath> (noun) and <cloth>, while with [ð] he notes <thou>, <breathe> and <bequeath>. Verbal/nominal distinctions are also made via the [ð]/[θ] contrast in the pure dialect in pairs like <sheath>/<wreath> and <clothe>/<cloth>. Pure versus Scotch voicing differences, on the other hand, are not all that numerous, but include the following:

PURE	SCOTCH
[θ]	**[ð]**
froth	froth as in *loathe*
oath	oath
both	both
[ð]	**[θ]**
thence	thence as in *thought*
thither	thither
heather	heather

The *Spelling Book upon a New Plan* (1796:vii) records as Scots and stigmatised a voiceless fricative in the plural *paths*, while Holmberg (1956:110) claims that 'A small point of great interest is James Douglas' [ð] sound in *with*..which is definitely non-Scots and confirms our already expressed view that Douglas' English is a London standard'. Burns (1766:16) from a long list of otherwise unremarkable instances, includes with voiced forms *beneath; frothy* and with voiceless *heathen*. Although he is not alone in doing so, Alexander Geddes tends to conflate *voicing* alternations with those involving *continuancy adjustment*. He tells us (1792:422-23) that 'the Scots, in borrowing words from other language [sic:CJ]), seems to have paid a just attention to the nicer and less discernible shades of sound (if I may so say), in the commutation and arrangement of consonants, generally preferring the softest of the same class, or those that coalesced the most readily with the following letter. Thus they said *descryv, luf, haif, optene, oblisit;* for *describe, love, have, obliged.*' While the 'foreign' status of some of these items is in doubt, Geddes' observation on voicing ([f]/[v]: [ʃ]/[ʒ]) and obstruency ([v]/[b]) alternations in his contemporary Scots is well attested in other writers in the period (Jones:1991:68-70). Yet, although he is careful to distinguish in his *Table* between <s> 'the same as 'soft *c*'' [[s]:CJ] and <z> 'its softer sound, or that of *s* in the English word *praise*', Geddes' use of the <s>/<z> symbol contrast in both the *Epistle* and his *Translations* appears to be unreliable and inconsistent. On almost all occasions he uses the <s> graph where we might etymologically expect [z]: <bus> '*boughs*', <mûs> '*muse*', <leis> '*lays*', <deis> '*days*', <reis> '*raise*', etc. which, if we take at face value, would represent a word final [z] → [s] weakening on a scale unrecorded by other contemporary commentators. That we should perhaps be wary in accepting such a state of affairs is suggested by rhymes such as <brûz/Mûs> (461/1/21-22) and <très>/<brèz> (460/1/11), although it seems possible that a substantial tendency towards word final fricative devoicing might have occurred. Evidence of a similar phenomenon involving dental/alveolar obstruents in past tense morphology contexts can be seen from such shapes as <luv't> '*loved*' (460/2/5); <remuv't> '*removed*' (460/2/6); <kâr't/fâr't> '*cared*'/'*fared*' (459/1/5-6) and <conténtit> '*contented*' (460/1/3) among many others. Phonologically related to such syllable edge devocalisations is the substitution of the less noisy [s] fricative for [ʃ] in items such as <bânis't> '*banished*' (459/1/1) and <sál> '*shall*' (459/3/8).

8.1.c [f]/[v] Alternations

In his description of labial fricative continuants, Sylvester Douglas distinguishes three distinct sounds: the sounds represented by the symbol <f> (Jones:1992:127):

> May be pronounced by the pressure of the lips together as in uttering *p* or *b*, but so as to leave some slight issue for the breath. In the act of blowing out a candle if done forcibly, an indistinct *f* is produced; if more weakly, a *v*. But the more usual way and more perfect, of pronouncing both is by pressing the edge of the upper teeth against the underlip.

Here Douglas seems to recognise the voiced and voiceless bilabial fricatives [β] and [ɸ] as well as their labio-dental congeners [v] and [f], but the former he sees as 'imperfect' pronunciations 'as when the *f* and *v* are pronounced by the compression of the lips instead of that of the upper teeth and upper [sic:CJ] lip' (Jones:1992:134). The bulk of Douglas' comments on the voicing discrepancy occur under the entry for the items CALF'S, WIFE'S, KNIFE'S (Jones:1992:180) where he notes: 'The genetives of *calf, wife, knife* are pronounced by most English people like the plurals of the same words, i.e. as if written, *Calves, wives, knives*. The Scotch, and some English people, retain in the genetive the same hard sound of the *f* as in the nominative.' Likewise, under his HOUSES (THE PLURAL OF *HOUSE*) entry he claims (Jones:1992:202) that 'The Scotch, and some provincials in England, pronounce the *s* hard in the plural, as it is in the singular; but it ought to be soft as in the verb to *house*; and in the singular and plural both, of *spouse, spouses*'. Again, under NEPHEW, we find: The *ph* in the pure dialect is pronounced as *v*. In Scotland & the North of England it has its usual sound of *f*' (Jones:1992:210). Elphinston notes too for him as Scottish alternants, whereby 'Affinity ov articulacion, accounts ezily for dhe chainge ov *us* to' *uz, az* to' *as, if* to' *of*' (1786:22-23).

8.2 Palatal and Velar Fricatives

Typical of many of his contemporaries, Nares (1784:105-106) notes the Northern-ness of these 'guttural' sounds as well as the 'difficulty' encountered in their pronunciation by those in whose phonological inventories such sounds do not appear:

> many words terminate in *gh*, in which situation those letters doubtless were originally the mark of the guttural aspirate, a sound long lost entirely among the inhabitants of the southern parts of Britain. It is still retained by our northern neighbours, who utter these letters, especially when followed by *t*, with a sound which we cannot readily imitate. For this reason, *gh* is wholly silent with us in general, as in *daughter, dough, high, night, slough, taught,* etc.

The phonaesthetic status of these 'guttural semivowels' or 'strong gutturals' is low in the estimation of all observers; for Sylvester Douglas they are 'so disagreeable to the English ear' (Jones:1992:160) and represent a 'barbarous pronounciation' to be 'got rid of' (Jones:1992:175). Adams' 'hard and remarkable gutturals' (1799:30) are a mark of the Scot: 'Polydore Virgil, in the remote reign of Henry VII, marks this difference even betwixt the English of those days and the Scotch, by the distinction of labial and guttural. English abounding in labial sounds, the Scotch with harsh gutturals, spoke their respective character to an Italian ear' (1799:133-34); yet his everywhere evident Scoto-Saxonphilia precludes and condemns any attempt at their modification (1799:153): 'We suppress the harsh gutturals, or convert them into single consonants. The Scotch retain them; and when they affect to soften them, the articulation or sound resembles that of a deep asthma, or last rattling of a fatal quinsy'. Although Elphinston (I795:5) too seems to share this dislike of the 'guttural' segments: 'Dhe guttural aspirate (*ch* or *gh*), essencial to evvery primmitive language, haz lost dhe aspiracion in dhe smoodhnes (or dhe softnes) ov dhe French and Inglish tungs', it is more muted: 'Dho dhe old guttural aspirate retain dhe direct foarce and form in dhe Scottish *loch*, and dhe depressive form (at least) in dhe Irish (az wonce Inglish) *lough*'(1786:242-43) and there is no outright condemnation of its occurrence in Scots (1786:23): 'hav not all Inglish, az all French, organs lost dhe power ov dhe guttural aspirate; saying *Baccus* and *Buccan*, for dhe old *Bacchus* and *Bucchan*?...and if manny livving languages preserv it inviolate; dhe Scotch and Irish ar dubbly interested to' gard dhe power dhey yet pozes, in dhe bold guttural emission ov at least dheir primmitive names: *Drogheda, Auchtermuchty*, and dhe rest'. He notes as well the tendency in English to vocalise this fricative (perhaps in the voice inducing intervocalic context), a tendency resisted (as it still is) in Scots (1786:66): 'dhe Welch, like dhe Inglish, hav smoodhed dhis guttural away; and so' retain onely *Bauan* and *Vauan* (or *Bawan* and *Vawan*) ov *Baughan* and *Vaughan*; hwich dhe Scottish *Strachan* (az if *Straughan*) joins Inglishly in *Strawan*; dhe oddher remnants ov dhe Gaulic tribes can stil, becauz dhey doo stil, emit dhe fool guttural, in such names az *Bucchan, Brechin, Drogheda*; *Lough-Ern, Loch-Lomond, Auchindinny, Auchtermuchty*, and dhe rest: dhe Scotch havving evver preffered dhe direct, az dhe just picture ov dhe guttural sound'. Never apologetic for the characteristic marks of Scotch pronunciation, Callander comments (1781:11): 'The German guttural pronunciation of *ch, g, gh*, is quite natural to a Scotchman, who forms the words *eight, light, sight, bought*, &c exactly as his northern neighbours...How much the English have deviated...'.

Beattie is unusual in explicitly recognising the existence of both [ç] and [x] palatal and velar fricative types. Noting that the letter C has two sounds (1788:34 and footnote): 'the one is heard in *came*, and the other in *come*', he postulates the existence of two related gutturals: 'while we articulate K, we let our breath pass with a pretty strong compression between the middle of the tongue and throat, there is formed that guttural sound, which in Scotland (where it is very common) is supposed to express the Greek C, and in the vulgar dialect of that country is annexed to the letters *gh* in the words *might, light, bright, sigh*, &c. In the same manner, by permitting the simple sound of G, as it is heard in *go*, to escape from between the tongue and throat, in the form of an aspiration, we pronounce another guttural, not unlike the former, which in Scotland makes the final sound of the word *lough* or *loch*, which signifies a lake. These two gutturals were certainly heard in the Anglo-Saxon (or one of them at least), but have been long disused in South Britain; and an Englishman finds it difficult to pronounce them; though to Scotchmen, who are inured to them from infancy, nothing is more easy', a description he further exemplifies in his footnote. Sylvester Douglas considers the pronunciation of these gutturals to be like that of 'all the semivowels, aspiration is in some degree performed. The fauces are made to approach, yet not so as to preclude entirely the passage of the breath' (Jones:1992:122). One such 'guttural semivowel' which 'has affinity to *k*' is exemplified in the item ACHILLES and probably represents the palatal fricative [ç], while a voiceless labial [x] fricative is to be assumed for what he sees as the 'barbarous' Scotch realisation of the <gh> in items like <sought>, <bought>, <thought>, <fought> and <drought>; 'the Germans and Dutch make the *g* a guttural semivowel, analogous to their *ch*, but softer in the same proportion as our hard *g* is softer than *k*' (Jones:1992:127). In this context we might note under James Gray's (1794:105) list of 'Words the same in Pronunciation, but different in Spelling and Signification' <Loch, or Lough> '*a lake*'/<Lock > '*of a door*'.

[θ]/[ç] alternation appears to be a common phonological phenomenon throughout the history of English phonology, evidenced from such Middle English spellings as <michty>/<mithty> '*mighty*' and presumably arises from the similarity between the acoustic 'fingerprint' of the two noisy segments. Nares (1784:105-6) notes both the Northern-ness of the 'guttural' as well as its association with the interdental fricative: '*Sigh* is by some persons pronounced as if written with *th*; a pronunciation which our theatres have adopted. Spenser has written it *sythe*, and rhymed it to *blythe*'. Burn too (1776:12) records the fact that <gh> sounds like 'the *th* in *drought*, [drouth]'. Sylvester Douglas notes [ç]/[θ] alternations under the item TECHNICAL, where the pure dialect [k] for <ch> is realized as [θ] in the Scotch dialect, a fact Douglas sceptically (but probably correctly) surmises arises from a 'resemblance between the Scotch guttural sound of *ch*, and the English sound of *th*' (Jones:1992:227). Walker's (1791:§393) observations are in a similar vein: '*Gh* in this termination is always silent, as *fight, night, bought, fought*, &c. The only exception is *draught*; which, in poetry, is most frequently rhymed with *caught, taught*, &c. but, in prose, is so universally pronounced as if written *draft*, that the poetical sound of it grows uncouth, and is becoming obsolete....*Drought* (dryness) is vulgarly pronounced *drowth*; it is even written so by Milton; but in this he is not to be imitated, having mistaken the analogy of this word, as well as that of *height*, which he spells *heighth*, and which is frequently so pronounced by the vulgar'.

The perhaps more commonly attested ([ç]:[x])/[f] alternation (Walker 1791:§391) is highlighted in the 'list of words in which the Natives of North Britain are most apt to err' of the *Spelling Book upon a New Plan* (1796:vii) where <roch>, <coch> and <lach> are listed as 'commonly pronounced' versions of the 'true' <rough>, <cough> and <laugh>. This phenomenon is also recorded by Sylvester Douglas, especially under his observations on the pure dialect syllable final [f] in items like <rough>, <cough> and <laughter>: 'while it is a provincial pronounciation in some counties of the west of England to say *oft*, and *thoft*, for *ought*, and *thought*. I know one instance of a man of education and eminence in a learned profession who retains this mode of sounding these words' (Jones:1992:127): an observation paralleled by the anecdote under BUFF (Jones:1992:176):

> I know a schoolmaster in Scotland who was fond of general rules, and thought because *tough* was pronounced like *stuff, ruff, huff,* that *bough* should be pronounced likewise. He taught his schoolchildren to pronounce it in that manner. But this sounded so ridiculous, even in their ears, that they gave him the nick-name of *Buff*, which, if alive, he probably retains to this day

It is most interesting however, to note that Alexander Scot in his *The Contrast* text shows spellings such as <meght> [mɛçt] and <reght> [rɛçt] representing '*might*' and '*right*', in an orthography which represents what the author claims 'fairly paints the present Caledonian English of the college, the pulpit, and the bar.' From such instances, it might be just possible to conclude that prestigious speakers of what we might see as some kind of standard Scottish English retained these 'barbaric' segments and that the condemnation of their use by other commentators merely demonstrates their disinterest in and disregard for regional linguistic norms in their over-riding concern to promote a standard based on some southern, metropolitan model.

Two other fricative alternations with [ç] are noted by Sylvester Douglas; the first with his observation that for the pure [ʧ] in the item RACHEL: 'many Scotch people substitute, in this word, for their vernacular and guttural sound of the *ch*, that of *k*' (Jones:1992:218); such an intervocalic [k]/[ç]/[ʧ] alternation might suggest an increased level of vocalicness for the obstruent in different sociophonetic contexts.

8.3 [l] Vocalisation

The effacement of syllable final lateral sonorants is a common feature of English and Scots contemporary as well as historical phonology. The acoustic similarity of [l] segments in general (with their relatively low F_2 frequency) and their highly periodic shape (well defined formant structure) often means that they are perceived as though they were themselves 'full' vowels, and full labial vowels at that; hence the common modern Glaswegian realisation of items like <Channel Tunnel> and <well> as [ʧæno^w tʌno^w] and [wɛo^w]. This is a phenomenon which Elphinston captures most effectively. Under his section dealing with *L* MELTED OR DROPT (1786:34) he spells out the rationale for the vocalisation as well as its popularity among contemporary Scots speakers: 'Next to' dhe vocal ar dhe articculating licquids meltabel; hweddher into' cognate effiscience, or into' quiescent gard.....Effective or servile, *l* final, somtimes medial, melts in dhe Scottish dialect. Dhus *ball* and *boll, pool* and *fool* (boath short) *bulk* and *sculk, allum* and *Allardice,* wer *bow* and *bow* (dipthong), *poo* and *foo, book* and *scoog, awm* and *Airdice*: *all won woll, aw, é, oo,* a figgurative Scotticism for *All won thing*'. The 'meltabel' liquid 'ov *bal* and *dal* feble' also 'Scottishly sinks in such names az Balfoor (Frenchly Balfour) or Dalkeith' (1786:35), and among a set of similar examples he notes: 'If we cannot now wonder at dhe contest between *faucon* and *falcon, Fawkener* and *Falconer* or *Falconar*; we may ezily reconcile *hawker* and *Halkerton*' (1786:141). Under his discussion of *Spurious Diphthongs* which, he claims, 'have so unfixed a sound in English, that the Scotch is [sic:CJ] much puzzled to alter them', Adams (1799:152-3) asserts that 'When coalescing consonants preserve the long, or broad sound of preceding vowels, then the vowel is changed, or the double consonant vanishes or receives the guttural sound, if combination admit it' and lists as Scotch usage *caw, saw,* or *cá, sá*' for English *câll, fâll,* where it is possible that his <aw> symbol represents [ɔ] or [ɒ] rather than a diphthong, while <á> probably realises [ɑ].

English observers like Walker (1791:47:§§401-5) show sets of items with [l] effacement, claiming that '*l* is silent likewise between *a* and *m* in the same syllable, as *alms, balm, calm, palm, psalm, qualm, shalm*', and the conditions for [l] retention appear to hinge upon what is perceived to be some constraint affecting syllable 'division' (see pp 235-239 below): 'but when the *m* is detached by the *l* by commencing another syllable, the *l* becomes audible. Thus, though the *l* is mute in *balm, palm,* and *psalm,* it is always heard in *bal-my, psal-mist, psal-mody,* and *psal-mistry*.' In much the same way, Nares (1784:111-112) lists [l] effaced items as per Walker, although his observation that *shalm* is 'written also *shawm*' may hint at diphthongisation concomitant with or preceding vocalisation. He suggests much lexical diffusion influence as well: 'In *fault,* the *l* is sometimes pronounced and sometimes dropped', while in the nominal forms of the items *vault* and *salve* the '*l* is sometimes suppressed' it is never so when they are used as verbs. Sylvester Douglas' remarks on [l] effacement as the first element in [lk], [lm], [lf] and [lp] syllable final clusters are disappointingly brief and fairly conventional. 'This semivowel and liquid' he regards as 'the most pleasing to the ear of all consonants' (Jones:1992:132) and records it as 'mute' in items like <half>, <walk>, <stalk>, <talk>, <salmon>, <psalm>, while it is 'generally sounded' in the pure dialect in <scalp>, <calm>, <balm> and <psalmody> (Jones:1992:221). He makes comment neither upon the peculiarities of the stressed vowel under conditions of [l] deletion/vocalisation nor of any idiosyncratic Scotch behaviour. Although discussed in a pure dialect context, his comment under the ALMOST entry: 'most good speakers sound the *l* in *almost*. In familiar conversation there are some who do not', might look like a genuine

Scotticism, especially since the phenomenon is also commented upon by Elphinston (Rohlfing:1984:312) - although not in 'solemn language' - and recorded by James Douglas (Holmberg:1956:108). Cortez Telfair (1775:153) under his section on *Silent Letters*, records with effaced [l] the items *'salve'*, *'falcon'*, *'Holburn'*, *'Malcolm'* and *'Bristol'*.

Although simple 'effacement' of syllable final [l] is well recorded in the period, commentators are rarely specific concerning the degree of 'residue' left behind as a result of the sonorant's vocalisation; perhaps what Elphinston intends by [l] sounds being 'meltabel......into' cognate effiscience'. Of the Scotch observers it is perhaps Drummond who (if only to disown it) most explicitly points to a genuine vocalisation of the lateral sonorant in syllable rhyme position (1777:23): 'some pronounce this letter [<o>:CJ] like the diphthong *ou* in *croud*, in the words *old, cold, scold, hold, molt, bolt, colt*, a practice not general, and therefore not to be imitated'. At the beginning of the next century, The English grammarian Smith (1816:16-17) seems to suggest too that [l] vocalisation brings with it the 'addition' of extra vocalic weight to the syllable in which it occurs, either in the form of stressed vowel or even sonorant lengthening of the sonorant itself. In the next section we shall see how this careful observer identifies two types of [r] segment, the *rough*; as in *rogue*, and what he calls the *smooth*, which he associates with the sound of the last syllable of *Messiah*, and therefore probably as some kind of centralised [ə] vowel. His comments on [l] effacement are very significant in this light: '*L* is changed into *m* in *salmon*; into smooth *r* in *almond, alm, calf, psalm*, &c, but in *could, should, would*, &c it is entirely silent' suggesting possible pronunciations as [ɑəm]/ɑɑm] *'alm'* and [kæəf]/[kɑɑf]/[kææf] *'calf'*, and so on. Surprisingly not in a Scots context, since the variable is such a common one in certain sociophonetic contexts in Modern Scots, Walker (1791:47) observes that: 'In *soldier*, likewise, the *l* is sometimes suppressed, and the word pronounced *so-jer*; but this is far from being the most correct pronunciation: *l* ought always to be heard in this word, and its compounds, *soldierly, soldiership*, &c.' Although it is obviously difficult to be certain precisely the kind of phonetic value he intends, Alexander Geddes' description of *l* at least suggests the possibility that it is readily vocalisable: it is 'the softest of all the liquids' and one which 'the Scots make..still more liquid than the English by retaining its Gaelic or Celtic sound; which is also common in Spanish, and expressed by *ll*. It is nearly the *ll* in French, and exactly the *gl* in Italian. It might in my alphabet have been denoted by a diacritic point - but as other three liquids are liable to a similar modification, and as one combination of vowels, namely *iou* after the single consonant, suits all the four, I thought it better to use that combination, than, without necessity, to multiply symbols.' We have already noted the possibility that in spellings like <goudin> *'golden'*, <fouk> *'folk'* and <gowd> *'gold'* just such an [l] vocalisation has taken place, leaving outputs such as [gɔudən] and the like.

8.4 [r] Segments

The period is replete with phonaesthetic descriptions of the [r] segment, for some reason viewed as the 'harsh guttural' and 'canine guttural.' Elphinston (1764:136;284) typically sees the segment as stemming from an 'irritated throat' and having an effect on the ear which is 'rough, harsh, horrid and grating' (1765:302). Walker too (1791:50) perceives the sound as 'but a jar of the tongue' and 'the most imperfect of all the consonants'. No less an observer than Buchanan (1762:22:footnote) comments: '*R*, a palatal; it is expressed by a Concussion, or Quivering of the Extremity of the Tongue, which beating against the Breath as it goes out, produces this horrid dog-like Sound', a negative interpretation shared by Kenrick (1784:48): 'the quibble of Abel Drugger in Ben Johnson's *Alchemist*, respecting the last syllable of his name, serving to shew that our ancestors considered it in the sense represented by Perius, who calls it *litera canina;* as bearing a resemblance to the snarling of a dog.' Elphinston sees as one of the virtues of modern prestigious pronunciation that 'dhe old aspirate ov R' has been replaced (1795:29): 'Som Greeks, followed by som Lattins, fancied to' ad rufnes to' dhe licquid *R*, or to' paint its innate rufnes more foarcibly, by subjoining aspiracion.....til at length harmonious *rezon* introduced *rime*, boath into' French and Inglish....Dhe very *rinosceros* disdains now alike to' ruffen hiz horn widh adscitious snorting, and to' stifel even hiz moddern sibbilacion'.

There is much comment throughout the 18th century on the regional characteristics of the *r* sound; for example, Adams observes (1799:49): '*R*: this letter is singularly rough in the mouths of Normans, and the inhabitants of the county of Durham, who cannot pronounce these words, without a disagreeable rattling of the throat, *Rochus Rex Maurorum*,' while Kenrick claims (1784:49): 'In the northern parts of England, particularly in and about Newcastle, we find the *r* deprived of its tremulating sound, and aukwardly pronounced somewhat like the *w* or *eau*. *Round the rude rocks the ragged Rachel run*, is a line frequently put into the mouths of the Northumbrians, to expose their incapacity of pronouncing the *r*, as it is sounded by the inhabitants of the southern counties' cf. Påhlsson (1972). Sylvester Douglas' comment that the English pronounce this sound 'the harshest of all letters....more softly' than the Scotch (Jones:1992:135) might infer a greater degree of voicing, but it is very likely that Douglas uses the hard/soft distinction on occasion not as an indication of voicing co-efficient, but - as we shall discuss further below - as a signal of obstruency versus (mainly affricative) continuancy. If this is at all a possible interpretation, then we might see the two [r] sounds as a 'hard' obstruent like [r] as against the alveolar voiced frictionless continuant [ɹ] (Anderson and Ewen:1987:159-60; Laver:1994:263-264). In his *Observations* to the *Table* Alexander Geddes (1792:423) records the fact that 'In some parts of Scotland this letter is pronounced with an aspiration, though not so hard as that of Northumberland. The Greeks seem to have given it the same sound', and what we might therefore interpret as some kind of frictioned, uvular [ʁ] can perhaps be seen in his <trhein> spelling for '*train*' (459:1/4). The fact that some kind of [ʁ] or perhaps [ʀ] segment is also recognised by Sylvester Douglas in the contemporary language seems clear from his statement (Jones:1992:134) that : 'What by the French is termed *grassayment*, in England the *burr*, and by the Scotch a *rattle* proceeds from pronouncing the *r* in the throat, without applying the tongue to the upper jaw, as must be done in the proper pronounciation. This guttural *r* it is that resembles the snarl of a dog.'

Although it is difficult to be certain whether Douglas intends to suggest that this [ʁ] is a pure or Scotch dialect characteristic, or both, the use of the 'epenthetic' or 'intrusive' [r] at syllable boundaries is put forward without any hesitation as the salient characteristic of Londoners, 'at least many of them, [who:CJ] make a very extraordinary use of this letter' (Jones:1992:134-135); see too Savage:1833; Matthews:1936; Flasdieck:1900. Observing that [r] is inserted between vocalic syllable terminations and initials at syllable and word boundary points, he condemns it as a 'barbarous pronounciation' but one which is nevertheless to be found 'in the mouths of some persons of education' (Jones:1992:135). Such a phenomenon, he claims, gives rise to realisations such as 'that is not my *idear* of the matter' and 'I shall be obliged to take the *lawr* of you'. A phonological 'sandhi' stratagem of this type is well attested in contemporary grammars, notably Elphinston (1787:264) who records that it is not merely to be associated with non-prestigious speech in the Capital 'But, nattural az it iz for a low Londoner to' shut dhe febel vowel ov *fellow* or *window*, in *fellor* or *windor*; so nattural iz it for an Eddinburrougher ov like (almoast ov anny) rank, to' warp dhe idea widh dhe sound (or dhe sound widh dhe idea) of *callow*, from warm, to' fresh, and even cool, in *callor oaster* (oister) or a *callor eg*' (1786:35). While we might see at least some of these 'intrusive [r]' instances as mechanisms for achieving ambisyllabicity in syllable interface contexts (Jones1989:300-1), others may be attributed to speakers' 'knowledge' of the propensity for syllables to show a vowel level reduced 'fade' at syllable boundaries, what Elphinston perhaps intends by his 'Dhe same cauz (febel vocalility in dhe end) haz made Grocenes assume *r* in (dhe colloquial) *idear* and *windowr*, for *idea* and *window*.' Phenomena like these are, of course, well attested still in the modern London and South East England dialect: cf [læst tæŋgər ɪn pærɪs] '*Last Tango in Paris*' in an otherwise non-rhotic phonology (Wells 1982: §§ 3.2.3, 4.1.4). Note too expressions like *your will be pleased* and *we hear your are among the best people in England* in the late 18th century Black American English recorded in the *Sierra Leone Letters* (1793-98) (Fyfe:1991). An almost near obsessive interest in this phenomenon is to be found in nearly all grammars and related materials throughout the nineteenth century, perhaps most typically in the complaint of 'Poor Letter R; its Use and Abuse' in *Mistakes of Daily Occurrence of Speaking, Writing, and Pronunciation Corrected*' (1885:6ff). A century before, Elphinston (1786:20) had complained of 'dhe grating *Arburthnot* for *Arbuthnot*, at Eddinburrough'.

Loss of syllable final [r] appears to be somewhat intermittently recorded throughout the 18th century record, and all the available evidence points to Scots being then, as now, universally rhotic. According to Walker (1791:50) the phenomenon was, however, observable in London (Hill:1940): 'In England, and particularly in London, the *r* in *bard, lard, card, regard*, &c is pronounced so much in the throat as to be little more than the middle or Italian *a*, lengthened into *baa, baad, caad, regaad*....But if this letter is too forcibly pronounced in Ireland, it is often too feebly sounded in England, and particularly in London, where it is sometimes entirely sunk.' Despite the fact that he disavows <verse>/<success> as a perfect rhyme: 'although the sound of the *e* in *verse* and *success* is not the same, the most offensive circumstance in this passage is the disagreement of the terminating consonants'. (Jones:1992:152), Sylvester Douglas rarely comments directly upon the possible effacement of syllable final [r] in the pure dialect. The only lexical context where he does appear to recognise the potential for post-vocalic [r] effacement (albeit by 'the English' only) appears under his observations on the item ASS (Jones:1992:165):

> This word is not inserted on account of any provincial manner of pronouncing it, but to illustrate the pronounciation of another, which the English sound so very like this, as to give occasion to numerous ambiguities of a very coarse nature. I remember a popular ballad several years ago, which was in great vogue for some time in the streets of all the great towns of the kingdom, and which was not deficient in humour. The burthen of it was this word *Ass*. But it was only used for the sake of an indecent equivocation in the sense, by its similarity in point of sound to the other word to which I allude. In Scotland, where I then happened to be, the joke was scarcely understood, because in that country, the sounds of the two words differ nearly as much as those of *pass*, and *pairs*.

Elphinston (1786:141) notes syllable final [r] effacement (perhaps accompanied by vocalisation producing some kind of [ɑu] diphthong) for the item '*Marlborough*': 'Nay *marl* wood yield to *maul*...and show herself onnestly *Maulburrough*; but for fear ov dhe learned laffers ov London, hoo so duly decide in difficult cases.' James Douglas appears to have only a single instance of deleted post vocalic [r] in <woosted> for *worsted* (Holmberg: 1956:109). Other evidence for the effacement of [r] is difficult to come by, although George Fisher's *The Instructor or Young Man's Best Companion* (1789:12ff) under his list of 'Words of the Same Sound' records: <Harsh> '*sever*'/<Hash> '*minced meat*'; <Marsh> '*low ground*'/<Mash> '*for a horse*'/<Mesh> '*of a net*', while Robertson (1722:47) has the pair <Torn> '*rent*'/<Tun> '*of wine*'. But by the early 19th century, there is ever increasing evidence of the effacement, and even the vocalisation, of syllable final [r]. We have noted already how Smith (1816), for instance, distinguishes two kinds of *r*, the rough sound, as in <rogue> and the smooth sound, in <hard>. That some phonetic difference between [r] types is not all that is intended by this terminology is clear from his observation that the aspirate *h* 'when it is final, and succeeds a vowel.....has the sound of smooth *r*, as in *Messiah*.' (1816:17), suggesting both [r] effacement and possibly vocalisation. Likewise, in his *Grammar and Rhetoric* ('being the First and Third Volumes of the Circle of Sciences') (1776:14) we have his statement that: 'The letter *r* has no variety of sound, is commonly pronounced, except in the first syllable of *Malbouough*. Some people sound it obscurely, or quite omit it, in the words *marsh, harsh*, and a few others.' We recall Douglas' assertion concerning [r] that 'In England it is pronounced more softly in general than by the Scotch.' If we choose to interpret his 'softly' nomenclature as equivalent to Smith's 'smooth', then this statement might just be used as evidence for his recognition of syllable final [r] effacement/vocalisation in the pure, and to a lesser extent in the Scotch, dialect.

8.5 Nasal Segments

All 18th century commentators recognise a tripartite bilabial, palatal and velar nasal segment distinction in [m], [n] and [ŋ]. Drummond (1777:8) provides his typically articulatory description: 'M - by putting the lips together and sending a sound through the mouth and nostrils, resembling the lowing of an ox, as *moan*'; N - is formed by placing the tongue nearly as in L, ['formed by the point of the tongue fixed to the roof of the mouth, sending forth a sound through the mouth, as *tale*':CJ] only a little flatter, and forcing a sound through the nose, as *drone*'; 'NG - is formed by putting the root of the tongue towards the latter part of the palate, directing a sound through the nose, as *sing*'. Sylvester Douglas recognises two types of non-bilabial nasal, the first, [n] 'is formed by applying the tongue just above the roots of the upper teeth, as in performing *d*, or *t*, and suffering a slight expiration to be performed through the nostrils' and is pronounced 'softly' (Jones:1992:132); the second, clearly [ŋ], he describes as 'more nasal' and is pronounced 'strongly', has a contemporary [ŋg] variant. Walker (1791:48:§409; 44;§381) uses the terminology 'finished, complete or perfect sound of *g*' and 'unfinished, incomplete or imperfect sound of *g*' for [ŋ] and [n] respectively. In common with Elphinston

(Rohlfing:1984:328), Dun differentiates the palatal and velar nasal using phonaesthetic terminology: '*Ng* has a ringing Sort of a Sound, as in *Among, Nothing, Offspring; Nk* has a clinking sort of a Sound....*Linking, Sinking, Drunken* ' (1766:22). Many observers in the period are ready to recognise the vowel-like qualities of nasal segments as well as their gesture relationship to a set of 'corresponding' stops, notably Sylvester Douglas (Jones:1992:132): 'It is a common circumstance relative to these two letters *m* and *n*, that if you stop the nostrils by pressing them together with your finger and then pronounce either the one or the other, it becomes a *mute* instead of a semivowel: that is, you can commence or terminate a vocal sound with it, as with *b, p, d* or *t*, but you cannot protract its own sound without a vowel, as you may when the nostrils are open'. Douglas makes many observations on [n] and especially on [ŋ] with which it can, on occasion, alternate. The set of items in the pure dialect showing the velar nasal pronounced 'softly' as [ŋ] and 'strongly' as [ŋg] are set out in some detail under the ANGER, ANGRY entry (Jones:1992:163), and are as follows:

[ŋ]	**[ŋg]**
<singer>	<anger>
<hanger>	<angle>
<ringer>	<angry>
<hanging>	<dangle>
<bringing>	<dingle>
<length>	<finger>
<lengthen>	<hunger>
<strength>	<single>
<hang'd>	<stronger>
<wing'd>	<surcingle>
	<wrangle>
	<manger>
	<linger>
	<longer>
	<danger>

where <clanger> would appear to be the only exception to what is current standard British English usage, although Douglas does observe that 'some vulgar persons in England, from a sort of affectation, sound the hard *g* at the end of *sing, thing, king*, etc. and rest their voice upon it. But this is to be carefully avoided' (Jones:1992:163; Dobson:1968;§412). However, he makes the claim that late 18th century Scotch vernacular usage seems to have been considerably at variance with this since 'In almost all cases where *ng* is found in the middle of a word, the Scotch sound it as in *singer*. Thus they make *finger* and *singer* a perfect rhyme, and *anger* and *hanger*' (Jones:1992:163). Likewise, he claims that in the Scotch vernacular

<longer> is pronounced as the pure <singer>, i.e. with [ŋ], not [ŋg] (Jones:1992:207). This possibly represents the antecedent of the still common Scots habit of realising a dental nasal in rhymes terminating in fricative consonants, as [lɛnθ] *'length'* and [strɛnθ] *'strength'*. Grant (1913:32) avers that these 'are probably derived from Scotch dialect and should be avoided', yet in other places his observation on a similar phenomenon is neutral: '*ng* in the middle of a word is a simple sound - no *g* follows it ; hence we say - '*sing-l*', '*lang-er*', '*hung-ry*', just as in Standard English we pronounce '*sing-er*' (Grant and Dixon:1911:xiv). Under his discussion of the LENGTH, LENGTHEN items Sylvester Douglas observes an [ŋ]/[n] contrast. The pure dialect he records as showing [ŋ], but the Scotch 'and inaccurate speakers among the English sound both words as if written *lenth, strenth*' (Jones:1992:205); Elphinston (1787:15-16) waxes quite lyrical on this Scots propensity: 'Dhe Scots must howevver be owned inclinabel to' suppres dhe guttural after dhe dental, and so to' simplify away dhe nazal sound. Dhus hear we *Launton* and *Monton* (*Munton*) for *Langton* and *Monkton; moarnen* and *murnen,* for *morning* and *moarning*: hwence dhe Scottish Shibboleth ov *lenth* and *strenth*, for *length* and *strength*. Nor can aught proov more sallutary to' Caledonians, boath for sense and for sound, dhan dhe frequent and attentive reppeticion ov dhe awfool cupplet: *Dhe yong diseze, dhat must subdue at length,/Grows widh our growth, and strengthens widh our strength*'.

James Douglas (Holmberg:1956:269) asserts that 'When *G* follows *N* at ye end of a Word it is always hard, as, BANG, HANG, RANG...CLING, STRING, SONG....LONGEST, BRINGING', where his 'hard *g*' represents a voiced obstruent, Elphinston also recording [ŋg] in *hanger, singer, longed, hanging, longing* in contemporary polite London speech (Rohlfing 1984:329). Nares' account (1784:113-4) records: 'In some provincial dialects, this final *g* is more distinctly spoken than it is among correct speakers; which mode of pronunciation sounds as if the *g* were doubled, thus, *sing-g, bring-g*.' Yet the devocalising of the nasal in the morphological <ing> to [n] as a Scottish characteristic is also prominent in the contemporary literature; 'G..is often dropped in the termination *ing*, as *hearing, speaking, working, smelling* whereby they are liable to be mistaken for *here in, speak in, work in, smell in*' (McIllquam:1781:16) and Elphinston's (1786:41) 'az in dhe addage *A wollen meddher maks a daw dochter*: A willing (or An active) moddher makes a lazy daughter'.

Elphinston records (the still current) [n]~[l] alternation in the item <chimney>, where 'Vulgar Inglish turns...*chimney*, into'...*chimley*' (1786:19), while Sylvester Douglas states (Jones:1992:182): 'This word by many vulgar people both Scotch and English is pronounced (very unaccountably) as if written *chimley*' (Jones 1989:123 ff.). Note too Beattie's (1788:33) comments on this kind of phenomenon: 'The liquids L and R are acknowledged by Wallis to be anomalous. He is inclined to derive them from D and N. He mentions a tribe of American Indians adjoining to New England, who cannot articulate R or L; but when they attempt either, fall into N, and instead of *lobster* say *nobsten*: I have met two persons, natives of Scotland, who did the same'. Interestingly too, in his list of 'Words like in Sound but different in Spelling', Robertson (1722:62) has as homophones: <appear>/<appeal> and <ail>/<aim>.

8.6 Cluster Simplifications

Almost all writers in the 18th century comment upon the 'simplification' of syllable final [kt], [nd] and [bt] clusters to [k], [n] and [t] respectively. The phonetic/phonological motivation for this phenomenon is complex (for some suggestions, see Jones 1990:187-190), but there is little doubt that social significance, in its widest sense, has been attached to alternations of this type throughout the history of the English language. McIllquam's (1781:16-17) [pɛrfɛt] and [ɛgzɛmt] for *perfect* and *exempt* are typical examples for the period recorded by many grammar and school book writers as well as dictionary compilers. Geddes' (1792:423) comments on *cluster simplification* are extensive, and rest on the phonaesthetic assertion that Scots shows 'fewer harsh combinations of consonants' than Metropolitan Court English, rendering *neglect, self, twelve, precinct, decerpt, tempt* and *kiln*, by what he represents as *neglek, sel', twel, precink, decep, temp, kil*. The anonymous writer of *A Spelling-Book Upon a New Plan* (1796) condemns as 'Commonly Pronounced' Scotticisms pronunciations such as <fack> '*fact*', <canle> '*candle*' and <suttle> '*subtle*'. Yet this sociophonetic judgement needs to be considered in the light of the fact that Alexander Scot (1799) records realisations like <aicsap> '*except*', <enstruck> '*instruct*', <raspacks> '*respects*' and <affack> '*effect*' in *The Contrast* which he explicitly states as representing a form of prestigious Edinburgh usage appropriate to 'the college, the pulpit and the bar'. That the sociolinguistics of these cluster reductions is complex is suggested too by the fact that Scot represents '*acknowledge*' by <aunoalege>, especially in the light of the severe strictures upon such a pronunciation of the word provided by Sylvester Douglas in his *Treatise* (Jones 1992:158):

> ACKNOWLEDGE
> As Scotchmen soon learn that the *k* is mute in *knowledge* and other words wherein it is followed by an *n*, they, for the most part, fall into the error of suppressing the *c* likewise in *acknowledge*, and pronounce it as if it were written *anowledge*, or *aknowledge*. But the English give this *c* its hard sound, and utter it distinctly...

The rather curious spellings for <known> and <knowledge> which appear in *The Contrast* text - <tnoan>, <tnoalege> - perhaps suggest that the effacement of the palatal obstruent in the pre-nasal context was neither immediate nor total; some degree of obstruency may have been perceptible syllable initially, perhaps in the shape of some level of glottal re-enforcement, orthographically captured by Scot's <tn> graph. What may be a similar phenomenon is recorded by Drummond (1767:26) under his *Rules for Pronouncing the Consonants*: 'C - sounds his first sound before *a, o, u,* his second before *e, i, y,* - his third before *i,* and another vowel. In some counties they pronounce *t,* for *c,* before *l,* as *tlear, tlay, tlout,* for *clear, clay, clout,* a dialect not to be imitated'. Grant and Dixon (1921:8) record an identical usage 'In Forfar and East Perth, *t* takes the place of *k* before *n* as

Scots	Phonetics	English
knee	tni:	knee
knife	tnəif	knife
knock	tnɔk	clock
knowe	tnʌu	knoll'

Yet Elphinston (1786:45) also notes that 'Colloquial Scotch somtimes lops a letter from dhe beginning; az we know in *ream* and *neze,* for *cream* and *sneze*'.

Much of Sylvester Douglas' observation concerning word initial cluster simplifications stems from his desire to point to orthographic inappropriateness (itself the product of earlier phonological change). For instance in <gnat> and <gnaw> the syllable initial obstruent is effaced (although in <gnome> and <gnomon> he records it as pronounced 'by most English people' (Jones:1992:127)). Likewise, he records *k* as mute in items like <knell>, <knight> and, as we have seen, <knowledge> (Kökeritz: 1950) and that this may have been a change initiated in Scotland is suggested by Elphinston (1786:14): 'If dhe Inglish keep an impracticabel *k, g,* or *w* in *know, gnaw,* and *write;* hware dhe onnest Scots hav long labored (widh hwatevver succes) to render dhose iniscials effective...dhe same North Britons, fond ov evvery harmony, hav begged a leve dhey hav not obtained on boath sides ov dhe Tweed; of sinking anoddher pallatal, a sibbilacion, and a dental, in *cream, sneze,* and *thwac;* hwich in *ream, neze* and *hwauk,* dhey wood gladly disembarras ov won iniscial articulacion'. Like many observers, Warden (175314) sees *ax* and *acts* as 'the same in sound', while Elphinston (1786:17-18) notes too: 'Dhe Scotch doo indeed, az littel az dhe French, lov clustering consonants in dhe cloze. Peculiarly ar dhey dherfore apt to' drop dhe final dental, after a shutting consonant: saying *ac, corrup, temp; acs, corrups, temps;* for *act, corrupt, tempt* (hwich can be but *temt*); for *acts, corrupts, tempts,* and dhe like...after *l,* or *n,* dhe nordhern Scots drop *d* final; saying *aul commauns* for *old commands.* Dhey dhus call dheir *boddhy,* or littel *boodh,* sometimes a *shiel* for a *shield;* and say *Dunkel* (strong on dhe latter), hware dhey see *Dunkeld*.....(Adams (1799:153) showing the Scotch form <chil> '*child*')....and dhe Scots say, in dhe

North, *cenner* or *thunner*; and evverihware, *temmer, nummer, tummel, sooroc,* for *cinder, thunder, timber, number, tumbel, sourdoc,* or dhe like...Simmilarly ezy, and totally French, iz dhe Scotch rejeccion ov dhe braud licquefier in dhe *lang-or* ov *lang-age,* for dhe *laguor* ov *language* (vertually, dhe *langgwor* ov *langgwage*)'. That he sees such deletions as phonaesthetically motivated is clear from his claim that 'From ruf, dhe organs run to' smoodh; not from smoodh to' ruf. Hence dhe Inglish tendency to' dilate *Henry* into' *Hennery;* and dhe Scotch insercion ov dhe dental, hwich harmoniously dividing, unites dhe licquids, in *Hendry* hwence *Henderson*' (1786:20). Observing that in the Scottish vernacular *fact* and *distinct* in turn rhyme to *attack* and *think,* rather than to *packt* and *linkt* (Dobson 1968:§§404-407), Sylvester Douglas, not unlike Elphinston - who records '*Fecles* dhus varied *featles,* in dhe sense ov hwat dhe Scotch name also *dooingless.* By oppozite chainge proovs *carracter carratter* in (dhe West ov) Scotland (1786:24) - likewise considers the basis of this Scotch phonological characteristic to rest upon considerations of what he calls *cacophonia* (Jones:1992:159). But he is clearly not wholeheartedly committed to the idea since he asks: 'How shall we explain the different instances where certain sounds appear harsh and are avoided in some languages or dialects and yet are admitted without difficulty in others, although of a genius equally musical and sonorous'.

Word and syllable finally too, cluster simplification is sometimes recorded by Sylvester Douglas as an instance of orthographic inconsistency; thus the 'mute' status of the syllable final [n] and [b] in such items as <damn>, <contemn>, <condemn> as well as <limb>, <womb> and <tomb>. Like most observers, he records the mute status of *g* in the prestigious pronunciation of <sign>, <benign>, <assignee>, <consignee>, possibly reflecting an historical process of a type where a syllable final [ç] or [ɣ] (orthographically represented by <g>) is vocalised, resulting in a stressed [ii] vowel space (Nares 1784:104-5). Under the item APOSTLE, Sylvester Douglas informs us (Jones:1992:164) that 'the *t* is in a manner mute in both dialects.' He notes as well that in *cognisance* the pure dialect also effaces the [g], pronouncing it 'as if written *conusance*', while in the Scotch dialect the [g] is retained (Jones:1992:185). However, it is important to emphasise that there is much evidence to suggest that consonantal cluster simplifications were subject to considerable lexical diffusion; for instance, while Sylvester Douglas records that in items like <tremble> and <humble> 'the Scotch are apt to suppress the *b* in this and other words ending in *ble*' yet 'in *member*...the *b* is to be sounded, both in this, and all other words of the same kind' (Jones:1992:229). Again, under his LONDON entry we find the observation that: 'The formal way of pronouncing this word, is to sound the *d*. The more usual and familiar method is to suppress it. Both are countenanced by the example of good, and unaffected speakers' (Jones:1992:206).

8.7 [h] Dropping and Adding

Sylvester Douglas comments upon the syllable initial loss of what he describes as a 'modification of articulate sound, which is merely a strong aspiration' (Jones:1992:128) or 'that effort of aspiration which precedes the pronounciation of the initial vowel in those syllables which are said to be aspirated ' (*Of the Provincial Accentuation of Particular Words*: folio 35). Such [h] effacement and addition he describes as a 'most capricious defect' in some English individuals, one which is apparently randomly spread throughout the lexicon and inter-regionally, some people pronouncing the '*h* in as complete a manner as other people, in words where it should be mute and not written. Yet such is the power of habit that if you desire them to try to pronounce the *h* in *hungry* or any word of that sort, they cannot do it, nor avoid doing it in *heir*, or adding it to *air*'; going on to record the hairdresser anecdote (Jones:1992:128):

> In the speech of some individuals in England there is this most capricious defect, that in words where others pronounce the *h*, at the beginning, they do not; and where others suppress it, or where it is not written, they pronounce it. This is one of the most unaccountable singularities I have ever observed. It does not seem to arise from imitation for I have not been able to trace it as a general habit among all the inhabitants of any place or district [It is however pretty universal among the lower ranks of people in Staffordshire, and some of the adjoining counties:footnote]. Neither can it be attributed to any particular configuration of the organs of speech, because these persons pronounce the *h* in as complete a manner as other people, in words where it should be mute or is not written. Yet such is the power of habit that if you desire them to try to pronounce the *h* in *hungry* or any word of that sort, they cannot do it, nor avoid doing it in *heir*, or adding it to *air*. I know a hair-dresser who has this singularity of pronounciation, and who often lays it down as a maxim to his customers, that nothing is so destructive to the *air*, as exposing it too much to the *hair*. I likewise know a Portuguese Lady who has been long enough in England to speak the language with great fluency, and to pronounce it in general tolerably well; but who has this extraordinary habit with respect to the *h*.

In common with most other observers in the period Sylvester Douglas highlights the lexical sensitivity of this alternation, in the pure dialect recording [h] as 'mute' in the item <herb>, but 'pronounced' in <heron>. While he claims the [h] to be mute in the pure dialect in <abhor>, <humble>, <humility> and <humbly>, it is realised in the same items in the Scotch vernacular; yet for the item <Leghorn>, the Scotch pronounce the [h], while it is suppressed in the pure dialect. Douglas presents a picture of wholesale lexical diffusion with insufficient data to point to real conditioning factors or lexical trends in either dialect, a characteristic of almost all other observers, with Nares (1784:108) claiming: '*H* is a mere note of aspiration, and is irregular only in being sometimes without effect; as in these initials, *heir, honest, hospital, herb, hour, humour, hostler*. In *herbage* I think it is usually pronounced, though suppressed in *herb*: nor is it dropped in *horal, horary*, &c. though it is in *hour*, the origin of which is the same'; very similarly, Walker (1791:46): 'This letter is no more than a breathing forcibly before the succeeding vowel is pronounced. At the beginning of words, it is always sounded, except in *heir, heiress, honest, honestly, honour, honourable, herb, herbage, hospital, hostler, hour, humble, humour, humourous, humoursome*'; and Smith (1816:16): '*H* is an aspirate sound; as in *house, horse*; but it is frequently silent, or nearly so; as in *humour, honour*; and an entire neglect of this distinction in the words *eat, heat*; *art, heart*; *ail, hail*, both in their primitive and derivative forms....may possibly produce *ridiculous*, and even *serious* mistakes, through the omission or misapplication of the aspirate *h*.' Cortez Telfair (1775:155) under his section on *Silent Letters*, declares <h> mute in examples such as *heir, herb, homage, honest, humor, humble, honor, hospital, annihilate, vehement, vehicle*, while James Douglas (Holmberg:1956:282) relates the appearance of [h] in pronominal forms to what is probably sentential stressing: 'The Consonant *H* is not sounded in the Beginning of the Pronouns, HE HER HIM HIS when they come in the middle of a Sentence in Common Discourse unless the Emphasis lies upon them'. Elphinston's (1786:254-255) exemplification of what he calls 'Dhis barbarous interchainge...common to' all dialects' under his '*Dhe umbel petiscion ov H*' surely smacks of parody:

> manny Ladies, Gentlemen and addhers, to' hoom *H* uzed to' find fair az free acces; hav now edher totally discarded dhat aspiring iniscial, or ridicculously associated him widh a company ov straingers. A yong Lady, to' dhe grait mortificacion ov *H*, obzerved dhe oddher day, dhat *ils* made a pretty *contract* widh dhe valleys below; dhat dhe *ouzes* wer butifoolly dispersed among dhe woods, and dhat she waz fond ov *earing* dhe *howls* in dhe *hevening*. From dhe verdant *harbor*, hware dhe birds chant so sweetly; she can admire dhe capacious *arbor*, hware so manny ships flote so safewly. She trembels at dhe prancing ov a *orse*, but fears him not drawing dhe *arrow*. She lovs dhe *harts*, az wel az dhe sciences; but iz constantly shooting *harrows hat* susceptibel *arts*. In summer preferring *hale* to' wine, she *heats hartichokes*; and in winter swallows *ot ashes*, widhout receiving anny *arm*. She *ates* warm weddher, yet likes verry wel a clear *evven, hespescially wen* santering among dhe *hashes* and dhe *hoaks*. So hamiabbel howevver iz dhis yong Lady, dhat, widh her fine *air*, sweet *hies*, quic *hears*, delicate *harms*, above all her tender *art*, she wood giuv anny man a *ankering* to halter iz condiscion. She even

> toasts a *andsom uzband*, next to' *elth* and *appines ere* and *erafter*; and dhis verry morning, perhpas meaning no *arm*, she made a gay yong fellow blush, by telling him he waz verry *hairy*.

All of this pre-empts the very similar and common comments upon [h] adding/dropping in the pronunciation manuals of a century later, notably *Never too late to learn: Mistakes of Daily Occurrence* (1855:12-13) where we find an almost stereotypical missive from Letter H to little *a, e, i, o,* and *u* complaining: 'Then I have heard a person, who was very well dressed and looked like a lady, ask a gentleman who was sitting by her, if he knew whether Lord Murray had left any *Heir* behind him: - the gentleman almost blushed, and I thought stopped a little, to think whether the lady meant a *Son* or a *Hare*'. However, despite Elphinston's claim that [h] dropping/adding is 'common to' all dialects', there is little evidence in the period for any peculiarly Scottish characteristics of the process. Almost all lists of 'Words sounding alike but different in meaning' contain examples of the phenomenon, yet even what is perhaps the most blatantly Scots leaning of these, the list of Robertson (1722:41ff) shows only: <Air> '*in the skyes*'/<Heir> '*of an Estate*'; <Arrass> '*hangings*'/<Harrows> '*to manure the Ground*'; <Hoar> '*with cold*'/<Hour> '*of the day*'; <Whore> '*a leud Woman*'.

8.8 #[hw]/#[w] Alternations

This last example prompts us to consider what we might see as a type of [h] dropping; the still current tendency of Scots speakers to realise word initial [w] as [hw]; compare Standard RP [wɑɪt] '*white*' with colloquial Scots [hwʌɪʔ]. What seem to be [hw] syllable onsets appear universally in Alexander Scot's *The Contrast* in items such as <whoch> '*which*', <whother> '*whether*', <whey> '*why*' and <whoa> '*who*'. However, there is no way of discovering to what extent his <wh-> graph represents the Scots use of a more fricativised onset suggested by the 'Commonly Pronounced' <chot> '*what*' and <chuen> '*when*' for the 'True Pronunciation' <w*h*àt> <w*h*ĕn> - where italicised *h* signifies non-realisation - of *A Spelling-Book Upon a New Plan* (1796) and highlighted too by Sylvester Douglas (Jones 1991:141): 'For by the true English method of sounding these words [*what, whelp, why*:CJ] the *h* is first heard......The Scotch pronounce the *wh* like their guttural *ch* [[x]/[ç]:CJ] followed in like manner by a *u*, losing itself in the succeeding vowel. When they endeavour to correct this fault they are apt to omit the *h*, so as to pronounce *whit*, and *wit*, *whig* and *wig* in the very same manner. Careless speakers among the English very commonly fall into the same error'. Walker (1791:46) too views this kind of *h dropping* with some concern: 'This letter [*h*:CJ] is often sunk after *w*, particularly in the capital, where we do not find the least distinction of sound between *while* and *wile*, *whet* and *wet*, *where* and *were*. Trifling as this difference may appear at first sight, it tends greatly to weaken and impoverish the pronunciation, as well as sometimes to confound words of a very different meaning.' Yet Smith (1816:17) still observes that the *h* 'has a weak sound in *where, when,* &c, as if written *hwere, hwen,* etc. It is not sounded after *r;* as, *rheum, rhyme,* &c' while Holmberg (1956:111) comments that 'For words like *when* James Douglas has a consonant combination which he transcribes *hw*. There can be no doubt that this is the same pronunciation as the [hʍ] or [hw] naturally used in the North of England and Scotland now...It is of course possible to consider Douglas' *hw* a Northern trait, but it must be borne in mind that even at the present time some people in the south of England consider [hw] a superior pronunciation. In Douglas' circles in London [hw] may have been general, but Douglas may also - like Elphinston and many Scotsmen speaking Standard English today - be anxious to teach this [hw]'. The characteristic modern Scots habit of realising an aspirated onset in items like '*why*' and '*where*' seems to be typical of Geddes as well, as is suggested by his spellings like <huyl> '*while*' (457/1/1); <hua> '*who*' (457/2/3); <huilk> '*which*' (458/2/3) and many others. Elphinston spells <hwich> <hwat> and <hwen> throughout, commenting on such items: 'That the *w* was subjunctively aspirated in them all..appears not only from the surviving pictures, but from the real aspirations being yet preserved by the ancient Britons, the Welch, Scotch and Irish; who, later in receiving, must be later in refining, the English articulations; while the language of London (in general the best) has lost the power with the practise' (Rohlfing:1984:339).

8.9 Continuancy Adjustments and Substitutions

Of all the consonantal alternations discussed in the 18th century Scotch grammar books, it is the tendency for consonantal segments to change their obstruency value, either in the direction of or away from relatively vocalic continuancy which perhaps attracts the most attention and discussion. The majority of instances cited are those where obstruent consonants come to be realised as noisy fricative continuants, although there are a few cases where the opposite process is recorded. For instance, Alexander Geddes observes (1792:423): 'The sound which we now express by *th,* and which almost all other nations, except the Spaniards, in vain attempt to utter, was changed by the Scots into *d* or *dd,* to speak more properly, they retained the ancient Saxon and Teutonic sound and symbol *d,* which the English have changed into *th,* as *fader, moder, broder, hidder, quhidder*', while Adams (1794), fanciful as ever, exclaims: 'ASTHMA sans H, bien raisonné! car H est dur aux asthmatiques' and Robertson's (1722:46ff) list of homophones includes <Either> '*this or that*': <Adder> '*a Snake*'. The record for fricativisation is very prominent in Elphinston too, as he notes the two way [ð]/[θ] - [d]/[t] and [p]/[f] alternations (1786:26-27): 'dhan for dhe Inglish *gahp, flap, skip, stripping, chop, trump; chub, gabel, caldron, Lauder, ladder, udder, considder*.....to' becom dhe Scotch *gahph* or *gahf, flaf, skif, striffin, chost, trumph, chuf, gavel....caudhron, laudher, laddher, uddher, considdher*', although he is careful to say that the obstruentising of the fricative is not just a Scotch characteristic, since 'dhe Inglish vulgar say *farden*...for *fardhing*' (Rohlfing:1984:242); however, Sylvester Douglas claims that the voiceless obstruent [p] in the pure dialect item <trumps> is made continuant (more vowel like) in the Scotch version pronounced 'as if written *trumphs*' (Jones:1992:230). It is interesting to notice too how Geddes appears to be one of the first to record what is now a common Scots characteristic - especially among Glaswegian speakers (Macafee 1900:126) - of substituting the voiceless alveolo-palatal fricative [ɕ] for [θ] especially in word initial position (1792:425): 'If the words *threes* and *fours* be pronounced with the deep northern guttural sound *chrees, fouhrs*, the *gh* in *soughand* as the Greek *c;* and *rescind* as it were written *reshind* (all after the Scottish pronunciation) I flatter myself that there will be found a feeble imitation of the original'.

Several commentators reveal what appears to be an alternation in the pure dialect between [d] and [ʤ], obstruent versus delayed release segments. Perhaps this is most clearly expressed by Sylvester Douglas under his EXAGGERATE item: 'Some English people pronounce the *gg* hard, as in *waggon*, but the most general pronounciation is like *dg* in *badger*' and again under SUGGEST, SUGGESTION (Jones:1992:225-26): 'The first *g* has its hard sound, as in *shrug, dug*. The second is soft like the *j* in *just*. *Sug-gest*. In the same manner as in *ac-cent;* the first *c* is hard and the second soft. The Scotch only use the soft sound of the *g* as the Italians in *suggerire*. The French sound the first *g* hard in *suggerer*'. Douglas rather inconsistently describes the intervocalic segment as a combination of the 'hard sound' (in the sense of non-continuant, rather than with its more usual reference to voicing)) of *g* and the 'soft' *j* in *just*: [ʤ], 'in the same manner as in *ac-cent;* the first *c* is hard and the second soft', where the hard/soft dichotomy must again represent some continuancy differential, rather than some voicing contrast like *[ækgɛnt] . He claims that it is only in the Scotch dialect that a shape like [sɣʤɛst] is countenanced, the obstruency element being suppressed (perhaps to achieve segment overlap at syllable boundary). Contrariwise, in syllable initial position, Sylvester Douglas observes that in the Scotch dialect, items like <zeal>, <zone> and <zenith> show a 'combined sound of *d*, and the soft *s*' (Jones:1992:142): i.e. [dz], compared to the more vocally sonorous [z] of the pure dialect. Intervocalic [ʧ]/[k]/[ç] alternations are also well recorded, no better so than by Sylvester Douglas under his RACHEL entry (Jones:1992:218) where we find the observation: 'The *a* as in *race*, the *ch* as in *Chester, church*. Many Scotch people substitute, in this word, for their vernacular and guttural sound of the *ch*, that of *k*'. Telfair (1775:152) also records <ch> as [k] in the items

'Rachel' and *'Charlotte'*. Elphinston (1786:27-28) is quite positive in this area: 'dhe Scotch stil loves even dhe simpel guttural, much beyond dhe moddern aspirate: retaining dhus *mac, thac* or *thic, sic, birk, kest, caf, cart, calk, streek; rig, brig, fike, dog;* for *match, thatch, such, birch, chest, chaf, chart, chalk, stretch; ridge, bridge, fidget,* and *dodge. Mac* may be less recogniz'd a match, remaining onely in such old phraze az *I nevver kenn'd (or kent) hiz mac*: I never knew hiz fellow'. Recall too current working class Glaswegian *To dog it 'to play truant'*. The two way alternation of the obstruent/fricative contrast in Scots is clearly shown by Elphinston (1786:46) where that dialect: 'swels dhe verb *scate* into' *sketch;* so making boath dhe *scate* and dhe *scater*, dhe *sketcher*: yet ballances exchange by diminnishing a *sledge* to' a *sled*'.

But perhaps the most commented upon continuancy alternation in the 18th century is that involving the voiced and voiceless obstruents [d]/[t] with the delayed release fricative [ʤ]/[ʧ], and the white noise fricative [š]. Buchanan provides lengthy descriptions of both segments (1757:12): '*ch* has a mute sound, which is expressed by first putting the tongue to the palate of the mouth, and then try to pronounce *itch;* it is very like *itch*, when *itch* is whispered: it is expressed in *cheap, church, which*, &c. The addition of (t) does not alter or increase the sound; for *snach* is the same as *snatch*, and *cruch* as *crutch*, &c. so that (t) is really superfluous'; he also notes (1762:25) that *ch* has 'a smooth sound like (sh) in Words derived from the Latin: as *debauchee, machine, chagrine, chaise, chevalier, champaign, chamade;* pronounce *deboshee, masheen, shagreen, shaise, shevalier, shampain, shamade'*. Again, '*Sh* has a smooth unvaried Sound very like (ish), when (ish) is whispered; it is expressed in *share, shame, dash, wash*, &c.' (1762:26). Dun (1766:21) sees [š] rather than [ʧ] in items like *'pinch'*, *'flinch'*: '*Ch* sounds as *sh* in *she*, in such as these, *danch, panch, blanch, branch, stanch, belch, filch, pilch, inch, pinch, bunch*...'. Although his post dental examples are perhaps not the most helpful, Elphinston too (1786:7) hears *ch* in a similar way: 'We must perceiv dhat after *l* or *n*, az after *t*, dhe Inglish *ch* emits no more dhan *sh*; and so coincides widh dhe French aspirate. Dhus *Welch, French, Scotch;* ar but *Welsh, Frensh, Scotsh;* dhe no les nattural contractives ov *Walish, Frankish, Scottish*. So ar *milch, batch,* and *branch*, merely *milsh, batch* and *branch*'.

In the period there is considerable debate about and some evidence for the reduction in vocality of the palatal vowel in <ium> terminations in items like *'medium'* to some kind of [j] semi-vowel, thus Cortez Telfair (1775:127): 'In such words as *medium, genius, Indian, i* may either make a diphthong with the next vowel or not, in poetry; But in prose, it makes always a diphthong; and then those words are pronounced as if written *meed-yum, geen-yus, Ind-yun*'. The author of *A Spelling-Book Upon a New Plan* (1796:26:footnote) makes a similar observation: 'The vowel *u*, in the terminations *ure* and *ute*, though marked with a circumflex accent, has not exactly the same sound as *ew*: - it sounds rather like *yŭ*, as, *creature*, (creatyŭr); *leisure* (leisyŭr), &c'; and commenting on his *lenient* (lēn ĭĕnt) entry, he states: 'Though *i*, in the terminations beginning with a consonant and in *ia* or *ie*, is marked as silent [italicised:CJ], it is not *wholly* so: - its effect is twofold. 1. It carries the preceding consonant, by a soft, and almost imperceptible transition, to the following vowel. 2. it affects the sound of the preceding consonant, if it be *d*, *l*, *n*, *s*, or *t*; making *d* to sound somewhat like soft *g*, as in *sol-dier* (sol-gier); *In-dia*, (In-gia): it makes the sound of *l* and *n* more liquid, as val*i*ant, len*i*ent; gives *s* a kind of musical sound, between that of *z* and hissing *s*, as in trans*i*ent; and makes *t* soft like *sh*, as in quot*i*ent, part*i*al: But a good teacher would do more to describe its power by one word of his mouth, than five pages in writing'. He seems to be suggesting pronunciations like [soldʒər]; [ɪndʒə] ; [valjənt]; [linjənt]; [tranʒənt]; [kwoʃənt] and [parʃəl]. Adams (1799:114-115) delimits the operation of the continuancy shifting of voiceless dentals to those instances where the [t] is part of the inherent structure of the lexical item: '*T* preserves its sound when it forms a radical syllable, for, on examination, it will appear not to be part of an expletive: as - *bast-ion, combust-ion, christ-ian, fust-ian*: Hence by strict rule (contradicted by use) *Egyp-tian* should be sounded, *Egypt-ian*, because the root *Egypt* is closed by *t*, and *ian* is the expletive; custom has made it yield to the rule of finals, *teon, tian, sion*, &c. which the above and similar words do not so readily admit, on account of a singular harshness they would thus produce'. Adams, in a typical anecdote, goes on to illustrate the English tendency to fricativise the [t] obstruent in such contexts through what he sees as its almost parodied use in Latin pronunciation: 'This hissing English contraction extended to Latin words, shews another absurdity in our pronunciation of Latin. In the year 1755, I attended a public Disputation in a foreign University, when at least 400 Frenchmen literally hissed a grave and learned English Doctor (Mr Banister) not by way of insult, but irresistibly provoked by the quaintness of the repetition of *sh*. The Thesis was the concurrence of God in *actionibus viciosis*: the whole hall resounded with the hissing cry of *sh* (*shi, shi, shi*) on its continual occurrence in *actio, actione, viciosia - ac-shio, vi-shi-osa*.' Present day speakers of Scots can be heard to alternate for '*media*' pronunciations like [midɪə]/[midʒə]/[midjə].

It is not always a simple matter to decide from the 18th century evidence whether we are witnessing a temporal sequence of change in this area of the phonology such that [ti] → [tj] → [tʃ], or whether observation was insufficiently sensitive to distinguish the second from the third 'stage' in the process. Walker (1791:55) describes the mechanism for the production of what he calls 'semi-consonant diphthongs' produced by the contact between [t] and a subsequent mainly palatal vowel as follows: 'Now the vowel that occasions this transition of *t* to *s* is the squeezed sound of the *e*, as heard in *y* consonant: which squeezed sound is a species of hiss; and this hiss, from the absence of accent, easily slides into the *s*, and the *s* as easily into *sh*. Thus mechanically is generated that hissing termination *tion*, which forms but one syllable, as if written *shun*.' Perhaps a more convincing explanation for the [t] → [ʧ] change might come from a consideration of what could provoke such a shift from the non vocalic end of the sonority hierarchy to a place on that scale where there is evidence of considerable vocality (observable periodic structure in the signal). Such an explanation may resemble the same kind of hypothesising we proposed for alternations such as [aʊ]/[ɔ] and the interpretation of [ju] as something approximating to [ʊ̈] (see pp. 156-157 above). Recall how, in the latter instance, we suggested that in place of interpreting the [ju] signal as comprising a palatal/labial *sequence*, listeners hear it as a complex or internally mixed phonetic segment comprised simultaneously of a labial (prominent) and palatal (subordinate) segment, the surface manifestation of such a mixture perceived as [ʊ̈] or [ɯ] (Anderson and Ewen:1987:212-214). In the same way we might argue that a *linear* sequence such as [t]+palatal vowel, might be interpreted as a single, composite and simultaneously expressed segment containing an internalised 'mixture' of a (prominent) palatal vowel and a voiceless obstruent; such a mixture is heard as a palatal-alveolar delayed release fricative such as [ʧ].

Walker provides extensive exemplification of this alternation, relating its occurrence to the placement of the accent: 'This pronunciation of *t* extends to every word where the diphthong or diphthongal sound commences with *i* or *e*. Thus *bestial, beauteous, righteous, frontier*, &c, are pronounced as if written *best-cheal, beaut-cheous, right-cheous, front-chier*, &c', although he roundly criticises Sheridan for generalising the phenomenon to 'non-accented' contexts: 'he has extended the change of *t* into *tch*, or *tsh*, to the word *tune* and its compounds, *tutor, tutoress, tutorage, tutelar, tutelary*, &c. *tumult, tumour*, &c. which he spells *tshoon, tshoon-able*, &c. *tshoo-tur, tshoo-tris*.....the words ought to be pronounced as if written *tewtor, tewmult, tewmour*, &c. and neither *tshootur, tshoomult, tshoomour*, as Mr Sheridan writes them, nor *tootor, toomult, toomour*, as they are often pronounced by vulgar speakers'.

Barrie (1796:3-5) asserts that 'Italic *e* and *i* sound like initial *y*, as in hid*e*ous, fil*i*al', while Italic *ce, ci, cy, si*, and *ti* sound *sh*, as in o*ce*an, so*ci*al, hal*sy*on, pen*si*on, ac*ti*on; Roman si sounds zh as in conclusion, also Italic *s* before *u*, as in plea*s*ure'. McIllquam (1781:18) modifies such a generalisation: 'T, when followed by *i* and another vowel, sounds as *sh* as; *nation, motion, satiate, satiety*; except when it is preceded by *s* or *x*, and derivatives from words ending in *ty*: as *suggestion, commixtion, mighty, mightier*'. The monosyllabic nature of the termination is categorically shown by Drummond's (1777:66) extensive lists of words showing *sh* for *c, t* and *s*; for instance 'Words where *c, t* sound *sh* before the diphthong *ia*, which sounds *a*[1] [[e]:CJ]: *Graciate, emaciate, affeciate, depreciate,* *officiate, vitiate, initiate, negotiate,*' etc. Likewise, '*c t s* sounding *sh* before the diphthong *ie*, which sounds e^2 [[ɛ]:CJ] *Ancient, omniscient, efficient, proficient,* etc.'; *c t* sounding *sh* before the triphthong *iou* which sounds o^2 [[ɔ]:CJ]: *adventitious, audacious, atrocious, pertinacious, malicious, fictitious* etc.'. Burn (1766:13) too seems to hear terminations in *-tion, -tial,* etc. as monosyllabic, representing *condition, partial, tertian, Grecian, coercion, halcyon,* and *division* as [condishun], [parshal], [tershan], [Greshan], [coershun], [halshun] and [divishun], as does Buchanan (1757:13:): 'Observe, that (si) before (on) at the end of words, takes the sound of (sh); as *division, occasion, evasion, mission,* &c. read *divishun, occashun,* &c. so that the terminations *sion* and *tion* have generally the same sound, *viz, shun* or *shon,* and are always, as they ought to be, pronounced as one syllable'. (However, Fisher (1789:20) in his list of 'words of the same sound' records *Gesture* '*Carriage*' and *Jester* '*a merry Fellow*' as homophonous.) Elphinston (1786:45-46) is his customarily expansive self on the issue:

> Into' won absurdity, howevver, dhe French hav not led us; nor hav dhey led us into' manny, or evver committed won equal to' dhat (we hav hiddherto' practised) ov prezenting before dhe aspirate licquefaccion, *i* occularly (az ettymolodgically) open, for *i* really (az auriccularly) shut! True it iz dhat, before *ti* belying *si*, or *ci*, no shutting dubbler cood be vizzibel; an irreffragabel argument, wer dhare no odher, against any such substitucion. Dhus dubbly impossibel iz dhe continnuance ov anny such picture az *ambition, ambitious; propitious, propitiate, propitiation; initial, initiate, initiation;* or az *Titian, Politian, Domitian,* or *Domitius;* for (dhe indispensabel az unexcepcionabel) *ambiscion, ambiscious; propiscious, propisciate, propisciacion; iniscial, inisciate, inisciacion;* hware dhe preceding *ci* remains dhe simpel sibbilant, atricculating dhe febel vowel. Nor iz *inisciate* more clearlly a word ov three syllabels, *i-nis-ciate;* dhan *inisciacion,* ov five: *i-nis-ci-a-cion*: dhe last being vertually *shate* and *shon*.

Sylvester Douglas (Jones:1992:217) notes the Scotch realisation of PRONOUNCIATION [sic:CJ]: 'The Scotch sound the *ou*, like the *u* in *Nuncio*. And the *ci*, like the hard *s*. As if the word were written *pronuncation*. But the *ou* has the proper diphthongal sound, as in *renounce, flounce* (in which words likewise, the vernacular Scotch method is, to sound it like the *s* in *Nuncio*) and the *ci* is either sounded, as in other cases, like *sh*, or often, to avoid the close repetition of that same sound twice in the same word, with the distinct sounds of the hard *s*, and the short *i* making it a separate syllable thus *pro-noun-ci-a-tion*'; a phenomenon noted too by Elphinston (1786:42): 'By making *i* (az of *e*) dhe mere softener ov *c*, dhe Scotch looz a syllabel ov *pronunciacion*, saying *pronunceacion* or *pronounsacion;* hwich corrupt Inglish utters in like manner *pronounceacion* or *pronounsacion*'.

Throughout the 18th century there appears to have been an alternation, especially word initially, between the less and more noisy fricatives [s] and [š], Walker (1791:54) criticising Sheridan for recommending pronunciations of *suicide, presume,* and *resume* 'as if written *shoo-icide, pre-zhoom, re-zhoom*', with Elphinston (1786:26) noting that the contrary interchange is a characteristic of Scots: '*shal, shood, wish, Scotch fasshion,* (or *fassion*), to' be herd Scottishly...*sal, sood* (or *sud*), *was, Scots fasson,* dropping onely dhe nazallity ov dhe French *façon*', and again (1786:23) 'Hence dhe Scottish *offisher* for *officer,* and *sal* for *shal;....plezer* for *plezzure,* and dhe like'.

There is surprisingly little record in the 18th century source materials of the Northern Scots [β]/[f] alternation, with the exception of Sylvester Douglas (Jones:1992:141) who sees the bilabial fricative as [hw]: 'In the North of Scotland *wh* is pronounced like *f*; so that *what,* and *fat, why,* and *fie,* form to the ear in that part of the Island, the very same words', while Elphinston (1786:32), commenting on the [v]/[w] interchange: 'If Londoners be liabel to' interchainge *wile* and *vile;* no wonder Abberdeens-men, to' prezerv dhe aspiracion (hwich Londoners often looz) shood be apt to' say *file* for *hwile.* More pardonabel iz *furl* for *hwirl,* dhan *worse* for *verse.*' The [v]/[w] alternation attracts more comment, notably from Sylvester Douglas who, under his discussion of the phonological relationships between stops and fricatives, hypothesises (Jones:1992:141):

> The analogy between the *b* and *v* might serve to explain the peculiarity in the speech of the Gascons, by which they always give the sound of *b*, to *v*. Saying *je l'ai bu* for *je l'ai vu*. *Bérité* for *vérité*. But if my memory does not deceive me they also pronounce like a *v* what is written with a *b*. As *veaux yeux* for *beaux yeaux*. This sort of exchange of the two sounds, is equally unaccountable with the habit of those people of whom I have already made mention, who pronounce the *h* where it is mute and suppress it where it ought to be pronounced. The continual substitution of *v* for *w*, and *w* for *v*, by the inferior class of citizens in London is an inexplicable phenomenon of speech, of the same nature with the two others of which I have just taken notice. I have known some individuals in Scotland have this last habit, and (if I am not mistaken) it is common to all the inhabitants of a small district of one of the Northern counties of that kingdom.

Commenting on <v>, Geddes (1792:437) notes that 'This letter is by the Scots often interchanged with *f*, and in some countries with *w*, as in London', although the author of *A Spelling-Book Upon a New Plan* is in no doubt that the use of [v] for [w] word initially is a Scotticism to be avoided, since he includes as 'Commonly Pronounced' under his list of words 'in which the Natives of North Britain are most apt to err' the items <werge> '*verge*', <vrote> '*wrote*', <vrung> '*wrung*' and <vrite>

'*write*' (Ohala and Lorentz:1977). While recognising this 'interchainge' as a common feature of London pronunciation, Elphinston (1786:32) also records its use in contemporary Scots: 'Dhe Inglish *how* waz indeed unfortunately varied into' dhe Scotch interjeccion ov expostulatory surprize, hweddher, *Ow! Vow!* or *Wow!* as in *Vow! man*; or, more coarsely, *Wow! man*'. It is Elphinston too who is one of the few commentators to record extensively the deletion of the [v] fricative in Scots, recording the 'colloquial' *guimme fippence hapenny* for *guiv me five-pence half-penny*, and everywhere seeing the deletion as non-standard: 'Dho *evil* runs also into' *il*, nedher Inglish nor Scottish stile wil be much exalted by dealing familliarly, edher widh dhe *devvil* or dhe *de'l*'. He goes on to complain that 'Certain it iz, dhat dhe Scotch did widh boundles fredom drop dhis aspirate. If won dialect stil mince *stove* and *shaiz* into' *sto'* and *shai'*, or *stow* and *shay*; Aberdeenish may wel shorten *preev* (for *proov*) into' *pree*'. Such deletion is not confined to [v] segments since 'Dhe dental aspirate also vulgarly sinks in boath dialects. Az Inglish vulgarrity hurries *hweddher*, no les dhan *hwiddher*, into' *hware*; braud Scotch squezes, simmilarly, *smoddher* into' *smo'r*'.

8.10 Metathesis

Under his HUNDRED entry (Jones:1992:203) Sylvester Douglas records the two classic contexts where [r] movement occurs in the internal structure of syllables: 1. where pre to post peak 'hopping' occurs in syllables whose rhyme component, when terminated by an obstruent consonant, is 'light', by this means achieving some kind of canonical configuration whereby maximal vowel prominence in the syllable is perceived as falling within the domain of the rhyme, thus [hɣndrəd] → [hɣndərd]. 2. The corollary of this process occurs when rhyme terminations are 'too heavy' vocalically, i.e. when they comprise two or more highly sonorous segments to the right of the peak as in the stressed syllable of '*Birmingham*'. One stratagem for the reduction of this 'over-vowelly' rhyme is the transposition of the [r] component of the rhyme into a pre-peak position: thus Sylvester Douglas' <Briminjam> example (Jones 1989:§3.2.3; Windross:1988). As we might suspect, Adams (1799:153) sees this [r] movement not as some kind of non standard deviation, but as a conscious and deliberate innovation by what he considers to be the superior Scotch dialect: 'Artful contrivance, not ignorance, has also introduced another singular deformation of our sounds, backed with the usual change, corruption of vowels, and interposition of new letters; as *burn, pin, thistle; brin, prin, thrustle*, &c.' Elphinston (1787:38) provides an extensive record of [r] as well as other kinds of metathesis: 'If, on boath sides dhe Tweed, dhe rifraf *acs*, for *ask*; and, particularly on dhe South, drive not dhe *wasps*, but dhe *wapses*, away; if dhe Inglish, even ov rank, talk of *childern* and *iorn*, for *children* and *iron*; if *film* twist into' dhe constitucion ov *flimsy* or *flimzy*...But entirely of Scottish warp ar *garse, corse, firth, thirl, guirn*, *orp, scart, birz* (*or* briz), *warstel,* and *terlis;* for *gras, cros, frith, thril, grin, throb, scratch, bruiz, wrestel,* and *trellis.* So (like dhe Inglish figgurative *brunt,* from *burn*) *brugh, crud, broad, wrat, scruf, truf, drouth, hwoml, kittel, forfet;* for *burg, burrough* or *burrow, curd, board, wart, scurf, turf, draught; hwelm, tickel, surfeit',* while *'Tirl, thirl,* and *skirl,* ar obvious transpozzitives ov dhe Inglish *tril, thril,* and *shril'* (1786:39).

9

SUPRASEGMENTALS: SYLLABLES, STRESS AND INTONATION

9.1 Syllables, their Definition and the Principles which Govern their Division

The majority of the genre of works which might loosely be called grammar books in the 18th century contain extensive comment on the theoretical status of the notion of the syllable as well as extensive rules as to how division of the component parts of the syllable was to be achieved. This concern did not spring primarily from any inherent interest in the status of syllables as phonological units, but largely from the conviction that a knowledge of syllable structure - especially the principles of syllable division - was an indispensable aid to good spelling, to clear and interesting oratorical delivery and to an understanding of the morphological and derivational structure of the lexicon: 'When the Scholar has learned the Rules for the Division of Syllables, care must be taken that he strictly conforms to them; and that he industriously avoid that random Method of dividing by the Ear, which is subject to mere jumble, as it must be continually fluctuating according to the various Dialects of different Counties. A strict Attention should also be paid to that advantageous Method of dividing derivative Words according to their primitives, i.e. that in the Division, the primitive Word be always kept whole; as it will be a Means of perfecting Youth in that very necessary Part of grammatical Knowledge, namely, the dependence that the English Language has upon itself with respect to Derivation' (Buchanan:1762:40:footnote). Again, McIllquam (1781:28) advises the young reader: 'If you do not know a word at first sight, do not guess at its pronunciation, but go over the syllables, one by one, and then pronounce it clearly and distinctly'. There is no doubt in the minds of many of the authors of school books that a knowledge of syllable structure and division is a *sine qua non* in any serious effort to improve spelling ability; typical is Dun's (1766:127) comment: 'This Method of teaching a Child to reach the Sound of a Word, Letter by Letter, as I said before, is certainly of very good Use to him; for it gives him a good Notion of the full Force and Sound of a Letter, and Syllable of a Word; it makes him more sensible of his Fault, when he adds the Sound of a Letter that is not in a Word, or takes away the Sound of a Letter that is in it: It helps his Spelling very much, and is the most immediate help to him, to divide Words into Syllables; that I can conceive'.

Pragmatic as ever, however it is Walker (1700:75-76) who recognises that 'Dividing words into syllables is a very different operation, according to the different ends proposed for it. The object of syllabification may be, either to enable children to discover the sound of words they are unacquainted with, or to shew the etymology of a word, or to exhibit the exact pronunciation of it', yet he realises too that such a division might be 'directed..by some laws of its own, laws which arise out of the very nature of enunciation, and the specific qualities of the letters'. Definitions of the syllable itself in the 18th century literature vary in detail and sophistication, and in general centre around the recognition of the syllable as a distinct unit of sound, which is vowel centred and describable in terms of the combinatorial qualities of the segments which occur at its edges. For Beattie (1788:52-53) 'The quantity of distinct speech that we pronounce with one effort of the articulating organs is called a *syllable*. In every syllable there must be one vowel sound at least; because without an opening of the mouth there can be no distinct articulation. A syllable may be a single vowel, as *a, o*; or a single diphthong, as *ay, oi*; or either of these modified by one or more consonants, placed before it or after it, or on both sides of it: as *to, of; boy, oyl; dog, foil; dry, art; swift, broils, strength*'. Beattie (1788:62-63) - under his discussion of 'emphatick syllables' - also recognises long and short syllables (which he relates to the degree of stress associated with the syllable); essentially these are CV and VC types: 'For, in our tongue, there are two sorts of syllabic emphasis. The one, terminating in a consonant, is formed by a stronger or smarter exertion of the voice: the other, which frequently ends in a vowel or diphthong, is distinguished by a longer continuance, as well as by a powerful energy. Thus, the first syllable of *study*, and of *passion*, though emphatical, is not long'. Syllable division is in general governed by a non-empty onset principle and an assignment, at syllable interface, of certain 'long' consonants (often on the basis of the orthography alone) to allow for the exemplification of contemporary views on the morphophonemics of syllable onsets and terminations. However, some imaginative theorising has to be employed by Beattie in squaring such principles with those syllables which terminate in two consonants: 'It is also true, that the other syllabick emphasis is sometimes long, as in *event, neglect*; but here the vowel is obviously short, and the protracted sound rests upon the consonants, and is owing to their duplicity, which forms a collision of the articulating organs, and a necessary delay in the pronunciation' (1788:63-64).

Perhaps similar motivations lie behind Perry's (1777:x) characterisation of syllables which are 'flat and slowly accented' (marked by a grave accent) as in *bŏr`der* and *wârn`ing*, as against those which are 'sharp and quickly accented' (marked by an acute accent) as in *bĕt´tér* and *wăsh´ing*, where syllable length is perhaps to be associated with codas terminating in sonorant initial clusters. However, syllable length is often conflated with 'long' i.e. diphthongal (even orthographic diphthong) versus 'short' monophthongal vocalic segments, notably by Dun (1766:142): 'Student: How shall I know whether a Syllable be short or long? Master: In every long Syllable there is either a Diphthong, as *Gain, heap*; or a Vowel only, of a long or broad Sound, as in *Gall, mate*. All other Syllables are commonly short, as *Bad, mat* &c'. In much the same vein McIllquam (1781:20) tells us under his *Rules of Quantity*; 'A long syllable takes double the time in pronouncing that a short one does, as *hāte, hăt; nōte, nŏt; tūne, tŭn*' where we once again see the customary 18th century conflation of length and vowel quality. Buchanan (1757:14) sees the syllable as 'a complete sound uttered in one distinct breath....no number of consonants can make a syllable without a vowel; as *strngth* can make no syllable by themselves, but if I put in (e) betwixt (r) and (n), thus *strength*, it makes a syllable and a proper word'. The author of *A Spelling-Book Upon a New Plan* tersely comments that 'A syllable is any one complete sound' (1791:126); Robertson (1752) 'one or more letters comprehended in one Sound'; Dun (1766:128) - who provides by far the most detailed treatment of all the Scotch authors on this topic - proposes 'any vowel or diphthong sounded by itself, or with one or more consonants, so as it may not mar the sound of the next letter'. His definition is clarified through the Student/Master question and answer routine so typical of his *Best Method of Teaching* (1766:129): 'S. Why do you say, there must be such a precise Number of these Letters united in one Syllable, as the Sound of the following letter may not be marred? M. Because young Beginners are very ready to mistake in the Division of Consonants, taking either too few, or too many of them to a Syllable, as in *Astonishment*; where the Child knows not that *hm* must be divided, and go to different Syllables, that he should say *A-sto-nish-ment*, not *A-sto-nis-hment*'. Clearly, as we shall see immediately below, his scheme of division entailed a knowledge of the morphophonemics of syllable initials and finals.

Rules for syllable division or boundary placement are provided by many commentators, notably Burn, Dun, Adie and Robertson and several of the works we have now become familiar with are composed of many pages containing lists of words of various syllable lengths showing syllable division and, as we shall see in the next section, stress placement as well. The rules proposed for syllable boundary placement primarily rest on two criteria: the first holds that, ideally, syllable onsets should be non-empty: this is especially the case in non word initial contexts - although even here, as we shall see the principle can be made to hold. That is, where there is an intervocalic consonantal segment, it should be treated as the onset to the second syllable, rather than as the coda to the first: thus an item like <about> shows a syllable division $[_1\text{a}_1][_2\text{bout}_2]$ or, in the representational system of most 18th century handbooks, *a-bout*. All observers appear to treat syllable division in bi- and polysyllabic words in this fashion, and all record an 'exception' where the intervocalic consonantal segment is represented by <x>: [ks]/[gz]. In such cases the consonantal cluster is seen as belonging in the coda position of syllable one: $[_1\text{egz}_1][_2\text{akt}_2]$, <exact>. No rationale is provided for this so commonly recognised exception to the general principle.

The second rule represents, in fact, a group of conditions dealing with situations where the intervocalic position is filled by more than one consonantal segment. Interestingly, in the context where these cases are being considered, there is very often a prior discussion of the morphophonemics of syllable initial clusters, with descriptions and lists of allowable English language groupings of consonants which can occur as syllable initiators and terminations. The combinatorial qualities of syllable structure in general are attempted most seriously by Dun (1776:134): 'Consider, that you can have no Syllable without a Vowel, and, consequently, if a Word begin with one, two or three Consonants, you must sound none of these till you come to a Vowel; I mean, that Vowel must make a part of the perfect, compleat Sound of those Consonants; And if it end with one, two or three Consonants, you must have all those sounded in the last Syllable, I mean, united in a Sound with the last Vowel, because none of them can sound by itself'. The rule for the division of consonantal clusters intervocalically hinges upon the extent to which all or part of the cluster can be an allowable syllable onset. A cluster or part of a cluster will be allowed to belong to the right hand syllable just so long as it is 'proper to begin a word' or 'proper to begin a syllable'. In this way items like <blandish>, <barter> and <instruct> will show a syllable division like $[_1\text{blan}_1]][_2\text{dish}_2]$, $[_1\text{bar}_1][_2\text{ter}\ _2]$ and $[_1\text{in}_1][_2\text{struct}_2]$ on the principle that *[nd, *[rt and *[nst are disallowed as syllable onsets (that they are so because they offend the sonority hierarchy principle of linear ordering of syllabic elements is a phenomenon apparently missed by 18th century scholars (Jones:1989:172)). But again, it is the principle of syllable onset non-emptiness which drives the division. The system is set out quite clearly by Dun (1766:132): 'S. What if there are, between two Vowels, three Consonants, that cannot unite in a Sound, with a Vowel immediately after them? M. If the first two can make an easy smooth Sound after a Vowel, then they end the Syllable, as in *Hert-ford;* and if the last two can be sounded with a Vowel after them, then they begin the Syllable, and the first of the three ends the former Syllable, as in *Mon-ster,* where *st* begins the latter Syllable, and *n* ends the former, because *nst* cannot begin a Syllable or Word'. The long lists of 'divided' words in *The Instructor* (1798:43ff) quite clearly illustrate these principles of division, with disyllabic splits like *a-ble, a-corn, a-gent,* while the principle that intervocalic consonant clusters are split between syllables *iff *[CC,* is also well attested by constructions like *ab-sence, ac-rid, ac-tor, al-der,* etc., although in this work medial [st] clusters are treated non-exceptionally, hence *mas-ter-ly.*

However, these lists also show cases where intervocalic consonants are assigned syllable membership in such a way as to offend the principle of coda non-empty-ness for syllable two. Instances are *ac-id, air-y, al-oes, bak-er, bal-ance, cab-in, chap-el, del-uge, dam-age, ech-o, sail-or.* It is difficult to find any single set of motivations for such a syllable bracketing, but they may be related to other sets of exceptions noted from the observations of some other writers, notably Robertson (1722:27): 'The third rule is, when several consonants come together in the Middle of a Word, they must be placed in the Syllables according to the distinct sounds, as in the Words *re-store, be-speak, a-skew, a-squint, fa-ble,* all the middle Consonants belong to the last syllable: but the very same consonants in *Mas-ter, whis-per, Bas-ket, Mus-quet, pub-lish,* must be divided, one to the first syllable, and the other to the latter, because they are so pronounced'. Robertson's rationale is difficult to grasp, although he may be suggesting that in the former instances the syllable division principles defer to lexical considerations; the [st], [sp] and [sk] clusters remain undivided when their placement in the second syllable produces a recognisable lexical item, otherwise they split. However fanciful this suggestion, it is interesting to note that these exceptions occur with the very consonantal clusters which uniquely show ambisyllabicity at syllable interface, since [st], [sp] and [sk] are alone among consonantal groupings which are simultaneously able to act as syllable onsets and codas, and thus allow a syllable bracketing like $[_1\mathrm{ma}[_2\mathrm{st}_1]\mathrm{er}_2]$ and so on (Jones:1989:104; 1978). There is also a third principle which just might show a sense among observers of the possibility of dual syllable membership of consonantal segments at syllable interfaces. All commentators cite a principle (again on the basis of the impropriety of the 'group' for syllable initial position) whereby those syllables showing double consonants intervocalically are divided, thus *ab-ba, wed-ding,* suggesting syllable boundary placement such as $[_1\mathrm{we}[_2\mathrm{d}_1]\mathrm{ing}_2]$. However, the inclusion of items like *ac-cent,* must make us incline to believe that the boundary placement is being driven by orthographic and not phonetic considerations on such occasions.

We have already commented upon the fact that Walker is very sensitive of the fact that the two main principles of syllable division should be somehow relatable to general phonological laws. He suggests that there is a direct co-relation between stress placement and syllabification; prominently stressed syllables contain a long, distinct vowel which should be 'open' and therefore ought to be coda empty, and syllable final consonantal material assigned to the onset of the following syllable. Likewise, weakly stressed syllables should show a short vowel, the universal sign for which is a syllable terminated by a consonant, a 'closed' syllable: 'These laws certainly direct us to separate double consonants, and such as are uncombinable from the incoalescence of their sounds: and if such a separation will not paint the true sound of the word, we may be certain that such sound is unnatural, and has arisen from caprice: thus the words *chamber, Cambridge* and *cambrick,* must be divided at the letter *m,* and as this letter, by terminating the syllable according to the settled rules of pronunciation, shortens the vowel - the general pronunciation given to these words must be absurd, and contrary to the first principles of the language. *Angel, ancient, danger, manger* and *ranger,* are under the same predicament: but the paucity of words of this kind, so far from weakening the general rule, strengthens it'.

The principles of syllable division seem also to have been sensitive to morphological and derivational criteria; 'Grammatical terminations, or endings, must be separated; as, *turn-ing, stand-eth.* the terminations *cial tial, cious tious, cion sion tion, cheon*; sounded *shal, shus, shun, shin,* ought not to be divided, as they form but one syllable' (McIllquam:1781:21). Gray's lists (1809:10ff) uniformly divide syllables according to morphological structure, regardless of other considerations, thus *zeal-ous, fool-ish, brethr-en,* as well as others such as *maid-en, ban-ish, man-age, vig-our* where the terminations may have some kind of quasi-morphological status. Considerations of this sort might account for divisions like those in *The Instructor* as *not-a-ble, nom-inal, nom-i-na-tion, no-men-cla-ture, sen-ti-ment-al.* Buchanan too, after a long section describing the rules for and long lists of examples of syllable division, comments: 'Have you no Exceptions from these general Rules? From these general Rules are excepted derivative and compound Words. How many sorts of Words are there? All Words whatsoever are either primitive or derivative, simple or compound....a primitive or simple Word is such as cannot be derived from any other Word in the same Language; as *man, good, kind, honest,* etc.....A derivative word is a primitive or simple Word, with the Addition of a Syllable or Syllables to the same; as by adding the Syllable (ly) to the primitive Word *Man,* is formed the derivative Word *man-ly;* so from the primitive *Good,* by adding (*ness*), comes the derivative *Good-ness'*. This is followed by a list of derivative words, divided according to their syllable structures: *commend-able, herb-al, accept-ance, read-ing, fool-ish, hero-ism,* etc., all of which is closely associated with a guide to the best method of producing 'true Spelling', and although as we have already suggested - many of the treatments of syllable division are tied in closely with matters pedagogical - Dun (1776:133) is careful to recommend that 'children should not be plagued by these rules'.

There are several places where we can find evidence for phonological change based upon some kind of motivation to realise a 'preferred' or even canonical syllable structure. In this context we might mention the alternation observed by Sylvester Douglas under his MEDICINE entry (Jones:1992:208-209):

> This word is constantly made a disyllable by the generality of the English, both in speaking and reading, whether prose or verse. There are some low people from vulgarity, and some few persons of learning, who sound the middle *i*. The old Poets make *medicine* a trisyllable in some instances....*Venison* is in like manner generally made a disyllable in pronounciation, though there are many English people who pronounce the *i*.

Disyllabic [mɛdsən] and trisyllabic [mɛdɩsən] shapes can be produced by both groups of speakers, a phenomenon also recorded by Cortez Telfair (1775:155). We might argue that the origin of this alternation stems from the speaker's 'desire' to achieve a bi-syllabic status for segments at syllable boundary. A parallel instance might be the Modern English [aθlit]/[aθəlit] *'athlete'* and the [rɛmnənt]/{rɛmənənt] '*remnant*' alternations. Configurations such as those like $_1$ath$_1$][$_2$lete$_2$] and [$_1$rem$_1$][$_2$ nant $_2$] show syllable interface as discrete. The 'splitting' of the consonantal clusters which appear at syllable interface by the additional of a vocalic segment has the effect of producing a lexical item whose post-vocalic (non word final) consonantal components are simultaneously the codas to their preceding and onsets to their following syllables, thus [$_1$a[$_2$θ$_1$]ə[$_3$l$_2$]it$_3$]. The trisyllabic *'medicine'* and *'venison'* instances cited by Douglas may have been motivated by factors like this, such that [$_1$vɛn$_1$]][$_2$ sən$_2$] → [$_1$vɛ [$_2$n $_1$]ɩ [$_2$ s $_2$] ən $_3$]. Of course, this phenomenon - well attested in the history of English in general (Jones 1989: §3.5.1; 1976) - can work across word boundaries as well. The 'epenthetic [r]' instances we have seen in 8.4 may also be accounted for along similar lines. In an phrase such as *'Law and Order'*, we might expect a syllable bracketing as: [$_1$lɔ$_1$]][$_2$ ænd$_2$]; the insertion of the [r] segment has the effect of achieving an ambisyllabic segment at syllable interface, such that we have: [$_1$lɔ [$_2$ r $_1$] ænd$_2$]. We might recall here Elphinston's (1786:43-44) comment that 'Evvery smoodh dialect haz avoided alike dhe needles clash ov consonants, and intergahp ov vowels...evvery diccion haz won or oddher insertive articulaccion, to' preclude dhe meeting ov vowels. Inglish, widh ezy propriety, subjoins to' dhe indeffinite artikel, preceding a vowel, dhe dental harmonious liquid....Dhust must we say, *an air* and *a hair...an owl, a howlet,* and dhe like. Did dhe Inglish, az dhe Scotch, drop dhe licquefier ov *u*, and utter insted ov *yoo*, only *oo;* dhey wood simmilarly say *an use, an university,* for *a use, a university*'.

We have already seen how one of the main principles underlying syllable division for 18th century grammarians was that of the non-empty onset. That is, while the central and unique portion of any syllable was its vowel segment, ideally it should also contain an onset to that vowel, a segment (or segments) which should show the morphophonemic characteristics of vowel reduction towards the syllable edge, thus an onset-peak combination like [tra is grammatical, while one like *[rta (with the vowel prominent [r] further away from the vowel than the voiceless obstruent) is clearly not. A well known feature of the phonology of English of all varieties is the tendency of speakers to 'fill' an empty onset slot with material which is as close as possible to the articulatory/acoustic character of the peak vowel in the syllable (Maddieson:1984:57). The instances of [h] insertion we saw in 8.7 could be regarded as examples of just such a phenomenon; the acoustic fingerprint of the [h] being the voiceless version of the peak vowel to its right, making it the ideal onset to the syllable. That other near-vowel segments (notably [w] and [j]) can perform such a syllable structure- preserving function is also well recorded: note the historical pathways taken by the Old English <an> *'one'* item, as [wʌn] and, in Scotland, [jun]. Elphinston (1786:10-11) scathingly records just such a Scotch tendency to use the 'unetymological' liquiefiers in syllable initial position: 'Dhe same rank, or rank ranklenes, vies in dhe two kingdoms, hweddher Scottish clowns shal prefix dhe slender licquefier to' *a* and *e*, or Inglish dhe braud to' *o* iniscial. From dhoze dherfore must stil be expected *ya, yen, yale,* or *yel, yabel* or *yebbel, yerth, yeternity;* for *a, an* (ainciently, az Greekly, *ane*) dhe indeffinite repprezentative ov *one*, hwich now iz *won; ale, abel, erth, eternity*. In Ingland may be simmilarly herd *yerth* and *yerb*, for *erth* and *erb;* no les dhan *Wo* and *Wokingham*, for *O*, and *Oakingham* or *Okingham*. So, on won side dhe Tweed, *hyame*, on dhe oddher *hwome*, iz *home*'. The phenomenon is well attested too in several of the lists of 'Words alike in Sound', for instance <Ear> *'of the head'* / <Year> *'twelve months'* (Gray:1809:105; *A Spelling-Book Upon a New Plan*:1796:147); <Year>/<Yearly>/<Early>; <Earn>/<Yarn>/<Yearn>; <One>/<Won> *'at play'* / <Own> *'to acknowledge'* (Fisher:1789:21-21).

9.2. Intonation

While many of the grammarians associated with Scotland in the 18th century have something to say about intonation (which they often refer to as Accent or Emphasis), none reaches the level of complex description to be found in the musical notation of Joshua Steele's *An Essay Towards Establishing the Melody and Measure of Speech* (1775). Beattie (1788:91) regrets that this is a work which is unread by him: 'An attempt has lately been made by Mr. Steele, to express certain accents of the English tongue by a new invented sort of written characters. This work, I hear, is very ingenious; but, as I have not seen it, I can say nothing more about it'. Beattie emphasises that 'every nation and province has a particular accent' and while he stresses that different accents must be treated with 'forbearance', not every accent is equally good and 'the language..of the most learned and polite persons in London, and the neighbouring Universities of Oxford and Cambridge, ought to be accounted the standard' (1788:92). Yet he points out that 'of all the peculiarities of a foreign tongue, accent is the most difficult for a grown person to acquire...Scotch men have lived forty years in London without entirely losing their native tone'. His views on contemporary intonation patterns are worth quoting at length (1788:90:footnote):

> Mr Sheridan, in those elegant Lectures which I heard him deliver at Edinburgh about twenty years ago, distinguished (if I rightly remember) the English interrogatory accent from the Irish and the Scotch, in this manner. His example was: 'How have you been this great while? - in pronouncing which, he observed, that towards the end of the sentence and Englishman lets his voice fall, an Irishman raises his, and a Scotchman makes his voice first fall and then rise. The remark is well founded; but it is difficult to express in unexceptionable terms a matter of so great nicety. I shall only add, that what is here said of the Scotch accent, though it may hold true of the more southerly

> provinces, is by no means applicable to the dialects that prevail in Aberdeenshire, and other parts of the north: where the voice of the common people, in concluding a clause or sentence, rises into a very shrill and sharp tone without any previous fall. 'You bark in your speech' says a man from Edinburgh to one of Aberdeen: 'and you growl and grumble in yours' replies the Aberdonian. In Inverness-shire and the western parts of Moray, the accents become totally different, and resemble the tones and aspirations of the Erse.

But, on the whole, comment upon and definition of intonational phenomena are rare and not particularly enlightening; fairly typical is McIllquam (1781:22): *What is meant by Emphasis and Cadence?* A proper modulation of the voice in reading; thus, emphasis raises the voice, and cadence lowers it on certain words of a sentence. - *Emphasis* and *Cadence*, or the proper rising and falling of the voice, are best attained by practice, and careful attention to those who read or speak well'. On other occasions, however, intonation is seen as inherently associated with vowel length, as for Buchanan (1770:46): 'Quantity regulates the tone of voice in words, as emphasis does in sentences. So that the voice of a North-Briton is easily distinguished from that of a South-Briton, though we do not see the persons nay, though we do not hear a word either of them says, the very tone will discover the country. The one of the former, though often rough with guttural sounds, is weaker, flatter, and less animating and approaches too much to a monotony. The tone of the latter is more grand and elevated, by the various sounds being uttered according to just quantity and accent; long or short, loud or low, grave or acute. There are Scotch gentlemen indeed in London, whose pronunciation, and consequently tone of voice, cannot be distinguished from natives of the place: but then they applied themselves rigorously to the study of it under the best masters, and with the advantage of not imbibing the least tincture of the provincial dialects, to which the generality of South-Britons are subjected'. Obviously, for Buchanan, being a North-Briton had at least, albeit occasionally, some advantages.

Emphasis and Cadence are seen as means whereby words and phrases can have their semantics altered through differential intonational patterns. Probably following upon the discussion by Sheridan (1762:58ff) in his Lecture IV *On Emphasis*: 'The necessity of observing propriety of emphasis is so great, that the true meaning of words, can not be conveyed without it. For the same individual words, ranged in the same order, may have several different meanings', Buchanan discusses the 'elevation of the voice upon a certain word or words in a sentence' whereby 'emphatical words...must be pronounced with a fuller and stronger sound of voice' (1770:53). However, it is probably true to say that most observers in the period see the same physical correlates underlying the perception of both word stress placement and intonational patterning: '*What is meant by accent*? Accent [`']is the raising of the Voice upon a Syllable in a Word; or, it is a remarkable Stress of the Voice upon a Syllable in a Word. *What is Emphasis*? Emphasis is the raising or depressing of the Voice upon a Word, or Words, in a Sentence' (Gray:1809:102). Beattie, again probably following Sheridan, not only equates Emphasis with stress marking in words, but also with the intonation shifts in sentences whereby changes in topic are identified (1788:59): 'Emphasis, which is a stronger exertion of the voice upon some words and syllables than upon others, is necessary to give spirit and propriety to pronunciation, by marking, first, the most important words in a sentence; and, secondly, those syllables in a word, which custom may have distinguished by a more forcible utterance'; he proceeds to illustrate through the sentence '*Do you walk to town today*?' the various topicalisation possibilities: 'If we exert our voice upon the pronoun, and say, 'Do *you* walk to town today?' the answer might be, 'No, but my servant does', and so on, applying in turn differential intonation to the verb and adverb in the sentence. Acknowledging Sheridan's exemplification, Drummond (1767:88-89) provides a similar definition of Emphasis: 'the pointing out some eminent word, with some little force and elevation of voice. The emphasis ought to be laid on those words which are the most weighty and important, as the emphatical word often determines the sense of a whole sentence.'

9.3 Stress and Stress Placement

Discussions, definitions and descriptions of stress and its placement in words of different syllable length are extensive in the 18th century grammatical cannon. The notion of stress is often associated with both accent and emphasis, Walker (1791:59) noting: 'Accent, in its very nature, implies a comparison with other syllables less forcible; hence, we may conclude, that monosyllables, properly speaking, have no accent: when they are combined with other monosyllables and form a phrase, the stress which is laid upon one, in preference to others, is called emphasis.....the accent always dwells with greatest force on that part of the word which, from its importance, the hearer has always the greatest occasion to observe; and this is necessarily the root, or body of the word'. However, he observes that while such a situation holds rather well for lexical items of native origin, it often fails with those derived from Romance sources, so that 'Accent...seems to be regulated, in a great measure by etymology'. Drummond is careful to distinguish between Accent and Emphasis, the latter being 'the pointing out some eminent word, with some little force and elevation of voice', illustrated very much after Sheridan's style, described in the last section. Accent, however, is for him (1767:88) 'a particular manner of distinguishing one syllable from another, either by dwelling longer upon it as, *móment, músic, tríal*; or pronouncing it quicker, as in *mánner, présent, sýstem*'. Buchanan (1766:50) sees a close relationship between stress, intonation, amplitude and vowel quantity: 'Accent is the elevation and inflexion of the voice upon a certain syllable in a word. The syllable, therefore, which takes the accent is both louder and longer than the rest; as in the noun *tórment*, the first syllable (*tor*) is louder and longer than the second (*ment*), thus *tōrmènt*. So in the word *reconcíling*, the third syllable (*cil*) which takes the accent, is louder and longer than any of the rest, thus, *reconcīling;* it is louder by the accent, that is, the elevation of the voice; and longer by quantity, that is, the inflexion of the voice'. For Elphinston (1786:47): 'Vocallity, somtimes Articulacion, az surely az Precizzion and Harmony, must graitly depend on dhat Emphasis, or enfoarcement (ov won syllabel beyond dhe rest), hwich iz propperly named *dhe stres*.....yet, az evvery word, in proparcion to' its number ov syllabels, iz liabel to' just so manny (at least possibel) varriacions ov ennergy; in notthing can distant dialects be suppozed more to' disagree'. Dun (1766:137ff) has a treatment of stress placement almost as full as that of Walker, and in reply to the question 'What is the Accent of a Word?' gives the response: 'It is a stronger and louder sound given to one Syllable than to another Syllable of the same word as in *Redréss*, where *dress* is pronounced with a stronger and louder sound than *re*'. However, 'definitions' of stress can often be cursory, as that given in the otherwise descriptively detailed *A Spelling-Book Upon a New Plan* (179125): 'Accent is a particular stress of voice that falls upon a syllable or letter in a word'.

Although several Scotch writers note the stress alternation between verbal and nominal types as in *óbject:to objéct; férment:to fermént; pérmit: to permít* and so on, it is only Dun (and that mainly following Walker) who gives any detail for the placement of stress in words of various syllable lengths and in combination with different types of terminations; indeed, it is the possibility of the construction of such 'general rules concerning accentuation' which so appeal to Sylvester Douglas as an alternative to the marking of stress placement in dictionaries and school books: 'Now there are three methods by which written instruction may be conveyed concerning the classical accentuation of English words. 1. By laying down general rules which apply to a great variety of individual words. 2. By marking with some visible sign or character the accented syllable of the word whose accent is to be ascertained. 3. By referring to verses of classical authors in which form the nature of our prosody, the position of the accent in such word [sic:CJ] must necessarily appear' (Appendix II). Dun's 'general directions' for stress placement seem to be necessary despite the fact that he claims that 'it is natural for one to pronounce one Syllable of a Word with a louder and stronger sound than another Syllable of the same Word, the accent is somewhat natural, and consequently will come easy...' (1766:137). The 'general directions' are made with reference particularly to nouns and adjectives only, with verbs treated somewhat in passing. Dun's main concern is to provide rules for stress placement in nouns and adjectives showing certain types of 'terminations'. Thus nouns and adjectives with endings such as *ial*, and *ion* will show penultimate stress placement, as in *mansion, jealous* and so on, while if the terminations are bi-syllabic, such as *uous,* then the stress is placed on the antepenult. Verbs terminating in *ize,* it is claimed, always show syllable final stress placement, thus *surmíse, surpríse, naturalíze.* Compound words and derivatives (especially of non-Romance origin) show the same stress patterning as their 'Principles': 'Saxon terminations, regardless of harmony, always leave the accent where they found it, let the adventitious syllables be ever so numerous' (Walker:1791:63). Dun asserts too that the greater the number of syllables in a word, the less likely is the stress to fall on the 'right hand' syllables, tending to be placed near the beginning of the word, thus *céremony, élegancy, abóminable,* while two syllable words tend to show stress on the first syllable rather than the second, save when they are 'compounds' *compléte, contríte* (Giegerich:1992:183ff).

Regional (and particularly Scotch) variation in stress placement is given some emphasis by only a few 18th century observers, notably Buchanan and Elphinston. Buchanan (1770:51-52) especially seems to regret the inconsistencies of Scots suprasegmental phonology in this respect: 'It is remarkable, that though the pronunciation throughout the several counties of England differs more or less from the purity of the best speakers; yet the accent is uniform overall. Hence arises another great disadvantage in speaking or reading, to which North-Britons, in general, subject themselves, namely, false accent. I shall here contrast a few examples. North Britons lay the accent wrong in the following words, and say

áccess		accéss
súccess		succéss
áffiance		affíance
alĭénate		álienate
alíenable		álienable
apostateéze		apóstatize
diffícult		dífficult
diffículty		dífficulty
chórography	for	chorógraphy
cósmography		cosmógraphy
démocracy		demócracy
excéllency		éxcellency
haráss		hárass
embarráss		embárrass
inexórable		inéxorable
intellígible		intélligible
unintellígibly		unintélligibly
irrevócable		irrévocable

Several of these examples suggest that 18th century Scots speakers rely more on end-stress than their English contemporaries (the *access* instance, for example) a phenomenon not unknown in modern Scots as well, thus *novél, mischíef* (Grant and Dixon:1921:62). While Elphinston (1786:51) assiduously records the differential nominal - verbal stress placement in items like *abstract, invalid,* he goes to some length to note that Scots speakers are inclined to favour end stressing (at least in a limited lexical set), regardless of syntactic category: 'Dhe Scots, perceiving dhat raddical verbs natturally emphatticize dheir ending; and dhat sevveral nouns becomming verbs, invert dheir stres accordingly; hav imadgined dhemselvs authorized to' uze dhe same fredom widh *bias, canvas, silence, sentence, triumph, comfort* and *sollace;* az in dhe North, widh *seccond*: much more widh dhe oridginal verbs *construe, rescue,* (resscue), *respite* or *respit* (resspit); *govvern, harras, ransac* and *cancel;* all Inglishly invariabel in prior strength: az iz *perfet* in evvery capacity, dho dhe Scotch hold it *perfite,* a rival to' dhe Inglish *polite*. Obzerving *practice* so nicely distinguished from *practise,* dhey cood not fancy dhe verb and noun (az dhey ar to' dhe Inglish ear) indiscrimminabel'. Another list of 'erroneously accented' Scots pronunciations is provided in the list of Philo-Orthologie in one of his letters to the *Edinburgh Magazine* (1722): see Appendix III.

Sylvester Douglas, while admitting that some differences between Scotch and English habits of word stress placement exist, agrees that they are not major and that they appear merely in the exceptions to general rules of stressing, not to the general principles themselves: 'The only difference between them and the English in this respect is that the exceptions in their dialect are different, and exceptions can only be ascertained by a particular enumeration' (Appendix II). He very much favours the use of visible distinguishing diacritic marks to delineate stress placement in the language, especially for provincial speakers, rather than any recourse to the learning of general rules: 'But foreigners and Provincials would derive great advantage from it, and written accents would also tend, like *rules* of accentuation, to give stability to the language itself....Our main dictionaries are, indeed, improved by the addition of the accentual mark to all the words, and Scotchmen have much oftener recourse to them for the accentuation than the meaning. But this sort of repository of accents does not supersede [sic:CJ] the convenience that would arise from accenting particular words in the Schoolbook in Scotland; for as the major part of the words in the language are accented in the same way in both parts of the island, the Scotch in reading as well as speaking acquire the habit of their provincial accentuations, without suspecting that they are provincial and therefore without endeavouring to ascertain the matter by an appeal to a dictionary'.

APPENDIX ONE: THE CONTRAST

A SPECIMEN OF THE SCOTTISH DIALECT, IN PROSE AND VERSE, ACCORDING TO THE LATEST IMPROVEMENTS

(Where a star appears, the term so used, is now more properly colloquial)

Moy oanast coarespoandant

Moast noat thenk oy aum ensanseble oaf thase enjaneous civeeletays woth whoch et haith daleited moy coampautreoats tow antarteen aw soajurner, aund rawaird hez veezet. Oy darfoir boot tow coanvence moy bast woshers thaut oy aum noat queit oonworday* aither oaf thaut janerous hoaspetauletay, oar thaut adefeeing coanvarsatione, whoch aquallay empruv aw mauns mainers, aund enspoir hez graitetud.

Oy min tharefor tow exibit, auz en aw merrour, foive oar sex, oaf fefty oar sexty, curaoazetays oy haiv mat woth; aund moast bag yur excuze foar troying whother ye oar oy oonderstaunds*, aumoang mainay laungages, wan must mautareaul tow uz aund ainay Scoatsmaun, bast. Et ez raither endid tow spic moy poalesh oaf steil, auz tow pruv moy encrass oaf tnoalege en moy thoats en aunswer tow yur wotty latter. Thes much oy shaul brifly afferm, noat dridding rabook, thaut moy dazein ez coanceezness, ev moy pan shud cary leecence thaut lenth auz tow fel moy péper.

Oy haiv sin, Ser, sence moy auroivaul en Scoatlaund, vauroietay oaf empruvments, baseids thaut oaf laungage; aund, ferst, aw glaureous enlairgement oaf Breetesh lebertay. Chaipels, woth mainay aw wecket laitin buke*, and saveraul proivat dwallens, oy seed* dalevered tow aw foiray troyaul, boy goadlay lauds aund lausses thereoontow muvved en sperret boy poious aupoastles, aund pretacket boy maugestrats aund airmays dauncing roond thase joayful coanflaugrationes. Ev ye ausk whey, wol* oy tal ye? Must raisonaubly ded thes hauppen, bacaze sarten empadant parsons haud damaunded lebertay oaf coanscience, en aw laund thaut toalarats ful lebertay auganst et.

Mein oys haiv bahall'd pritchers, thaut ware noat thoat tow prauctoise; yay, mainay notted titchers, thaut coold noat rid; mainay plidders thaut audoarned aw baur, aund ware man oaf pairts, tho' noat pairts oaf spitch. Oy haive heerd evven oaf salabratted outhours, thaut caun naither spic, rid, noar wreit.

Oy haiv bin cradeblay enfoarmed, thaut noat lass auz foartay amenant samenaurays oaf lairnen enstruck cheldren en ainay laungage boot thaut whoch auloanne ez nidful, aund nurter tham en ainay haibet oonlass thaut oaf civeeletay. Oy haiv massalf tnoan dip-lairned professours oaf fowr destengueshed oonavarsetays, caupable oaf coamoonicatten airts aund sheences* auss w-al auz laungages auncient oar moadarn, yet endefferent auboot, aund froam thance oonauquant woth thaut sengle laungage whoch ez auboov ainay laungage alz; aund en whoch auloanne thase maisters ware tow empairt tnoalege. Foar moy share, oy moast aunoalege oy caunnoat winder ev Cauladoneaun paurents sand cheldren tow Yoarksheir foar leeberaul adecatione, aund paurteekelarlay foar thaut poalisht *lengo*, whoch ez noat spoc en Scoatlaund.

Mainay aun oad theng meght oy aud, thaut moast serproize aw traiveler, whoa, haiving bin loang aubsent, raveezets hez mautarnaul laund; wharen et haiz rajoayz'd aund ragaul'd hem tow parsave noo cettays, vellauges, vellaws, gairdens, poands, canauls, &c. oaf ooteeletay aund maugneefacence bayoand eemaugenatione; tow feind trad, nauvegatione, augriculter, maunoofaucters, buzness en shoart, flooreshen; lairnen etsalf premotted en ainay lein, aicsap ets naiteraul chaunnel.

Those pleezers aund pauraudoaxes oy caunnoat boot coanfass, ev moy coanfassione woold prevoack hem thaut endaivoured tow prevoack hez freend, tho' noat oontow wraith, parhops oontow jalousay; aund, whoever mescheevous wroang amoolatione moast pruv, reght amoolatione, leik doimont oan doimont, shaul haiv proaper affack en poaleshen swit freendshep.

Ma loard, laddy, aund faimelay, prasant coamplaments woth those moy raspacks. Ma laddy caunnoat boot aupruv oaf thase eeneetiautoray buckays, aund shaul oarder coapays froam Ambrugh woth airlayest oapoartunetay. Ainay outhour, aspaciauly aw famale outhour, ev noat raither aun outhorass, (though thes mambar ez poasseblay plaonaustic), moast w-al raloy oan moy sempauthay, auz ye tarm et, oar auss dipplay tow dep, moy femmauchay.

Noatheng haiv oy tharefor tow sebjine, oonlass thaut oy aum hopful craddit shaul autand thes aurdant sensaretay, whoch, faur froam empitching moy chaurater, shaul oaparat en ma favours, whan et wol spic those aufactionat ragairds woth whoch oy moast, en ainay pronunsatione, alweis steil masalf,

Moy oanoured freend's
Must obadiant sarvaunt
tow coamaund,

AULAXAUNDAR SCOAT:
Cleidbaunk, Mey 1. 1779

APPENDIX TWO: OF THE PROVINCIAL ACCENTUATION

CAP 1

Of the Accented Syllables in Words of More Syllables than One

In every word of more than one syllable, one is always uttered in a more marked and distinguished manner than the next. In *Fancy* the first syllable is so pronounced. In *assist* the last. In *retirement* the middle. This is not peculiar to any one language. No one ever heard of a living dialect spoken where he could not at once, fix on a particular syllable in every word which was thus distinguished. I mean when such a word was pronounced distinctly and by itself. The same thing is observable in the dead languages, as pronounced either by the English or other nations. If we try to avoid it in uttering any given word and to sound all the syllables of which it is composed in the same manner in which we usually sound that one which I have been describing, they seem to lose their relation and dependence upon one another as parts of one whole and each strikes the ear as a distinct independent monosyllable. In the word *Dayly* the first is the distinguished syllable. Try to mark the other with the same sort of utterance and you will resolve this disyllable into two monosyllables *day* and *ly*. That affectation of the voice, which occasions this distinction we call *accent*. The distinguished syllable is said to be *accented* or to have the accented [sic:CJ] placed upon it.

What originally determined the choice of the accented syllables in different languages, we cannot ascertain. In part perhaps it depended upon the nature of combined articulate sounds. Where the same word was employed to express two different ideas, the accent being placed on one of its syllables when it was used in one sense, it became convenient to distinguish the other sense by a different position of the accent. In derivative words the accentuation of the primitive was frequently the guide, in words adopted from other languages, the Etymology. But these three last cases presuppose a choice already made. For what reason determined the accentuation with regard to the primary sense of the same word or with regard to vernacular words from which derivatives have been formed, or foreign words in the language from which they have been adopted? Accident and caprice had probably the principal share in this as in all other circumstances belonging to the formulation of language, for the position of the accent cannot *necessarily* depend on the nature of words otherwise we could not vary it, if at pleasure; the same word, though with different meanings would never be accented in a different manner and that not even in different languages, or different dialects of the same language. In the same word when used in the same sense, the accent is uniformly placed on the same syllable. No Englishman ever accents the first syllable of *Fancy* today on the second tomorrow. No more than he sounds the *a* in one way at one time and in another way at another. This adherence to the same mode of accentuation is in some measure necessary for the main end of speech, viz. a distinct communication of ideas. Change the accentuation of a word and you in a degree change the word itself, and if every man were to assume the license of altering the audible signs of his ideas as whim should suggest, language would soon become unintelligible.

But one of the characteristics of a provincial dialect is the accentuation of certain words in a manner different from that which obtains in the pure idiom - Thus the words *success, event, magazine* are not are not accented in the same manner in Scotland as in England. Now there are three methods by which written instructions may be conveyed concerning the classical accentuation of English words. 1. By laying down general rules which apply to a great variety of individual words 2. By marking with some visible sign or character the accented syllable of the word whose accent is to be ascertained. 3. By referring to verses of the classical authors in which form the nature of our prosody, the position of the accent in such word [sicCJ] must necessarily appear.

CAP 2
Of General Rules Concerning the Accentuation of Words in the English Language

Though we have observed that caprice or accident seem chiefly to have directed the original position of the accent, yet it cannot but have happened that when once it was fixed on a certain syllable in any particular word it should also in general be placed on the corresponding syllable in other words which were of a similar nature, either in respect of the quality, and quantity of their vowels, the number of their syllables or their terminations. From this principle, from the difference in the signification of the same word, and from Etymology, and derivation, Dr Johnson has deduced certain general rules, which he has inserted in his grammar. A complete system of such rules, accompanied with an enumeration of the exceptions (which as in all languages so particularly in ours, take place with regard to every general rule) would be of signal service to foreigners in the acquisition of the English tongue. Such a work would also contribute to the stability and permanence of accentuation. Although I have said that the same word is always accented in the same manner, that remark is subject to considerable restriction. In the course of years little alterations with regard to particular words are by degrees introduced. The whim of some individual, a minister, a fine lady, a favourite actor, a popular preacher, displaces the accent of some one word. Their private acquaintance either induced by the love of novelty or the desire to flatter, adopt the innovation, and this sometimes from mere affectation, sometimes from the remains of a provincial barbarism, sometimes perhaps from a defect in the organs of speech. The Vulgar, and even the learned, give way by degrees to the authority of fashion, and the new accentuation is thoroughly established. But this sort of fluctuation is not near so common in the accentuation of words as with regards to the sounds of their vowels and consonants. The reason is that there always has been a sort of criterion in our language by which disputed accentuation might be in most cases decided. I mean the practice of the classical poets. Where there is such a criterion whose authority is tacitly established by general consent it is not so easy for a mere unnecessary innovation to gain a permanent footing. The misfortune is that authority of verse, could not formerly be readily and easily produced because till Dr Johnson's dictionary appeared no attempt had been made to collect classical evidence not only of the verse but also the accentuation of the different words in the language. Still there is much wanting to render that branch of English grammar perfect, and after all though a collection for that sole purpose would afford the best part of the truth of general rules, still the rules themselves would be of more general use for the purposes of easy retention and ready and immediate application. But with regard to the Scotch peculiarities of accentuation, they do not seem to be such as require any particular attention to such rules. They, as the English, do from habit and education, observe in most instances the Rules which have been laid down by Dr Johnson. Nor do I believe any other could be pointed out which they err against in all cases. The only difference between them and the English in this respect is that the exceptions in their dialect are different, and exceptions can only be ascertained by a particular enumeration.

CAP 3

Of the Accentual Mark

To ascertain the accented syllable in every word by a visible character, has never been practised in the written language of any nation, while it continued also a living language. If the Greek furnishes an exception to this observation, it is to be remarked that even the Greek accentual marks, which we shall have occasion afterwards to mention more at large, were not in use till a late period, and were unknown in the days of the great Poets and Orators. Many reasons concurred to occasion their omission, or neglect of written accents. If we carry our imagination back to the Epoch when writing may first supposed to have begun we shall think it possible, though the simple sounds of which distinct words were composed must have been previously analysed because otherwise distinct characters would not have been employed representing each of those elementary sounds. Yet that, at the time when the accentuation of words had never been the subject of accurate consideration. Habits, imitation and convenience led one man to accent words in the same manner as his neighbours, and when, by the written signs he knew what word was meant, he naturally accented it in reading in the same manner that he would have done in discourse. How few people are there now know, by abstract reflection, that every polysyllable is accented in their own pronunciation as well as in that of others. They speak and read with the proper accent, as Molier's Bourgeois Gentilhomme made prose. Written language having been found to answer its purpose without this appendage, it was thought unnecessary to introduce it when musicians and grammarians had observed its existence and the order upon the nature of accent in audible speech. One objection to the general use of accentual marks is that they would clog and perplex the arrangement of the letters, and spoil in some measure the beauty of elegant writing and printing. They would also increase the labour and expense. From the reasons just mentioned it is manifest that to natives and those who hear and speak the pure dialect of a language from their infancy, such assistance is not immediately necessary. But foreigners and Provincials would derive great advantage from it, and written accents would also tend, like *rules* of accentuation, to give stability to the language itself. If the constant use of an accentual mark might appear superfluous and perhaps a blemish in books in general, they should at least be employed in all those designed for the instruction of foreigners in our tongue and in the school books in Scotland, those words should be accented in which the provincial is different, in this respect, from classical pronounciation [sic:CJ]. Some of the editors of Milton have marked in this manner the syllables in the [sic:CJ] Paradise Lost which he accents differently from the present usage, though it will appear afterwards that such a precaution is not often necessary in verse. Our modern dictionaries are, indeed, improved by the addition of the accentual mark to all the words, and Scotchmen have much oftener recourse to them for the accentuation than the meaning. But this sort of repository of accents does not supersede [sic:CJ] the convenience that would arise from accenting particular words in the School book in Scotland; for as the major part of the words in the language are accented in the same way in both parts of the island, the Scotch in reading as well as speaking acquire the habit of their provincial accentuations, without suspecting that they are provincial and therefore without endeavouring to ascertain the matter by an appeal to a dictionary.

Sylvester Douglas
Signals MS 104c.32
Signet Library
Parliament Square
Edinburgh

APPENDIX THREE: THE WEEKLY MAGAZINE OR EDINBURGH AMUSEMENT

The Weekly Magazine, Volume xviii, 1772

Sir,

It was but lately that I had an opportunity to peruse an Essay in your Magazine, signed *Philo-Orthologiae* (Vol. xviii:p.101) concerning the different modes of pronunciation in Scotland. Meeting with two or three friends I read the essay to them; and the following, as nearly as I can remember, was the substance of our conversation, which I would chuse to throw into the form of a dialogue, to avoid the insipid repetitions of *he said*, and *answered the other*, &c.

A. I am much of Mr What de-cal-lum's mind. It is most certain, that when we attempt to pull out the mote of the south-country dialect, we see not the very great beam in our clipping way of speaking.

T. We are not at all singular. Every county sneers at its neighbours. I have heard people in *Dundee*, otherwise very sensible, wonder how the folks of *Perth* could compare themselves to them in propriety of pronunciation. Could anything be more ridiculously laughable?

P. I have often had occasion to remark that Aberdeen seems to be the central point where the north and south-country dialects meet (I should have said *broad Buchan* and south-country dialects; for our speech in Aberdeen is only a sort of polite broad Buchan). The variation is most sensibly observed as we go south. At Stonehaven it begins; at Bervie the variation is strongly marked; but in Montrose the accent is *toto caelo* different from ours.

Whereas when we go north, we are not sensible of the Highland accent, till we come to Keith; it keeps a little softer in Elgin, and throughout that part of Murray; but in Forres it is strong; stronger in Nairn; but in Inverness it exceeds all our powers of nose to imitate them: For though they speak good grammar, or, as they call it, *speak proper*---

S. By your leave, Sir. I beg pardon for interrupting you, but I cannot allow them even *that*. There are as great barbarisms in grammar there as any where. I don't mean only among the lowest class, but even among the bettermost, for *Exempli gratia*: When we would say *give it to him when he comes*, the most polished Invernesian of them all expresses himself thus, *give it unto him when he would be coming. I beg a very great pardon*, is another choice phrase of theirs. And where we express our consent by *certainly, to be sure*, &c. they almost universally say, *what then*?

C. Stop Mr. - you're running into invective.

S. No; by no means: I only mean to show that they are not such excellent grammarians in common speech as they would make us believe they are.

P. I believe the reason why the Greek 'υπσιλον or French *u*, prevails so much in the *south*, and not at all in the **north** of Scotland, to be the very great intercourse in former days with the French; an intercourse mostly confined to the southern parts of this kingdom. It is certain that the French left behind them not only the last mentioned peculiarity of pronunciation, but even many of the words of their language, which are used to this day, only mutilated or corrupted in pronunciation: for instance;

A Servet,	a towel
Rouser,	a watering-pot,
A Chosser,	a chaffing-dish,
To Fash,	to trouble,
Orlich,	a dial-plate,
Cannel,	cinnamon,

From

Serviette	
Arroser,	to water.
Chausser,	to warm.
Facher	to trouble, vex.
Horloge,	a dial or clock.
Cannelle,	cinnamon

But I might mention five hundred instances of the same kind. Further, many of those modes of expression, or phrases commonly called Scotticisms, are strictly speaking, Gallicisms, or literal translations from the French.

N. True: but we wander from the point. Have you never remarked, that in some parts of Banff-shire they change the *v* for the *w*, and contrariwise, as the Cockneys do, saying *Prowerbs, wines, conwinced,* &c for *Proverbs, vines, convinced*? Not to mention that through Banff-shire, and almost all Murray, *it* is pronounced *hit.*

E. To a person acquainted with the dialects of the different counties, no other landmark or boundary but the speech of the people would be required to acquaint him where he was: It is impossible to ride six miles into the country without observing a sensible variation.

P. I'll tell you a story which I read the other day in a jest-book to illustrate the case in hand: A German and an Italian were disputing in London concerning the beauty, sweetness, and harmony of their respective languages; says the German, Dere is no language in de vorld so shweet as de Sherman: Vor de Italien vorts break my toot, and make me to gape - *O-o-liva - Pa-a-du-ua - Ma-an-tuua*: But de Sherman vas so charming - *Van Schwartzen-bachez-sdorff - Die Verruchtekeyt - De Ditschmahlsdorff. Dere vas de Sound, vere dere is de Armony.* Against this there was no disputing.

D. And yet, to do the German justice, it must be allowed, that he found more sweetness in the rough rumbling of his native consonants, than in the soft and liquid vowels of the Italian. His language resembled his natural disposition, noisy, rough, hardy; as the Italian did that of the other, effeminate, luxurious, and enervated.

N. No county in Scotland has reason to be ashamed of its dialect, when compared with that of the north-west counties of England. An English man will understand, and be understood in any part of Scotland (except where they speak Erse, which is out of the question); but I defy him to know what they would be at in Westmoreland and some parts of Yorkshire. Their Lingo is beyond measure barbarous.

The sum of all is, that none of us could ridicule another for real or supposed peculiarities in dialect or pronunciation. It is a trite, but a true observation, that to a stranger our sounds are as uncouth as his to us. I never heard two people of different counties (suppose a Dundee and an Aberdeen man), making game of one another, but it put me in mind of these lines of Pope:

Thus one fool lolls his tongue out at another
And shakes his empty noddle at his brother

Let us, when conversing with a stranger, endeavour to accommodate ourselves as much as possible to his dialect; not by the silly method of *taking him off* to his face, but by divesting ourselves of our pativinity, and approaching as near as we can to the true standard of pronunciation, which is as free of affectation as of canting. And if -

Here the ladies called for cards, and all sense and reason was drowned by the noise of mattadores, vole, poole, counters, and other such politely-uncouth names. I left the company as soon as I decently could, and retired to my chambers, where I employed myself in writing down what I now send you.

Si digna haec, populo quamprimum mitte legenda,
Sin aliter, foculo trade voranda tuo.

Yours, &c.

Philo-Orthologiae Secundus
Banks of Dee, Dec. 26. 1772

The Weekly Magazine, Volume xix, 1772

Sir,
It is a matter of much surprise, that among all ranks of people, even those of good education, a rooted prejudice in favours [sic:CJ] of the particular dialect of their own country, and even parish, exists to a degree that blinds them to the grossest absurdities in their own, and makes them condemn that of all dissenters as ridiculous and improper. This prejudice has several inconvenient tendencies; it lessens a stranger in our opinion merely on account of his accent, as it is vulgarly termed; let his behaviour be ever so unexceptionable, and his parts considerable, when his pronunciation agrees not with ours (as faulty perhaps), instead of attending to his sentiment, we ill-mannerly sneer at the uncouthness of his sounds. Sometimes, it produces a competition and warm debate, on which occasions dogmatical assertions only take place on both sides; ill blood is raised, and a convert is seldom made by either party. But not withstanding its general bad effects, it was productive of good to myself. Being early removed to a considerable distance from my native abode, for the benefit of education; to a place differing greatly in its dialect from that of my own country, I was very soon attacked for what may be termed Pativinity; this I did not relish, and resolved to try some method to elide such mortification. As I could discern no beauties in the language of my accusers preferable to those of my own, I could not think of adopting it, especially when I considered the like censure would await me upon a change of situation. I then judged the best method was to endeavour acquiring the *proper* English pronunciation, renouncing the peculiarities of my own and companions, so that, if attacked again on the same score, I might have book and leaf to adduce in my vindication. The expedient succeeded almost to my expectation, but with exceptions too; for having called Ab---a, where I had resided some time before, after spending some months in the metropolis, I was told by a gentleman of that city, 'Fat ivir ye've impriv'd in, Sir, weel I wite, its ne i' your langige'. Though I was confident of not having carried away a single metropolitan phrase or accent, and equally so of the impropriety of an attack by this gentleman of beam-filled eyes, I replied with silence, knowing that reasoning the point would have been in vain. After this instance, I shall briefly endeavour to point out what may be called the characteristics and defects of the various dialects to be met with in different parts of North-Britain, as far as I am acquainted, both in respect of tone and pronunciation.

First, the general sound or tone of the southern counties, Edinburghshire, Fife (and the Orkneys with a little variation), may be called *canting*. That of the west and north Highlands *plaintive*; that of Shetland isles savouring of the Danish *affectionate monotony*. Next, with regard to the pronunciation, that of the Borders differs little from the adjacent northern English counties; a little farther to the northward, and all the way to Angus (by the east side) it is marked by the frequent occurrence of the sound peculiar to the French *u*, and the Greek *υπσιλον*, and intirely foreign to the English language; therefore cannot be exemplified by any combination of our alphabet, but is the sound given in these parts to *moon, soon*, &c. which, by the Greek alphabet, is exactly expressed thus, *μυν*, *συν*, &c. Also by the broad *a* or *au* taking place often where it ought not, and indeed almost always where the letter *a* is used; thus for *hand*, which is a short syllable, they say *haund*, for *land laund*, &c. That of Aberdeen, Banff and Caithness-shire, by an uniform conversion of the sound of *oo* into that of *ee*: Ex. for *moon*, *meen*, for *soon*, *seen*; and of *wh* into *f*, thus, for *what*, *fat*, for *why*, *fy*, &c. and lopping off all final *d*'s, when preceded by the letter *n*, for instance *comman* for *command*, &c. Murray, by converting the *oo* into *eu* in some instances, for *smooth*, *smeuth*, &c. Inverness I think with justice claims the most proper pronunciation in Scotland; at the same time it is hurt by an over-lengthening many of the vowels and retaining the general plaintiveness of the Highlands. The northern isles pronounce much like the metropolis in all other respects, but that you seldom hear broad *a* so frequent in it, as already observed. Ex. a *ball*, which should be pronounced *bawl*, they call *ball*, making it a short syllable.

In these observations I must be understood to have in view only some of the first, the second, and lower classes of people: those of the most liberal education, I know, are generally masters of the true English pronunciation and idiom, divested of its barbarisms.

Should these hints of the peculiarities and defects in the several dialects rouse the attention of those deficient in orthology, to obtain a less exceptionable stile of language, renouncing the prejudices in favours of their own, and abating their contempt of that of all dissenters, I should esteem myself extremely happy: but as so great and good effects are not to be expected from so feeble an attempt, I shall be amply satisfied if I become the means of exhorting the more pertinent remarks of your *ingenious* correspondents on this subject, from whose abilities I have reason to hope great reformation in the sentiments and language of my countrymen. Please put the above on the blue or white parts of your Magazine, as you find it merits, and oblige,

Yours, &c.
PHILO-ORTHOLOGIE
Shetland, Sept. 20.
1772

The Weekly Magazine, Volume xviii, 1772

Sir,

The reception you were pleased to give a well-meant attempt, I made some time ago, to characterise, and point out the essential differences in the several dialects of the English language in Scotland, emboldens me now to offer something further in gratification of my signature, being strongly compelled to contribute my mite towards the improvement of that inestimable faculty, whereby man is, in an eminent degree, distinguished from the rest of his fellow-creatures.

I shall here confine myself to that part of grammar called *accent*, not in its general and vulgar acceptation, by which is understood that tone or pitch of voice distinguishing the inhabitants of different countries and provinces, described by me, *canting, affectionate*, &c.; but, as defined by grammarians, 'that peculiar stress of the voice laid upon any syllable of a word, whereby that syllable is made more remarkable than any other in the word'; the great use of which, not only in distinguishing the import of words, alike wrote, of different significations, as *prèsent, presènt*, but likewise in producing that pleasing and most beautiful variety in the modulations of the voice, is so well known, that I need say nothing in favour of it. As rules for placing this accent are to be met with in most English grammars, I shall offer none here, but only give an alphabetical list of those words on which almost all Scots people agree in misplacing the accent, in two separate columns, the first showing what syllable ought to be accented, and the other what syllable is erroneously accented. In order to distinguish the accented syllable the more clearly, I have put it in *Italics*, and have included the consonant of the succeeding syllable in those words which have the *double* accent; so called, because that accent in the pronunciation doubles the succeeding consonant, whereby the vowel in that syllable, being placed between two consonants, retains its close or short sound: Thus dis*tri*bute, on account of the double accent, is pronounced dis*tri*bute: but, when the accent does not include the succeeding consonant, the accented vowel ending the syllable assumes its long sound: thus ho*ri*zon is pronounced ho*ry*son; which it does likewise when the next syllable begins with a vowel: thus A*bi*athar is pronounced A*by*athar. In the above list [see Table: Appendix Three below] I have avoided inserting words, concerning whose accent there is any uncertainty, and those whose accent is optional, as *A*cademy or A*ca*demy; also such whose accent I think does not please the ear, though to be found in very reputable authors, but which I cannot wish to see generally adopted, as *Arch*angel, *Ber*lin, *Cey*lon, for Arch*an*gel, Ber*lin*, Cey*lon*.

After all, I am sensible many of your readers will think I have made a vast pother about nothing, as I have known several who, from inattention, or a bad ear, could not distinguish the accented syllables of words they had with propriety pronounced themselves.

Depending chiefly on the merit of my *pains*, I flatter myself soon to observe in the *Weekly Magazine*,

Yours, &c.
PHILO-ORTHOLOGIE

TABLE
Appendix Three

List of words which ought to be accented on the syllables marked below in *Italics*	but which	are erroneously accented in the syllables wrote also in *Italics* below
On the 1st.		
*Ab*raham		Abra*ha*m
*Al*exander		Alex*an*der
*A*rabic		A*ra*bic
*Ba*laam		Ba*laa*m
*Fes*tival		Fes*ti*val
*Har*ass		Ha*rass*
*In*jure		In*jure*
*Is*rael		Is*ra*el
*Ju*dicatory		Ju*di*catory
*Lu*natic		Lu*nat*ic
*Ma*nila	some say	Ma*ni*la & Ma*nil*a
*Phil*istines		Phi*lis*tines
*Pol*itic		Po*lit*ic
*Ty*rannize		Tyrann*ize*
On the 2d.		
A*bi*athar		Abi*a*thar
Ac*cess*		*Ac*cess
Al*lies*		*Al*lies
Ap*os*tatize		Apostat*ize*
A*rith*metic		Arith*met*ic
Ca*per*naum		Caper*na*um
Ca*tas*trophe	*some accent and pronounce*	*Cat*astroph
Com*mit*tee		Commit*tee*
Con*trib*ute		*Con*tribute
Dis*ci*ple		*Dis*ciple
Dis*trib*ute		*Dis*tribute
Em*bar*rass		Embar*rass*
En*quiry*		*En*quiry
Es*quire*		*E*squire
Eu*phra*tes		*Eu*phrates
Ex*pi*ry		*Ex*piry

Ho*ri*son	*Hor*ison
In*con*solable	Incon*sol*able
In*ev*itable	Ine*vi*table
Ir*rep*arable	Irre*pa*rable
Ir*rev*ocable	Irre*voc*able
Le*vi*athan	Levi*at*han
Re*main*der	*Re*mainder
Re*spec*tively	Respec*ti*vely
Sa*be*ans	*Sa*beans
Suc*ces*sively	Succes*si*vely
On the 3d.	
Magaz*ine*	*Ma*gazine

REFERENCES

Abercrombie, D. 1979. The Accents of Standard English in Scotland.

Abercrombie, D. 1965. Forgotten Phoneticians. *Studies in Phonetics and Linguistics*. 44-53. London. Oxford University Press.

Abercrombie, D. 1965. Steele, Monboddo and Garrick. *Studies in Phonetics and Linguistics*. 35-43. London. Oxford University Press.

Adams, J. 1799. *The Pronunciation of the English Language. English Linguistics 1500-1800*. No. 72. Alston . R.C. (ed.). Menston. 1968.

Adams, J. 1794. *Euphonologia Linguae Anglicanae. English Linguistics 1500-1800*. No. 112. Alston . R.C. (ed.). Menston. 1968.

Adie, William. 1769. *A New Spelling-Book: In which the Rules of Spelling and Pronouncing the English Language are exemplified and explained*. Paisley.

Aitken, A.J. 1979. Scottish Speech: a Historical View. with Special Reference to the Standard English of Scotland. In A.J. Aitken and T McArthur (eds.) *The Languages of Scotland*. 68-84. Edinburgh. Chambers.

Aitken, A.J. 1981. The Scottish Vowel Length Rule. In M. Benskin and M.L. Samuels (eds.) *So Meny People Longages and Tongues*. 131-57. Edinburgh University Press.

Aitken, A.J. 1971. Variation and Variety in Written Middle Scots. In Aitken. A.J.. McIntosh. A. and Palsson. H. (eds.). *English Studies in English and Scots*.. 177-209. Longman. London.

Allardyce, A. 1888. *Scotland and Scotsmen in the 18th Century from the MSS of John Ramsay. Esqu. of Ochtertyre*. 2 vols. Blackwood. Edinburgh and London.

Anderson, J.M. and C.J. Ewen, 1987. *Principles of Dependency Phonology*. Cambridge University Press. Cambridge.

Anderson, J.M. and Charles Jones, 1974. *Phonological Structure and the History of English*. North Holland. Amsterdam.

Anderson, J.M. and C. J. Ewen. 1987. *Principles of Dependency Phonology* Cambridge University Press. Cambridge.

Angus, W. 1800. *A Pronouncing Vocabulary of the English Language: Exhibiting the Most Appropriate Mode of Pronunciation. Glasgow. English Linguistics 1500-1800*. No. 164. Alston. R.C. (ed.). Menston. 1969.

Angus, W. 1800. *An Epitome of English Grammar*. Glasgow.

Angus, W. 1814. *English Spelling and Pronouncing Dictionary*. Glasgow.

Angus, W. 1800. *A Pronouncing Vocabulary of the English Language*. Glasgow.

Angus, W. 1814. *An English Spelling and Pronouncing Vocabulary*. Glasgow.

Angus, W. 1814. *An Introduction to Angus Vocabulary and Fulton's Dictionary*. Glasgow.

Anon, 1885. *Mistakes of Daily Occurrence of Speaking, Writing, and Pronunciation Corrected*. London.

Anon, 1784. *A General View of English Pronunciation: to which are added EASY LESSONS for the use of the English Class*. London.

Anon, 1796. *A Spelling-Book upon a New Plan*. Glasgow.

Anon, 1795. *The Child's Guide* . Aberdeen.

Anon, 1798. *The Instructor: or An Introduction to Reading and Spelling the English Language*. Glasgow.

Arsleff, H. 1967. *The Study of Language in England. 1780-1860*. Princeton.

Bailey, R.W. 1987. Teaching in the Vernacular: Scotland, Schools, and

Linguistic Diversity. In C. Macafee and I. MacLeod (eds.) *The Nuttis Schell.* 131-142. Aberdeen University Press.

Barrie, A. 1794. *A Spelling and Pronouncing Dictionary of the English Language for the Use of Schools.* Edinburgh.

Barrie, A. 1796. *A Spelling and Pronouncing Catechism.* Edinburgh.

Barrie, A. 1799. *A Spelling and Pronouncing Dictionary of the English Language.* Edinburgh.

Barrie, A. 1800. *An Epitome of English Grammar.* Edinburgh.

Barrie, A. 1800. *The Tyro's Guide to Wisdom and Wealth with Exercises in Spelling.* George Caw. Edinburgh.

Bartsch, R. 1987. *Norms of Language.* Longman. London.

Basker, James. G. 1993. Scotticisms and the Problem of Cultural Identity in 18th Century Britain. In John Dwyer and Richard B. Sher (eds.) *Sociability and Society in 18th Century Scotland..* Mercat Press. Edinburgh.

Beattie, James. *The Theory of Language.* 1788. *English Linguistics 1500-1800.* No. 88. Alston, R.C. (ed.). Menston. 1968.

Bickley, F. 1928. *The Diaries of Sylvester Douglas* (2 vols.). Constable. London.

Bliss, A.J. 1952-3. Vowel quantity in Middle English borrowings from Anglo-Norman. *Archivum Linguisticum.* 4. 121-47; 5. 22-47.

Boggs, W. Arthur. 1964. William Kenrick's Pronunciation. *American Speech.* 39. 131-34.

Bronstein, A.J. 1949. The vowels and diphthongs of the 19th century. *Speech Monographs.* 16. 227-242.

Brown, T. 1845. *A Dictionary of the Scottish Language.* Simpkin and Marshall. London.

Buchanan, J. 1770. *A Plan for an English Grammar-School Education.* London.

Buchanan, J. 1762. *The British Grammar: English Linguistics 1500-1800.* No. 97. Alston, R.C. (ed.). Menston. 1968.

Buchanan, J. 1757. *Linguae Britannicae Vera Pronunciatio: English Linguistics 1500-1800.* No. 39. Alston, R.C. (ed.). Menston. 1968.

Buchanan, J. 1766. *An Essay Towards Establishing a Standard for an Elegant and Uniform Pronunciation of the English Language throughout the British Dominions.* London.

Buchmann, E. 1940. Der Einfluss des Scriftbildes auf die Aussprache im Neuenglischen. *Anglistische Reihe* 35. Breslau.

Burn, J. 1766-99. *A Practical Grammar of the English Language..for the Use of Schools.* Glasgow.

Burn, John. 1786. *A Pronouncing Dictionary of the English Language : English Linguistics 1500-1800.* No. 173. Alston, R.C. (ed.). Menston. 1969.

Callandar, John of Craigforth. 1782. *Two Ancient Scottish Poems; the Gaberlunzie-man, and Christ's Kirk on the Green.* Edinburgh.

Campbell, George. 1776. *The Philosophy of Rhetoric.* Edinburgh.

Catford, J.C. 1957. Vowel Systems of Scots Dialects. *Transactions of the Philological Society.* 107-117.

Chomsky, N and M. Halle. 1968. *The Sound Pattern of English.* Harper Row. New York.

Cockburn, H. 1856. *Memorials of His Time*. Black. Edinburgh.

Cohen, M. 1977. *Sensible Words. Linguistic Practice in England. 1640-1785*. Baltimore.

Collin, A. Z. 1862. *An Essay on the Scoto-English Dialect*. Lund.

Collin, Zacharaias. 1862. *An Essay on the Scoto-English Dialect*. Berlings. Lund.

Colville, J. 1899. The Scottish Vernacular as a Philosophical Study. *Proceedings of the Philosophical Society of Glasgow*.. 39 ff.

Complete Peerage *of England, Scotland, Ireland, Great Britain and the United Kingdom*. 1892. George Bell. London.

Crompton Rhodes, 1928. *Sheridan; Plays and Poems*. Oxford.

Danielsen, B. 1955-63. *John Hart's Works*. Part I. Almqvist and Wiksell. Stockholm.

Davies, C. (ed.) 1934. *English Pronunciation from the 15th to the 18th Centuries*. London.

Dixon, Henry. 1728. *The English Instructor*: *English Linguistics 1500-1800*. No. 47. Alston, R.C. (ed.). Menston. 1967.

Dobson, E.J. 1968. *English Pronunciation, 1500-1700*. Oxford University Press. Oxford.

Donegan, P. 1978. *On the Natural Phonology of Vowels*. *Working Papers in Linguistics*. 23. Department of Linguistics. Columbus. Ohio. Ohio State University.

Dorow, K-G. 1935. *Die Beobachtungen des Sprachmeisters James Elphinston über die schottische Mundart*. Dissertation. Weimar.

Douglas, James. 1956. *Treatise on English Pronunciation* (c 1740): see Holmberg.

Douglas, Sylvester (Lord Glenbervie). 1822. *The First Canto of Ricciardetto, translated from the Italian of Forteguerri, with an Introduction Concerning the Principle Romantic, Burlesque, and Mock Heroic Poets...and Notes...Critical and Philological*. London.

Douglas, Sylvester. 1773. An Account of the Tokay and other Wines of Hungary. *Philosophical Transactions*. vol. lxiii. part 1. London.

Douglas. Sylvester. 1768. Experiments and observations upon a blue substance, found in a Peat-moss in Scotland. *Philosophical Transactions*. vol. lviii. London.

Douglas, Sylvester. c 1779. *Of the Provincial Accentuation*.

Douglas, Sylvester. 1820. *Occasional Verses, Translations and Imitations, with Notes, critical and biographical*. Smith. Paris.

Drummond, John. 1767. *A Grammatical Introduction to the Modern Pronunciation and Spelling of the English Tongue*. Edinburgh.

Dun, James. 1766. *The Best Method of Teaching to Read and Spell English, Demonstrated in Eight Parts*. Edinburgh.

Dunlap, A.R. 1940. Vicious pronunciation in 18th century England. *American Speech*. 15. 364-7.

Dwyer, J. 1987. *Virtuous Discourse*: *Sensibility and Community in late 18th Century Scotland*. Edinburgh University Press. Edinburgh.

Ekwall, E. 1975. *A History of Modern English Sounds and Inflexions*. Oxford. Blackwell.

Elphinston, J. 1766. *The Principles of the English Language Digested for the Use of Schools*. London.

Elphinston, J. 1786/87. *Propriety Ascertained in her Picture, or Inglish Speech and Spelling Rendered Mutual Guides, Secure Alike from Distant, and from Domestic, Error*. London.

Elphinston, J. 1790. *English Orthoggraphy Epittomized*: *English Linguistics 1500-1800*. No. 288. Alston, R.C. (ed.). Menston. 1971.

Elphinston, J. 1795. *Miniature of English Orthography* . *English Linguistics 1500-1800*. No. 28. Alston, R.C. (ed.). Menston. 1967.

Emerson, O.F. 1921. John Dryden and a British Academy. *Proceedings of the British Academy*. London.

Emsley. B. 1933. James Buchanan and the 18th Century Regulation of English Usage. *Publications of the Modern Language Association*. xlviii. 3. . 1154-66.

Ewen. C.J. 1977. Aitken's Law and the Phonatory Gesture in Dependency Phonology. *Lingua* 41: 307-29.

Ferguson. Robert. 1773. *The Poems of Robert Ferguson*. (ed.) M.P. McDiarmid. Scottish Text Society. Edinburgh. 1956.

Fisher. George 1789. The *Instructor or Young Mans Best Companion*. Rivington. London.

Flasdieck. H. 1936. Zum lautwert von ME ę̄ im 18. Jahrhundert *Anglia*. 60.

Freeman. E. 1924. A Proposal for an English Academy in 1660. *Modern Language Review*. vol. 19.

Fulton and Knight, 1813. *Principles of English Pronunciation: A General Pronouncing and Explanatory Dictionary of the English Language*. Edinburgh.

Fyfe, C. (ed.) 1991. Our *Children Free and Happy: Letters from Black Settlers in Africa in the 1790s*. Edinburgh University Press. Edinburgh.

Gabrielson, A. 1913. The Development of Early Modern English ĭ/r (+ cons). *Minnesskrift till Axel Erdmann*. Uppsala och Stockholm.

Geddes, A. 1792. Three Scottish Poems. with a previous dissertation on the Scoto-Saxon dialect. *Transactions of the Society of Antiquaries of Scotland*. vol. 1. 402-68. Edinburgh.

Georgian Era, (The: Memoirs of the Most Eminent Persons, who have Flourished in Great Britain). 1832. 4 vols. Clarke (ed.). London.

Giegerich, H. 1994. *English Phonology: An Introduction*. Cambridge University Press. London.

Gil, A. 1621. *Logonomia Anglica.*: *English Historical Linguistics 1500-1800*. No. 68. Alston, R.C. (ed.) Menston. 1968.

Grant, W. 1913. The *Pronunciation of English in Scotland*. Cambridge University Press. London.

Grant, W. and J M Dixon. *Manual of Modern Scots*. Cambridge University Press. Cambridge. 1921.

Gray, J. 1794. *A Concise Spelling Book*. George Caw. Edinburgh.

Gray, J. 1809. *A Concise Spelling Book for the Use of Children*. Edinburgh.

Grieg, J.Y.T. 1932. *The Letters of David Hume*. Oxford University Press. Oxford.

Grierson, H. J. C. 1934. *The Letters of Sir Walter Scott: 1821-1823*. Constable. London.

Haggard, M. 1973. Abbreviation of consonants in English pre- and post-vocalic clusters. *Journal of Phonetics*. 1. 9-23.

Hart, J. 1569: see Danielsen, B.

Hewitt, D. 1987. James Beattie and the Languages of Scotland. In J.J. Carter and J.H. Pittock (eds.) *Aberdeen in the Enlightenment*.. 251-260. Aberdeen University Press. Aberdeen.

Hill, A.A. 1940. Early loss of [r] before dentals. *Publications of the Modern Language Association*. 55. 308-21.

Hodges, Richard. 1644. *A Special Help to Orthographie*. London.

Hodgson, M. 1770. *A Practical English Grammar for the Use of Schools and Private Gentlemen and Ladies*. London.

Holmberg, B. 1956. *James Douglas on English Pronunciation C. 1740*. Gleerup. Lund.

Hooper, J.B. 1976. *An Introduction to Natural Generative Phonology*. Academic Press. London.

Hooper, J.B. 1972. The syllable in phonological theory. *Language*. 48. 525-40.

Horn, W. and Lehnert, M. 1954. *Laut und Leben*. 2 vols. Deutscher Verlag. Berlin.

Horn, W. 1901. *Beiträge zur Geschichte der englischen Gutturallaute*. Berlin.

Hornsey, John. ND. *A Short Grammar of the English Language in two Parts. Simplified to the Capacities of Children, with Notes and a Great Variety of Entertaining and Useful Exercises*. Newcastle.

Hume, 1760: see Greig, J.Y.T. 1932.

Innes Smith, R.W. 1932. *English Speaking Students of Medicine at the University of Leyden*. Oliver and Boyd. Edinburgh.

Johnson, Samuel. 1747. *A Plan of a Dictionary for the English Language; Idler*.

Johnston, P. 1980. *A Synchronic and Historical View of Border Area Bimoric Vowel Systems*. Unpublished Ph.D. Dissertation. Edinburgh.

Jones, C. 1976. Some constraints on medial consonant clusters. *Language*. vol. 52. 121-30.

Jones, C. 1989. *A History of English Phonology*. Longman. London.

Jones, C. 1992. (ed.) *A Treatise on the Provincial Dialect of Scotland by Sylvester Douglas*. Edinburgh University Press. Edinburgh.

Jones, C. 1991. Some Grammatical Characteristics of the *Sierra Leone Letters*. in Fyfe. C.

Jones, C. 1993. Scottish standard English in the late 18th century. *Transactions of the Philological Society*. Vol. 91. 95-131.

Jones, C. 1994. Alexander Geddes. an 18th century Scots orthoepist and dialectologist. *Folia Linguistica Historica*. xvii. 71-103.

Kaffenberger, E. 1927. Englische lautlehre nach Thomas Sheridans Dictionary of the English Language (1780). *Beiträge zur Erforschung der Sprache und Kultur Englands und Nordamerikas*. 3.1. Breslau.

Kennedy, A.G. 1926. Authorship of *The British Grammar*. *Modern Language Notes*. vol. 41. 388-391.

Kenrick, W. 1784 *A Rhetorical Grammar of the English Language*: *English Linguistics 1500-1800*. No 332. Alston, R.C. (ed.). Menston. 1972.

Kerswill, P. Babel in Buckinghamshire? Pre-school children acquiring accent features in the New Town of Milton Keynes. In G. Melchers and N.L. Johannesson. *Non-Standard Varieties of Language.* Acta Universitatis Stockholmiensis. Almqvist and Wiksell. Stockholm.

Kinghorn, A.M. and Alexander Law. 1944-1974. *The Works of Allan Ramsay.* 6 vols. Scottish Text Society. Edinburgh. .

Kiparsky, P. 1973. How abstract is phonology? In O. Fujimura (ed.). *Three Dimensions of Linguistic Theory.* 5-56. Tokyo.

Koel, E. 1901. *Spelling Pronunciations.* Quellen und Forschungen. Strassburg.

Kohler, K. J. 1966. A late 18th century comparison of the Provincial dialect of Scotland and the pure dialect. *Linguistics.* 23. 30-69.

Kohler, K.J. 1966. Aspects of the history of English pronunciation in Scotland. unpublished Ph.D. Dissertation. Edinburgh.

Kökeritz, H. T. 1950. The reduction of initial *kn* and *gn* in English. *Language.* 21.

Langley, H. 1963. Early nineteenth century speech: a contemporary critique. *American Speech.* 38. 289-92.

Lass, R. 1984. *Phonology: An Introduction to Basic Concepts.* Cambridge University Press. London.

Laver, J.M.H. 1994. *Principles of Phonetics.* Cambridge University Press. London.

Law, A. 1965. *Education in Edinburgh in the 18th Century.* Publications of the Scottish Council for Research in Education. 52. University of London Press. London.

Lehiste, I. 1970. *Suprasegmentals.* MIT Press. Cambridge. Mass.

Lettley, Emma. 1988. *From Galt to Douglas Brown: 19th Century Fiction and Scots Language.* Scottish Academic Press. Edinburgh.

Lieberman, P. and S.E. Blumstein, 1993. *Speech Physiology, Speech Perception and Acoustic Phonetics.* Cambridge University Press. London.

Lloyd, R.J. 1921. Glides between consonants in English. *Die Neueren Sprachen. Zeitschrift für den neusprachlichen Unterricht.* 12. 14ff. Frankfurt. 1904.

Luick, K. 1921. *Historische Grammatik der englischen Sprache.* 2 vols.. Chr. Herm. Tauchnitz. Leipzig.

Macafee, C 1983. *Glasgow.* Varieties of English around the World. Text Series 3. Amsterdam.

Machyn, H. 1550: see Nichols, J.G. 1848.

Mackintosh, Duncan. 1797. *A Plain, Rational Essay on English Grammar.* London.

Maddieson, I. 1984. *Patterns of Sound.* Cambridge University Press. London.

Matthews, W. 1936a. Some 18th century phonetic spellings. *English Studies.* 12. 47-60. 177-188.

Matthews, W. William Tiffin. 1936b. An 18th century phonetician. *English Studies.* 18. 97-114.

McIllquam, William. 1781. *A Comprehensive Grammar.* Glasgow.

McMahon, A.M.S. 1991. Lexical phonology and sound change: The case of the Scottish Vowel Length Rule. *Journal of Linguistics.* 27. 29-53.

Meyer, E. 1940. *Der englische Lautstand in der zweiten Hälfte des 18.*

Jahrhunderts nach James Buchanan. unpublished Ph.D. Dissertation. Berlin.

Michael, I. 1970. *English Grammatical Categories and the Tradition to 1800*. Cambridge University Press. London.

Milroy, L. 1980. *Language and Social Networks*. Blackwell. Oxford.

Monboddo, J.B. (Lord) 1774. *Of the Origin and Progress of Language*. London.

Monroe, B.S. 1910. An English Academy. *Modern Philology*. vol. 8. 107-116.

Mossé, F.1952. *A Handbook of Middle English*. Johns Hopkins. Baltimore.

Müller, E. 1914. *Englische Lautlehre nach James Elphinston. 1765. 1787. 1790. Anglistische Forschungen* 43. Heidelberg.

Nares, R. 1784: *Elements of Orthoepy. English Linguistics 1500-1800.* No. 56. Alston, R.C. (ed.). Menston. 1968.

Nichols, J.G. 1848. *The Diary of Henry Machyn. Citizen and Merchant Taylor of London*. Camden Society 42. London.

Ohala, J.J. 1974. Experimental historical phonology. In J.M. Anderson and C. Jones. (eds.) *Historical Linguistics II*. 353-89. North Holland. Amsterdam.

Orton, H., S. Sanderson and J. Widdowson. 1978. *The Linguistic Atlas of England*. Croom Helm. London.

Pahlsson, C. 1972. *The Northumbrian Burr: a Sociolinguistic Study*. Gleerup. Lund.

Parker, W.M. 1971. (ed.)*The Heart of Midlothian*. Sir Walter Scott. Dent. London.

Perry, W. 1776. *The Only Sure Guide to the English Tongue or a New Pronouncing Spelling Book*. Edinburgh.

Perry, W. 1775.*The Royal Standard English Dictionary*. Edinburgh.

Pollner, C. 1976. *Robert Nares: Elements of Orthoepy*. Europäische Hochschulschriften. Reihe xiv. Angelsächsische Sprache und Literatur. Bd. 41. Frankfurt.

Ramsey, John. of Ochtertyre. see Allardyce. 1888.

Raphael, I.J. 1972. Preceding vowel duration as a cue to the perception of the voicing characteristic of word final consonants in American English. *Journal of the Acoustical Society of America*. vol. 51.1293-1303.

Read, A.W. 1938. Suggestions for an Academy in England in the latter half of the 18th century. *Modern Philology*. vol. 36. 145-156.

Robertson, James. 1722. *The Ladies Help to Spelling*. Glasgow.

Rogers, P. 1991. Boswell and the Scotticism. In Greg Cligham. (ed.) *New Light on Boswell*. 56-71. Cambridge University Press. London.

Rohlfing. H. 1984. *Die Werke James Elphinstons (1721-1809) als Quellen der englischen Lautgeschichte*. Heidelberg.

Savage, W.H. 1833. *The Vulgarities and Improprieties of the English Language*. London.

Scot, Alexander. 1779.*The Contrast: A Specimen of the Scotch Dialect. In Prose and Verse. According to the Latest Improvements; With an English Version*..

Scot, Alexander. 1776. *An Exercise for Turning English into French, with Grammatical Rules*..

Scot, Alexander. 1777. *Fables Choisies a l'usage des Enfans; Nouveau Recueil ou Melange Litteraire. Historique, Dramatique, et Poetique*..

Scot, Alexander. 1792. *Collection Académique, tirée des auteurs françois les plus renommés, en Prose et en Vers*. Edinburgh.

Scot, Alexander. 1781. *Rudiments and Practical Exercises. for Learning the French Language, by an Easy Method.* London.

Scott, John. 1774. *The School-Boy's Sure Guide; or, Spelling and Reading Made Agreeable and Easy.* Edinburgh.

Scott, William. 1793. *A Short System of English Grammar.* Edinburgh.

Scott, William. 1807. *A New Spelling and Pronouncing Dictionary.* Edinburgh.

Scott, William. 1796. *An Introduction to Reading and Spelling*. Edinburgh.

Scott, William. 1807. *A New Spelling. Pronouncing. and Explanatory Dictionary of the English Language*. Edinburgh.

Sheldon. E.K. 1971. Pronouncing systems in 18th-century dictionaries. *Language*. vol. 22.

Sheldon, E.K. 1938. *Standards of English Pronunciation According to the Grammarians and Orthoepists of the Sixteenth. Seventeenth and 18th Centuries.* Unpublished Dissertation. University of Wisconsin.

Sheridan, T. 1762. *Course of Lectures on Elocution.* London: *English Linguistics 1500-1800*. No. 129. Alston, R. C. (ed.). Menston. 1968.

Sheridan, T. 1780. *A General Dictionary of the English Language*. London.

Sheridan, T. 1781. *A Rhetorical Grammar of the English Language.* Dublin: *English Linguistics 1500-1800.* No. 146. Alston, R. C. (ed.). Menston. 1969.

Sichel, Walter 1910. (ed.) *The Glenbervie Journals*. Constable. London.

Sinclair, Sir John. 1782. *Observations on the Scottish Dialect.* London.

Smith, G.G. 1908. *The Scottish Language: The Cambridge History of English Literature*. vol II. Cambridge.

Smith, J. 1816. *A Grammar of the English Language Containing Rules and Exercises*. Norwich.

Spence, Thomas. 1775. *The Grand Repository of the English Language*. Newcastle.

Spence, Thomas. 1782. *Crusonia: or Robinson Crusoe's Island* (A Supplement to the *History of Robinson Crusoe*). Newcastle.

Stampe, D. 1972. On the natural history of diphthongs. *Papers from the Eighth Regional Meeting of the Chicago Linguistics Society.* 578-90. Chicago.

Steele, Joshua. 1775. *An Essay Towards Establishing the Melody and Measure of Speech.: English Linguistics 1500-1800.* No. 172. Alston, R.C. (ed.). Menston. 1969.

Stephen, L and S. Lee. 1908. *Dictionary of National Biography.* Smith, Elder and Co. London.

Sturzen-Becker, A. 1942. Some notes on English pronunciation about 1800. In *A Philological Miscellany Presented to Eilert Ekwall.* . 301-30. Uppsala.Swift, Jonathan. 1712. *A Proposal for Correcting. Improving. and Ascertaining the English Tongue* . London.

Telfair, C. 1775. *The Town and Country Spelling Book.* Elliot. Edinburgh.

Thomson, H.W. 1927. *The Anecdotes and Egotisms of Henry Mackenzie. 1745-1831.* Oxford University Press. London.

Tucker, Abraham. 1773. *Vocal Sounds.: English Linguistics 1500-1800.* No. 165. Alston, R.C. (ed.). Menston. 1969.

Tuite, Thomas. 1726. *The Oxford Spelling-Book (Being a Complete Introduction to English Orthography)* : *English Linguistics 1500-1800*. No. 41. Alston, R.C. (ed.). Menston. 1967.

Turner, J.R. 1970. *The Works of William Bullockar: Booke at Large 1580*. Leeds University Press. Leeds.

Valk, C.Z. 1980. *The Development of the Back Vowel before [ɹ] in early Modern English*. Unpublished PhD Dissertation. Muncie. Indiana.

Verney, Lady F.P. 1892. *Memoirs of the Verney Family*. 4 vols. London.

Vianna, M.E. 1972. A study in the dialect of the southern counties of Scotland. Unpublished Ph.D. Dissertation. Edinburgh.

Walker, I.C. 1968. Dr. Johnson and *The Weekly Magazine*. In. *Review of English Studies*. xix. 14-24.

Walker, I.C. 1981. Scottish nationalism in *The Weekly Magazine*. In. *Studies in Scottish Literature*. xvi. 1-13.

Walker, J. 1791. *A Critical Pronouncing Dictionary*: *English Linguistics 1500-1800*. No. 117. Alston, R.C. (ed.). 1968.

Wallis, J. 1653. *Grammatica Linguae Anglicanae*. Oxford.

Warden, J. 1753. *A Spelling Book*. Edinburgh.

Wells, J.C. 1982. *Accents of English*. 3 vols. Cambridge University Press. London.

Whitehall, H. and T. Fein. 1941. The development of Middle English ŭ in early Modern English and American English. *Journal of English and Germanic Philology*. 40.

Wyld, H.C. 1937. *A Short History of English*. John Murray. London.

Wyld, H.C. 1953. *A History of Modern Colloquial English*. Blackwell. Oxford.

Zettersten, A. 1974. *A Critical Facsimile Edition of Thomas Batchelor*. Part 1. Gleerup. Lund.

Index